SUPERVISION:
Emerging Profession

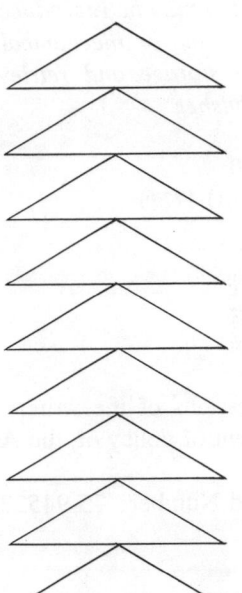

Readings from
Educational Leadership

Edited by
ROBERT R. LEEPER

Introduction by
FRED T. WILHELMS

Association for Supervision and Curriculum Development, NEA
1201 Sixteenth Street, N.W., Washington, D.C. 20036

Copyright © 1969 by the
Association for Supervision and Curriculum Development, NEA

All rights reserved. No part of this publication may be reproduced or transmitted in any form or by any means, electronic or mechanical, including photocopy, recording, or any information storage and retrieval system, without permission in writing from the publisher.

Price: $5.00
NEA Stock Number: 611-17796

The materials printed herein are the expressions of the writers. They do not represent endorsement by, nor a statement of policy of, the Association.

Library of Congress Catalog Card Number: 75-94523

Acknowledgments

SPECIAL acknowledgment is made to the authors for permission to reprint the articles appearing in this book of readings. Robert R. Leeper, Associate Secretary and Editor, ASCD publications, was responsible for final editing and production of the selections. Nancy Olson and Lana G. Pipes compiled the index. Technical production was handled by Lana G. Pipes, Nancy Olson, Mary Albert O'Neill, Karen T. Brakke, and Teola T. Jones. Cover design is by Brooke Todd & Associates.

Contents

Foreword
    An Emerging Profession   *Robert R. Leeper*   vii

Introduction
    Leadership: The Continuing Quest   *Fred T. Wilhelms*   ix

PART I
LEADERSHIP: TALENT FOR GROWTH

The Human Dimensions of Supervision	*Earl S. Johnson*	3
The Critical Shortage of Educationists	*Fred T. Wilhelms*	8
"Most of the Change"	*Robert R. Leeper*	11
A More Wholesome Balance	*Stephen M. Corey*	13
Poise Under Pressure	*Richard L. Foster*	15
Leadership for Human Change	*Harold D. Drummond*	21
Supervision: Loneliness and Rewards	*Alice L. McMaster*	23
When Supervisor and Principal Work Together	*Nicholas J. Vigilante*	27
Effecting Change Through Leadership	*Luvern L. Cunningham*	30
New Leadership and New Responsibilities for Human Involvement	*Ben M. Harris*	35

PART II
ISSUES IN PROFESSIONALIZATION

Role of the Supervisor	*Gordon N. Mackenzie*	41
In-Service Education of Supervisors	*Reba M. Burnham*	45

Preparing Education Supervisors   *James R. Ogletree,*
   Fred Edmonds, Pat W. Wear   49
Preparation and Certification of Supervisors   *Margaret Flintom*   53
Professionalization of Supervisors and
   Curriculum Workers   *James R. Ogletree*   56
What Does the Flexner Report Say to ASCD?   *Harold T. Shafer*   59
Role and Function of Supervisors and
   Curriculum Workers   *Rowannetta S. Allen*   62
Preparatory Programs for Supervisors   *Maurice J. Eash*   65
Identifying Potential Leaders for Supervision and
   Curriculum Work   *Robert S. Thurman*   69
Certification Requirements for General Supervisors and/or
   Curriculum Workers Today—Tomorrow   *H. Irene Hallberg*   72
Selection and Recruitment of Supervisors   *Johnnye V. Cox*   75
Professionalization of Supervisors and
   Curriculum Workers   *Barbara A. Hartsig*   77

Part III
Research: Instrument for New Knowledge

How Is Supervision Perceived?   *Carolyn Guss*   83
The Supervisor at Work   *Johnnye V. Cox*   87
Instructional Improvement: Considerations
   for Supervision   *William H. Lucio*   90
Personalities, Teachers, and Curriculum
   Change   *Ronald Urick, Jack R. Frymier*   94
Need for Research on Instructional Supervision   *Ben M. Harris*   98
Supervision and Action Research   *Mary Columbro Rodgers*   102
Emergence of Technical Supervision   *Ben M. Harris*   107
Knowledge About Supervision:
   Rationalization or Rationale?   *James B. Macdonald*   110
Supervision: Focus on Thinking   *Mary Lou Usery White,*
   Muriel Radtke, Louise M. Berman   113
Supervision: An Attempt To Modify
   Behavior   *John J. Koran, Jr.*   118

Part IV
The Supervisor at Work

Coordinating a Supervisory Program Muriel Crosby	125
The Supervisor Reports H. Leroy Selmeier	128
Improving the Skills of Teaching John Prater	132
The New Teacher—and a New Kind of Supervision? Alexander Frazier	136
Strategies for Instructional Leaders Frank Gerhardt	142
Supervisory Visits Locate Teachers' Needs George C. Kyte	146
To Improve Instruction, Supervision, and Evaluation . . . Thomas A. Petrie	149
The Supervisor's Part in Educating the New Teacher Roy A. Edelfelt	153
Supervision and Continuing Education for Teachers of English Robert F. Hogan, James R. Squire	157
Supervisory Techniques with Beginning Mathematics Teachers Sandra Noel Smith	163
Supervision and Team Teaching Ward Sybouts	165
The Supervisor's Role in Personnel Administration James E. Rutrough	168
Merit Rating: Have the Issues Changed? Frances R. Link	172
Supervisor: Coordinator of Multiple Consultations Pat W. Wear	176
Supervising Supervisors in an Urban School District Harvey Granite	180

Part V
Supervision: Its Potential

New Frontiers for Supervision Marcella R. Lawler	189
What Should Be the Crux of Supervision? Louise M. Berman	193
The "Guese" of Supervision Bernard J. Lonsdale	196
"Osmosis"—The New Supervision? William C. Jordan	200
A Challenge to the Supervisor Doris G. Phipps	203

vi • Supervision: Emerging Profession

A Supervision Experiment with the
    Disadvantaged   *Gertrude L. Downing*   206

Supervising Teachers of the
    Disadvantaged   *Marcia R. Conlin, Martin Haberman*   209

The Powerlessness of Irrelevancy   *Larry Cuban*   214

Beyond the Status Quo: A Reappraisal of
    Instructional Supervision   *David T. Turney*   218

Supervisors: A Vanishing Breed?   *Maurice J. Eash*   223

Is Systems Analysis for Supervisors?   *Maurice J. Eash*   227

Supervising Computerized Instruction   *William Van Til*   232

The Supervisor and Media   *Elwood E. Miller,
    DeLayne Hudspeth*   235

Curriculum Negotiations: Present Status—
    Future Trends   *William F. Young*   238

Negotiations: Inevitable Consequence of
    Bureaucracy?   *Robert L. Saunders, John T. Lovell*   241

The Supervisor We Need   *Richard F. Neville*   244

A Necessary Frame of Reference   *John T. Mallan,
    Frank Creason*   250

Social Planning and Social Change   *Frances R. Link*   253

Index   257

Foreword

An Emerging Profession

THIS anthology on supervision grows out of a need, long recognized by school people, for background materials in a single volume treating this special kind of instructional leadership. Represented in the volume are articles from a decade of writings (1960 through 1969) by leaders in the emerging profession of supervision.

This rich panoply of writings on supervision shows the experience and insight of many contributors to *Educational Leadership,* the official journal of the Association for Supervision and Curriculum Development. These contributions appeared in an era marked by changes that have stirred, tested, tried, and shaken older institutions not only in education but in all areas of society. Writing in such a time, the authors have without exception shown marked ability to analyze current needs and to project sound proposals for meeting them in the perspective of the future.

Today supervision itself is being challenged both from within and from outside the profession. The continued existence of the supervisor as an instructional leader is at issue. We may, therefore, find a great sense of pride and of reassurance in reviewing a record such as that presented here.

Supervision: Emerging Profession

The word "emerging" in the title of this anthology does not represent a last gasp of the holders of an anachronistic professional role. Rather the supervisor is emerging from this decade with a clearer self-knowledge, a deeper insight, and a broader perspective in the realm of instructional improvement.

Sixty-five articles are included in this anthology. The materials represent an exciting and sweeping panorama as they treat the various aspects, motivations, techniques, and goals of supervision. The essays fall rather naturally into five major sections. Within these sections the articles are arranged partly in chronological order and partly in accordance with the special aspects of the topics treated.

- "Leadership: Talent for Growth" presents the seminal concept of the leadership function, especially as this relates to the role of the supervisor. Stressed here are the ideas that the supervisor must provide a humane and supportive leadership that will skillfully and as rapidly as possible enable the recipients of supervision to proceed "on their own."

- "Issues in Professionalization" includes the essays that were planned and written by the ASCD Commission on Problems of Supervisors and Curriculum Workers. Problems treated here range from recruitment through the preparation, the certification, and the continuing education of supervisors and curriculum workers. These articles represent a new and more sophisticated approach by supervisors and curriculum workers to the authority, dignity, and responsibility of their own professional role.

- "Research: Instrument for New Knowledge" reflects a growing recognition by supervisors and curriculum workers of a need for creating or adapting means by which to study their own efforts. Only in this way can they improve and make more responsible and responsive their own methods, techniques, and goals. Accounts of research on supervisory processes included here represent a promising beginning.

• "The Supervisor at Work" brings clear and poignant pictures of supervisors at work as instructional leaders in classrooms and school systems. These essays show professional persons working in supportive relationships with teachers, principals, parents, and superintendents.

• "Supervision: Its Potential" projects the ideals and possibilities of supervision into the future. This future is at present only darkly glimpsed, but it does seem to offer promise of ever-widening vistas of need and potentiality for supervision. Special needs in the areas of research and of theory are identified as among the most pressing concerns of the supervisory profession.

This book is intended for use with students in teacher education who want to learn about some of the areas that lie "out there" in the broader education profession. Some of the challenge, excitement, and lure of adventure can be glimpsed in these pages. Graduate students, teachers in service, and supervisors themselves, whether general or in special fields, will find in these writings new inspiration, keener vision, and practical help.

Above all, they will find a deepening sense of pride in and commitment to the emerging and growing profession of supervision.

June 1969

ROBERT R. LEEPER, *Editor
and Associate Secretary
Association for Supervision and
Curriculum Development, NEA*

Introduction

Leadership: The Continuing Quest

IN A time when great changes are being made, and even greater changes are impatiently demanded, leadership mounts to a new importance. One can sympathize with a public hard pressed by financial demands if it wonders whether there is not too much superstructure of officials who do not actually teach children; yet one must say to that public that the improvements it wants will not come of themselves, will not come without the help of coordinated analysis and planning. One may sympathize even more with the mature, highly educated teacher who rebels against being told what to do and how to do it; if that was all there was to supervision, he would be right; but, again, one must say that the single classroom teacher, no matter how wise and skillful he is, stands in a poor strategic position to bring about major change by his lone efforts. There must be coordinating leadership if the institution itself is to reach new heights as the superior teacher does.

Yet to stake out a bold claim for educational leadership is only to start the mind whirling with questions. Even at the simplest levels of supervision the questions are more abundant than the known answers.

For instance, there *are* teachers—especially among the beginners—whose immediate needs are at the level of routine skills. They need to learn how to manage a classroom, how to keep records, and so on. Even at this level the question arises: What is the best way to "teach" them? Is it just to *tell* them? Is it to *show* them, by demonstration? Is it to get them the sympathetic help of a more experienced "buddy"? Or what?

A little further along the questions become even more insistent. There *are* teachers who can manage fairly well but whose "methods" are inadequate. They need to learn how to teach fractions in arithmetic or use phonics in reading. This is the sort of thing most people think supervision is all about. But how effective is the traditional system of visitation-cum-critique at even this relatively simple task? Would it be more effective to let the teacher visit around and see good models, or to view films and video tapes? Would a problem-solving seminar with some expert do it better? The questions flow on and on.

The rate of question-flow accelerates tremendously, even within this basic area of methodology, if what we are after is a more radical shift to, say, the development of an inquiry system of teaching. How can we help a teacher move away from the generations-old system of "telling" and assigning and quizzing—the system that is so firmly imbedded in his imagery of what teaching is? Will some form of interaction analysis, micro-teaching, and self-activated video-taping help him most? Or what?

And then we step up to the truth that teaching is, at base, a webbing of human interactions; that the climate of a classroom is more than the sum of all the best methods. Suddenly we are dealing with something far harder to influence than even the most complex skills. What will it take? Sensitivity training?

Even in writing this we seem to have assumed that supervision is something done to the teacher by some wiser, perhaps more experienced, superior. Yet we know that in all the dimensions that matter most it is *growth from within* that really counts. The most "efficient" methods of improving a teacher's skills may only leave us with a dependent, possibly frustrated person, little able or motivated to plow ahead on his own steam as a mature professional. Thus a whole new order of questions arises: How can we set a teacher free, help him toward autonomy, get him engaged on his own initiative? How can we help create a climate for growth? And what will that take in our own growth? Should the sensitivity training be first of all *for us*?

Still, even these hard questions assume that what we are concerned about is the individual teacher. They largely ignore that greater order of problems that has to do with the system itself. In a concerted way, how do we decide what our school system stands for, what its goals are, and its priorities among its goals? If we decide we want a comprehensive program of health education woven through the whole curriculum, how do we move toward it? And how do we do it so that everybody engaged in it grows in the process?

These are only a few of the questions which haunt any sensitive person in a position of supervisory leadership. Time is always short. He is terribly busy himself, and many of the people with whom he must work are even more harshly confined by set schedules. The demands upon his wisdom are numerous, for there are choices to be made which only an insider even knows to exist. The demands upon his moral stamina are at least equally great, for much of the time he operates amid conflict, engendered sometimes by honest differences in values and opinion, sometimes by personal antagonisms, fears, and the defense of vested interests.

His situation in recent years is further complicated by a variety of pressures. Teachers, asserting their growing independence, are often hostile to anything that smacks of direct supervision. Students and others are growingly restive and demand radical program change in the direction of greater "relevance." Parents press for direct accountability to them as to what their children should study and how well they learn. Roles are changing; staff organization is swirling; titles and functions are shifting. But whether his title is "principal," "supervisor," "curriculum coordinator," or whatnot, the person in a position of supervisory leadership is caught in the middle.

It is into such a world of genuine intellectual puzzles and social conflict that *Supervision: Emerging Profession* comes. It is one record of a decade of groping by a group deeply concerned for true democratic leadership. Some of the questions it deals with are technical, some philosophical, some social. The decade of its formation in the pages of *Educational Leadership* has been one of great ferment and growth—and that is reflected in its make-up.

But one thing this book never pretends to have—not on a single page—is the final answer. The quest for true democratic leadership, though it is an old quest in its way, is still only beginning. We are coming into a period when studies in leadership are intensifying and we can expect new help. The use of the newer media looks promising. Perhaps the various forms of interaction analysis will open new doors. Perhaps, too, the growing movement for sensitivity training will bring new resources.

However all that may turn out, one truth stands firm. The need for organized leadership, always great, is going to increase. The forms will change; the structure of staff organization will change; the nature and extent of participation by teachers and others will change. But the need for trained, dedicated leaders will not change—except to grow.

Too little has been made of this. The best educational leaders have often been, by the very nature of their sophistication in leadership, self-effacing and low in visibility. Just because of their sophistication, they are often the least "sure" people in the whole world of education. The quick, pat answer may serve everybody else, but not them; they know how little we know on the great questions of learning and teaching. Consequently, they are often hesitant and open to many choices. In lesser minds their doubt and hesitancy can all too easily be seen as weakness and lack of expertise. And their services can be seen as expendable.

Yet the truth is that the whole forward motion of education depends, to a fantastic degree, upon this little band of "supervisors." At best they are only a handful, these lifelong students of teaching and learning and leading. They deserve to be cherished, and ASCD cherishes them. We hope that the next ten years will see their numbers grow and their resources enriched. We hope that in 1980 another collection of "the best of *Educational Leadership*" will show that we have moved far ahead—even though then, too, the quest will still be only beginning.

June 1969

FRED T. WILHELMS, *Executive Secretary Association for Supervision and Curriculum Development, NEA*

PART I

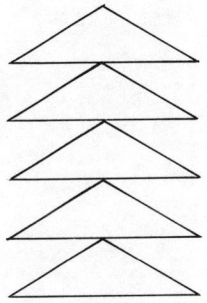

Leadership: Talent for Growth

The Human Dimensions of Supervision

Earl S. Johnson

IN SPEAKING about "the human dimensions of supervision,"[1] perhaps we can relieve the term "supervision" of its quite formal and even formidable coloration by speaking of a *person* who is a teacher-leader. Let us refer to such a person much more from the perspective of "acquaintance with" than from the perspective of "knowledge about." The difference between these two perspectives is near to profound because *appreciation,* which comes from "acquaintance with," must precede *understanding* which comes from "knowledge about." This order is, for me, the first law of pedagogy for I believe that we have little to *understand* unless we *appreciate* or *feel* something.

For the human dimensions and the obligations and risks of the role of teacher-leader let us turn to Martin Buber, the greatest living Jewish theologian. Following are some lines from the section on "Education" in his writings:

If education means to let a selection of the world affect a person through the medium of another person, then the one through whom this takes place, rather, who makes it take place through himself, is caught in a strange paradox. What is otherwise found only as grace, inlaid in the folds of life—the influencing of the lives of others with one's own life—becomes here a function and a law. But since the educator has to such an extent replaced the master, the danger has arisen that the new phenomenon, the will to educate, may degenerate into arbitrariness, and that the educator may carry out his selection and his influence from himself and his idea of the pupil, not from the pupil's own reality.[2]

Let me now restate what I understand to be Buber's "strange paradox" as it is set in the difficult role of teacher-leader. It is the paradox of "authority and freedom," for the questions which we must all resolve as teacher-leader are these: "How much of what kinds of authority shall we employ?" and "How much of what kinds of freedom shall we permit?"

My answer to these questions, if answer it be, is that authority and freedom must always be kept in balance. What that balance is, can be, or should be, I shall not undertake to state in terms of any principles, for these would have to rest on "knowledge about." Let me, rather, share with you, as my meager experience permits me, something in the nature of "acquaintance with" such a balance.

Let me begin sharing with you my feeling-knowing about the role of teacher-leader by saying something about the context in which that role is played. This context

[1] This article is based on a paper read at the 10th Annual Spring Convention of the Wisconsin Association for Supervision and Curriculum Development, May 2, 1960, at Marinette, Wisconsin.

[2] Martin Buber. *Between Man and Man.* Boston: Beacon Press, 1955. pp. 99-100. (Reprinted by permission of The Macmillan Company.)

Earl S. Johnson, Emeritus Professor of the Social Sciences, University of Chicago, and Visiting Professor, Social and Philosophical Foundations, School of Education, University of Wisconsin-Milwaukee

is, of course, the context of human association—groups of various sizes, engaged in a variety of cooperative tasks, and made up of individuals who, because they are individuals, are different in talents, in interests, in skills, and in knowledge. Being different in these respects they are *unequal* in these respects. But, being unequal, they are not unworthy!

Subject to Each Other

For the purposes of our concern, the most important feature of human association is that the members of it, the participants, *take each other into account*. I do not mean that they are simply polite to each other, although that relation is not ruled out. I mean, rather, that each is aware of the other, identifies him in some way—as able, friendly, confused, coarse, concerned, informed, ignorant, sympathetic, or whatever; makes some judgment or appraisal of him, identifies the meaning of his action, tries to find out what he has on his mind, tries to figure out what he is doing, why he does it, or what he intends to do. Note that each does this to the other; thus flies the shuttle which weaves a fabric of understanding, subject always to correction. Let me make it clear: I speak not of the relation of object to object, of subject to object, or of object to subject. I speak of the relation of subject to subject. Each is, if you will permit a play on words, "subject to each other." Each takes the other into account as the one who is taking *him* into account. Both are active; neither is passive. Both are influencing and being influenced. Their relations are in the nature of a transaction except that here each is buyer and each is seller.

In this account of human association I mean to suggest a moving process in which the participants note and gauge each other's actions and attitudes. Each, likewise, organizes his actions and attitudes with regard to the other—he inhibits, exhibits, encourages, guides, and directs himself, in short, *disciplines* himself and builds up those patterns of action and attitude which he believes to be appropriate to the situation which is, itself, constantly in change. That some are more adept at these things than others are does not gainsay that all engage in them.[3]

Such a process of organizing patterns of action and attitudes is the group process, *par excellence*. Each is a member of it to the degree that he takes the attitudes of the others and controls his conduct—overt and covert—in terms of their attitudes. This does not mean, at all, that he agrees with or capitulates to the attitude of others. The fact is only that he is aware of them and, in that awareness, structures for himself his unique actions and attitudes.

Yet, this account requires an important amendment. This is that here is enacted the *democratic* group process in the measure that participation is fully shared, to the degree that compulsion is absent in each one's coming to his own patterns of action and attitudes, and to the degree to which these patterns serve goodness and wisdom as defined and understood in the democratic image of collective and individual life. Dewey's words to this effect are these: "Regarded as an idea, democracy is not an alternative to other principles of associated life. It is the idea of community itself." Here, Dewey's statement about a fact is also a statement about a value.

If this account presents something not only quite complex but even mystical, such is the nature of the process of human association which is the process of *communication*—whether or not it takes verbal form. We may now better understand Dewey's observation that "... of all things communi-

---

[3] See: Herbert Blumer. "Psychological Import of the Human Group." In: M. Sherif and M. O. Wilson. *Group Relations at the Crossroads*. New York: Harper and Brothers, 1953. p. 194.

cation is the most wonderful ... that the fruit of communication should be participation, sharing, is a wonder by the side of which transsubstantiation pales." [4]

Traits of the Teacher-Leader

Within such a context the role and status of teacher-leader emerge. This means that I conceive this role and status to be a thing *earned,* rather than *assigned.*

Let me state what I understand to be the minimal conditions for the emergence of the role and status of teacher-leader. They are these:

1. A human association, democratic in its self-image

2. A common task or call it, in the somewhat heavy language of our craft, goal-oriented activities which are good and wise

3. Democratically disposed individual members with differing talents, skills, interests, and knowledge.

The teacher-leader is, then, the person who comes to be set apart from the other members of a human association by reason of the superior influence which he exerts upon the goal-setting and goal-achieving activities of such an association. How far such a person is from the one who is *officially* designated as teacher-leader, I leave to your own insight. I trust that the distinction between earned and assigned teacher-leader role and status is thereby confirmed. It is a real, not a titular designation. It is the role and status of teacher-leader, not of chairman or boss.

Such an interpretation of the teacher-leader role and status reveals that it does not reside alone in any personality trait taken singly, or even in a constellation of so-called teacher-leader traits. It reveals itself as the *function of a personality in a situation.* One cannot be teacher-leader in a social vacuum. Furthermore, certain personality types interact better and more effectively within certain kinds of group situations than do other personality types. Thus the role and status of teacher-leader is a relative rather than an absolute one. However, this fact of relativity should not be taken to mean that there is no similarity in the attributes which make for effective teacher-leader behavior in quite different group situations.

What these constants in teacher-leader traits or attributes are is difficult to state with either precision or certainty. Nevertheless let us hazard a sampling of them. They are such as these: respect for individual differences; the ability to initiate and an unwillingness to dominate; the skill and tact necessary to strike the "right" balance between *effectiveness,* which is the cooperative accomplishment of intended group objectives, and *efficiency,* which is the feeling by individual group members that they have been rewarded; and the ability to feel what the Quakers call "the sense of the meeting." Yet even these assumed-to-be teacher-leader attributes require the "right climate" of human association for their effective manifestation.

And now to these add the following: the gift of listening with "the third ear"— the ear of deep and sympathetic insight; one who is slow to anger and plenteous in mercy; one who does not command, for commandments anticipate only blind allegiance; one who shows and *teaches* but does not exhort; one who does not seek disciples, for the teacher-leader does not require servitude of one who, when the occasion arises, will supersede him; one who is virtuous and, in being so, knows that virtue is not an alternative to power but is, rather, the skillful and decent use of it; and one who understands

---

[4] John Dewey. *Experience and Nature.* La Salle, Illinois: Open Court Publishing Company, 1926. p. 166.

the import of the paradox that "since I am their leader I must follow them."

Each of these, whether far or near as universal attributes of the teacher-leader, will depend for its best expression on the type of human association to which it is appropriate, because these traits in some degree both arise in and are effective only in those human associations in which they *can* arise and function. The role and status of teacher-leader are, thus, always a kind of "back-inference" from demonstrated and proven abilities in given situations.

Yet, even as I recite these little-better-than hunches about the constants in the person whom I have called teacher-leader, I feel that one attribute has slipped through my fingers—perhaps one of the most significant. I share it with you in Count Tolstoi's delineation of the gray and aged commander of the Russian troops at the battle against Napoleon at Borodino. That the setting was military rather than civil or academic I believe is relatively unimportant:

> He gave no orders, but only assented to or dissented from what others suggested . . . when he listened to the reports it seemed as if he were not interested in the import of the words spoken, but rather in something else—the expression of face and tone of voice of those who were reporting . . . he knew that the result of a battle is decided, not by the orders of one commander-in-chief . . . but by that intangible force called the spirit of the army, and he watched this force and guided it as far as that was in his power.

Let me give you another conception of the role and status of teacher-leader: this time from civil affairs. I share with you the words of Edmund Burke:[5] "For my part, in what I have meditated upon the subject, I cannot, indeed, take it upon myself to say that I have the honor to *follow* the sense of the people. The truth is that I met it in the way I was pursuing their interest according to my own ideas."

From the attributes which have come out of my perceptions of the role and status of teacher-leader, to which are now added two classic conceptions of leadership in military and civil affairs, perhaps you may be able to construct an image of the teacher-leader most proper for the varying forms of human association whose theatre is the school.

I think of these varying forms lying within two major categories of human associations: those of teacher-and-students, and supervisor-and-staff. I remind myself, and you, that I have been trying to shed some light on the "right" balance between *authority* and *freedom*.

Communicating an Idea

These observations bring me to comment on what I believe to be the central intellectual problem facing the teacher-leader—the communication of an idea. I choose to present this problem through the poetry of the Persian poet, Kahlil Gibran, and the prose of the American educational philosopher, John Dewey. Although each refers to, or implies, only the role and status of teacher, their wisdom is quite as apt to the role and status of teacher-leader. Gibran writes:

> No man can reveal to you aught but that which already lies half asleep in the dawning of your own knowledge. . . .
>
> If he is wise he does not bid you enter the house of his wisdom, but rather leads you to the threshold of your own mind.
>
> The astronomer may speak to you of his understanding of space, but he cannot give you his understanding.
>
> The musician may sing to you of the rhythm which is in all space, but he cannot give you the ear which arrests the rhythm nor the voice which echoes it.

---

[5] Burke has been accused of opposing democracy. He opposed only its Jacobin form and manifestation which he saw, and correctly, as producing a totalitarian mass state of despotism rather than genuine democracy.

And he who is versed in the science of numbers can tell of the region of weight and measure, but he cannot conduct you thither.

For the vision of one man lends not its wings to another man. . . .[6]

I hope that you will wish to add this to your own collection of "the poetry of pedagogy"—the art to which we are all devoted but whose literature is so lamentably blind to its artistic, and hence poetic, nature.

Now, John Dewey's view and language on the same problem—whether ideas can be taught, *as ideas*. I share with you some lines from *Democracy and Education*:

> . . . *all* thinking is original . . . no thought, no idea, can possibly be conveyed as an idea from one person to another. When it is told, it is, to the one to whom it is told, another given fact, not an idea. The communication may stimulate the other person to realize the question for himself and to think out a like idea, or it may smother his intellectual interest and suppress his dawning effort at thought . . . Only by wrestling with the conditions of the problem at first hand, seeking and finding his own way out, does he think.[7]

I cannot forbear remarking here on the most redundant of redundancies, but one heard often in teacher circles: "We must teach them to think for themselves." The truth is, of course, that they can think *for* themselves only if they can think *by* themselves. The help we may give them is implicit in Gibran's and Dewey's wisdom.

But I see the role and status of teacher-leader in yet another context—that of priest and prophet. At the more elementary levels, our task is perhaps exclusively that of priest—to communicate the truths of the past, the culture's inheritance from past cultures. But, progressively, as these levels are left behind, our role becomes increasingly that also of prophet—to examine the relevance of the cultural inheritance for present times.

In the priestly role we are, in the best and most exacting sense of the term, soothsayers, that is, truth-sayers. In our prophetic role we are examiners, judgment-makers, and critics. Severe injury to the idealism of our students will certainly follow if we play the prophetic role before an immature audience. But, just as surely, our failure to play the role of prophet at the proper stage of our students' maturity will leave their critical capacities undiscovered, unchallenged, and undeveloped. Our obligation as teacher-leader is to play the roles of priest and prophet in helpful and proper balance. Both are called for more often than we think.

Our Faith in Progress

In these roles we serve the *beliefs* of our culture and *reasoned insight* into their meaning and usefulness. The beliefs are our convictions. These dictate the priestly role. This is our debt to the Hebrews. Reasoned insight takes the form of criticism of our convictions; this dictates the prophetic role. This is our debt to the Greeks. Thus, in these roles, we confirm the values on which not only our craft but also the civilization which it seeks to serve are founded.

May I now identify what is for me the prime virtue of the teacher-leader? This is the faith that we can bring every participant in the associations in which our professional life is cast to the top of his level of achievement and this, not by outdoing someone else but by coming into his largest intellectual and spiritual stature.

This is the faith that there is a yet undiscovered and unachieved dignity and worth in everyone. This is the grain of mustard seed which is "indeed the least of all seeds; but when it is grown is the greatest

---

[6] Reprinted from: *The Prophet* by Kahlil Gibran with permission of the publisher, Alfred A. Knopf, Inc. Copyright 1923 by Kahlil Gibran; renewal copyright 1951 by Administrators C.T.A. of Kahlil Gibran Estate, and Mary G. Gibran.

[7] John Dewey. *Democracy and Education*. New York: The Macmillan Company, 1916. p. 188.

among herbs and becometh a tree, so that the birds of the air come and rest in the branches thereof."

Such a faith is a faith in *knowing* and *loving*. Of the nature of knowledge we hear and know much. It is the nature of love of which we stand in great need of better understanding. I refer to love of self as well as to love of others, for they are not alternatives and they are not separable. When I speak of "love of self" I speak not of self-renunciation or selflessness. I speak in affirmation of the scriptural injunction to "Love thy neighbor as thyself." If to love my neighbor as a human being is a virtue, then it must be a virtue rather than a vice to love myself since I am a human being. Self-love does not exclude, indeed it includes, self-knowledge. How pathetic it would be if it were said of us, as King Lear's daughter said of her father, that "he hath ever but slenderly known himself" which condition was, I gather, cause of his inability to love himself. We know, by reason of this lack, what manner of man he was.

Thus the components of the democratic character, developed in a democratic social order, come to view. These are thinking and loving. These are the human dimensions of supervision. ☐

The Critical Shortage of Educationists

FRED T. WILHELMS

WHAT does "educationist" mean? For years it was an epithet hurled derisively at something like the group Conant now calls "the establishment." But that doesn't make sense if—as thoughtful people from the President on down are daily proclaiming—education is Number One on America's agenda. It is nonsense to cry the need of physics for physicists and of biology for biologists, and then to deny that the foremost of all our enterprises needs its own students and scholars—and that is what educationists are.

Why do we not make the title a proud one by defining it with tough realism and raising high the qualifications to earn it? I propose three basic tests:

That one is a lifelong, career student of the educating of human beings

That he looks at it whole, and is dedicated to its entire improvement

That he is *engaged* in it, working actively with its realities.

This is an exclusive definition. It will not admit to the title many of those behavioral scientists who make studies of learning, for example, or of group relations, but do them in isolation from the general context of education. Neither will it admit most of those scholars from other learned disciplines who labor so vigorously to improve the content of some curricular field.

Fred T. Wilhelms, Executive Secretary, Association for Supervision and Curriculum Development, NEA, Washington, D.C. In 1965, Associate Secretary, National Association of Secondary School Principals

The contributions of both groups are great and they are powerful allies; educationists depend upon them, and should be lastingly grateful for their work. But, as psychologists, anthropologists, historians, or linguists, they are best identified by their own proud titles.

Neither, regretfully, will the definition admit to the title many of the practitioners in education—classroom teachers, administrators, supervisors, etc. Again, their contributions are enormously valuable, and educationists depend upon them for steady, responsible proficiency as well as for a wide range of inventive innovations. But, under the grinding pressures of their daily tasks, all too few of them take that ultimate step from educator to educationist which depends upon the career-long, deep study of the educating of human beings.

Finally, the title is not to be bestowed automatically upon all those professors who teach in schools of education. Far too many of them are making a career of mouthing a few eternal generalizations which they learned in graduate school; far too few are genuinely engaged either in pushing out the frontiers of theoretical insight or in the hard, grimy business of solving the real problems of real schools.

Who are left, then, to earn the name? A small, tough-minded, hardly idealistic band! They come from every source: Some of them are classroom teachers, administrators, and supervisors who somehow—despite the demands of their daily realistic whirl—keep boring into the eternal inquiry, combining scholarliness and public statesmanship with their practical skill. Some are behavioral scientists and members of other learned disciplines who, having perhaps begun on a narrower base, become identified with the whole enterprise. Some are professors and researchers in the schools of education who spend their lives expanding and mobilizing what is known and thought, and getting the best of it applied to reality. And some, one is tempted to add, come from the ranks of the laymen—in citizens' commissions, for example, and in the PTA—individuals so driven by their zeal and their divine discontent that ultimately they make themselves authentic experts.

It does not greatly matter whence they come—there are all too few of them. We are in a time when the general commitment to education towers to unimaginable heights. But the very excitement of fine, devoted men leads to precipitate ventures, to shooting from the hip, to near-reckless promotion of pieces without regard to pattern, to answers without questions. In terribly short supply are educationists able to move from clearly articulated questions and problems, through the best that is known in theory and practice, toward integrated solutions. It is as if one suddenly had to staff an enormous enterprise and there were plenty of people with the know-how to do this or that part—but no one who knew what the whole thing was about. "The harvest truly is plenteous, but the laborers are few."

If this seems overdrawn, put yourself for a moment in the position of staffing the great nascent movement for reform of the social studies, with its many special projects in geography, anthropology, history, and other fields. Given the money, it may not be too hard to find excellent specialists, field by field. But where will you find sufficient supply of those who can see even the social studies whole—let alone their place in the entire curriculum—while at the same time bringing to bear what is known from the behavioral sciences and from experience as to learning and teaching and evaluation, as well as the whole philosophical *corpus* of what schools are for? To produce fragments is easy if one is willing to settle for narrow objectives; to produce a whole is something else again.

It is no wonder that educationists are

few, for the true educationist is a weird and wonderful combination. He has to be a gritty realist. He is the one who always has to remember all the youngsters. Others can go off for a few years' luxurious kick on behalf of the gifted—and then, just as suddenly, become sob sisters for the dropout; he was remembering both all the time. Others can seize onto one simple, pat answer—the phonetic method, team teaching, nongraded schools, or whatnot. He always has to go the hard, lonely way, living with uncertainty, knowing that the evidence is all too scanty—and yet be willing to place his bet on *some* way of moving in the meantime.

To assess even the evidence there is, he has to cover an enormous amount of ground, not only by study of theory and research but also by alert awareness of pioneering practice. Haunted by the desperate need for research, he lives in a world that respects research in almost every field except his own; tortured by his knowledge of what is already securely possible, he lives with a mass of mediocre performance in schools stifled only partly for want of money; zealous to live by the best findings of research and practice, he has to subject himself to the interminable politics of the catch phrase and the sententious tradition.

And yet he is no good at all if he loses his vision, if he cannot go on pressing after each rebuff, if he cannot take his ideas down into the marketplace of educational politics and mobilize campaigns he may never wholly win, wringing the sustenance of his life out of some small inches of gain.

Miraculously, a few do manage the combination. Scarred by many a conflict, they are as idealistic as the day they came out of college dewy-eyed and sure that they were going to reform the world. Even if they are practical schoolmen pushed by every day's exigencies, they still carry on the great inquiry and acquire a remarkable depth of insight. Or, if they are specialists in inquiry, they still retain a remarkable awareness of what is going on in the front lines and regularly move out there to fight for real effect.

I submit that this handful of seasoned students and campaigners—the real educationists—are a national resource unparalleled. It is time that they learned to speak with a firmer voice. It is time that the public learned to listen. It is time that we moved to produce more of them with at least the concern we show for producing more medical experts. It is time that the teachers colleges—particularly those with great graduate schools—be seen for what they are: the nerve centers and the generative dynamos of the best it will take to create a worthy education.

It is time that every school system—partly by the planned release of time and money, but even more by the creation of a climate—make itself a comfortable home for those educators who wish also to be educationists, to study as well as to act. It is time to end school reform by cliché and hunch and guess, and to put together a combination of all the resources it will take to develop sound inquiry and apply it to integrated action.

ASCD is not the only home of educationists—like gold, they are to be found where they are. Yet it is the outstanding home. It has never been away from the thick of action, but it has never wavered in its respect for inquiry, and it has never cravenly reefed its sails in the face of winds of contrary opinion. Yielding very little to any quest for popularity, it has persevered in tacking its way into those winds as best it could. The headway may be small at times, great at others, but it keeps on going. The typical ASCDer has joined its ranks precisely because his intellectual honesty drove him to love both inquiry into the truth and vigor in applying it. And his position tends to be one that gives him a better than average chance to see education in the large, to study it, and at the same time be engaged in action.

One could read this in self-congratulation, to say, "What a wonderful organization ASCD is!" We had better read it in the sobering thought, "What an awful responsibility ASCD bears!" We do not need to think ourselves alone. We do not even need to think invidiously of other organizations which serve their own groups and purposes well.

And yet the fact remains: No other organization has put together quite the same combination of people, to push the frontiers of educational thought and knowledge and apply what is learned unflinchingly to the whole of education. No other large organization has developed quite the same tradition of using all its membership and staff resources democratically to work its way through the toughest problems without giving an inch because of timidity.

And if this be so, what do we do now to use the brain and muscle we have grown? Within our own ranks we are an exceptionally congenial group, good at even painfully honest intercommunication. Can we consciously build on this resource to get ourselves more adequate preparation for a role so demanding that it is terrifying? (As I wrote this I questioned increasingly whether I met the qualifications; I wonder whether you haven't had the same reaction.) Can we consciously facilitate the mutual interpenetration of inquiry and practice, of specialization and wholeness?

Beyond our ranks, how can we best give our nation the help it needs in these days of high demand and short supply? Can we, and should we, deliberately build up the image of the educationist who is more than practitioner, more than abstract scholar, a person with a unique contribution? Can we bring him to be sought for by the public and by officials, so that he will be used where he is most needed? And can we make the unique role so attractive to the profession that more and more of the best young educators will also aspire to meet the tests of the educationist? ☐

EL 25 (4): 283-85; January 1968
© 1968 ASCD

"Most of the Change"

(An Editorial)

ROBERT R. LEEPER

*Most of the change we think we see in life
Is due to truths being in and out of favor.*[1]

[1] Robert Frost. "The Black Cottage." *Complete Poems of Robert Frost*. New York: Holt, Rinehart and Winston, Inc., 1958. p. 77. Copyright © 1930, 1939 by Holt, Rinehart and Winston, Inc. Copyright © 1958 by Robert Frost. Copyright © 1967 by Lesley Frost Ballantine. Reprinted by permission of Holt, Rinehart and Winston, Inc.

THIS editorial focuses upon "the introduction of something new" (which is one definition of *innovation*) in education. We will look at change and at some of the effects of certain truths being in and others being out of favor. We will also be concerned with *why* the "something new" is introduced, and with the results of its introduction.

Robert R. Leeper, Editor, Educational Leadership, *and Associate Secretary, Association for Supervision and Curriculum Development, NEA, Washington, D.C.*

Education is a deliberate relating of people, usually younger or less experienced with older or more experienced, in a setting that is contrived to produce change. Here we are concerned with the origin and the content of the "something new," the innovation—whether it be an idea, a fact, a method, a system, a body of knowledge, an object, or a technology. We are also concerned with the conditions under which the "something new" is made available to persons in the educational setting, and with the effects and the direction of such relating.

In a sense, we are dealing with the process by which the cultural invention is introduced in the school, with the manner, the content, and the effects of its introduction. Innovations will be self-defeating and futile if their advocates fail to take into account the feelings, motivations, values, and needs of the people concerned.

We have come to a time, in the evolvement of our democratic, industrial, scientific, and technological society, when we are becoming increasingly enriched by the creation of new inventions, especially in the realm of content, ideas, processes, products, and machines. We have for some time been in the early stages of seeking to comprehend what these new inventions are and what they mean and to apply these to people in the setting of the school. Many wise and well-informed persons have been involved in attempts to make this application in the school setting. Not always, however, have the attempts proved successful.

In several instances, the staffs of national projects, in updating the various content areas, have completed their massive endeavors, breathed a sigh of relief and leaned back, expecting the new materials, content, and approaches to transform practice. When such transformation did not begin at once to be apparent, staffs of these projects looked again at their implementation procedures. In some instances, the elements that needed most attention were those surrounding the point at which the innovative factor is brought into relation to the teacher and the learner in the school setting.

A Soil for Growth

Of prime importance in education are the factors which control the act of relating, the point at which teaching and learning take place in the setting of the school. Our society and culture have found it easier to provide the things and the content with which this educational setting is furnished than to influence and to enhance the intangible elements that surround this setting-for-learning. Some of these "intangible" elements that are so crucial to the success of education are psychological and social, while others are aesthetic, political, and value-based.

Perhaps it is easier to manage and to manipulate the tangible elements in the school setting than it is to provide a climate in which the intangible elements of teaching and learning will have a natural and responsive soil for growth.

Individuals—whether pupils, teachers, supervisors, principals, superintendents—cannot be manipulated into insight, into mastery, into wisdom, save at great cost, both to the manipulator and to the manipulated. And when such insight is achieved, it is likely to be infused with bitterness, or resentment, or other qualities so negative that society's cost for such a manipulative approach must be reckoned as too great.

One example of a very significant truth has been in favor at brief moments in certain schools in our nation and in other democratic lands. This truth is that innovation, the "introduction of something new," can best be accomplished in the schools of a democracy when the setting exemplifies the finest and best of respect for the individual, whether teacher or learner.

Not all innovation needs to derive from

the "great thinkers" or the status leaders or the specialists or the executives of business or industry or government. When a teacher or principal or supervisor gains insight and the confidence to introduce a change that he believes to be for the enhancement of the teaching-learning situation, this is innovation at the point of greatest need and significance. Such innovation should be supported and encouraged.

In an atmosphere reasonably free of threat, generally supportive, and confidently democratic, innovation is a continuing and expected process. In such a setting, innovation is not "new and different," it is the texture of each day's planning and working together for learning and for growth.

The innovative idea is not squelched because it is new and different—and therefore disturbing to routine practice. Consciously and selectively, the novel idea or approach is noted, discussed, shaped, fashioned lovingly and insightfully so that it will have a fair chance to be tried in a supportive atmosphere.

Some of the approaches that have been tried in innovation must be examined. Experienced educators must look at various aspects of theory and practice in innovation, at desirable objectives, at policy matters related to change, and at issues of public understanding and support.

As we think about innovation, its purpose and effect, let us not permit the glamour of the new and the novel and the manipulatable to blind our vision to some of the older truths that were dearly bought. Such truths might conceivably lend an invincible power to the "something new" that is being related *by* human beings *to* other human beings in an educational setting.

Above all, this setting must be contrived with, and be characterized by, intelligence and wisdom and love. ☐

EL *21 (2): 67-68, 136; November 1963*
© 1963 ASCD

A More Wholesome Balance

(An Editorial)

STEPHEN M. COREY

IN COMMON, I suspect, with a number of professors of education who write and talk about supervision I have had no personal, firsthand experience with it, as does a school teacher, for a long time. No "supervisor" has tried recently to get me to do my work more effectively, nor have I been thought of as a supervisor by those of my colleagues whose work I have tried to influence.

This being, in a sense, on the outside of the whole complex apparatus of supervision, with its status differences and its group identifications and its anxieties and resistances, can probably be only in part compensated for vicariously. One thing, though, has impressed me from my work with supervisors, my reading about what they do, and especially my experience with people trying to get me to do my work better and my

Stephen M. Corey, Emeritus Professor of Education, Teachers College, Columbia University, New York, New York, and Professor of Education, University of Miami, Coral Gables, Florida. In 1963, Professor of Education, Teachers College, Columbia University

attempts to get some of my colleagues to do better. This is that while modern supervisors may function in many different ways, and increasingly use a language of their own, and work with more sophistication in groups than they formerly did, the main purpose of supervision has not changed much, if at all, through the years. The primary job of the supervisor is still to do whatever he thinks will be successful to get *someone else* to work more effectively, more productively.

What has changed in connection with supervision, and this most members of ASCD are aware of, is that more and more people recognize that the method of getting another person to do his work better that had seemed so straightforward and reasonable and has been in use for a long, long time is not very effective. This time honored method has defined a supervisor as one who knows what ought to be done, and how, by those people he is supervising, and is able to get them to do what he thinks they should. The assumption is made that after hearing about and seeing what ought to be done, or submitting to some training in the new and better ways of working, the worker will do what the supervisor thinks is best even though this may seem to require more effort. If he does not do what he should, in this sense, he is stubborn or recalcitrant or unprofessional or something else bad.

As I have suggested, many students and practitioners of supervision doubt that this way of bringing about improvement in the work of another person can be very successful no matter how tactfully or gracefully it is attempted. In my experience, and I am sure it is not unusual, one central reason for this skepticism is not far to seek. When someone in my organization has as one of his main responsibilities getting me to do better, whether or not he is called a supervisor, this does something to our relationship. I rarely consider him a member of the group of my peers whose norms have much to do with my productivity. I realize that his success is judged differently from mine by the people who render these important judgments. His success comes, in large measure at least, from his ability to see what it is that I am not doing well, or getting me to see this, and his skill in bringing about change, presumably improvement, in my professional behavior. This is what his superiors expect of him no matter what euphemisms are used about our working together on the same tasks. The person who is trying to get me to do better will not like this perception of him because he knows it interposes a barrier between us. It makes his job harder because I almost *must* resist him in order to keep my self respect. He would rather I regarded him as a friend and co-worker and help giver. He could then be more influential with less effort.

One reason for what is often a resistant attitude toward many well intentioned supervisors who try to tell other people what to do is the built-in implication that they are constantly judging other people. We all make evaluative judgments about one another more or less continuously, of course, and this includes the way our associates do their work.

Whenever we suspect we are judged to be professionally inept, however, this sets in motion many mechanisms we have learned can protect somewhat our threatened self respect.

This is especially marked in our relations with a supervisor because by trying to improve us we know he thinks we are not doing what we should. Our defense is to believe that he, or any one else judging us unfavorably, is himself even more inept, or he is prejudiced, or he overlooks the favorable evidence, or he resents us personally. If we look closely we can usually find some evidence to support each of these accusations.

I am almost always surprised when some experience tells me again how very sensitive I am to criticisms of my own work, explicit or implied. Often when I ask for criticism I actually want commendation and am disappointed if I do not get it. Like most others I try to cover up this sensitivity because it is generally considered to be a weakness. The fact remains, though, that if someone wants to help me do better, he had better not let me know if he thinks I am doing poorly. If he does think so, I am almost certain to find out.

For another person to be very influential so far as my professional work is concerned, he must realize I am now doing as well as I can, all things considered, and these things may be legion. This assumption that workers, the teacher, you and I, actually want to do as well as we can, *in our own view,* and are constantly striving to live up to these higher expectations in those areas in which we seem not to be achieving as well as we believe we should, is not sentimental, of course. It is one of the important realities supervisors often overlook. Even when this is "known" to be true the conviction is often insufficiently internalized to make behavior consistent with it.

If I am in a mood to be helped by a supervisor or anyone else, and no one can do much with me along this line unless I am, it is not necessary that the person wanting to help me also judge me. I have already done that. What I need is a person who can help me think more penetratingly about what I am trying to do, the way I go about it, and the evidence I use to estimate my success. This requires quite a different kind of supervisor, it seems to me, from the one who believes his task is to know what I should do and then get me to do it. The help I need most is with a process and I regret that attention to processes has diminished in the recent emphasis on a product that is usually in the form of knowledge. I hope that ASCD can accelerate the return to a more wholesome balance. ☐

EL 22 (3): 149-54, 193-94; December 1964
© 1964 ASCD

Poise Under Pressure

RICHARD L. FOSTER

THIS paper will present three vignettes or backdrops. Some principles or hypotheses will be developed in relationship to these. These principles will then be shown in operation.

Three Vignettes

The first backdrop comes from the work of Chris Argyris of Yale, an industrial psychologist who has done most of his work with industry. Argyris states that in the typical business organization one finds at the top a president, some vice-presidents, and the directors. Next come the supervisors, and finally, the workers. In the schools we have boards of trustees, superintendents, assistant superintendents and directors, supervisors, and teachers.

Argyris says that in these typical or-

Richard L. Foster, Superintendent, Berkeley Unified School District, Berkeley, California. In 1964, District Superintendent, Jefferson Elementary School District, Daly City, California

ganizations there are specific human problems at the lower level. As one gets down the hierarchy, people at this lower level feel they do not belong to the organization—they are just there. What happens to these people? They leave! They get discouraged with what is going on, they realize they are not actually a part of the process—and they leave. Some of them stay but take sick leave. Some of them do not leave, and they do not take sick leave—they leave psychologically—they come to work every day, but they are not there.

Argyris did an interesting follow-up on this last group. He talked to some of these people about their supervisors—most of the responses were pretty negative. Occasionally Argyris ran into a worker who said he liked his supervisor. Investigating this response, he came upon an interesting phenomenon. He found that the supervisors who were liked were the ones who were not seen very often!

While Argyris' study does not treat the schools, his inclination is that schools have the same problem as industry. Company newspapers, company parties, higher salaries—none of these devices seems to ameliorate the situation. According to Argyris, the only solution comes through commitment in which there is inner personal trust and confidence.

Backdrop number one then seems to say: Something has to be done about the organization of schools if people who work in them are to develop a sense of commitment.

Let us move on to vignette number two. The Rockefeller report on *The Pursuit of Excellence* [1] states that no educational system will be any better than the quality of its teachers. In the effort to bring about improvements, schools can do all kinds of things with such administrative arrangements as "ungraded schools" and "team teaching" and bring in machines and any new device available—experience shows that it will not make much difference unless there is a change in the quality of the teachers in the system. Moreover, this quality has to embrace many types of diversity if a rich kind of school system that most of us would like to enjoy is to develop.

A brief history seems to fit in here. A year or two ago I went to the opening meeting of the teaching staff with whom I work. One of our new teachers showed up with a beard. The president of the Board of Trustees, after the meeting was over, said to me, "What are you going to do about that beard?" I said, "Ah, nothing. I'll just wait and see what it means." In about three weeks the principal of that school came to me and said, "Would you like to know about that beard?" I said, "Not particularly." He said, "Well, let me tell you about it anyhow. This teacher is in a Shakespearean play. He's one of the actors in the play, and that's why he's got the beard." I said, "Oh." A few weeks passed, the play was over, and the teacher shaved his beard. I saw the principal about a month later and he said, "Hey, Dick, the guy's growing a beard again. You know what? The kids liked him better with the beard than they did without it!"

Our conception of excellence is going to have to include many kinds of people who can do many kinds of things. Bruner reports that Whitehead has said that education should be "an exposure to greatness." It seems to me the only real exposure of any lasting depth that children get in the public environment called the school is with teachers. You can rig your school system with a lot of individuals called counselors, supervisors, principals, and superintendents, yet it is a one-to-one relationship with the teacher that makes the difference.

---

[1] Rockefeller Brothers Fund. *The Pursuit of Excellence.* New York: Doubleday & Co., Inc., 1958. 49 pp.

Harold Clark at Teachers College, Columbia University, conducted a broad research project in his study of "quality education." When he came to analyze the data, he found an interesting fact. Whenever a teacher was using any kind of reasonable method, and was enthusiastic about that method, pupils learned. Of course, somebody is going to ask, aren't some methods better than others? Probably; but not as important as enthusiasm.

That is picture number two. Now let us move to number three and discuss the dynamics of change. There are many people in school systems who believe that change can be ordered by authority. Occasionally a trustee says to me: "Couldn't you put out an order on this item?" I point out that I could, but that probably nothing would happen. Teachers are very bright. They know which of the notices that I send out are important and which are trivial.

A system can develop a curriculum guide which may or may not be opened during the year. Guides per se do not develop behavioral change. How then does change take place if not by order, by curriculum guides, or by a state adoption—although any of these may exert some influence? It seems to me that change takes place when one has new experiences in a creative environment in which there are tremendous opportunities for perceptions in an open society. People act on what they perceive, and this is what makes the difference.

Change is a very interesting thing. Change means that one has to set new levels of aspiration—one must get a little bit anxious again about what he is doing. Change is a drain on energy. By the way, a certain amount of resistance to change is a healthy thing. If everybody changed on what everybody else thought was good for them, we would all be schizophrenic. So, in my dimension, change comes in an interesting, perceptive, aroused, creative environment in which one gets goose pimples simply because he works there.

The questions raised in these first three parts may be summarized by an additional question: How do we create an educational environment in which people are committed to the task, are open to change, and in which they are free enough to respond enthusiastically?

Leadership Style

Let me now introduce my concept of leadership. I use one that Gross advocates. He says that there is a leadership style in which the only conversation is: "What can I do to help?" I am in total agreement with the Rockefeller report on the importance of the teacher as the critical factor in how fine a school system we have. I am also amused at Herbert Thelen's comment in *Education and the Human Quest*:

Teachers are of all sorts, too: they range from nimble piccolos to thumping basses, from mellow horns to clashing cymbals; from sparkling champagne to flat beer; from lovable lizzies to champing Cadillacs.[2]

It seems to me that the most important contribution to come from those in leadership roles is the achievement of keen insights in the selection of personnel for a school district. In our district we have been using, in our interviewing and hiring, the three criteria recommended by David Ryans in his research on characteristics of teachers. According to Ryans, some of the criteria seem to be more important in the elementary school than in the high school. In my judgment, however, these criteria are as much needed in the high school as in the elementary school.

Pattern X: Understanding, friendly,

[2] Herbert Thelen. *Education and the Human Quest.* New York: Harper & Row, Publishers, 1960. p. 16.

warm teachers *vs.* aloof, egocentric, restricted teachers.

In interviewing an applicant, the first thing I look for is to see if this is a warm, loving human being. If it is a male, I look to see if he is male-like; and if it is a female, I want her to be female-like. One of the questions I sometimes ask in an interview is, "Do you see yourself as a real female (or a real male)?" It is surprising how many people are afraid of this question, almost as if they are afraid to reveal that they are human beings.

Pattern Y: Responsible, businesslike *vs.* evading, slipshod, unplanned behavior.

What is a good day in the fourth grade and how would you plan for it? Is this a person who plans in the broad sense? (This does not mean lesson plans.)

Pattern Z: Stimulating, imaginative, surgent, enthusiastic people *vs.* dull, routine sorts of human beings.

That word "surgent" is one that moves for me. What do you get excited about? Can you laugh? Can you cry? Can you feel? Can you touch? Are you a real human being? With the help of a college, a person can be taught techniques and methods and even the structure of knowledge; but it is extremely difficult to make human beings out of people who have worked for 20 some years at being inhuman.

Using these criteria we can find the warm, sensitive, enthusiastic young teachers. However, some of them will only be around for two or three years, because if they are warm, enthusiastic, sensitive young girls, they are soon going to become wives and mothers. That is one of the risks one takes when one works with human beings.

After we have found and employed these wonderful, "human" persons, what do we do about it? I have some hypotheses that many people may not agree with, but here they are.

Four Hypotheses

First, you have to operate within a decentralized hypothesis. This can be terribly debilitating if you have been working with a centralized concept of school organization. Learning takes place in the individual classroom in the individual school; it does not take place in the central office. This means that the individual school should make the decisions on what its in-service program is going to be and what it is going to work on. The school has a right to hire its own consultants without central office consent and the school should make the decisions on which consultants from the central office, either city or county, it is going to use. This means that various schools will be moving at different paces on different things.

The second hypothesis is that supportive personnel are not responsible for producing change in others. As human beings working with teachers we have only one responsibility—to communicate openly what our feelings are and to interchange in the communication. We cannot be responsible for other people. They are responsible for themselves, to be their own self-actualizing instrument. They have this prerogative, and we have no right to deprive them of it.

The third hypothesis has to do with consultation. In my judgment, consultation is a unique professional relationship between peers in which either of the two persons involved has the right to terminate the consultation at any time. It is a healthy environment if a teacher, in consultation with his supervisor, feels he can say, "I think I am now ready to move by myself, with support." Supervisors do not rate, they do not evaluate, they do not praise, they do not reward, they do not punish. They *interact with*. This is the only kind of support that human beings should have.

My fourth hypothesis is one with which many readers may be familiar: It is that principals sometimes cast long shadows on schools. The Ohio State University study in regard to which characteristics in principals make a difference is one that ought to be considered in the selecting and hiring of people. This study suggested that there are three characteristics that make a difference.

One characteristic was comprehensiveness: The ability to see the educational cosmos in a broad sense; having intellectual and emotional stamina to stand the press of the immediate; the ability to tolerate theoretical considerations; the ability to see that a day was good in its big sense, not because the football team won a game, and not because some pupil did something spectacular, but because of what is going on in a big, comprehensive picture. When we are near a principal like this, we get the feeling that "something is happening here."

The second characteristic was penetration: The ability to ask questions about things which everyone else is taking for granted; the willingness to penetrate into a problem and ask, what really makes the difference here? If we had done this, we would not, for example, have so many unused language laboratories around the country at present. For a time, it almost became a cultural symbol of accomplishment to buy a language laboratory whether it was usable or not.

The third characteristic was flexibility: "Flexibility," in the study, was defined as absence of psychological rigidity, a tolerance for tentativeness. Let me emphasize: A tolerance for tentativeness—so many people want the answers right now, as though the answers are always evident!

Recently a psychologist made a recommendation in regard to the placement of a youngster in one of our hard-of-hearing classes. After I listened to all the technical presentations that went on about I.Q.'s and scores and hearing and all the rest, I asked him: "What is your clinical 'hunch' as to what this youngster will do in the classroom?" He answered, "I had a feeling you were going to ask me that question, and I don't know. After all this technical data, I haven't formed my clinical 'hunch.'" I said: "Why don't you take another day and formulate a clinical 'hunch' and come back and let's talk about it? You now know so much about this child that you really don't even see him. Get an idea as to what's going on here in a tentative sort of way. We don't care if you're wrong. We care if you care enough to have a 'hunch' about this youngster."

These four hypotheses then make up the second part of this paper. Now let us see how they work.

A Technique of Change

About three years ago, in a conference with the consultants, we were discussing the fact that our school district was getting large—about 9400 children. We were reaching the point at which it was impossible for consultants individually to contact all the schools. The suggestion was made that perhaps a more effective method of operation could be arrived at. Maybe a consultant could find some teachers and a principal who were interested in a particular area, and the consultant could then work with them in depth.

Two or three of the people at this meeting seized this idea enthusiastically. One of these was our health consultant. We have been using a magnificent health series in the district. It is one of those series in which we can teach nutrition from the first to the sixth grade, and can guarantee at the seventh grade, when the kids are turned loose, they will buy a coke and candy bar for lunch! Our health consultant decided that she would like to find a few teachers and a principal who would be interested in having youngsters at the fifth and sixth grade level study about their hearts and circulatory systems in depth.

She found two teachers who were interested in such a study and a principal who wanted to work with them; and with these people she developed a program. Every day she co-planned, she co-taught, she team-taught, she did all of the things that one is supposed to do in teaching. She worked with small groups, she worked with large groups, she worked with the teachers. One of the things she found out, she said, was that you have to think through what makes a difference in knowledge before you can help anybody gain knowledge.

What about the children involved in this program? They were fifth and sixth graders, not homogeneously grouped, from middle-class environment, with average I.Q.'s—probably about 105 or 106. Every child in the group, by the time the work with the program was over, could trace a drop of blood through the entire circulatory system. They could tell you in technical terms, and they usually wanted to be more technical than we wanted to be, the anatomy of the heart. They could tell you the difference between a normal and an abnormal heart. They made all kinds of charts and diagrams. They could tell you what happens in a stroke and a thrombosis and a coronary and how the system recovers and what takes place in the capillaries and why it takes place. They could talk with you in depth about the importance of mental health or the effects of alcohol, tobacco, or stress.

More interesting was the fact that these children *wanted* to do all this studying; they were enthusiastically interested in learning all they could about the heart. Parents reported that the children were asking for models of the heart for Christmas presents. Children who had never before been really excited about anything in school became so enthusiastic that they were reading books all the way up to college level in order to find the information they needed. We have done the same thing in other areas of the curriculum.

When this heart program had progressed to the point at which it really made sense to the two teachers, the principal, and the consultant, we decided to put on a demonstration. Other teachers in the district were notified that we would hold an open meeting and that anybody who wanted to come was welcome. These teachers were assured that they were not expected to do anything about the fact that they were there—just to come to see what other people were doing.

As a result of this initial effort, at the present time (three years later) approximately four-fifths of our teachers in the fifth and sixth grades are voluntarily teaching a depth unit dealing with the heart.

This technique of change works equally well in many areas. In order to be able to support these efforts on the part of our teachers, we yearly hire five to ten more teachers than are needed in the classroom. We use them as substitutes, but we use them primarily to release teachers who can then go to see other people at work. It is so simple, yet it brings results. Moreover, working in this small kind of teacher-to-teacher relationship allows us to cut down considerably on the large group meetings most districts find so necessary.

In our district we have about 75 student teachers a year. When teachers come to work for us, they are told that within three years they are expected to be able to handle student teachers. We try to work so that teachers who have been with us for a year or two get a chance to do one of the demonstrations with somebody working with them in depth. We try to rotate the number of teachers who work with new teachers a couple of weeks before school starts. We recently put on a curriculum fair in which we presented some 18 different demonstrations for parents.

When every teacher has been a master teacher for student teachers, has put on a number of demonstrations for other teachers, has worked with new teachers before school started—then a staff seems to emerge that is motivated by excitement and commitment.

The program I am suggesting in curriculum change has a basic investment in people. First, "I really believe that people want to perform well if they are free enough to perform well, and this performance is not based on any kind of gimmick."

Second: "I have tremendous faith that individual schools will make adequate and dependable decisions on what they want to do and that each school will become its own broken front."

Third: "I believe that an environment that is dedicated to growth and to development of people, in which everyone is free to move, finds less resistance. When people suddenly discover they are free, they do not have to fight against things but can put their energy to the things they want to do."

I must warn you that if, after thinking these suggestions through, you should decide to try them, you are going to come up against new pressures. There are those who will want you to issue directives—they will want to know when you are going to make the district adoption, which means "When will we fixate at a certain point so we do not grow?" They will want you to emphasize homework and A B C's and phonics. Hemingway had a definition of "courage" which was: " 'Courage' is grace under pressure." I have a definition which says, " 'Courage' is poise under pressure." You are going to need a lot of poise under pressure when you begin to invest in human beings in an interesting, creative, consultative way. □

Leadership for Human Change

(An Editorial)

HAROLD D. DRUMMOND

AS THIS is written, the American people are being bombarded through our marvelous communication media with myriad appeals made by candidates of our two major parties. The political struggle is being waged to determine which of the parties shall provide leadership for the next four years. Long before this is published the political decision will have been made in typical American fashion by each interested person voting his own convictions. This experiment has worked well for us as

Harold D. Drummond, Professor of Elementary Education, University of New Mexico, Albuquerque. In 1964, Chairman of the Department and President, ASCD

a people and as a nation for 175 years—not perfectly by any conceivable yardstick—but well. Through the technique of the ballot box and the voting machine we have chosen our leaders. They have, in the main, provided leadership for human change.

Educational leadership even more than political leadership *must* be oriented to human change. The basic goal of education *is* change—human change—in desirable directions. We welcome young children, most of whom cannot read, or write, or figure, into our elementary schools. About twenty years later some of these same individuals will have a hood, signifying the doctorate, placed upon their shoulders—symbol of high academic achievement and superior scholarship. What enormous changes have taken place in these individuals between these two points in time! The frightened, mother-oriented kindergartners have become the poised, confident, effective scholars. Not all of the credit for the changes can be assumed by the schools the scholars attended; but the schools are the social agencies specifically charged in our culture to accomplish such miracles. That such changes do occur regularly in our society is a tribute to parents, to teachers, and to our political and cultural systems.

Unfortunately, undesirable changes also frequently occur as young people move through our system. Some youngsters never seem to develop the aspirations, the drives, and the skills needed to achieve at a level near their potential. Some of them become the well-advertised dropouts. A few will undoubtedly repudiate authority and acceptable norms of behavior to become the beatniks, the juvenile delinquents, the rapists, and the gangsters of tomorrow. Not all of the blame for such changes should be placed upon the schools these individuals attend; but, as the social agencies specifically charged in our culture to accomplish other changes, schools must accept considerable responsibility for such failures.

Changing People

We must focus attention upon the school as a change-agent—and the specific focus is on changing *people*. Quite generally, the adults in this nation accept behavior change as an important function of the schools. Not all adults agree, however, on the specific behaviors desired. Clearly, one of the major responsibilities of educational leaders in such a situation is, therefore, *to help build sounder understandings of what constitutes desirable behavior* at every step in the educational process.

Certainly, we can all agree that behavior deemed acceptable for a five-year-old is not acceptable for a high school senior. A major problem is that well-meaning parents and teachers sometimes expect adult-like behavior from youngsters, and build such pressures on them that undesirable behavior is almost sure to occur. Contrast such leadership with that described in the ASCD yearbook *Perceiving, Behaving, Becoming:*

Perhaps the one over-all implication for education drawn from the discussion of fully functioning people by our four authors is that education must value change. As people are ever-moving and ever-becoming, education needs to move into the future with them. We need to de-emphasize tradition and the past and devote more energy to the present and the future. Schools should be places where students can grow and change as total personalities. Most of the suggestions in the preceding paragraphs call for change—for the valuing of change. Educators can no longer afford to deplore and resist change. Too many teachers are still insisting that things must be done the "right" way. In such an atmosphere, goodness becomes synonymous with conformity. Messiness, noise, confusion, and mistakes, out of which may come originality, creativity, and genius, are suppressed in favor of neatness, quiet, order, and "being right," out of which can come conservatism, cowardice, rigidity, and smugness.

We have spoken of the importance of

teachers who value change. It is even more important in supervisors and administrators. If administrators desire courageous and creative teachers who are forward moving and open to experience, they must welcome, value, and encourage change. Experimentation must be facilitated and even, sometimes, protected. Differences in teachers must be appreciated and encouraged, not just tolerated. To do this, supervisors, administrators, and teachers will, themselves, need to overcome their fear of making mistakes. Change will only occur in an atmosphere where change is valued, difference is warmly appreciated, and mistakes, which are the inevitable concomitant of trying, are accepted as a normal part of the price of growing. Each person can only behave in terms of what seems to him important. To induce values in others, then, administrators and supervisors need to be sure that they really hold the values they say they do and that this message is getting through to those they supervise.[1]

Effective leadership for desirable human change comes from those persons who themselves are open to life, growing, and fully functioning. They see ahead limitless possibilities for man—a world of peace, justice, harmony, plenty—and they face that future with hope, with joy, with commitment. Leaders with such vision and commitments provide settings within which young people can grow in confidence and competence; can learn to accept the hard knocks of defeat and discouragement as well as the thrilling experiences of success and achievement; and can develop self concepts which will enable them to face the world as secure, free, creative, courageous persons.

The basic and continuing task of leadership for human change is to develop educational institutions which surround learners with love, patience, support, understanding, guidance toward responsible use of freedom, opportunity to make mistakes without loss of standing, and challenges commensurate with their maturity and abilities. Within such settings, commitment to basic human values will continue to be developed in succeeding generations of young Americans. Within such settings, human personality will be treasured, differences will be accepted and cherished, hard work will be willingly undertaken because of goals clearly perceived, and feelings of goodwill toward all men will naturally grow. □

[1] Arthur W. Combs, Chairman. *Perceiving, Behaving, Becoming*. Washington, D.C.: Association for Supervision and Curriculum Development, 1962. p. 207.

Supervision: Loneliness and Rewards

ALICE L. MCMASTER

I would not exchange the sorrows of my heart for the joys of the multitude. And I would not have the tears that sadness makes to flow from my every part turn into laughter. I would that my life remain a tear and a smile.
KAHLIL GIBRAN (1)

THERE are elements within the framework of the role of the supervisor which bring a rich return and there are elements that seem to make it a lonely quest. On some occasions, it is difficult to distin-

Alice L. McMaster, Contra Costa County Department of Education, Pleasant Hill, California

guish "east from west" and to know where one set of elements begins and the other leaves off. Feelings become mixed. At other times, the reward or the loneliness appears distinct and the feelings are clearcut. The supervisor's role is both "a tear and a smile."

Although the school personnel who share responsibilities for supervision have much in common, the material contained in this article relates specifically to the role of a curriculum supervisor or consultant working at a district level. The intent is not to be theoretical or abstract, but to share some personal thoughts about the nature of the supervisor's role and how it relates to feelings of reward and moments of loneliness.

Supervision: A Shared Function

Much sincere, direct, and provocative writing has been done on the topic of modern supervision. Attention has been directed to its definition, purpose, scope, and unique values, as well as to its central problems and issues.

The use of well defined terms assists in counteracting the tendency to stereotype the general term, "supervision." Such an effort has been made in *Supervisory Behavior in Education,* by Ben M. Harris (2), with whom, some years back, the writer had many happy and rewarding experiences in the curriculum work of a local school district.

The terms and their distinctions are given as follows: "instructional supervision," conceptualizing supervision as a part of a larger entity; "supervisory behavior," describing the tasks, skills, and processes involved; "supervisory personnel," referring to all personnel sharing responsibility for leadership in supervisory activities regardless of position, title, status, or amount of responsibility; and the term "supervisor," being reserved for those whose major responsibilities are for providing leadership in supervisory activities.

According to Harris, many new terms have been created to replace or substitute for the word "supervisor" in order to reflect more precisely the nature of the work and the newer concepts of supervision. Among the host of such terms are coordinator, instructional leader, and consultant.

Much of the professional literature reveals that supervision is a shared function, that it should be viewed as a part of the total operation of the educational system, and that its primary purpose is for the development and improvement of the total teaching-learning process.

Modern supervision is positive, dynamic, democratic action designed to improve classroom instruction through the continual growth of all concerned individuals—the child, the teacher, the supervisor, the administrator, and the parent or other lay person (3).

Nature of the Supervisor's Role

For the most part, the supervisor's feelings of reward or loneliness revolve around some unique feature of the role. The purpose here is to discuss some of these features, not to define, describe, or defend the position.

There are certain factors which are basic to the effectiveness of the supervisor's task. Among the most crucial are: (a) the supervisor himself—his personality for the role, his feelings toward other people, his background of experience, and his convictions concerning what the role has to offer; (b) the belief in and the support given to the position by the administration, the school board, and the community; and (c) the personal and working relationships established among the personnel of the school district, including a team approach involving teachers, principals, parents, children, and members of the supervisory personnel.

The work of the supervisor involves the lives and feelings of people—with different backgrounds, experiences, and opinions. "Principles of individual differences, acceptance, and self-understanding—as well as the results of other contributions to the study of human beings—should be applied to instructional leadership" (4). The work is on a "feeling" level, and continuously calls for sensitivity to situations, for intuitive responses, for patience with time, and for wisdom to know when to lead and when to follow, when to speak and when best to remain silent. It is a matter of having an open mind, being an "open self" (5), seeing the worth of others and having a good image of self.

In the ASCD 1962 Yearbook titled, *Perceiving, Behaving, Becoming: A New Focus for Education* (6), Earl C. Kelley says that the "fully functioning person" not only thinks well of others, but thinks well of himself—"the oneness of the self-other relationship." He goes on to say that "it is doubtful that there can be a self except in relation to others, and to accept one implies the acceptance of the other."

These qualities of being able to see through the eyes of the other person, to place oneself in another's shoes, to exemplify warmth and mutual trust, and to reflect a "we are in this together" feeling are often the factors in supervision which determine whether or not another person is willing to take a second look or give something another try. This way of working, although not always easy to do, can provide the most satisfaction for others and can, at the same time, give the supervisor his greatest feeling of reward.

If he is indeed wise he does not bid you enter the house of his wisdom, but rather leads you to the threshold of your own mind (7).

Decisions are often made on a moment-to-moment basis. Certain occasions call for extemporaneous thoughts. Intuition and a good night's sleep may be the best preparation. Other contributions allow for more time and for planning, not over-structured, but thorough enough to present a relaxed feeling of oneness with the group.

Situations may vary; roles become blurred; changes are in order; one's sense of timing cannot always be accurate. The strength of the contribution may depend on another's strength of leadership. The scope of the work can be wide or narrow; the purposes can be alike or different; distinctions are often subtle. Some work can be held in the hand—a guide or a handbook. Other work can be held only in the heart—a suggestion made in a principal's office or a smile from a teacher as she hands you some children's stories.

In operation the supervisor's role often loses its identity. The how's, what's, and when's can be vague. The why's are usually relative to the situation. What one does is difficult to define. I was visiting a fifth grade classroom not too long ago. A vivacious youngster at the back of the room looked at me and asked, "What do you do for a living?" His attention was called to the front of the room and I drew a deep breath. As I walked down the hall, I wondered what I would have said if time had allowed.

The results of the supervisor's work are often measured in someone else's success. Many times the best job a supervisor can do is the job that helps someone else to succeed. The better his work, the more accurately another's performance may be judged. The irony is that the very essence of the role can lead to misunderstanding and misconception, and perhaps negative evaluation, as related to "the need for" or "the help from" a curriculum supervisor. This feature is abstract and subtle and must be understood and accepted by the supervisor as an inherent and positive part of the role. Acceptance of this paradox can bring reward; lack of acceptance can cause frustration and long moments of loneliness.

A Personal Note

It is a soul-searching experience to think back over the happenings in one's work which have given feelings of reward, and about those which have brought loneliness. Recently, as I have heard friends in the field of supervision speak about their experiences, and as I have recalled my own, I have been reminded that the greatest satisfaction for a supervisor comes from the type of work that brings him in contact with people.

Following are some kinds of opportunities and experiences which I feel bring feelings of gratification. Although this changing role has both joys and sorrows, loneliness would come to me if circumstances did not afford these types of satisfactions. The experiences listed have been jotted down as I have thought "out loud" about my work as a curriculum supervisor in a school district.

1. Being a part of a school district where value is placed on the roles of the supervisory personnel, where the "team approach" of working is established as vital to the service, and where some balance is maintained between the direct work in the schools and the work on a district level

2. Working in a school where the principal plans and makes the best use of a supervisor's time

3. Assisting a teacher with methods, materials, techniques, etc., which may help to make her experiences and those of the children more rewarding

4. Talking and working with the children in a school

5. Helping with the planning and holding of in-service meetings around school or district needs

6. Taking part in the development and try-out of new approaches to the teaching-learning process

7. Having such opportunities as: making a visit to a classroom, reading and reviewing the new materials for teachers and children, reading a set of original stories, watching a group of children put on a puppet play, etc.

8. Helping with the planning and decision-making procedures as related to the curriculum program within the district

9. Having opportunities to take part in activities outside the school district which provide means of gaining knowledge and which, in turn, can be of assistance to the district

10. Having a personal feeling from day to day of being of help to someone in some way.

In times of change, which can bring depersonalization, pressures, and fragmentation, there is need for ways of working which bring people close together.

This can be a part of a supervisor's contribution and at the same time can be the source of his greatest reward. Howard Thurman (8), educator and theologian, has expressed his feelings in these words: "In this atomic age, the only refuge a man has is another man's heart." ☐

References

1. Kahlil Gibran. *A Tear and A Smile*. New York: Alfred A. Knopf, Inc., 1950. p. 3.

2. Ben M. Harris, *Supervisory Behavior in Education*. New Jersey: Prentice-Hall, Inc., 1963. pp. 6, 11, 12, 23-24.

3. Ross L. Neagley and N. Dean Evans. *Handbook for Effective Supervision of Instruction*. New Jersey: Prentice-Hall, Inc., 1964. p. 17.

4. Luther E. Bradfield. *Supervision for Modern Elementary Schools.* Columbus, Ohio: Charles E. Merrill Books, Inc., 1964. p. 8.

5. Charles Morris. *The Open Self.* Chicago: University of Chicago Press, 1956.

6. Earl C. Kelley. "The Fully Functioning Self." In: *Perceiving, Behaving, Becoming: A New Focus for Education.* Washington, D.C.: Association for Supervision and Curriculum Development, 1962. p. 18.

7. Kahlil Gibran. *The Prophet.* New York: Alfred A. Knopf, Inc., 1945. p. 62.

8. Howard Thurman. From a speech at a banquet in his honor, San Francisco, 1964.

When Supervisor and Principal Work Together

NICHOLAS J. VIGILANTE

LEADERSHIP problems, notably resistance to change at the principal-supervisor level, generally occur because the attitude balance in the principal-supervisor relationship has been disturbed. As educators, we frequently see disturbances as we work with principals and supervisors.

In order to determine imbalances in principal-supervisor relationships, we must first closely define a balanced relationship. The optimum balance is one of mutual respect. A mutual respect balance exists when each is respected and is encouraged to practice and pursue the satisfactions of his position until that pursuit infringes on the right of the other to do the same. Inherent in this relationship are an awareness of role definition, leadership skills, status, intellectual honesty, communication skills, empathy, and other personality dynamics.

Role Perception

As we strive toward mutual respect, a close examination of the current views of the perceived role of the principal and supervisor as seen by the supervisor and principal is a critical need in any analysis of the working relationships of these two related positions. To what degree does congruence or incongruence exist? Research and theory dealing with the nature of human behavior in social settings illustrate that an individual's personal philosophy, his way of looking at the world and people around him, determines his success as a change agent. In effect, the quality of human relations determines the productivity level of people more than any other single factor.

Optimum relationships can be developed when one is as fully conscious of his own basic commitments or assumptions as he is of the basic commitments or assumptions held by others. The supervisor's and the principal's perceived view can function as a hidden source of disagreement and friction or it can serve as a catalytic agent which brings about change. Inaccurate sensory data can greatly impair the effectiveness of an entire staff while accurate sensory data can accelerate positive human behavior.

Nicholas J. Vigilante, Associate Professor of Education, University of Florida, Gainesville

There are many ways in which we might approach the mutual respect philosophy. Determining the leadership style employed by both the supervisor and the principal as they work together is but one of the many possibilities. What part does status, authority, personal philosophy, and process vs. product orientations play in directing the principal's behavior as he interacts with the supervisor? The same question can be asked of the supervisor as he interacts with the principal.

Leadership Style

A study [1] conducted in one midwestern state was concerned with the leadership style of elementary principals and elementary supervisors. Basically, this research was an attempt to answer the question, how do elementary principals and elementary supervisors view their respective role and the role of the other in four dimensions of interpersonal relations. As defined by Seeman,[2] these four dimensions of interpersonal relations leading to role conflict are deeply rooted in American life and contribute much to the complex leadership patterns found in our democratic society.

The four dimensions of role behavior are: (a) the status dimension (success ideology vs. equality ideology), (b) the authority dimension (dependence vs. independence), (c) the personal dimension (friendship obligation vs. institutional obligation), and (d) the means-ends dimension (product vs. process). The extremes of this bipolar arrangement parallel the Getzels-Guba Model,[3] which provides an excellent interpretation of distinct types of leadership style: the "idiographic" style, which stresses the personal needs and dispositions within the individual, and the "nomothetic" style which is characterized by a role and role-expectations orientation. The "transactional" style is characterized by behavior which is neither idiographic nor nomothetic but which rests on a continuum somewhere between both extremes.

Leaders who report themselves as relatively high in ambivalence—that is, who sense the dual demands of their position—or who are seen by others as transactional, tend to be rated as more effective leaders. With this viewpoint, it becomes obvious that the role of the principal or supervisor is one filled with moments of apprehension. Both roles are very complex and therefore most difficult in resolving the conflict of people orientation vs. things orientation, person vs. product, humanism vs. technocratic. While each position demands that either nomothetic or idiographic leadership is required for the moment, there are situations in which the transactional behavior is expected.

Supervisors as Seen by Principals

As a result of the study, the role of the elementary supervisor as perceived by the principal for each dimension was characterized in the following manner:

1. For the status dimension, the elementary principal expects the elementary supervisor to identify with his peers; identification with subordinates, the desire to "go along" with the group, to be considered as "just a member of the group," is reflected rather than identification with authority or

---

[1] Nicholas J. Vigilante. "A Role Perception Study of Elementary Principals and Elementary Supervisors in the State of Ohio." Unpublished Ph.D. dissertation. Columbus, Ohio: The Ohio State University, 1964.

[2] Melvin Seeman. *Social Status and Leadership*. Bureau of Educational Research and Service. Monograph No. 35. Columbus, Ohio: The Ohio State University, 1960.

[3] J. W. Getzels and E. G. Guba. "Social Behavior and the Administrative Process." *The School Review* 65: 423-41; Winter 1957.

increased status. The primary objective is to keep the subordinates happy and contented within a highly individualistic relationship.

Consider, for example, the supervisor's position with regard to joint professional staff meetings with principals. The principal might view the supervisor as one who rotates the job of chairmanship, and who solicits ideas from the group membership when planning the agenda for the meeting rather than the one who presides over the group after his planning the agenda for the meeting. The principal's view of the supervisor seems to be decidedly equality rather than success oriented.

2. For the authority dimension, the elementary principal expects the elementary supervisor to display actions that he takes on the authority of others and actions he takes on his own authority. His behavior stresses goal accomplishment. Yet also, he is expected to make provisions for individual need fulfillment.

A conspicuous example of this dimension is found in the degree of initiative taken in improving the instruction. Principals expect supervisors to receive authority from a superior prior to initiating any experimental program as well as to instituting some experimental programs in various schools to gather evidence in support of his ideas before presenting them to his superior. The value of dependence and independence is a source of considerable ambivalence. This tendency appears more apparent in medium size communities, with school populations between 5 and 10 thousand pupils.

3. For the personal dimension, the elementary principal expects the elementary supervisor to display behavior which expresses a loyalty to the organization—living by the book—as well as behavior which is the result of personal friendships and social and personal contacts.

A possible example between institutional dedication and personal friendship might be illustrated using the following situation. When a principal, whom the supervisor likes and admires, has violated a board policy, the elementary principal expects the supervisor to follow the procedures that he has used before in similar situations, regardless of his personal feelings. At the same time, the principal expects the supervisor to ignore the situation as long as no one makes a complaint. Such a conflict in standards of judgment accentuates the difficulty of either role.

4. For the means-end dimension, the elementary principal expects the elementary supervisor to take actions which are prompted by the requirements of immediate problems and the actions which are prompted by the desire to improve the future operations of the organization.

This dimension might be characterized by the following example. In the process of working on curriculum development, principals expect supervisors to attend to specific problems that affect the teachers as well as to work on the development of a scope and sequence program based upon the trends of education. This dual focus is an attempt to find a balance between the emphasis on group process and group product.

In summary, there is no doubt in my mind that those of us who are working in the field of human relationships and trying to understand the basic orderliness of that phenomenon are engaged in a most complicated and crucial endeavor. This can best be accelerated in an atmosphere where mutual respect is in evidence. If we are thoughtfully working to understand our relationships as co-workers, then we are working toward ends which will be more productive to the children who are involved in the programs which are developed as a result of this relationship. It becomes clear that we must not only be interested in *what* people do, but the *why* of their behavior.

The principal and supervisor must seriously consider analyzing and revising their own behavior according to the principles they advocate for the other person. Each must adopt the analysis of his behavior as an object of exacting, continuous study. □

EL 21 (2): 75-79, 111; November 1963
© 1963 ASCD

Effecting Change Through Leadership

Luvern L. Cunningham

MANY American schools have seen fit to build into organizational and administrative structures a host of "helping" or "facilitating" professional roles. Staff members such as principals, consultants, supervisors, special teachers, helping teachers, psychologists, and the like, all eagerly await their respective opportunities to help teachers. Other school systems, the British, for example, have not found it as important to surround British teachers with coteries of well trained, highly specialized "helping" personnel. As a consequence, in some school systems in the United States, we may have contributed to a dependency relationship of teacher on superior, as well as on other staff personnel, that has had less than a positive effect on teaching.

We seem to have created extensive educational bureaucracies and there appears to be little hope that we can shed the mantle of bigness and complexity. Apparently we find it difficult to conceive of the teacher as a professional person capable of comprehending the totality of the teaching role. The complexity of the institution in which many of our teachers are imbedded seems to conflict with our larger purpose of "improving instruction." All protestations to the contrary, we do not place much confidence seemingly in our teachers' capacities to reflect upon their own teaching behavior, to assess their own progress in teaching, and to render modifications in their teaching based on self and situational assessments. Thus we increase the dependency on supervisory and administrative leadership.

If these are accurate observations, the problems of those who perform supervisory functions in our school systems are increasing in difficulty as dependencies and interdependencies grow. Whereas supervision in the past may have been directed at maintaining levels of performance within schools, now the supervisory function includes defining and redefining goals, clarifying personnel relationships, elevating levels of aspiration of people in our schools, assessing the

Luvern L. Cunningham, Dean of the College of Education, The Ohio State University, Columbus. In 1963, Profesor of Educational Administration, University of Minnesota, Minneapolis

performance of teachers and other staff members, and, most important of all, establishing a climate for innovation and change.

The "leader" emphasis is pronounced in supervisory behavior today. Concomitantly the expectations for effecting change are growing. Given these circumstances, what notions are available to the supervisor who is willing to lead and who wishes to understand more clearly the dimensions of his role? A description of concepts helpful in creating change is the purpose here.

Supervisor as Change Agent

One useful way for a supervisor to conceive of his leadership responsibility is to define his role as that of "change agent." Dissatisfaction with the status quo is given in such a definition. The "change agent" concept is not new, although it may not be understood generally among supervisors in schools. The notion was first described by Kurt Lewin[1] and has been used exensively since that time by many others.

As an agent of change, three additional concepts are helpful. These are *social system, diagnosis,* and *intervention*.[2] Each of these will be described briefly and then applied in one example.

The concept *social system* is a powerful and valuable concept for the supervisor. For our purposes a social system might be defined as an interrelated, interdependent assemblage of persons, objects, and ideas that tend to function, operate, or move in unison, often in obedience to forms of authority or control.[3] School systems are complex social systems. The concept of social system is a solid analytical tool because it permits the supervisor to look at his work environment in a dispassionate way.

Supposing a principal wants to think about his school as a social system, how is this of value to him? He may choose to think of his school as a large, involved social system made up of many subsystems. Getzels and Thelen[4] have described classrooms as subsystems; familiarity with their systems analysis of classrooms would provide insights into social systems in general. In secondary schools, departments may be considered as subsystems or the administrator's cabinet can be thought as a different order of social system, which ties together or integrates other subsystems within the school. In terms of the earlier definition, one must keep in mind that social systems and subsystems within broader systems are interrelated, interdependent, and tend to operate in response to various forms of authority.

People with supervisory responsibilities should be able to set themselves apart from their schools, to get outside of their professional settings and look at the whole as well as the parts of their enterprise. Schools are in motion, dynamic; and in the everyday conduct of school affairs the person with supervisory responsibilities can be swept along with the tide. The appeal here is for the person to separate himself conceptually from his work and think about his situation and himself in new terms.

---

[1] Kurt Lewin. "Frontiers in Group Dynamics: Concept, Method, and Reality in Social Science; Social Equilibrium; and Social Change." *Human Relations* 1: 5-41; June 1947.

[2] These concepts have been described by the author in "Effecting Organizational Change," Report of the 1962 Principals Leadership Course, Department of Educational Administration, University of Alberta, Edmonton, Alberta, Canada, 1962; and in "Viewing Change in School Organization," *Administrator's Notebook,* Vol. 11, No. 1; September 1962.

[3] *Ibid.*

[4] Jacob W. Getzels and Herbert A. Thelen. "The Classroom Group as a Unique Social System." In: *The Dynamics of Instructional Groups,* 59th Yearbook, National Society for the Study of Education. Chicago: University of Chicago Press, 1960. pp. 53-82.

By combining the two terms *change agent* and *social system,* we are ready then to consider the two other notions—diagnosis and intervention.

Diagnosis and Intervention

Superintendents, principals, supervisors, and all other personnel with supervisory responsibilities are "internal" change agents. That is, they are parts of the social system, and subsystems, of the school. As internal agents of change they are seeking to direct, control, or modify a social environment of which they are very much a part. Because they are a part of the broad social system that is the school, as well as many subsystems within the school, they are not as capable of seeing the "big picture" as would an external change agent. A consultant, for example, who might be invited in to view a school, or a problem within a school, functions as an external change agent. Lippitt[5] and his colleagues have studied at length the impact of external change agents on various kinds of organizations. For our purposes we are interested in supervisors as internal change agents essentially, although professional people who travel about a district, working in many schools, can be conceived of as external agents of change to particular buildings, but internal to the total system.

Supervisory leadership requires continuing reflection upon the status or performance of the organization for which the leader is responsible. The concept of diagnosis, which has to do with the art of discerning the current state of affairs within an organization at any given point in time, is appropriate.

[5] Ronald Lippitt, Jeanne Watson, and Bruce Westley. *The Dynamics of Planned Change.* New York: Harcourt, Brace & Co., 1958. For further help in understanding the change agent concept see the volume: Warren G. Bennis, Kenneth D. Benne, and Robert Chin. *The Planning of Change.* New York: Holt, Rinehart & Winston, 1961. pp. 193-94.

Diagnosis calls for:

> ... skills in observation, listening, analysis and assessment of forces and factors, and the prediction, as best one can, of trends, potentialities, and apparent, current directions. It is not unlike what doctors engage in with their patients, except that in the case of school leaders, the tools for diagnosis are much more primitive than those available to our doctors. The concept "diagnosis" is an action concept; it is something that change agents ought to do.[6]

An important part of situational diagnosis is self-diagnosis. Of value to most leaders would be the thoughtful review of three leadership styles described by Moser:

1. The *nomothetic* style is characterized by behavior which stresses goal accomplishment, rules and regulations, and centralized authority at the expense of the individual. Effectiveness is rated in terms of behavior toward accomplishing the school's objectives.

2. The *idiographic* style is characterized by behavior which stresses the individuality of people, minimum rules and regulations, decentralized authority, and highly individualistic relationships with subordinates. The primary objective is to keep subordinates happy and contented.

3. The *transactional* style is characterized by behavior which stresses goal accomplishment, but which also makes provision for individual need fulfillment. The transactional leader balances nomothetic and idiographic behavior and he judiciously utilizes each style as the occasion demands.[7]

The terms *nomothetic, idiographic,* and *transactional* may sound like some new kind of gibberish designed to confuse rather than clarify. This is far from the case. Leaders do differ in terms of their behavior. Although

[6] Cunningham, "Effecting Organizational Change," *op. cit.,* p. 108.

[7] Robert P. Moser. "The Leadership Patterns of School Superintendents and School Principals." *Administrator's Notebook,* Vol. 6, No. 1; September 1957.

space does not permit full dress review of the three styles described here, it should be emphasized that familiarity with these descriptions and research thereon enhances a leader's insight into his own leader behavior. It would be unfair to say that one leadership style is superior to another leadership style. Under one set of circumstances one style may work well; under other circumstances another style may be needed.

On the basis of the diagnosis a change agent makes of the social system in which he is imbedded, and after he has decided on the nature of the change he wishes to effect in his school system, he must decide "when," "where," and "how" he will intervene in the ongoing processes of his organization to achieve his objective. The systems and subsystems that make up his school are dynamic, not static. People are at work, or should be at work. Patterns of behavior have been established; roles have been defined; formal and informal communication systems have been formed; expectations for performance have been developed. The introduction of change introduces disequilibrium into the social system and may be threatening to many persons who occupy important roles in the school. The consequences of intervention in an ongoing enterprise should be weighed carefully. The "when," "where," and "how" of intervention are crucial matters. The meager evidence that exists relative to the introduction of the notion of merit salary plans suggests that intervening with the merit notion is hazardous indeed but may be less so if leaders diagnose their organizations properly and consider carefully problems related to intervention.

Applying the Concepts

Let us try to apply the concepts used thus far. Some of the most perplexing problems facing America's schools are those found in our large school districts where our bureaucratic structures frequently work against the achievement of the schools' purposes rather than in support of the schools' objectives. School social systems behave in ways identical to, or at least similar to, other large social systems. Business and industrial enterprises, hospitals, public agencies of various kinds can become sick, even pathological. Schools too can become sick or pathological in terms of how persons behave in the social systems and subsystems of the school. Morale can deteriorate; performance levels can be reduced; personnel turnover rates can increase; community dissatisfactions with the school can mushroom.

Deterioration of the effectiveness of any organization can be organization wide, or it can be limited to one unit within the organization.[8] School districts too can experience district wide deterioration or it may be confined to one or a few buildings within a system. Suppose I have just been appointed supervising principal of a school that is known to be deteriorating. What do I as the person with supervisory responsibility for this building do? Can the concepts introduced in this article serve me in any way?

I might begin by becoming familiar with the notion of internal change agent. To accept this notion I would have to accept simultaneously the idea that if affairs in my school are to be changed, I am going to have to be the pivotal figure—this is my job in fact.

As change agent I need to understand the nature of complex social organizations; and to expedite this understanding the concept of social system and subsystems within larger social systems will be useful to me.

[8] For a most insightful analysis of the problems of supervisory leadership in a "sick" organization read: Robert H. Guest. *Organizational Change: The Effect of Successful Leadership.* Homewood, Illinois: Richard D. Irwin, 1962.

Having clarified my understanding of myself as change agent and my environment as a complex social system, I am ready to proceed with diagnosis. Before arriving on the job I have probably been reflecting on my situation and intuitively I have arrived at some understandings of what has been happening in the building. But intuition may not be enough. If the organization is deteriorating, it is apparent that something has gone wrong. As indicated earlier, a sound place to begin is for me to examine myself. Although I may be reluctant to admit it, I may become my organization's biggest problem if I fail to include myself in diagnosing the situation. If I were to assess my leadership style, this might in itself give me some valuable insights. And for that purpose it would be beneficial to study the Getzels-Guba model and some of the research generated by the model.[9] Earlier reference was made to Moser's study of three leadership styles derived from the Getzels-Guba formulation.

Suppose my diagnosis of the state of affairs in my building reveals that teachers are dissatisfied with their working environment, parents are raising questions about their youngsters' progress, the central office is increasing its demands upon the leader, and I have discerned that my leadership style is highly nomothetic or goal oriented. When, where, and how do I intervene in this situation to change present conditions?

By understanding more clearly my own supervisory behavior, I may have made a beginning. Further, having diagnosed my situation, I might have been able to establish some priority on the problems with which I am faced. Priority for problem consideration and the importance of problems in the long range are not the same, so I need also to think through problems in terms of their importance. With problems identified, priorities established, and importance discerned, I am in position to face intervention.

It would seem obvious that I cannot lick all of the problems by myself. I must involve my faculty and staff. If I am accurate in my self perceptions relative to my leadership style, if I am nomothetic in my orientation, I probably should continue to direct energies toward attaining the schools' goals. It is doubtful that anyone can shift his leadership style dramatically. Therefore, it would be incumbent upon me to capitalize on my strengths in dealing with problems facing my schools. Possibly one of the dangers in the idiographic or personalistic style is over-personalizing relationships with teachers and failing to clarify expectations for teachers. As a goal oriented leader, I am capable of delegating and defining roles. Intervention then may best be achieved with the faculty and staff as a group in a setting where I can make my position clear and where I can share my objectives with my colleagues. The question of "when" is one of timing; the question of "how" is partially answered in the "where" response. After a few weeks a special evening faculty meeting following a dinner might be an appropriate beginning. On such an occasion the administrator might share his concerns for the school and invite faculty and staff participation and support in a program of self study and improvement.

Recognition of a deplorable state of affairs in a building will not come as a surprise to the staff. A confident and vigorous plan for solving some of the problems may be a surprise. People as a rule are more comfortable when their personal status is clear.

A supervisor must realize that definitive sets of rules do not exist to cover all of the "hows," "whens," and "wheres" that arise

---

[9] Jacob W. Getzels and Egon G. Guba. "Social Behavior and the Administrative Process." *The School Review* 65: 423-41; Winter 1957.

in effecting changes in schools. If the supervisor approaches his problems intelligently, thoughtfully, and persistently, drawing upon the concepts described above, he should be able to effect the changes he desires. The brief example given here is not a suggested pattern; it may not even be a desirable one. It is cited only as an example of the process a supervising principal might follow as he thinks through the problems of taking a new position in what seems to be a deteriorating school. ☐

New Leadership and New Responsibilities for Human Involvement

(An Editorial)

BEN M. HARRIS

THE "in" word nowadays in education is *new*. Everything has to be new, bright, different, innovative. A decade ago the "in" word was *leadership*. A whole series of leadership studies in government and industry caught our fancy, and teachers, counselors, principals, and supervisors all lost their identity to become "leaders." A decade earlier the "in" word was *involvement* as a result of the group dynamics movement. We sought many silly and superficial ways to get people involved, even though we were able to adopt some worthwhile ideas.

Properly enough, I plucked these three "in" words from the several titles suggested to me for this guest editorial. I wanted to try to revive the big ideas represented by these terms—*new, leadership,* and *human involvement*. The fourth word of my title is *responsibility*, and it has never been an "in" word in supervision circles. My main thesis is that it should be!

U.S. education is often described as being in the throes of a revolution. We have new curricula, new people, new money, new forces, new agencies, new hardware, new militancy, new challenges, and a new breed of student all thrust upon the educational scene. A closed, tradition oriented, locally dominated institution may be rapidly becoming open, change oriented, and federally dominated. If so, it is indeed a revolution in the making!

Revolutions come in many forms. Some are violent; others are peaceful. Some relate directly to the changing needs of a society; others are abortive. Some produce only short periods of chaos and uncertainty; others produce lingering wounds of hatred and insecurity which seem never to heal. What kind of revolution will this one in education come to be? Who is responsible? Who will lead? What will the new developments be? Will human needs be well served?

These questions are still clearly un-

Ben M. Harris, Professor, Department of Educational Administration, The University of Texas, Austin

answered in USA 1969. ASCD'ers can (and I think should) help answer these questions in ways that assure a productive revolution with a minimum of undesirable side effects.

Responsibility for Leadership

The word *leadership* refers to showing the way and guiding the organization in definitive directions. New leadership is needed in this sense of the word. Two kinds are required:

1. Those in status positions must lead out with new boldness and find better ways of influencing the schools toward rationally planned, timed change.

2. New leadership positions must be created, staffed, and coordinated to facilitate the enormously complex job of leading instructional change.

Where instructional change is concerned, there is no substitute for supervisors who know children, instruction, and how to work with people. Nearly every instructional innovation that has experienced any success has had supervisors closely connected with its implementation.

This is not an argument for more of the same. It is an argument for an experienced core of instructional generalists in high status positions with courage, authority, responsibility, and freedom from concern for the daily operation of the school. No combination of school principals, resource teachers, assistant principals, department chairmen, college professors, or curriculum committees will satisfactorily take their place.

The need for new leadership positions in education has been growing increasingly obvious with every passing year since Sputnik. Stimulating, creating, initiating, facilitating, controlling, and assessing revolutionary changes on many instructional fronts is not a job for principal and supervisor alone.

Technical support of many kinds is needed. Gradually we are seeing media, research, psychiatric, and computer specialists on the staffs of our schools. A nationwide movement to create regional educational service centers with staffs of instructional specialists is well under way. The reorganization of state departments of education is beginning to provide supervisory support to schools in master planning, curriculum development, and program evaluation. Research and development centers and regional laboratories are coming to recognize that supervision is their business in a real sense.

The big question in all of this concerns *coordination*. As disparate individuals and groups pursue worthy but uncoordinated goals and objectives, they tend to produce confusion; potentially significant developments fail to bloom. The general supervisor, regardless of title, must provide the leadership for unification of efforts on the part of these many new leaders.

Responsibility for Newness

We often doubt that anything is really new. But old or new, change has no intrinsic worth. Values and related criteria must be applied to every change to provide a basis for accepting, rejecting, or promoting it. Who shall provide the leadership for valuing proposed changes in instructional practice? We cannot continue to rely on trial and error approaches; the errors are too numerous.

We cannot leave the valuing process up to each individual teacher or school with neither guidance nor relief; the changes are too numerous and persistent. Surely we cannot allow responsibility for valuing changes to rest as it has in the past with proponents, pressure groups, and commercial interests!

The generalist in instruction must assume responsibilities for initiating, guiding, and coordinating rigorous evaluation procedures. This is not to suggest that supervisors' values must prevail. Quite to the contrary, the challenge to supervisors is to accept responsibility for seeing to it that every point of view is represented, that children's interests remain central, that critical questions are asked, that data are not only gathered but analyzed and interpreted.

Every new development which has a theoretically plausible base needs to be guaranteed ample opportunity for development and testing. Yet each must be subjected to critical analysis and the test of consistency of values must be applied. *Only those in key leadership positions with interests vested in quality instruction and in possession of broad-gauge supervisory competencies can assume such responsibilities.*

Responsibility for Involvement

Like newness, *involvement* is not an end in itself, but a means to an end. As opportunities for improving education present themselves in increasingly complex forms, the problem of implementation looms large. Simple changes require little of those affected. When the textbook is revised or a new one is published, it matters little who is involved in the selection process. Good teachers rarely rely on textbooks, poor teachers memorize them, and it won't help or hurt the kids much either way. About the same thing can be said for many changes of the recent past.

Increasingly, however, we are flirting with changes in instruction which would profoundly affect teacher, child, parent, and society. When we contemplate the individualizing of instruction in any genuine sense, or providing for discovery learning, or confronting pupils with the real social issues, or cultivating antonomous, emotionally congruent persons, a new set of requirements for involvement emerges. When large, complex instructional changes are introduced, teacher behavior, pupil behavior, and parent behavior are all affected. These changes in behavior produce counter-currents which challenge and disrupt. Who is responsible for the involvement of all those likely to be affected by dramatic instructional change?

The kinds of changes mentioned here will, if well implemented, produce reverberations of great magnitude throughout the system. How naive we will be if we assume that revolutionary changes are greeted with open arms when they are "good for kids"! We are human beings and creatures of habit. Changes in the system create new problems, deny old satisfactions, demand new skills, and introduce uncertainties.

Involvement in many aspects of the change process can dampen such resistance. Involvement needs to be functional, however, not just an intellectual exercise or a form of tokenism. Involvement must cut across the subsystems to teachers, students, parents, and other people who are likely to be affected.

Who can assume responsible leadership for producing this more elaborate kind of involvement? Can the general supervisor, who specializes in working with people, who knows the larger complex of the system, who understands instruction and the behavioral consequences of major changes in program, provide such leadership?

Leadership has meaning only when it leads to desirable goals. Goal-seeking behavior implies change, seeking that which is different from what is. In education, and especially in instruction, goals are human and means are human. Hence, involvement of people as we lead is inescapable.

New leaders emerge to take up old and new challenges. Supervisors have their golden opportunities for productivity as the group with a long tradition of concern for instruction, change, and people. *Let no one suggest that the day of the generalist is past!* ☐

PART II

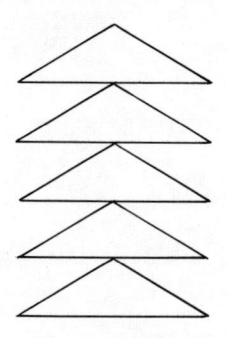

Issues in Professionalization

Role of the Supervisor

GORDON N. MACKENZIE

IN THIS age of unrest and revolution, the school supervisor has not been left undisturbed. Forces are at work which are reshaping supervisory positions and placing new demands on all instructional leaders who would not be bypassed in the rush of new educational developments. Before detailing the changed pressures and demands, two key words will be defined.

Chronology of Role Influences

"Supervisor" is here used as a generic term to include all whose unique or primary concern is instructional leadership. Supervisors may be called helping teachers, curriculum consultants, curriculum directors, or assistant superintendents in charge of instruction. The word "role" is used to indicate what the holder of a position does. While there are clear differences among the holders of various instructional leadership positions in respect to what they do, their professional activities are certainly interrelated and it is the contention here that all are being profoundly influenced by several recent developments.

The influences operating to shape the supervisor's role may be clarified, in part, by a glance backward at the roles of the supervisor during the past 50 years. During the first two decades of the century, the supervisor was primarily concerned with quality control in respect to the teaching process. Teacher preparation was at a minimum and supervisors were charged with visiting classes, observing and conferring with teachers. Demonstration lessons and institutes on the content and method of various subject fields reflected the level of preparation of teachers as well as the introduction of new areas to the curriculum. Individual supervisors, in many instances, had a narrow range of responsibilities such as handwriting, music, art, or reading. Their appointment resulted from a new addition to the curriculum or from a trouble spot in previous offerings.

By the 1920's concern was developing for the impact of the total educational program and much attention was focused on over-all objectives such as the Cardinal Principles of Education. Course-of-study development as a means of reorganizing the curriculum was the usual approach. Supervisors often became course-of-study writers, first with the help of outside consultants, and later with the assistance of committees of teachers. The general supervisor gradually became increasingly common.

What had been viewed as a task of clarification of purpose and realignment of content in the 'twenties came to be seen by the 'thirties and 'forties as a more complex task of changing teaching and teachers. The inadequacy of course-of-study revision alone became apparent and new approaches of numerous kinds were invented. Central to many of these were the ideas of participation

Gordon N. Mackenzie, Professor of Education, Teachers College, Columbia University, New York

and involvement of teachers in the process of curriculum change. By force of circumstances the supervisor became a specialist in group dynamics. American business and industry, with help from the social psychologists, had done the pioneering, and in many school systems group work supplanted close, individual supervision, as well as course-of-study writing, at least in the public and popular discussions among instructional leaders. The changes toward increased preparation of teachers as well as longer average periods of professional service went almost unnoticed. "Curriculum change as social change" or "curriculum change as change in people" became the slogans. The hectic pressures and deep fears of the depression 'thirties were largely forgotten as professional educators turned inward upon themselves in their preoccupation with "groupness," "consensus," "belonging," "morale," and the means of lifting oneself by one's bootstraps. Educators were seeking to understand themselves and the social system within which they operated, and significant progress was made.

The outer world was not forgotten. There was much concern for lay participation. The rights of parents and other citizens to determine the purposes of public education were loudly proclaimed, and much attention was focused on the complexities of doing this.

Second World War a Turning Point

But supervisors as well as those in other walks of life lost contact with the substance of what was happening. The Second World War and its attendant developments had shocking consequences for all of us which were not fully evident until we were well into the 'fifties. The rise of automation, of electronics, and of nuclear power during the war years, along with the injection of large private foundation funds into the education stream, hastened new developments.

Following the Second World War, there were many criticisms of education, some of which were linked with the patriotism-communism theme. Some were pointed at the claimed failure of the school to focus effectively on intellectual development or the teaching of so-called fundamentals. Increasingly supervisors became involved in interpretations of the educational program to the public.

As the problems of youth, especially in our large cities, began to shock the public and haunt the educators, and as the fear of communism rose, the nature of the numerous fundamental changes in our society became more widely understood. The importance of education, as well as the difficulties in providing it for ever larger segments of our population, became abundantly clear. The popular demand for more and better education rose to new heights.

Concern with Politics of Curriculum Change

The sources of curriculum change largely shifted to the public and to the professors in the academic disciplines. In some instances, the supervisory staffs in school systems were not even consulted as changes of various kinds were introduced by boards of education. It is probably safe to say that thousands of supervisors felt bypassed. Whereas they had regarded themselves as forward-looking professionals, sometimes impatient and weary in their efforts to bring about curriculum change, they suddenly realized that now they were being regarded as reactionaries who were blocking "progress."

The specific nature of some of the influences was clear, although the precise channels of influence were not always discernible. The vast sums set aside in foundation grants to support specific proposals for reform or to finance a careful study of particular aspects of the curriculum were obviously a new and powerful influence. The federal government became a financially generous party to changes at both the elementary and secondary levels. The revived interest of the academicians in elementary and secondary education lent new force and prestige. American industry saw potentials for the sale of products of modern technology to the schools.

For a time educators were literally assaulted by a great host of proposals of differing kinds. Some of these fostered especially by one of the foundations struck at the "things" of education. Organization and method were manipulated in an effort to reform the educational system. Varying proposals for new means of staff utilization, educational television, advanced placement, teaching machines, and testing to identify scholarship winners exemplified this approach. The precise influence on the curriculum and on the learning products in the schools of these organization, materials, and methods emphases is difficult to determine.

Most of the claimed considerations were not directly educational in nature. Instead they focused on the teacher shortage or on such general claims as the need for excellence. Clearly there has not been adequate consideration of the curriculum implications of this great concern with the "things" of education.

Another category of proposals which has had a greater variety of sources of support, including foundations, has focused on a reexamination of the subject fields. The rapid increase in knowledge has made urgent a reconsideration of what should be taught through the various disciplines as well as how they should be taught. Significant developments within several disciplines in respect to content, structure, and method have resulted in great demands for extensive in-service education of elementary and secondary school teachers. Both types of changes, those coming through the "things" and those coming through changes in the disciplines, appear to be moving public education toward greater uniformity, toward national as distinct from local initiative and determination. The politics of curriculum change which have emerged since the Second World War make new demands on supervisors. Fresh kinds of thinking as well as unfamiliar skills are called for. Board of education and internal school system policies not previously thought of are needed for dealing with the influences operating on the curriculum today. Skills are required for dealing with the rising power sources as well as for coping with the current in-service education demands. Several kinds of specialization within the supervisory group will certainly be required.

Reactions to New Role Developments

While reactions among educators to the present politics of educational change and improvement have been varied, one significant development is the widespread tendency for professional groups to reexamine their qualifications, their preparation, and their responsibility for professional improvement. The NEA's New Horizons Project has helped to lay much of the groundwork for this effort.[1] ASCD has established a Commission on the Preparation of Instructional Leaders and is actively coordinating its efforts with those of the American Association of School Administrators, the Department of Elementary School Principals, the National Association of Secondary School Principals,

[1] Margaret Lindsey, editor. *New Horizons for the Teaching Profession.* A report of the task force on New Horizons in Teacher Education and Professional Standards, 1961. National Commission on Teacher Education and Professional Standards, 1961. National Commission on Teacher Education and Professional Standards, National Education Association. Washington, D.C.: the Association, 1961.

and the University Council on School Administration.

The ASCD Commission has in preparation a policy statement which will be discussed widely during the 1961-62 school year. By July of 1962, the Commission hopes to recommend a policy statement to guide ASCD actions in the area of further professionalization of supervisors during the years immediately ahead. While it is too early to predict the exact form of these statements, it is possible to indicate what may be the major areas of attention. The Commission is of the opinion that action in at least six areas is required at the present time.

First, the qualities and abilities essential to effective operation as supervisors and curriculum workers need reexamination and redefinition. The functions, activities, and areas of required competence of those whose unique task is that of serving other staff members on instructional matters require clarification. This is no simple task in view of the changing climate within which schools are operating and the shifting requirements of specific assignments of those holding such widely varying positions as helping teacher, consultant, supervisor, curriculum worker, and assistant superintendent in charge of instruction.

Nevertheless, an effort is being made to define, in terms that will be helpful to supervisor-preparing institutions as well as to school systems, the expectancies held for those who serve in supervisory and curriculum improvement positions.

Second, standards for the selection of supervisors are an essential consideration in assuring competent personnel. Selection is viewed as a continuing process, starting with those who as teachers serve in curriculum improvement roles and continuing through initial identification of individuals who have the promise which is likely to be enhanced by further preparation, selection for specific kinds of preparation, tryout in leadership positions through internships, and selection for appropriate supervisory positions throughout a professional career.

Third, criteria for planning programs for the preservice and in-service preparation of supervisors are greatly needed. Many now enter supervisory positions without specific preparation or after having met only meager and inadequate certification requirements. At least a year and possibly two years of preparation are needed to foster development in the various areas of performance which are significant for today's supervisor. This should include various kinds of study and learning activities with careful attention to substantial, well-supervised field experiences.

Fourth, if programs of preparation are to be fully effective, accreditation of higher institutions that provide appropriate programs for the preparation of supervisors appears to be an important cornerstone in professional advancement. Assurance that supervisors will have satisfactorily demonstrated their competence through approved programs of preparation should be given the American public. A national accrediting agency, National Council for Accreditation of Teacher Education, is now ready and competent to implement this phase of the professionalization program.

Fifth, procedures for licensing of supervisors is in need of reexamination. Licensing of professional personnel and of workers of many kinds has long been a state function and several states have requirements for supervisors. Licensing might well be based primarily on the satisfactory completion of an approved or accredited program of preparation. Both the absence of requirements and the prescribing of two or three courses, the two most common practices, appear to be quite inadequate.

Sixth, professional organizations themselves should take action through membership policies and other programs to assure quality performance of their members. Self-policing by a professional group presents complex problems.

There is little experience within the field of education to guide action in this area. It appears wise, however, for ASCD to recognize and identify those of its members who have its stamp of approval as being qualified members of the profession.

Recent developments relative to the role of the supervisor stem from changes in education and its increased importance in our rapidly shifting world order. Greater demands will be made on education in the years ahead and one of the most important responses of supervisors is to be certain that they are adequate to the task. To do this is no simple undertaking, but supervisors can do much to improve the quality of their own group by taking responsibility for clarifying their role, improving selective admission, setting standards of preparation, and developing requirements for licensing and for quality performance. The challenge to ASCD is clear. What will its response be? □

EL 19 (2): 103-106; November 1961
© 1961 ASCD

In-Service Education of Supervisors

Reba M. Burnham

SUPERVISORS are challenged today as never before to continue their study on the job. The many demands for rapid changes in the instructional program have brought about this challenge. New insights as to how learning occurs, new discoveries in the content fields, developments in research methodology, and numerous proposals for curriculum change make such adjustments mandatory. Supervisors, therefore, must seek opportunities to increase their understandings and improve their skills in providing leadership toward a more effective instructional program.

What are some ways in which supervisors can improve their skills and understandings through in-service education? This article contains some examples of opportunities provided for the in-service education of supervisors in Georgia.

Internship

The internship is one kind of learning opportunity provided for supervisors in service. During the period of the internship the supervisor is employed as a full-time supervisor in a school system. An advisor from the state university is assigned to work with each supervisor for the period of the internship. The advisor visits the supervisor at least three times during the school year and assists him in planning and evaluating his supervisory activities.

The visits to the supervisor are cooperatively planned, as to time and purpose,

Reba M. Burnham, Professor of Education, University of Georgia, Athens

by the supervisor and the advisor. The advisor gives help with the problems about which the supervisor is concerned. The supervisor participates in a program of individual instruction based on the real problems which he encounters.

During each visit to the supervisor, the advisor spends some time in reading and discussing the supervisor's diary or daily log, and other materials prepared by the supervisor, and discussing activities in which the supervisor has participated or plans to participate. The visits help the supervisor to determine progress that he is making toward improving his needed skills and understandings. Other activities are planned for the supervisor in terms of his needs. He may be advised to visit a supervisor in a nearby system, visit schools in which experimentation is being carried on, confer with a particular person, or read certain professional material. The visits enable the supervisor to identify other learning opportunities he should seek following the internship.

Seminars in Geographical Areas

For the past three years the University of Georgia has offered seminars for experienced supervisors in certain geographical areas of the state. The supervisors requested the seminars and assumed responsibility for making the necessary arrangements regarding place of meeting, time and length of each session. Members of the seminar and a staff member from the University met once a month for a six-hour session.

The seminar was planned on the assumption that members of the seminar have familiarity with basic principles of supervision, of teaching and learning, and that supervisors feel fairly "comfortable" in applying these principles. The specific purpose of the seminar was to assist supervisors in "raising their sights and undergirding their understandings" regarding these basic principles.

It was the belief of the staff members in supervision that one way to help supervisors "raise their sights and undergird their understandings" was to help them gain better understanding of *themselves* and the *people* with whom they work. It was further believed that as supervisors gain such understandings, their work as supervisors will be affected positively.

In terms of these beliefs, the seminars were organized to provide opportunities for individual investigation of one or more specific *personal* problems and concentrated group study of selected theories which would assist with a better understanding of the personal problem selected.

As a means of helping individuals in the identification of personal problems, the following questions were presented to the members of the seminar:

1. What are some of the tensions or pressures that come from your job? For example, are you frustrated by lack of time, information, know-how, or skill?

2. What are some of the tensions or pressures that you place on yourself? For example, do you want to be the kind of supervisor that Mr. X is? Do you wish that you were different in disposition, attitudes, values, and general appearance?

3. What are some of the tensions or pressures that others cause? For example, does the superintendent or principal expect you to do the "impossible"? Does your family make demands that you can't meet? Does it bother you when *everyone* is not enthusiastic about and accepting of your ideas?

4. What are some of the tensions or pressures that come from your relationships with others—administrators, teachers, parents, children, other supervisors?

5. What are other pressures or tensions that you have as a supervisor? or as a person?

Each member of the group identified one or more specific pressures or tension points relating to his own behavior which he wished to "ease" during the year. Some tensions identified were ones to be investigated in an individual's private world. Some tensions were presented to members of the group for their help.

Sessions of the seminar were devoted to a study of specific topics, such as the nature and meaning of perception and learning, beliefs, values, needs, self-concept, experience, threat, and the implications of these for education and, more specifically, supervision. As each of the areas was explored, members of the seminar investigated readings in philosophy, psychology, social psychology, anthropology, sociology, as well as educational literature, and assumed responsibility for sharing their readings with members of the group. Other staff members from the University, representing various disciplines, met with the group frequently to assist in the "raising of sights and undergirding of understandings."

Each six-hour session consisted of three blocks of time. The first block, approximately three hours, was referred to as the *theory session*. During this block, the major topic for study provided a basis for discussion. The second block of time was devoted to discussion of the *personal* problem. The remaining time was spent in testing ideas for action programs in the participant's back-home situation.

Weekend Seminars

A weekend seminar, consisting of five weekend sessions, was offered during 1960-61 to supervisors at an advanced graduate level at the University of Georgia. Each session consisted of approximately 10 hours of work. The sessions began on Friday evening and ended on Saturday afternoon. The purpose of this seminar was to provide an opportunity for supervisors to identify, describe, and investigate causes of problems in supervision and to study research related to problems identified. Each member of the seminar kept a written account of his problem. Each account contained a statement of the problem, description of significant events that demonstrated the problem, and the supervisor's role in the problem situation—his behavior, feelings, relationships, and additional outside factors affecting the problem. These descriptions evolved into case studies in supervision which were used for discussion in the seminar.

A second purpose of the seminar was to provide an opportunity for supervisors to increase their knowledge and skills in writing for professional journals. Each member of the seminar prepared an article for a professional journal. Time was spent in the seminar for members to edit materials. Many of these articles were submitted and accepted for publication in state and national journals.

A second weekend seminar being offered during 1961-62 is the seminar in group development. This seminar is planned for persons interested in further training in group leadership. Major emphasis is given to helping individuals increase sensitivity, awareness, and understanding of self and others in groups; improve behavioral skills in interpersonal relations, group leadership, and membership roles; and to improve methods used in planning and conducting conferences and educational programs.

Special attention is given to helping groups analyze and experiment with their own group processes. Opportunities are provided for members to practice behaving skillfully in a variety of common and difficult interpersonal and group situations.

Institutes

A six-week Mathematics Institute for supervisors was held at the University of Georgia during the 1961 summer session. The institute was cooperatively sponsored by the University of Georgia and the State Department of Education and staffed by faculty members from the Mathematics Department and the College of Education of the University of Georgia. The purpose of the institute was to help supervisors become more literate in mathematics and to help them provide leadership in the field of mathematics education. A second purpose of the institute was to build readiness for a new state guide in mathematics which will be ready for trial this fall. As a follow-up of the institute, each participant will conduct a two-week workshop in mathematics during 1961-62, in his local system, and will give leadership to a "pilot school" in the "tryout" of the new state guide in mathematics.

A Curriculum Research Institute was conducted during the 1961 summer session. This institute was planned for experienced supervisors at the advanced graduate level. The purposes of the institute were to help curriculum workers identify and examine curriculum areas in need of study, analyze various approaches to curriculum planning, curriculum designs, and teaching procedures. Enrollees in the institute developed outlines for research projects to be carried out during 1961-62. These students will enroll in appropriate field courses and have the assistance of members of the faculty of the College of Education as plans are executed.

Additional supervisors enroll in regular college courses to strengthen their professional competencies. They enroll in local workshops with teachers to study problems of the local system, and they carry on individual research activities. These are only a few of the ways in which the supervisor can strengthen his own professional work through participation in an in-service program planned to meet his needs.

The illustrations given thus far are descriptions of learning opportunities for supervisors in service, for which college credit is given. Supervisors avail themselves of many other opportunities to continue their professional growth for which college credit is not earned. The following are examples of such programs.

Continuing Education

Supervisors meet regularly in their district to study problems of common concern. Principals, superintendents, and teachers often meet with them to assist in the study of selected problems.

Some of the most important opportunities for the supervisor to grow professionally on the job are those that exist in the local school system. Classroom teachers, principals, superintendents, other school personnel as well as lay persons have much to contribute to the continuous education of the supervisor. As these persons identify their problems and plan cooperatively for ways of working toward the solution of these problems, the supervisor gives and receives help.

Experimental programs at the local level afford opportunities for in-service education of supervisors. During 1961-62 thirty-nine school systems in Georgia are experimental centers for nongraded programs. In each of these systems the supervisor is involved in helping a school faculty to study and develop plans for initiating a nongraded program.

Supervisors utilize opportunities to participate in state and national conferences as in-service education programs. Supervisors are often involved in helping to develop guides in the various curriculum areas. In many cases, they may assume major leadership responsibility for the project.

Finding time and maintaining a schedule for professional reading and study are highly essential for the supervisor's growth on the job. Keeping informed of new developments through professional reading is a *must* for the supervisor.

Certain conditions must exist for the development of an effective in-service education program for supervisors. The first and perhaps most important condition is that the supervisor has a zest for knowledge and seeks opportunities for learning on the job.

Time must be provided for the supervisor to participate in in-service education programs. The local administration must recognize the importance of the supervisor's participation in these activities and willingly release him for this purpose. ☐

Preparing Educational Supervisors

JAMES R. OGLETREE
FRED EDMONDS
PAT W. WEAR

PROGRAMS of preparation for educational supervisors exist to help students acquire knowledge, understanding, and skills for their work as instructional leaders.

Such programs are based on certain assumptions and subsequent operational decisions. These are the: (a) end-product image or purposes held for the program; (b) selection and admission of students; (c) content deemed necessary to produce the desired end-product; (d) institutional arrangements for courses and/or experiences facilitating the development of the end-product; (e) availability and utilization of materials and resources contributing to the learning of the desired content; and (f) staff behavior in the teacher-learner relationship with students.

Changes in preparatory programs can be achieved through modifications in any one or all of these six aspects. This article provides a brief summary of an experiment aimed at assessing, clarifying, and relating all of these variable aspects in an effort to develop more effective preparatory programs for supervisors.

A Cooperative Program

For four years, 1957-61, Berea College and the University of Kentucky engaged in

James R. Ogletree, Professor, and Fred Edmonds, Associate Professor, College of Education, University of Kentucky, Lexington; and Pat W. Wear, Chairman, Department of Education, Berea College, Berea, Kentucky

a cooperative experimental program that was partially financed through the Fund for the Advancement of Education. This program had as its primary objective the development of improved processes and procedures for preparing educational supervisors.[1] Within this basic aim were several operational objectives which served as guidelines throughout the project.

Foremost among these purposes was a desire to utilize recent research findings in the areas of learning and human behavior to develop individualized programs for each of the students. Such individualized programs required the student with staff to obtain accurate and detailed information concerning his needs, perceptions, and capabilities and to use this information to develop appropriate learning experiences for his preparation as a supervisor.

A second purpose was aimed toward identifying the competencies normally demanded of a supervisor, and toward the examination and exploration of processes for helping each student acquire these.

A third purpose was to utilize both on-campus and on-the-job experiences to determine how these activities could be aligned, synchronized, and utilized productively in the preparation of supervisors.

Another purpose, made even more necessary because of the developmental nature of the experimentation, concerned the constant and thorough evaluation of both the preparation program purposes and the implementing activities related to these purposes.

The experimentation was also committed to aiding the individual student: (a) to develop a sound theory of education; (b) to develop a concept of supervision consistent with that theory; (c) to acquire the skill and ability to apply supervisory functions (instructional improvement) to supervisory tasks; and (d) to develop personal attitudes, beliefs, and values for: (1) continuing self-improvement, (2) increasing self-direction, (3) developing self-confidence in working things out for himself, (4) increasing ability to solve problems, (5) increasing ability to acquire and utilize knowledge relevant to the solution of supervisory problems, (6) increasing respect for the worth of others, (7) increasing ability to work for purposes which contribute to the improvement of society, and (8) increasing ability to work with others in the solution of educational problems.

During the four-year project, thirty persons completed two-year preparation programs. These persons participated as members of one of three groups, with six students in the first (1957-59), twelve in the second (1958-60), and twelve in the third (1959-61). Admission to the project was contingent upon: (a) eligibility for provisional licensing upon completion of the initial summer; (b) employment as a full-time supervisor in a local school district; and (c) recommendation by the superintendent of the employing school district.

While the two-year programs were extremely flexible in operation, each was organized in terms of four blocks of time. As the student entered the project, he participated in an all-day seminar with the other members of his group for eight weeks. During this phase, efforts were made to develop a climate in which the student felt accepted as a person of worth, capable of directing his own program of growth and development. The members of the group (supervisor-interns) were encouraged to work on questions and issues important and relevant to them as supervisors.

---

[1] For a full report of this project see: "Program of Experimentation in Preparing Educational Supervisors." *Bulletin of the Bureau of School Service,* Vol. 24, No. 4, June 1962, College of Education, University of Kentucky, Lexington.

The second phase of the program was the first-year internship, an academic year, in which the supervisor functioned on the job with assistance from a project staff member. This one-to-one relationship of staff to student provided opportunity for the student to assess his own level of development, recognize his own preparation needs, and develop processes for improving himself as a supervisor as he functioned in a specific setting. Concurrently, he participated in all-day, biweekly meetings with his group where his supervisory problems were shared and the help of the group was sought.

A third phase of the program was the student's second summer on the University campus. During this time he was engaged in college course work in areas related to supervision and maintained continuing contact with the members of his group. He also worked closely with the staff of the Program of Experimentation in Preparing Educational Supervisors (PEPES) through periodic group meetings and individual conferences.

The final phase of the program was a second-year internship, another academic year, in which the supervisor and his staff member were engaged in continuing the relationship begun during the first year. Here again an effort was made to use the task of developing a local supervisory program as a base for providing learning experiences for the student.

As indicated here, the project was in part integrated into the normal preparatory programs of the University. For example, each student was granted graduate credit for his efforts. He could earn six to nine semester hours of credit during the first summer, six semester hours during the first year internship, six to nine semester hours during the second summer, and six semester hours during the second year internship. However, with the exception of the second summer's related classwork, the experimentation was conducted within a unique framework developed by the PEPES staff.

Behavioral Efforts

The traditional teaching method in which the staff predetermined the content and scope for student study was replaced by six behavioral efforts in which the staff sought: (a) to behave in a manner that would focus upon the personal growth and development of the individual student; (b) to behave in a manner which would help the students draw an analogy between the way staff performed and the way supervisors might perform with teachers; (c) to create a climate conducive to optimum learning for both students and staff; (d) to replace the typical textbook-oriented classroom teaching situation with a learning situation in which the problems, concerns, and needs of the students determined the content of the program; (e) to use these problems, needs, and questions as vehicles to move more deeply into study areas which could help the students gain a broader understanding of human behavior as a base for effective supervision; and (f) to involve themselves in appraising and assessing their own behavior and modifying it in terms of this assessment.

Evaluation

At the conclusion of the four-year period of experimentation, many changes could be identified as a total or partial consequence of PEPES. For example, while some students did not respond as adequately as others, most of the students did exhibit behavioral changes in keeping with the preparational purposes of the project. The program was most effective with those students with whom the staff was able to establish a warm, continuous relationship in which students and staff were able cooperatively to identify areas of need and to develop appropriate experiences to meet them.

Each student was a fully employed supervisor, with all the responsibilities and opportunities which such a condition produces. Therefore the staff member, in effect, became a partner-in-action with the supervisor, maintained frequent and purposeful contact with him, and provided assistance as he sought to increase his effectiveness on the job. However, the staff member at all times had to focus his attention upon helping the supervisor mature toward the stated preparational purposes.

The internship also produced ample evidence to support an assumption that a local school district and its personnel have an important function to perform in the preparation of their own supervisory staff. It showed that preparation programs, rather than being confined to a college campus, should be developed in terms of experiences provided both on campus and on the job. The campus experiences can be directed toward bringing groups of supervisors-in-preparation together to utilize institutional resources and toward providing specifically needed information, to share experiences, to develop plans of action, and to work on common needs and problems. The local setting provides a natural laboratory which supplies real problems, real needs, and real learning opportunities for supervisors in preparation.

Staff participation in this type of preparation program demanded knowledge, understandings, and behaviors quite different from those required in typical programs. Because of participation in all phases of the program, and because of the extended period of contact with each student, the staff constantly had to evaluate its own levels of development, identify areas needing improvement, function with students in a manner consistent with the way they believed the students should function as instructional leaders, and develop experiences to provide the competencies they themselves needed to behave effectively as staff members.

PEPES demonstrated that two institutions with uniquely different backgrounds can cooperatively develop and implement experimentation which results in improving the quality of preparation programs for supervisors within a state. As a result of the experimentation, preparation programs for all school leaders at the University were modified to include certain aspects of the extended internship concept. These programs also were modified to allow for different role projections on the part of staff members who help prepare school leaders, and were clarified in terms of preparative purposes.

In brief, PEPES was a four-year experimentation dedicated to the development of more adequate procedures for preparing educational supervisors. As with all preparatory programs, it began with a series of operational assumptions and decisions. It had a set of educational purposes, a series of assumptions about supervision, people, and preparation, and a tentative plan of operation. PEPES, unlike most programs, held these as tentative hypotheses to be tested through their implementation.

As staff gained experience and as evaluative data became available, the operational plan and procedures were revised and modified accordingly so that the experimentation itself was developmental in nature. This flexibility, this continuous evaluation and modification of procedures, was a significant characteristic of PEPES, a characteristic which may have important implications for future experimentation aimed at developing more adequate instructional leadership programs. ☐

Preparation and Certification of Supervisors[1]

MARGARET FLINTOM

RECENT efforts to improve the schools of North Carolina have involved cooperation by the State Board of Education, the State Department of Public Instruction, and several professional organizations. This joint endeavor has resulted in state-wide curricular studies, improved learning situations, increased salaries, and a plan aimed at producing better qualified professional personnel.

Good administrators, supervisors, and teachers are considered essential in all schools. Attention, therefore, was directed to ways of recruiting persons with desirable qualities and of providing programs that would enable them to become confident, growing, creative people with adequate preparation in general education, academic specialization or concentration, and professional education. This goal naturally led to a study and revision of certification requirements.

The task of bringing about changes in certification became a responsibility of the State Advisory Council on Teacher Education and Professional Standards. This group of 72 members included representatives from private and public teacher preparatory institutions, persons from professional organizations, and the lay public. The council decided that certification should be based upon the recommendation of teacher preparatory institutions that meet definite standards and have approved programs that are planned within the framework of designated guidelines, rather than upon the completion of stipulated numbers of hours of credit and certain specified subjects.

The next step was to obtain the approval of the plan by the North Carolina College Conference and the State Board of Education. The College Conference is composed of representatives from colleges in the state, the State Department of Public Instruction, and the State Board of Higher Education. The State Board of Education has the final authority in matters concerning educational policies and is the legal State agency for the certification of the professional school personnel.

After the North Carolina College Conference and the State Board of Education had adopted in principle the approved program approach, subcommittees were appointed to set up guidelines and standards

[1] The statement which serves as the basis of this article was prepared by a committee appointed by the State Advisory Council on Teacher Education. Members of this committee were the following: Mrs. Carrie Abbott, Mrs. Eloise G. Eskridge, Mrs. Mildred T. Miller, Miss Sarah Yoder, Miss Margaret Flintom, chairman.

Margaret Flintom, formerly Elementary School Supervisor, Charlotte-Mecklenburg Schools, Charlotte, North Carolina

for the approval of institutions and programs of work leading to various types of certificates. More than a thousand individuals were involved in planning the program which will go into effect September 1, 1964.

Although the committee appointed to propose guidelines for the preparation of supervisors consisted of supervisory staff members, other people were invited to attend and participate in committee meetings. These included representatives from colleges, the State Department of Public Instruction, and the North Carolina Education Association. Karl Openshaw, Associate Secretary of ASCD, served as a consultant.

All prospective supervisors will be encouraged to complete the sixth-year program. However, until more people are available to fill positions in the state, a certificate based upon the master's degree will be issued. Additional compensation is planned for supervisors having the advanced preparation.

Preparation Program

The complete text of the committee report, "Criteria for Approved Program for the Preparation of Supervisors," follows:

The program for each candidate should be planned as a logically organized whole in the light of his previous study and experience and of his performance on the screening procedures of the institution. It should be designed to assure that he becomes knowledgeable about the total school program, but should permit concentration of interest at the elementary or secondary levels or in special subjects such as art, music, and library science.

The program should be developed in such manner that the master's degree and the sixth-year programs together meet the guidelines which follow. The master's degree program should provide preparation called for by each guideline and the sixth year should be designed to develop both breadth and depth in the same areas.

Guideline 1: *The program should give the prospective supervisor a thorough understanding of the nature of the learner and the psychology of learning.*

Preparation in this area should include a thorough understanding of the learning processes, individual differences, adjustment, behavior, readiness, attitudes, ideas, beliefs, motivation, and growth and development; individual and group instruments for individual appraisal (tests, inventories, anecdotal records); case study techniques; management of cumulative records; procedures in securing, recording, interpreting, and using pertinent information about the individual.

Guideline 2: *The program should provide the prospective supervisor a comprehensive study of the dynamics of human behavior.*

Preparation in this area should include a careful study of the variety of ways in which people work successfully. Emphasis should be given to an analysis of both individual and group behavior in order that the applicant might know how people may be helped in their personal adjustments and interpersonal relations. In addition, study in this area should include knowledge of and considerable practice in the use of group processes and their specific applicability to the work of the supervisor. The program should provide experiences designed for fostering and nurturing appreciation of individuality and sensitivity to the feelings of others; opportunities for trying out and evaluating leadership skills; opportunities for self-expression as a means of promoting creativity and initiative.

Guideline 3: *The program should give the prospective supervisor an understanding of curriculum development, including the bases for decision in curriculum changes.*

Preparation in this area should include a study of philosophy, sociology, anthropology, and psychology as these disciplines relate to curriculum development. It should include a study of curriculum development in both large and small school systems, including an understanding of the role of the supervisor, the role of other professional personnel, and the role of lay persons; should give consideration to ways in which decisions are made and implemented; should provide a thorough understanding of the purposes and objectives of the school, the curriculum, and the relationships of the community to the program of the school.

Guideline 4: *The program should include for the prospective supervisor a thorough grounding in the techniques of supervision.*

Preparation in this area should include careful study of the uses of various techniques of supervision; orientation of teachers; in-service programs for the growth of teachers; classroom observation and individual follow-up conferences with teachers. Emphasis should be on ways in which teachers can be helped in working with children and youth, including grouping, provision for individual differences, methods, and techniques for teaching, selecting, constructing, procuring, and using instructional materials.

Guideline 5: *The program should acquaint the prospective supervisor with the various phases of organization and administration involved in the operation of a school.*

Work in this area should provide the supervisor with a knowledge of the principles of organization and administration; understanding of and respect for the roles of all persons concerned with the educational process, including the responsibilities and relationships of teachers, principals, and other administrators, other supervisors, and members of governing boards in the organization of the school system and in the profession. Preparation should include some attention to general finance planning, budget allocation, school plants and equipment, school law, and personnel to enable the supervisor to advise in these areas.

Guideline 6: *The program should provide for the prospective supervisor opportunities for graduate work in related areas, including work in his subject of specialization.*

Preparation in this area should include electives in academic subjects to meet the needs and interests of the individual. There should be preparation directed toward experiences in such fields as speaking, writing, and engaging in various forms of intercommunication with individuals and groups, including practice in oral and written reporting, speaking to community groups, writing press releases, and preparing supervisory bulletins. Preparation should be required at the graduate level in the area of specialization in which the supervisor expects to devote the major portion of his time. At the secondary level, the word "specialization" is intended to apply to a teaching field or fields and, at the elementary level, to refer to academic courses in teaching fields which prepare for supervisory leadership in the elementary area.

Guideline 7: *The program for the prospective supervisor should include an emphasis on research and appropriate statistics.*

Work in this area should assist the prospective supervisor in gaining greater insights and skills in the use of techniques of action research, and in designing and carrying out research projects. Included in the program should be adequate opportunities for experiences to provide knowledge of significant educational research, its implications, and its use.

Completion of program: The fifth-year program of preparation should entitle one to the master's degree. When a sixth-year program is involved, the institution should grant appropriate recognition for completion of program.

Recommendation of institution: Each candidate for a certificate must be recommended by the appropriate college official. The recommendation must certify that he has completed the program for the preparation of supervisors (master's degree level or sixth-year level) and it must be accompanied by a transcript of credit.

Authorization of service: The supervisor's certificate authorizes the holder to be a supervisor of instruction in elementary and secondary schools, but area of preparation should determine his field of work. □

EL 23 (2): 153-55; November 1965
© 1965 ASCD

Professionalization of Supervisors and Curriculum Workers

JAMES R. OGLETREE

AS NEVER before, American education is "alive" with excitement, enthusiasm, and hope. Permeating the entire spectrum of societal affairs is the recognition and support of education as the generative power for human progress. More specifically, the professional family itself is experiencing something of a renaissance as to its own worth as a critical force in social preservation and advancement.

Included in this professional renaissance is an increasing sensitivity to educators' responsibility to improve the quality and quantity of the services rendered to the larger society. The National Education Association's Commission on Teacher Education and Professional Standards has made substantial contributions which have resulted in many states' increasing the standards of qualification of teachers. The American Association of School Administrators for more than fifteen years has actively sought to raise the quality of preparatory programs for those who become its members. This organization has been extremely successful in regard to the preparation and certification of school superintendents. Similarly the Department of Elementary School Principals has for ten years expended its energies at an increasing rate to raise the competence of elementary

James R. Ogletree, Professor of Education, University of Kentucky, Lexington

school principals. While not quite so actively, the National Association of Secondary School Principals has also been seeking to extend the professionalization of its members.

In 1959, the Association for Supervision and Curriculum Development, by a resolution adopted at its national meeting, created a Commission on the Preparation of Instructional Leaders. Early in its deliberations, the Commission outlined a research and writing program from which emerged a recognition that preparation of instructional leaders could not be treated intelligently in isolation from a number of factors, all of which were integral parts of a larger and more complex problem—namely, professionalization.

In response to the query of ASCD's responsibility in the movement of supervisors and curriculum workers toward self-discipline and professional maturity, one of the Commission's working papers [1] stated:

> By its very nature, ASCD exists for the purpose of assisting in the continued development of instructional leaders. Such leaders are considered to be any persons who are interested and involved in the improvement of instructional programs. Membership in the Association is open to all such persons. However, among the professional educators who are members, only supervisors and curriculum workers have no other organization through which they can work or speak as a national group on such matters as professional maturity and self-discipline.
>
> Other professional organizations and lay groups look to ASCD as an organization for leadership in the areas of supervision and curriculum development. They listen with respect when ASCD speaks for its members. Therefore to offer supervisors and curriculum workers an opportunity to develop plans for their

[1] Mimeographed Working Paper of the ASCD Commission on the Preparation of Instructional Leaders, 1960.

own self-discipline and professional maturation and to allow them to speak out through the Association seems to be not only an important function for ASCD, but, more significantly, a primary responsibility.

A Significant Step

Upon the recommendation of this Commission, the Executive Committee of ASCD committed itself in 1961 to cooperating with the American Association of School Administrators, the Department of Elementary School Principals, and the National Association of Secondary School Principals in establishing a Joint Committee on the Professionalization of Administrators and Supervisors. While this Joint Committee has not yet been overly productive, its creation was and is a major step forward in inter-organizational cooperation in an area of primary significance to each.

In 1963, a second significant step was taken by ASCD's Executive Committee. Upon the recommendation of its Commission, the Executive Committee designated the National Council for the Accreditation of Teacher Education as the agency for accrediting preparing institutions. Subsequently a budgetary allotment was made for NCATE to develop standards for use in its accrediting procedures.

Similarly, in 1963, the Commission's final report recommended that the Executive Committee appoint a Standing Committee on Professionalization of Supervisors and Curriculum Workers. Subsequently this Committee has extended the original work of the former Commission.

The Committee's first year was spent in gathering information about the professional status of supervisors and curriculum workers. Surprisingly such data proved almost nonexistent at the national level. Consequently, literary sources were searched, assistance was sought from NEA's Research

Division, from State Departments of Education, and from Presidents of State ASCD units. From these sources the earlier Commission's manuscripts were updated in each of the following areas: (a) Roles and Responsibilities of Supervisors and Curriculum Workers, (b) Recruitment and Selection, (c) Preparatory Programs, and (d) Certification.

It was soon apparent that while working papers were important, no significant progress could be made at the national level in absence of comparable action within each state. Consequently State Unit Presidents were encouraged to create State Committees on Professionalization of Supervisors and Curriculum Workers.

Each state unit was invited to send such committee co-chairmen (a field person and a college person) to one of six regional meetings sponsored by the National Committee. Approximately 70 percent of the states responded, and representative groups in five regional meetings discussed the Committee's working papers, to check normative data collected by the Committee and to plan together on ways of working together during 1965-66.

From these regional meetings over 15 state units have specific operations under way to determine the current status of supervisors and curriculum workers, and from such studies to project action programs to advance the quality and status of such persons.

The Committee's experiences with the state units indicate a widespread and deep-seated interest in the problem of improving the quality of services rendered and the professional status enjoyed by supervisors and curriculum workers. Consequently, this year's work will include: (a) a continuation of the regional meetings, (b) the preparation of a bulletin which will include the working papers and a suggested survey guide for state use, (c) an increased involvement with the Joint Committee (ASCD, AASA, DESP, and NASSP), (d) a closer working relationship with NCATE to develop standards for accrediting preparatory programs, and (e) the publication of a series of articles, of which this is the first, on issues faced by the Committee.

This brief introductory article will be followed by others which deal in order with the following descriptive working titles: How One Profession Did It; What the Literature Says About Supervisors' Roles; Supervisors' and Curriculum Workers' Preparatory Programs; Recruitment and Selection of Potential Members; Certification Practices; How One State Does It; and Where From Here?

In retrospect, this initial article has sought to confirm the position that the Association for Supervision and Curriculum Development does provide a framework within which its supervisors and curriculum workers, as members, can exert concerted effort at the national level. Second, it is hoped that this article has communicated a renewed faith that responsible action of mature people can result in productive effort to produce improved services for the youth we serve and that only as these services are improved can supervisors and curriculum workers move toward a higher level of professional maturity.

Finally, it is hoped that each reader leaves the article with many questions. How can one such organization contribute to such a professional group? How does a group move toward professional maturity? What controls can be exercised? What problems should be anticipated? What lessons can we draw from other professions? The next article in this series will attempt to draw comparisons between the route followed by the medical profession and those routes open to supervisors and curriculum workers. This article, too, will raise questions which deserve consideration. ☐

What Does the Flexner Report Say to ASCD?

HAROLD T. SHAFER

OVER the past eight to ten years the Association for Supervision and Curriculum Development has been formally concerned about the professionalization of supervisors and curriculum workers. The past work of the Commission on Professionalization, the present purposes of the Committee on Professionalization, and the ASCD 1965 Yearbook [1] all attest to this major interest. Within the total family of educators—teachers, administrators, teacher trainees, and specialists, the question of how we relate to the definition of a profession has been a historical issue as well as one of contention with the lay public.

What are some of the major problems in the upgrading of performance of all educators, especially of the group known as supervisors and curriculum workers whose ranks are growing each year?

Regardless of a general definition of a profession, there are agreed-upon characteristics, be it in the fields of medicine, law, theology, architecture, dentistry, pharmacy, or others. Some of these common factors are: entrance requirements, preparatory training, clinical or field experiences, accreditation, licensure or certification standards of performance, and ethical practice. Generally, all these component parts constituting a profession are controlled and policed by the membership.

As educators pursue the professionalization of educational workers, they turn to other professions for analysis as a base for comparison, hoping that from such study we may better understand the qualities that illustrate desired standards common to all. The medical profession is considered to be the classic example with overtones of the ideal as a pattern for emulation.

The history of the development of the medical profession both in America and Europe supports the "test tube approach," for the quality level of modern day medicine is the result of much research and action within its ranks. It is a colorful story, filled with much soul-searching and self-criticism. The use of its experience in total and direct application to the educational profession is not suggested or implied here, rather, it is recommended that in describing the progress of medical education, we achieve a perspective for our own.

Observer and Critic

Much credit for the professional upgrading of the medical profession is given to one man, Abraham Flexner, who at the time of his death in 1959, at the age of 92, was revered for his contribution to medical education and to education in general. In

---

[1] Robert R. Leeper, editor. *Role of Supervisor and Curriculum Director in a Climate of Change,* 1965 Yearbook. Washington, D.C.: Association for Supervision and Curriculum Development, 1965.

Harold T. Shafer, Superintendent of Schools, Wyckoff, New Jersey

this fact there is a modern day parallel, in that even as the educational profession has its critics outside its ranks, so A. Flexner, a prime observer and critic, was not a member of the medical group. In reference literature he is identified as an educator.

Mr. Flexner gained some national attention in 1908 for a report entitled, "The American College: A Criticism," which brought him to the attention of the Carnegie Foundation for the Advancement of Teaching. At the invitation of the Carnegie Foundation that he undertake such a project, he published in 1910, after two years of visitation and study, a report, "Medical Education in the U.S. and Canada." This document is known as the "Flexner Report."

The reading of his autobiography [2] is interesting and of value to all educators, for Flexner spent more than seventy years of his life contributing to American education and research.

In 1908, at the time Mr. Flexner launched his study of medical schools, the calibre of medical practice and the preparation of medical training attributed to the medical schools in the U.S. and Canada were being questioned. "The practice of medicine, long a professional calling in Europe, was then (1910) still a trade in America." [3] The well known motive of the founders and operators of medical schools was profit making. Cutthroat competition for students was unbounded.

As Flexner approached his visitation of operating schools, centered mainly on the east coast and in the midwest, two factors characterized his efforts. One, Flexner went totally unprepared as to survey methods and instruments. Two, his point of view was that medical training was a form of education and not a mysterious process of initiation or professional apprenticeship.

He found that a lack of basic training due to inadequate facilities and teaching aids was universal. It was not uncommon for Flexner to discover classrooms completely devoid of charts, apparatus, and equipment.

Flexner thought it necessary that clinical training be obtained through contact with patients in local hospitals. He found this need either not being provided for or hospital facilities and staff for this purpose, in his own words, "in wretched condition."

Working upon the assumption that a medical school related to a college or university should measure up to the institution's standards for training, he found these standards only weakly integrated and correlated.

After a number of visits to medical schools, Flexner began to approach his inspection in an organized manner and he shortly formulated a set of criteria. In his report, Flexner summed up what he called the decisive points, which, when known, were conclusive as to the quality and value of a medical school.

First, the entrance requirements. What were they? Were they enforced?

Second, the size and training of the faculty.

Third, the sum available from endowment and fees for the support of the institution, and what became of it.

Fourth, the quality and adequacy of the laboratories provided for the instruction of the first two years and the qualifications and training of the teachers and the so-called preclinical branches.

Fifth and finally, the relations between medical school and hospitals, including particularly freedom of access to beds and freedom in the appointment by the school of the

---

[2] Abraham Flexner. *Abraham Flexner, An Autobiography*. New York: Simon and Schuster, 1960.

[3] John Lear. "Who Should Govern Medicine?" *Saturday Review,* June 5, 1965. p. 39.

hospital physicians and surgeons who automatically should become clinical teachers.[4]

Parallel in Education

With slight modifications of this list, mainly by changing a few words and terms such as "preclinical branches" and "relations with hospitals" to "research and demonstration centers" and "field experiences," one can readily apply the decisive criteria to any aspect of the training and practice of teachers, administrators, or curriculum workers.

The American Medical Association, through its Council on Medical Education and Hospitals and the American College of Surgeons, is the influential watchdog of medical training in medical schools and hospitals.

Accreditation of these institutions is crucial to their existence. Also, the number of such schools is controlled through the rigid standards set.

Through the professional organizations, state standards for examination before a board of examiners and the granting of a license to practice all hinge upon meeting the requirements set by the profession. Such conditions also exist in other professions mentioned earlier, i.e., law, pharmacy, dentistry.

In an earlier generation it was practically necessary for a physician to go to Europe for postgraduate work. Today the U.S., along with England and Scandinavia, is outstanding in postgraduate studies and medical research. The influence of the Flexner Report can be credited also for this development.

The study of the history of the medical professionalization and the career of A. Flexner is exciting and informative. However, drawing direct implications from the evolution of the medical field for a professional group in education is fraught with danger.

Nevertheless the history of fifty-plus years of conscious analysis and improvement of medical training does supply us with clues as to major factors involved in professionalization of any group of workers.

As supervisors and curriculum workers, we should give serious attention and united effort in analyzing our own professional growth in the following areas:

1. We need a nationwide systematized study of current conditions hindering professionalization.

2. We need to consider setting standards for recruiting and selecting future supervisors and curriculum workers.

3. We should work to strengthen preservice training specialization programs to insure concreteness in the program which needs both the theoretical classroom studies and field work.

4. We should ask for and assume a definite role in setting standards for certification by working with certification agencies.

5. The association should take steps to study taking direct responsibility for policing the rank and file membership for violations of acceptable practice.

6. We should develop a specific program nationally, statewide, and locally to improve the public image of supervision and curriculum work.

7. We can note the fact that professional preparation is an expensive venture in which the amount of financial support and investment in training is directly related to the quality of such preparation.

To those who seek a fresh viewpoint and one that is substantiated by experience, especially as they probe the progress of instructional workers' self-evaluation and efforts to professionalize themselves, we suggest that the foregoing summary of medical professionalization may offer a perspective and a hopeful direction. ☐

---

[4] Flexner, *op. cit.*, p. 79.

Role and Function of Supervisors and Curriculum Workers

ROWANNETTA S. ALLEN

THE current period of sweeping changes in education is bringing about corresponding changes in the role of the supervisor and curriculum worker. This role, which at one time seemed clear-cut, is becoming more complex and could become more significant. The role is more complex because of the many persons at local, state, and national levels who are actively demonstrating an interest in public education; it is potentially more significant because of the state of flux which currently characterizes curriculum development.

No longer is curriculum development a simple matter; this, too, is becoming more involved and often places the supervisor and curriculum worker in the position of either standing between the school system and the general public or serving as the agent of the school system to encourage public involvement and support. Inherent in the current situation is an urgent need for competent, courageous, professional leadership.

In the face of this challenge to educators to contribute vital leadership, there is an obvious lack of professional unity. In fact, there is apparent confusion among supervisors and curriculum workers, as well as administrators, as to (a) the accepted purpose of supervision; (b) who is qualified to perform this function; and (c) how supervision shall be accomplished.

Need for Clarification

School systems differ, it is true, but with all of their differences, there is usually a singleness of purpose, namely: to provide the best possible education for children, youth, and adults served by the system. There is no single set of curriculum guides that can be used to prescribe a dynamic, changing program, nor can there be, if education is to keep abreast of the times. The urgent need of school systems throughout the country, therefore, is for an adequate number of professionally trained supervisors and curriculum workers who are prepared to assume leadership in continuing curriculum revision.

Supervisors and curriculum workers have been added to the administrative staffs of school systems purportedly to facilitate the development of and the implementation of improved educational programs. For example, as early as 1922-23, the State of Maryland, by act of the legislature, authorized the local units to employ "supervising teachers or helping teachers"[1] as professional appointees to the staff of the county superintendent of schools to assist him with the prescribed responsibilities of his office as expressed in the law: "The county super-

[1] The Public School Laws of Maryland. Vol. 34, p. 137, January 1955.

Rowannetta S. Allen, Supervisor of Teacher Personnel, Prince George's County, Maryland. In 1966, Assistant Superintendent of Schools for Elementary Education, Prince George's County

intendent shall visit the schools, observe the management and instruction and give suggestions for the improvement of the same." [2]

As public school systems recently have been confronted with the problems of providing for rapid increases in enrollment and adjusting to the mobility which has accompanied this growth, many new job titles have appeared on the staff roster. Frequently existing personnel have been asked to assume new or additional responsibilities. In assuming the various titles assigned to them, and consequently performing the functions associated with the titles, the role of the supervisor and curriculum worker has often become ambiguous.

In material recently prepared by Gordon N. Mackenzie on "Roles of Supervisors and Curriculum Workers" there is confirmation of this:

> There is wide range in both the titles used and in the assignment of responsibilities to supervisors and curriculum workers. The diverse origins in the positions, some being in administration and others being in teaching, curriculum, and the improvement of instruction, cause initial difficulty. A strong supervisory or administrative lineage is apt to result in a stress on such functions as quality control, the provision of needed information for administrators, and the management and coordination of various kinds of organizational activities. The teaching, curricular, and instructional improvement lineage suggests a possible emphasis on direct assistance to teachers, curricular planning, and in-service education. The local variations in skills and interests of holders of various positions, and the differing patterns of organization further cloud the picture as to what any specific individuals do and how the supervisory and curriculum improvement functions are performed. In fact, to diagnose the manner in which supervisory and curriculum improvement functions are performed, it may be necessary in specific school systems to analyze the functioning of such diverse but related performers as the chief school administrator for instruction, directors, coordinators, general and special subject supervisors, principals, building curriculum coordinators, and department heads.[3]

Compounding the problem of identifying and clarifying the role of supervisors and curriculum workers, according to Mackenzie, are "the underdeveloped state of the theory of the fields of supervision and of curriculum as well as the low levels of preparation of some supervisors and curriculum workers. Certainly if there were well developed descriptive theories as to the nature of curriculum and of supervision, as areas of knowledge, there would be more clarity and understanding as to the functions which the workers in these areas could perform to maximize the output of the educational program. However, the present absence of this knowledge does not excuse the tendency on the part of many to oversimplify the nature of supervisory and curricular work and to assume that any good teacher or any good administrator with sound professional intentions can perform the implied functions effectively." [4]

A little over a decade ago the purposes of supervision, as represented by a review of the titles listed in *Education Index* (June 1950-May 1955) and stated in general terms, were counseling teachers, helping beginning teachers, inspiring professional growth, improving instruction, and providing educational leadership. Ten years later the titles listed seem to indicate more purposes, more persons involved, more ways of getting supervision done, and more inherent problems.

Emerging from the writings on super-

---

[2] *Ibid.*, p. 135.

[3] Gordon N. Mackenzie. "Roles of Supervisors and Curriculum Workers." Statement prepared by Mackenzie as a former member of the ASCD Committee on Professionalization of Supervisors and Curriculum Workers for discussion by State ASCD groups.

[4] *Ibid.*, p. 2.

vision of this period are the questions: Whose responsibility is the improvement of instruction and the development of curriculum? Does this responsibility rest with the superintendent? the principal? the department head? the generalist? or the specialist?

Analysis and Description

In the recent literature there is a recognizable trend toward making curriculum development a cooperative undertaking and toward using a team approach to supervision. Each of these trends reinforces the urgent need for trained professional leadership to give direction and guidance to the group effort.

Some of the problems reflected in the titles appearing between 1950 and 1955 sound strangely familiar today. Mentioned among them were such problems as resolving conflicts in supervision, changing the attitude of teachers toward supervision, discovering an effective approach to supervision, agreement on basic principles of supervision, training for supervision, delineation of responsibilities, certification requirements, and group-centered supervision.

Newly stated, the concerns of a decade ago are still with us. Among them are the following: determining what techniques are worth while, effecting a wholesome balance in supervision, meeting the needs of experienced teachers as well as those of beginning teachers, up-dating the theory of supervision, human relations in supervision, clarifying the purpose of supervision and the roles of persons involved, how supervision is perceived, the "guese" of supervision, and the need for cooperation in supervision.

From a cursory review of the titles of articles on supervision, it is evident that there is growing interest in the topic, that supervision is being presented from many differing points of view, that the volume of writing on supervision is increasing, and that most of the current writers are new to the field.

Obviously the literature deals more with an analysis and description of supervision as it exists rather than of supervision as it ought to be. Constantly recurring is an expression of the need for clarification of role.

This is further substantiated by Roy Wahle's review of titles of dissertations listed in *Research Studies in Education* for the period 1957 through 1962. While serving as a member of the ASCD Committee on Professionalization of Supervisors and Curriculum Workers, Wahle prepared a report which reveals a total of eighty-four dissertation titles dealing with varied aspects of supervision and curriculum development. Of this total nearly a third deal with role, status, and duties of the different persons performing the supervisory function. These include the principal, the general supervisor, the instructional vice-principal, the superintendent, and, in the case of student teachers, the supervising teacher. Nineteen titles relate to techniques, activities, services, and practices of instructional supervisors. A third major group of titles centers around studies of supervisory relationships, perceptions, and attitudes.

Implicit in these titles is the continuing need for clarifying the role of the supervisor and curriculum worker. The local variations in assignment of supervisory functions mentioned by Mackenzie are evident here, and while not mentioned specifically as problems, there is the recurrence of such key words and phrases as attitudinal perceptions, administrative organization, leadership, cooperative programs, critical competencies, principles and basic assumptions, personal characteristics, competency patterns, and inservice education.

Out of this situation what can and should arise?

In a previous article in *Educational*

Leadership, Harold Shafer called the attention of supervisors and curriculum workers to the Flexner report, suggesting that the experience of the medical profession in achieving professionalization may offer a perspective to engage educators in active pursuit of comparable standards as a professional group.

Professionalization implies the possession of a certain and particular know-how which can be brought to bear on problems. It implies concerted action to raise the level of practice within the profession and to maintain a mutually acceptable level of performance through policies enforced by the professional group. It implies selective admissions, specialized training in duly accredited institutions, and certification procedures approximating licensing.

As we realize the urgency of the need for trained professional leadership in education and as we become more keenly aware of the unanswered problems which could be resolved if we, as a profession, took action, is it too much to hope that we may strengthen our efforts in that direction now?

Succeeding articles by members of the ASCD Committee on Professionalization of Supervisors and Curriculum Workers will alert readers to existing conditions and will suggest some reasonable possibilities for concerted action. ☐

EL 23 (5): 358-62; February 1966
© 1966 ASCD

Preparatory Programs for Supervisors

MAURICE J. EASH

WE LIVE in a time when the professional ranks are more numerous than in previous years. Yet most professions are unequal to the demands from the public for action or advice. Correspondingly the elevation in public status has made the position of being a professional highly sought by many groups, and a goodly portion of time is devoted in annual conferences to trying to establish the boundaries and requirements, or to justify being called a profession.

The conference antics which the thrust toward professionalism prompts offer considerable latitude for jest, and usually the group is trying to emulate the queens of the professions, law or medicine. Underlying these surface activities, however, is a serious response to a social demand, a demand for broader competency, better application of knowledge in every area of human affairs, and the belief that experimental and theoretical knowledge is superior to lay advice founded upon myth and/or folklore.

It has been suggested that the professional trend is closely associated with the bureaucratic. In a bureaucracy, further differentiation of function encourages the building of specialization and amassing of the esoteric, developing separateness in the organization, but also provides more elaborated specialties with new knowledge on

Maurice J. Eash, Associate Professor of Education, The City University of New York, Hunter College, New York

complex problems. Bureaucracy, which, contrary to a widely circulated public opinion, is not necessarily opprobrious, has characterized the larger school systems and become commonplace in public education. Consequently separate specializations within the field have instituted drives to upgrade their areas of inquiry to professional status.

In the December issue of *Educational Leadership,* Harold Shafer dealt with a dimension of the problem of professionalization in his brief review of the major steps involved in the rise of a recognized profession, that of medicine. It is the contention of this paper that the roots of many of the problems in preparatory programs reside in the major issues involved in professionalization. Since one of the dominant characteristics of a profession is the possession of a general and systematic knowledge not readily available to the public, preparation programs for the aspirants to the profession have received much attention.

The detailing of programs, insofar as selection of courses and their sequence is concerned, has been a major preoccupation in graduate programs of higher education. Seldom has so much faith been invested in so little empirical evidence. In a time when scientific investigation has moved far past the bits and pieces observation stage, the formulation of programs of professional preparation still resides in the realm of the occult. To cushion the lack of knowledge, an occasional euphemistic disguise is employed in pronouncements of programs, "expert opinion," but such pronouncements rarely define what constituent components served as the basis of the opinions.

A Systems Approach

In the past education has progressed in many areas through making applications from related disciplines. I would suggest that in the problem of building improved programs of preparation, we can gain substantially from similar application of theory from theoretical computer designs used in analyzing new problems.

At the present stage of development in preparatory programs for supervisors and curriculum workers, the programs can best be defined as combinations of idiosyncratic projections of staff and compromises generated by the exigencies of academic politics. The wide variation in programs bears out the lack of systematic foundations. Some curriculum and supervisory programs parallel almost exclusively the programs for school administrators; others do not define any specific program; some mandate specific courses, others outline broad experiences, or attempt to predicate programs on desired behavioral outcomes. In short, systematic approaches to investigating and defining suitable programs have been lacking and the landscape of preparatory programs viewed as a whole reflects the resultant chaos.

The lack of agreement on professional role is reflected in preparatory programs as they are mirrored in certification. Certification for supervisors alone ranges from fourteen states which have no certification to four states with four separate certificates. If added to these figures are certifications for curriculum workers, the number of certificates is further multiplied. The chaos is further compounded when the bases for certificate preparation programs are examined in further detail. In some cases the supervisory certificate is an ancillary licensure to the administrative certificate, requiring little or no preparation; in others it is an extension of the classroom teachers certificate.

Most commonly when a special certificate is awarded for supervision or curriculum it represents the taking of some courses, usually limited in numbers, and as an additive to some other program. At this time the preparation does not appear to be either specific to a function or specialized in program. Consequently the licensure of supervisors and curriculum workers, being vague and supplementary to other licenses and goals, frequently results in a serious imbalance of number of preparing institutions, and of number of licenses issued in relation to market demand. As examples underscoring this imbalance, one state has issued over 7,000 licenses and counts only a little over 260 positions; another state has twenty-eight institutions offering preparatory programs for supervisors, when in all likelihood one would produce a sufficient number. Even these normative figures do not disclose what is believed to be the most serious resultant, the quality of preparatory programs.

At this stage of development, programs of preparation present the black box problem which faces a systems researcher in beginning stages of exploration of a system.[1] In systems research terms, a black box is a system wherein we can determine inputs and outputs but are unable to describe effectively or accurately the interactions which transpire among the inputs to produce the outputs.

The inputs, primarily students, faculty, material resources, are global knowns; the outputs, graduate students who assume responsibility in supervisory and curriculum positions, are identifiable. The ineluctable component of the system has been any accurate analysis and measurement of the interaction of the global variables in input, and the resultant changes in the output. The black box problem in programs of preparation may be diagrammed as in Figure 1.

Typically the building of a program for preparation has proceeded from some assumption of desired outputs. Output descriptions have ranged from strictly normative job analysis of practitioners, to theoretical role formulation, and behavioral descriptions stemming from a philosophical basis. Output description, being a massive exercise, displays inherent weakness as the means (programs of preparation) are derived to execute the ends (output). The connections between inputs and outputs are exceedingly tenuous at best and not exposed to any sophisticated analysis which is a first step in evaluation. Methodological myopia has indeed been a major stumbling block in every profession, even the ones held up as exemplars and models. Except for rare examples the quality of product in practically all professions has exhibited the infinite variety of the human species.

Can progress be made in preparation programs through the rise of a systems approach? I believe it can. We have in a vague sense, without benefit of refinement or formalization, instituted partial use of a systems approach, especially with the great preoccupation with input variables. The past experience of other professions would tend to substantiate the worth of such efforts.

---

[1] A system has been defined as "complexes of elements in interaction to which certain system laws can be applied." (L. Von Berlatanffy. "Problems of General Systems Theory." *Human Biology* 23: 307; 1951.)

Inputs { Students, Faculty, Material resources }   (System) Programs of preparation   { Supervisors, Curriculum workers } Outputs

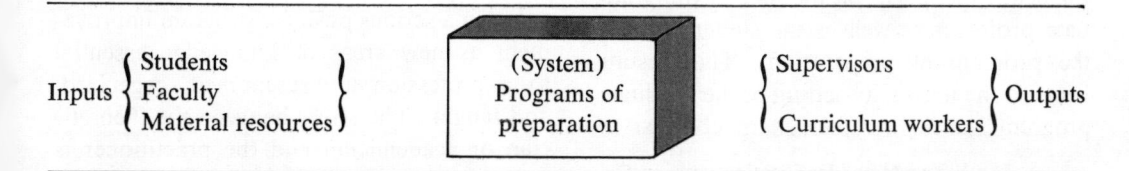

Figure 1. A Systems Approach to Programs of Preparation

For example, the medical profession has utilized a heavy emphasis with input variables as the way to improvement. Banking on highly intelligent students, rich material resources, and a faculty tested through experience, medical practice has made giant strides forward.

Attaining Identity

In suggesting that programs of preparation move into the black box stage, I do not wish to imply that we stay there. Almost every research begun under the gross paradigm of the black box advances in knowledge and discloses internal subsystems which can indirectly yield more explicit data on specific problems. The literature on the study of the professions provides some inklings of subsystems within the total preparation program that may exist within the box.

One potential subsystem that has been studied and reported on is identification with an occupation.[2] The scattered evidence from this, and from other studies, would suggest that the subsystem of graduate student-graduate professor interaction is quite crucial to attainment of professional identity and the professional attributes which accompany professional status. One example of a professional attribute which might be developed through identification, and one which is considered a characteristic of all professions, is the ability to think objectively and inquiringly about matter which, for the layman, may be subject to orthodoxy and sentiment. As an interesting aside on identification, one can speculate about the necessity for field experiences on the part of the graduate professor as well as the student during the program of preparation. This results because the university setting of the graduate program stands in rather sharp contrast to the field of practice of the student, assuming he will enter the public school system.

Further division of the black box into subsystems is a necessity. As suggested here, some of the search in sociology on professions indicates that organized experiences which place students in the position of working under conditions that correspond to the functional environment of the practitioner are crucial to professional development. Of subsequent interest to programs of preparation is the finding that student identification with a profession is influenced by working in a close relationship with a practitioner, and in areas where the close relationship does not exist identification is slow in developing, if at all.

An attendant problem in present programs of preparation organized around a course or two in supervision and/or curriculum is that few staff members are involved full time in the concerns of the area. Pursuing a divided responsibility is not conducive to development of the specialty or identification of the graduate professor with the area.

Utilizing the fragmentary clues from allied research in the behavioral sciences, the black box could with further research become amenable to subsystem analysis. Once this secondary stage is reached studies probing the interaction of the global components of faculty, student, and physical materials could be designed. Through evaluation of outcomes, subsystems could be manipulated and tested.

This is only one of the major problems in preparatory programs. Other types of problems arise from the stresses which develop in a serious push for program improvement as new areas of knowledge essential to a profession are researched, organized, and taught. The stress between the theoretician or academician and the practitioner is a very common concern. The former, pulling and tugging, exercising a critical, analytical approach, utilizing and developing new

---

[2] "The Elements of Identification with an Occupation." Howard S. Becher and James Carper. *American Sociological Review* 21 (3): 341-48; June 1956.

knowledge; and the latter, consumed with the pressure of ever present duties, resenting the constant urge for improvement and upgrading of practice. Yet from such stress is progress fashioned. Since these are natural outcomes of the advancement to professional status, the academician and practitioner must channel the conflict productively, exercising care to avoid the enshrinement of dogma and the punishment of the unorthodox.

Under the present state of knowledge, a variety of patterns of programs including knowledge from the allied behavioral sciences would seem to be suggested as helpful. Until the time when the component variables can be more accurately sorted and symbiotic influences carefully traced, the evaluation and development of programs will need to rely on assessments of major input variables and their organization.

Some sample questions for preparatory programs might be: On standard measures, what is the quality of the students being admitted to the program? Are there periodic evaluations of student progress and on what basis? Are there follow-up studies on graduates? What types of opportunities for experience are planned for the students: courses? field work? Does the staff actively participate in research, writing, and professional organizations? Do physical facilities at the university and in adjacent public schools exist for the program? How many graduate students are assigned to a major professor, and what is the work load? These and other similar questions on input variables will have to serve as a guide until resolution of the more fundamental questions on professionalization is attained. ☐

EL 23 (7): 587-93; April 1966
© 1966 ASCD

Identifying Potential Leaders for Supervision and Curriculum Work

ROBERT S. THURMAN

ONE of the most serious problems facing the education profession is that of finding persons with leadership ability. Ryder predicts that although the general population of the United States will increase by one-third during the next two decades, the age group from which leaders emerge will remain constant.[1] This means the competition for these leaders will become keener than it is at the present time. The demand will be greater not only by different groups within the education profession but by private enterprise and by governmental agencies.

A second serious problem is that of finding people within the leadership pool who have the personal attributes, intellectual abilities, and professional commitment to fulfill the roles of supervisors and curriculum workers. The profession can no

[1] N. B. Ryder. "Demography and Education." *Phi Delta Kappan* 41: 379; June 1960.

Robert S. Thurman, Associate Professor of Education, Department of Curriculum and Instruction, University of Tennessee, Knoxville

longer afford the luxury of hoping that enough persons with promise will decide to prepare to be supervisors or curriculum workers but must take decisive steps to identify persons with the potential talent and to encourage them to consider the opportunities in the field of supervision and curriculum.

Selection Is Critical

The problem of selection is a troublesome one. At present there is no specific criterion supported by research which can be used to predict in advance whether or not a person will be an effective supervisor. William Bagley's statement is even more appropriate today than in 1939 when he said that "if three-fourths of the time, energy, and money spent . . . in carrying through elaborate programs of curriculum-revision had been spent in a determined effort to raise the standards of selecting and training teachers . . ." education would have been more effectively improved.[2]

Although little has been written on the problem of selecting qualified persons and less research has been done in this area, this is not to say that writers have failed to describe the qualities they believe supervisors should possess. Any text on supervision includes lists. And according to these lists a supervisor should among other things love children, be student-centered, group-centered, have the courage to take a stand, have teaching experience, listen to opinions of others, and be guided at all times, not by opinion, but by research findings. Any person attempting to develop these, and the many other characteristics listed by writers, would soon be a paragon of virtue.

The reality of the matter is that little has been done to determine the areas in which a person must have knowledge, skills, and insights in order to be an effective supervisor or curriculum worker. Only until these areas are thought through can steps be taken to set up any kind of selective admission to programs of preparation.

As a result, it appears that currently there are only two kinds of selection procedures being carried on in most of the preparing institutions. One is self-selection. The decision is left to the individual to decide whether or not he has the background, talent, or commitment to become a supervisor or curriculum worker. If he decides he does have such qualities, the second step of the screening procedure is employed. He needs only to meet the general requirements for admission to graduate study, which are basically the same for English, supervision, or any other field.

Careful consideration should be given to the roles supervisors and curriculum workers must play and to the program of preparation needed to carry out these roles. Are there any personal characteristics which would enable a person to be more effective in his work? Are there academic and professional abilities the person should have? What skills are needed? What professional qualities and capabilities are necessary for these positions? Which of these should a person have prior to entering a program? Which can be sharpened during preparation? Which can be developed as a result of preparation?

These are questions the profession, and specifically the Association for Supervision and Curriculum Development, should be concerned with. These questions are not purely academic. The quality of the educational program of the decades ahead will depend greatly on the answers given to them.

The responsibility for searching for the answers does not lie only with preparing institutions. Granted in the final analysis these institutions must determine who will

---

[2] William C. Bagley. "An Essentialist Looks at the Foreign Languages." *Educational Administration and Supervision* 25: 250; April 1939.

enter and complete the programs. Nevertheless, people in local school systems have an important stake in the quality of these persons. These school people can contribute much to the selection process by working with selection committees of colleges and universities, by serving on graduate committees, by observing and evaluating the prospective supervisors in field situations, and by assisting in research projects designed to study the characteristics of identified effective and noneffective supervisors.

Recruiting Potential Leaders

Related to the problem of selection is that of recruitment. The establishment of high standards does little good unless there is a reservoir of talented prospects from which to choose.

As already stated, the decision to prepare to be a supervisor has been left largely to the individual. Although little research has been done in the area of why people choose to become supervisors, it appears that many drift into the position rather than entering on purpose. A study of supervisors in Kentucky reports that only 11 percent of the participants entered a graduate program for the purpose of specializing in supervision.[3] The writer surveyed a group of male undergraduate prospective secondary teachers, asking what they hoped to be doing in ten years if not teaching. Most of them said they wanted to be a principal or a superintendent. Upon further questioning, it became evident they either were not aware of opportunities in the areas of supervision and curriculum or they did not know what a person did in these jobs, thus were not interested.

Self-selection will doubtless continue to be an important means by which people will decide to become supervisors or curriculum workers. It cannot, however, be the only means. There needs to be an organized program designed to identify persons with promise.

As in the selection process, both the personnel in local school systems and those in teacher-preparation institutions should work together in identifying these persons. Together they can establish machinery which allows talented people to be identified. Such prospective leaders may be in the preservice program preparing to teach, they may be teachers or administrators, or they may be in related areas such as guidance. The important feature is that people *consciously* will be looking for individuals who have promise. They must also consider that group that is so frequently overlooked—women.

Identifying persons with promise is just part of the task. They must be made aware of the opportunities in supervision and curriculum work. This calls for the development of a wide variety of materials—brochures, pamphlets, films, filmstrips, and perhaps advertisements for use in mass media. These should describe the functions and responsibilities of supervisors and curriculum workers, the nature of the preparation required, and the job possibilities.

Expense doubtless has been an important factor in keeping some very promising men and women from pursuing advanced study in these two areas. Although the individual may continue to bear a large share of the financial cost involved, it seems clear that more assistance will have to be provided from other sources. Currently, preparing institutions are providing the bulk of financial assistance to such students in the form of scholarships, fellowships, and assistantships. Other sources must be found, however.

As in other aspects of selection and recruitment, the local school system can

---

[3] Ray Alexander and others. *Educational Supervision in Kentucky, 1961-62.* Lexington: Bulletin of the Bureau of School Services, College of Education, University of Kentucky. 35: 1; September 1962. p. 42.

play an important role. For example, the system can provide leaves of absence with partial pay for individuals who will move into these leadership positions.

Providing Leadership

In such a quest for talent, the Association for Supervision and Curriculum Development can provide much leadership at the national level. Through the Committee on Professionalization of Supervisors and Curriculum Workers, it can continue to work with state units. In addition, the Association can develop materials to be used for recruitment which would be too expensive for a state unit to prepare. For example, it might produce a film which presents the many roles a supervisor plays. It can encourage and support studies which might give some direction in the selection process.

An ASCD affiliated unit can also provide much leadership within the state. It can make annual studies of the supply and demand of supervisors and curriculum workers; it can encourage preparing institutions and school systems to cooperate in identifying, recruiting, and screening men and women for these positions; it can assist in the development of materials which describe opportunities in these fields; and it can help develop ways of providing financial assistance to those who need it.

Now is a time to re-file the old saw so that it goes: "Those who can, do. And those who do with unusual ability and insight become leaders in supervision and curriculum work." ☐

Certification Requirements for General Supervisors and/or Curriculum Workers Today—Tomorrow

H. IRENE HALLBERG

RECENT articles in this journal have explored the meaning of professionalization as it relates specifically to supervisors and curriculum workers. Harold T. Shafer's article in December looked backward to the Flexner Report on education in the medical profession to gain a better perspective of preparation in our own field. In Rowannetta S. Allen's article in January it was apparent to the reader that the unique role of the supervisor needs clarifying. The approach of defining the supervisor's role by functions seems to offer promise. Maurice J. Eash in the February issue presented criti-

H. Irene Hallberg, Staff Member, United Methodist Group Ministry of the Rogue River Valley, Medford, Oregon. In 1966, General Consultant, State Department of Education, Olympia, Oregon

cal issues found in the preparatory programs for supervisors. Robert S. Thurman's article in April highlighted the need for identifying and selecting potential supervisors and curriculum workers.

Another necessary criterion for a profession is the establishment of quasi-legal policies and regulations which establish minimum requirements for the certification of individuals. These certification requirements affirm the individual's competency and serve to regulate the quantity as well as the quality. A profession must also have the means for enforcing the professional ethics and standards through provisions for revoking certification for cause.

Certification requirements for general supervisors and/or curriculum workers must be strengthened if professionalization of this category of educators is to be attained. A study of the certification requirements for supervisors and/or curriculum workers completed in 1964 revealed wide discrepancies in these standards among the 50 states. There was a total of 71 certificates for supervisors and/or curriculum workers available in 36 of the 50 states. Some certificates entitled the holder to supervise at either the elementary or secondary level, or both, with a few certificates undesignated. Twelve of these 71 certificates were for supervision of special subject matter areas and two entitled the holder to supervise both general and special subject areas.

Suggested Principles

If stronger certification requirements are the hallmark of a profession, then certain principles should be developed. The following are suggested:

1. Certification requirements should give recognition to the unique role of the general supervisor and/or curriculum worker needed for today's schools.

At present supervisors are certified under the administrator's certificate in eight states, while in one state the teacher's certificate was the basis under which the supervisor worked. In another state, which had a certificate for supervisors, a supervisor could actually work under any certificate—teacher's, principal's, or superintendent's.

2. Certification should be based on the development of a planned program by the training institution, approved by the licensing agent, the State Department of Education.

This planned program should provide for a balance among theory, observation, field work, and practice in research skills.

At present the supervisory programs of the education institutions were approved in 13 states. However, it was not clear, from the stated requirements, what the approving agency was. In one state an internship was required while another state had a permissive program for internship.

In only one certificate was the phrase "planned program" found.

3. Certification should be granted automatically upon recommendation of the training institution when the planned graduate program has been successfully completed.

At present, certification is generally based on completion of course work and specified experience. However, 16 of the 71 certificates issued in 1964 had no major courses required. Fifty-one certificates required courses in supervision, 32 certificates required curriculum courses, and 24 certificates required courses in administration.

Eleven of the 71 certificates had no experience requirements listed.

Over half of the 71 certificates required teaching experience ranging from 2 to 5 years, 7 certificates required supervisory experience, and 3 called for teaching or supervisory experience. The remaining certificates called for various types of administrative experience.

4. *The number of training institutions should be limited in order to bring a balance between supply and demand to assure an adequate program.*

Two states have as many as 27 institutions offering classes needed to meet certification requirements for supervisors' certification. In another state (Kentucky) in which there are 8 institutions offering course work for supervisory certification, the supply is far in excess of the state's needs.

5. *Certification requirements should provide for continuing professional growth and be issued for specified lengths of time.*

Life certificates are not recommended unless there is some provision to assure continuing professional growth, use of certificate, and revocation.

Forty-four of the 71 certificates had no requirements stated for renewal of the certificate. There were 8 certificates granted for life, while 15 certificates were issued for specified lengths of time, the range being 3 to 10 years. Of the remaining 4 certificates, each had a different requirement for renewal.

Some certificates were renewable if a certain specified number of class hours had been earned. A few certificates were renewable on evidence of professional service and growth. (Several states had a requirement of supervisory services within a specified length of time to keep the certificate valid.) Only one state indicated that the certificate could be revoked.

6. *It is desirable to have both provisional and professional or standard certificates.*

The provisional certificate should be for the beginning supervisor, have less stringent requirements, and be valid for a limited period of time.

A professional or standard certificate should represent continued professional growth, contributions to the profession, and effective and efficient performance and be valid for a longer period of time. Provision should be made for renewal of the latter certificate as long as the holder meets the requirements for it. Means for revocation of either type of certificate on moral, ethical, or professional grounds should be clearly stated.

Among the 36 states issuing certificates for supervisors, 12 have two types of certification for general supervisors.

7. *In a society characterized by a high rate of mobility, it would be desirable to have reciprocity for the supervisors' certificates among the states.*

This principle calls for appraisal of the programs of the preparing institutions by a national accreditation organization.

The 1964 study gives no indication that there is any degree of reciprocity of this kind among the states.

The incongruence between the principles as stated and the findings in the 1964 study of certification requirements for supervisors and/or curriculum workers dramatizes the great need for a concerted attack upon the matter of the certification requirements in the 50 states.

We suggest the following questions for study and action:

1. To what degree do the certification requirements for general supervisors in your state meet the principles as stated above?

2. After pinpointing the strengths and weaknesses in the certification requirements for general supervisors, what plan of action would you devise?

3. What organization and/or persons could be enlisted to strengthen the certification requirements for general supervisors in your state? ☐

Selection and Recruitment of Supervisors

JOHNNYE V. COX

SELECTION for leadership positions is an established and accepted procedure in business, industry, government, education, and the other professions. The selection processes vary in quality and effectiveness from one of these groups to another and within segments or divisions of each group. On a continuum extending from "poor" practices or processes to "good" practices or processes, these parent groups and division groups would probably be located from one extreme pole to the other. However, on a continuum describing *effort* and *progress* in improving practices we would probably find each large and small group a considerable distance from the "low" pole.

This activity to improve selection practices appears to stem from, or certainly to include, a concept that "leaders are both born and made." Stated differently, this concept involves finding persons who have already demonstrated leadership ability and helping them to develop further these competencies through programs designed especially for preparation for a specific task. There is no longer a question of whether there should be selection for leadership but of how it should be done and who should do it.

It is the purpose of this report to describe policies and practices of recruitment and selection for supervision in Georgia as they were originally established and as they have been adapted to meet changing conditions. A brief historical statement about the development of the total supervisory program is presented as background information.

The late 'thirties saw many educational developments in Georgia take shape and flourish. One of these developments was a cooperative approach to the task of improving teaching and learning in Georgia schools. It was believed by forward-looking educators of that time that providing supervisory assistance for teachers in service would be an effective approach to the task. However, to provide supervisory assistance for teachers almost meant starting from the beginning. At this time there were fewer than six persons employed as supervisors in Georgia schools. There was no program of preparation for supervisors at any institution in the state.

The Georgia Teacher Education Council, an agency created in the early 'forties, assumed the sponsorship of a program for preparing school supervisors. An advisory committee of the Council gave leadership and direction in developing policies of the program. A three-pronged approach was made. Simultaneous activity was directed toward (a) recruiting and selecting personnel to prepare themselves for supervisory positions, (b) developing a program of education for the selected persons, and (c) providing for the employment of these persons in supervisory positions.

Recruitment for positions that existed mainly in hopes and dreams demanded con-

Johnnye V. Cox, Director, Georgia Programs for the Education of Supervisors, University of Georgia, Athens

siderable enthusiasm, effort, and time. The advisory committee of the Council assumed major responsibilities for this task. Criteria for selection were established. The committee was guided by the concept that if a good teacher already exhibited *good* leadership qualities this person could be helped to become an even better teacher and leader.

Procedures

The criteria were informally stated and informally applied. There was more concern that the items on the list "fitted together" in a person than that they could be identified within a person. The criteria included such items as evidence (a) of leadership among children and adults, (b) of "getting along with" students, fellow teachers, administrators, and people of the community, (c) that he likes teaching and that he demonstrates effective teaching, and (d) that he is tolerant and respectful of persons with whom he differs. Evidence of intellectual ability, emotional stability, and social adjustment was sought. Chronological age was not considered to be too important but "age in spirit" was important.

The next task was to find teachers who seemed to meet the established criteria. The advisory committee assumed this responsibility. Contacts were made with administrators, teachers, and other school leaders to secure names of teachers who might become prospective supervisors. Applications for study in supervision were sent to the prospects.

As applications were received visits were made to the teachers by one or more members of the committee for observation of classroom procedures and for conferences with the teachers and their associates. Letters of inquiry were sent to other persons who knew the teachers. Questions relating to the criteria for selection were asked of the teachers and of persons who knew them.

The materials about each prospective supervisor were carefully reviewed by a small group of the advisory committee. This selection committee made recommendations for approval or nonapproval. Invitations were extended to persons who were recommended. Other applicants were advised of the committee's decisions.

Needless to say, making these contacts for recruitment was a time-consuming process on the part of several persons—especially for the Executive Secretary of the Council and the chairman of the advisory committee. However, making contacts for recruitment provided opportunities for giving information about supervisory services to administrators and teachers, thus assisting with creating supervisory positions and with placement of supervisory personnel. These close personal contacts in the early years of the program also helped many people to become familiar with criteria for selecting prospective supervisors.

Patterns of Selection Change

In these early years, by now the mid and late 'forties, the committee worked toward recruiting, training, and placing in employment about twenty persons each year. As a general pattern these persons came into the education program without a commitment for employment. Again the advisory committee gave assistance in this phase of the program by helping administrators and prospective supervisors to arrange interviews and visitations with each other. These contacts usually resulted in employment for the supervisor.

By the early 'fifties administrators and other school leaders had been approached many times for names of prospective supervisors and had been asked for recommendations concerning them. These leaders had become familiar with the selection criteria and their recommendations were usually quite valid.

This acquired competency on the part of school leaders relieved the advisory committee of making as many contacts as formerly with the prospective supervisors.

Another change of practice caused a shift of responsibility for selection for study in supervision. In the early years of the program most administrators made nominations of persons "to work in school systems other than ours." As time passed and as the program of supervision was recognized for its merit, administrators began to nominate persons "to come back to our own system." Generally these nominations were made by teachers and administrators selecting a person or persons from their own system "because they know us and our situation."

The practice of presenting these nominations to the selection committee is continued. However, the committee does not collect as much information as it previously required. Only seldom does the committee find much to question about a candidate who has "passed the test" of being nominated by his peers to be a supervisor in that system.

Has the selection process broken down or become weaker? The persons connected with the Georgia program do not believe it has. The selection procedures have been shifted in part from a state educational agency and institution to the local school staff and administrators. These persons are perhaps more concerned that the supervisory personnel meet accepted criteria than even are the members of the advisory committee.

This shift in "who does the selecting" has almost eliminated the need for seeking and creating positions for employment. It is seldom that a person who enters the program of preparation has not already been selected for employment.

This report has discussed "selection for supervision" from the standpoint of "selection for *study* in supervision." This is the point at which selection is made in the Georgia program. Selection for employment presents no problem if selection is made at entry of study or preparation for supervision. ☐

EL 24 (3): 268-71; December 1966
© 1966 ASCD

Professionalization of Supervisors and Curriculum Workers

BARBARA A. HARTSIG

WITH the recent increase in the need for supervisors and curriculum workers, superintendents and personnel officers in many school districts have been asking such questions as, "Where can we find persons for these positions? What qualifications should we look for? What preparation can we expect them to have?" Naturally, the Association for Supervision and Curriculum Development, the only organization for all

Barbara A. Hartsig, Professor of Education, California State College at Fullerton

supervisors and curriculum workers, is expected to provide answers to these inquiries, to give assistance in the search for qualified supervisors and curriculum workers, whether for positions in general areas or in special and subject fields. Supervisors and curriculum workers too are interested in the problem of professionalization in order to improve the quality of their services.

To help supervisors and curriculum workers focus on the problem and decide on a course of action the ASCD Committee on Professionalization of Supervisors and Curriculum Workers has studied the situation.

During the past year members of this Committee have presented seven articles in *Educational Leadership* under the heading of "Issues in Professionalization." In four of these articles the point was made that if supervisors and curriculum workers are to improve the quality and quantity of their services they must work toward defining their roles and functions, developing procedures for selection and recruitment, establishing preparatory programs based on research findings and best available knowledge, and securing appropriate certification requirements.

In other articles, ways by which the medical profession proceeded to professionalize itself were described, steps taken by the Georgia Teacher Education Council to professionalize supervisors in that state were presented, and the work that ASCD has done in the area of professionalization of supervisors and curriculum workers was reviewed.

What must all supervisors and curriculum workers do if the goal of their professionalization is to be achieved? This concluding article in the series attempts to summarize the preceding articles and working papers of the Committee and to point a direction for the profession.

Characteristics of a Profession

Shafer [1] set forth the following factors as characteristics of a profession: specific entrance requirements, preparatory training, field experiences, certification standards, and ethical practices all of which are controlled and policed by the membership. A brief examination of the ways the profession of supervisors and curriculum workers meets these criteria and some suggestions of steps to be taken are given below.

Entrance Requirements. At the present time there appear to be no specific requirements for admission to the profession, but rather "there are only two kinds of selection procedures being carried on in most of the preparing institutions. One is self selection . . . [The other is] to meet the general requirements for admission to graduate study." [2] Such procedures certainly are inadequate and inappropriate for a profession.

Identification of prospective supervisors and curriculum workers should be the responsibility of individuals in school systems and in preparing institutions. Preparing institutions, in cooperation with school districts, should develop a plan for selective admission and retention of persons of professional promise. Standards for selection and in preparing institutions. Preparing invious academic and professional preparation, commitment to professional goals, and intellectual ability. Only those who are admitted to the program should be permitted to study in the program.

Preparatory Training and Field Experiences. Currently preparatory programs for supervisors and curriculum workers are ex-

[1] Harold T. Shafer. "What Does the Flexner Report Say to ASCD?" *Educational Leadership* 23 (3): 235; December 1965.

[2] Robert S. Thurman. "Identifying Potential Leaders for Supervision and Curriculum Work." *Educational Leadership* 23 (7): 589; April 1966.

tremely varied and appear to reflect the lack of agreement on professional role. "Some curriculum and supervisory programs parallel almost exclusively the programs for school administrators; others do not define any specific program; some mandate specific courses, others outline broad experiences, or attempt to predict programs on desired behavioral outcomes."[3]

Even though extensive research is needed to determine the nature of effective preparatory programs for supervisors and curriculum workers, there are some guidelines which are recommended at the present time. In preparatory programs sufficient opportunities should be provided to develop a broad orientation to educational and social theory, learning theory, personality theory, and research design. Preparatory programs also should provide a background of knowledge in the related areas of educational administration, guidance, pupil personnel, and measurement and evaluation.

In addition, a student preparing for supervision or curriculum work in a special or subject area should have advanced work in that area. The professional sequence should demand a minimum of two years of study beyond the bachelor's degree and should combine formal academic classwork with supervised field experience, a combination which bears a rather direct relationship to demands that all supervisors or curriculum workers will face. It is highly recommended that the number of preparatory institutions be limited in order to bring a balance between supply and demand and to assure adequate programs.

Certification Standards. Through certification a profession sets about to eliminate the incompetent from its ranks and to increase the competency of those admitted to the profession. Certification requirements are extremely varied from state to state. A 1964 survey revealed that in 36 of the 50 states there were 71 certificates for supervisors and curriculum workers and that, of the 71 certificates, twelve "were for supervision of special subject matter areas and two entitled the holder to supervise both general and special subject areas."[4] With not quite three-fourths of the states requiring some kind of certification for supervisors and curriculum workers, there is much to be done if professionalization is to come about. Of course, certification in itself is not enough. The requirements for the certificate must be evaluated too.

Certification must reflect the role and function of supervisors and curriculum workers and should be based on a preparatory program developed by a college or university in cooperation with school districts and approved by the state department of education. In the article already mentioned, Hallberg enumerates seven principles to consider in establishing and revising certification requirements.

Ethical Practice. In the establishment of certification requirements, provision must be made for the profession to enforce professional ethics and standards. Provisions should exist to revoke a certificate when the profession has determined that an individual does not meet established criteria. Reasons for revocation would include: inability to perform competently, personal behavior detrimental to the profession, and/or professional behavior in conflict with an established code of ethics.

From its study of the professionalization of supervisors and curriculum workers,

---

[3] Maurice J. Eash. "Preparatory Programs for Supervisors." *Educational Leadership* 23 (5): 359; February 1966.

[4] H. Irene Hallberg. "Certification Requirements for General Supervisors and/or Curriculum Workers Today—Tomorrow." *Educational Leadership* 23 (8): 623-24; May 1966.

the Committee found that some criteria for a profession seem to be met in part but not enough to assure qualified and competent supervisors and curriculum workers. This certainly means that the profession has much work to do.

Concern of the Profession

In establishing entrance requirements, preparatory programs, and certification standards, reference is frequently made to the nature of the work of supervisors and curriculum workers, and to the tasks that they perform. The roles and functions of supervisors and curriculum workers determine to a large extent who enters the preparatory program, the nature of that program, and the license to be received. It follows then that a study of the roles and functions is imperative. It is an essential first step. Allen points out, though, that these roles and functions keep changing, that during the decade from 1955 to 1965 there appeared to be "more persons involved [in supervision], more ways of getting supervision done, and more inherent problems" than during the previous ten years.[5]

This would make it impossible to outline once and for all the duties of supervisors and curriculum workers. Rather, it is necessary that roles and functions be examined periodically and systematically in order to modify and change selective procedures, preparatory programs, certification standards, and in-service programs to be sure that supervisors and curriculum workers can carry out the tasks facing them and can function in new roles as these emerge. This is no small task, but it is an important one, one which all supervisors and curriculum workers, whether field persons or college persons, whether generalists or specialists, must face.

[5] Rowannetta S. Allen. "Role and Function of Supervisors and Curriculum Workers." *Educational Leadership* 23 (4): 332; January 1966.

The Committee on Professionalization of Supervisors and Curriculum Workers will attempt to give leadership in the matter of professionalization through (a) publication of a booklet dealing with major areas of concern in professionalization; (b) preparation of a list of recommendations in the areas of role, selection, preparation, accreditation, and certification; (c) development of a working kit for use by state units; and (d) regional conferences for chairmen of state professionalization committees. Upon the request of unit presidents or chairmen of state committees on professionalization of supervisors and curriculum workers, members of the ASCD Committee will be willing to assist affiliated units in an attempt to bring about professionalization of supervisors and curriculum workers in their states. Names of ASCD Committee members are listed at the conclusion of this article.

If complete professionalization really is to come about, however, each affiliated unit and each member of ASCD will need to assist. Only through a united and concerted effort of all can the professionalization of supervisors and curriculum workers be accomplished.

ASCD Committee on Professionalization of Supervisors and Curriculum Workers

Harold T. Shafer, Wyckoff Township Public Schools, Wyckoff, New Jersey, Chairman; Marion Beckwith, Montgomery County Schools, Silver Spring, Maryland; Leo Black, Colorado State Department of Education, Denver; Ben Harris, University of Texas, Austin; Barbara Hartsig, California State College at Fullerton, Fullerton; Fred Edmonds, University of Kentucky, Lexington; Bernard Kinsella, Pittsford Central School, Pittsford, New York; John Prater, Maywood Public Schools, Maywood, Illinois; J. T. Sandefur, Kansas State Teachers College, Emporia; Robert Thurman, University of Tennessee, Knoxville; Roy Wahle, Bellevue Public Schools, Bellevue, Washington. ☐

PART III

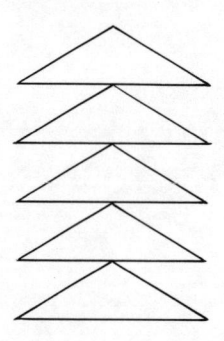

Research: Instrument for New Knowledge

PART III

Research: Instrument for New Knowledge

How Is Supervision Perceived?

CAROLYN GUSS [1]

WHAT should be the function of supervision? What duties performed by supervisors are being noted? Of these, which are the most important and which are the least important? How can the effectiveness of supervision be improved?

These questions, among others, have been and are of great interest to supervisors themselves. They are likewise of concern to college and university faculties responsible for educating future supervisors and, in some degree, to the persons who are affected by the process of supervision—namely, teachers, pupils, parents, and other members of the community. Answers have been sought by various methods. These answers should prove helpful in clarifying the role of supervision and contributing to its improvement. A need for answers to these questions was one of the reasons why the Indiana ASCD undertook a three-year study of perceptions of supervision.

Psychological research and theory have indicated that an individual's behavior is determined largely by the individual's perception of himself and his role and that the expectations of others create, in part, this self-image which directs behavior. It seemed reasonable, therefore, that answers to these questions would lie, in part, in perceptions held by supervisors themselves and by others of the role of supervision.

The Research Committee of the Indiana Association for Supervision and Curriculum Development, therefore, decided to derive whatever answers it could to the foregoing questions from replies received from six groups of persons. Members of these groups were considered influential in creating the expectancy level for school supervision—school administrators, principals, university faculty members in schools of education, parents, supervisors, and teachers.

A Perception Study

The idea of a perception study of supervision was approved by IASCD. Members were given a questionnaire asking them to suggest areas of knowledge or areas of function which might be determiners of how supervision was being perceived.

An opinionnaire was constructed on the basis of suggestions received from the IASCD membership. Also considered were the findings of six doctoral researchers,[2] a Ball State Teachers College committee, a previous IASCD research committee, and several school city committees that had investigated various facets of the subject within the preceding five years. The instru-

---

[1] Carolyn Guss served as Chairman of the Indiana ASCD Research Committee which conducted the study reported in this article. Members of the committee included Daisy Jones, Director of Elementary Education, Richmond Public Schools; Joseph C. Payne, Supervisor of Educational Research, Indianapolis Public Schools; and Doris Young, Associate Professor of Elementary Education, Purdue University.

[2] These researchers were: Lucy Bachman, R. Burdett Burk, Agnes Dodds, Joe Lowe, James Mitchell, and Wayne Palmer.

Carolyn Guss, Professor of Education, Indiana University, Bloomington

ment was deliberately developed as an open-ended, very broadly conceived, short and succinct device in order not to prestructure the replies. It was tried out experimentally. On the basis of the report on the pilot study, the committee was instructed to proceed.

Copies of the opinionnaire were sent to a random-stratified sample of 50 persons in each of six groups in Indiana—administrators, principals, faculty members teaching elementary and secondary education courses, parents, supervisors, and teachers. Over 50 percent of the administrators and supervisors returned completed opinionnaires. Only 16 percent of the parents responded with replies that were sufficiently complete to be included. Twice as many replied but did not attempt to answer the questions, indicating that they did not feel qualified to do so. Replies from the other three groups—principals, faculty members, and teachers—totaled 28, 21, and 14 respectively. Thus 139 completed replies were received in response to the 300 requests.

Analyzing results was no small task. As indicated earlier, the instrument was unstructured. The committee members found themselves with a vast array of replies variously worded and ranging from very broad, all-inclusive comments to very specific, narrowly structured responses. Decisions had to be made. Insofar as possible, grouping of replies was based upon careful judgments and not on arbitrary decisions. It must be admitted, however, that the lines of demarcation and shades of meaning were not always clear. Whether the differences were a matter of semantics or of meaning constantly plagued the committee.

Findings

The following findings represent an effort at objectively and accurately analyzing and summarizing the thousands of individual replies in the raw data. Statements reported as being held by the group were made by more than 40 percent of the respondents. Those reported as representing a minority point of view were held by less than 10 percent of the respondents.

Functions of Supervision. The question of what *should* be the functions of supervision was designed to elicit philosophical speculation from the six groups. Functions mentioned by a majority of respondents were:

Develop curriculum to meet the needs of the community

Help teachers achieve the most effective learning environment

Improve instruction

Inspire teachers

Render expert advice concerning methods and materials

Serve as consultant or coordinator.

Duties Being Performed by Supervisors. The second question was intended to find out what the six groups of respondents perceived as the duties that were being performed by supervisors. Whether or not supervisors in Indiana are actually doing these things is speculative. The study, however, shows that a representative sampling of professional and lay persons concerned with supervision believe they are performing these duties:

Compiling library and audio-visual materials

Giving professional advice and assistance to teachers

Improving the curriculum

Taking care of paper work

Testing and evaluating.

Most Important Contributions of the

Supervisor. Here again a wide range of value judgments was expressed. The contributions of supervisors considered most important were:

Help teachers, especially new ones, improve classroom instruction

Hold individual conferences with teachers

Provide teacher guidance and improve morale

Serve as leader in curriculum development.

Least Important Contributions of the Supervisor. It should be noted that 40 percent of the parents replying to the questionnaire did not answer this question. Several wrote, in effect, that they considered everything supervisors do as important. The following contributions were considered least important:

Creating an unnatural situation in the classroom

Doing the teacher's work

Evaluating teachers (checking up, inspecting)

Performing clerical jobs (ordering, counting, delivering)

Writing reports and keeping records.

Recommended Improvement in Supervision. This question received more individual replies than any other. Perhaps it is human nature to seize an opportunity to tell others how to do their jobs more effectively. It may be, however, that improvement is needed. Suggestions for improvement included:

Create a better understanding between teachers and supervisors

Define goals of supervision more clearly

Increase clerical assistance to supervisors

Increase number of supervisors; i.e., decrease number of teachers and classrooms per supervisor

Describe more specifically the role of supervisor

Raise training and salary standards.

Supervision Defined. Some may believe that the sixth question should have been first. The committee held that respondents should give their definitions of supervision last. On the basis of having answered the first five questions, respondents had done some critical thinking about supervision before giving their definitions of supervision as a process of:

Observing, evaluating, and implementing the educational process

Improving instruction by working with teachers

Directing the curriculum

Cooperating in providing a wholesome learning environment for children

Critically evaluating and directing education

Overseeing, checking, comparing, and helping.

Functions of Supervision

A single study, of course, can answer only a few of the questions asked. We believe, though, that this study has served to give supervisors an insight into how their work is perceived by a number of groups which affect or are affected by the work of the supervisor. Wherever this perception agrees with the picture supervisors hold as their ideal, supervisors may feel safe in continuing the same principles of supervision. Wherever these perceptions vary from the ideas expressed, supervisors may wish to consider how to function so that their work will be perceived more nearly in terms of their objectives. Following are brief summaries of the replies by the six groups of respondents:

Administrators: The function of supervision is that of improvement of instruction. The most important contribution is curriculum development. Goals of supervision should be more clearly defined so that supervisory effectiveness can be improved.

Principals: The function of supervision is that of helping the teacher achieve the most effective learning situation. The least important contribution is that of doing the teacher's work, and the effectiveness of supervision would improve if there were a better understanding between teachers and supervisors.

University Faculty: The function of supervision is to facilitate the work of teachers and help improve the learning situation; emphasis should be placed on curriculum development, mechanical routine activities must be de-emphasized or completely dropped. Supervisors should be mightily concerned with the human relations role they play and the human powers they wield. They should be trained and inclined to help teachers reach their highest potentials.

Parents: In replies from parents, four functions of the supervisor received equal emphasis—passing on new materials and methods to teachers, visiting classrooms, supervising teachers, and developing a curriculum to meet the needs of the community. Teacher guidance and assistance is their most important contribution. Generally there were no suggestions for improvement and the more common definition of supervision was to oversee, check, compare, and help.

Supervisors: The function of supervision is helping teachers to improve instruction. The individual conference with the teacher is very valuable, while clerical jobs are least important. Suggestions for improvement include more clerical help, more supervisors, and closer relationship between supervisors and principals.

Teachers: They tended to want to avoid being the object of supervision. Some of them considered supervision as an attack on them personally. Others thought of supervision as a program dealing with materials, ideas, and schedules rather than with the teaching-learning situation as it affects personal relationships.

To inspire teachers and to improve morale were given as functions and contributions of supervision. This aspect of supervision, however, was not recognized by respondents as being performed. In the opinion of the committee, herein lies one of the most significant implications for possible behavioral changes on the part of supervisors.

Just as the role of the classroom teacher is changing, because of such factors as modern technology being applied in the classroom, various sized groups and types of grouping being used throughout the school day, an increasing amount of information to be conveyed to an increasing number of students, so the role of the supervisor is changing. Recurring references to improvement of the curriculum, community needs, evaluation, creating a better understanding, and raising standards suggest a very important implication of the study—supervisors cannot perpetuate the *status quo,* they must be sensitive to changes, and must be prepared to help teachers adjust to change. They must instill in teachers a desire and a zeal to dig deeper, to extend their horizons, and to advance the frontiers of knowledge. ☐

The Supervisor at Work

JOHNNYE V. COX

MOST studies of supervision describe this work *as it is perceived by an observer*. There is a trend, however, in recent studies for the supervisor himself to be one of the observers of the supervisor's behavior. Moreover, as supervisors research the role of the supervisor they are involving more and more people in the process of cooperative research. This research is directed toward action for clarifying and improving the services of the supervisor. Such trends are evident in the studies described here. Implications of these studies for the supervisor are also evident. However, in each study reviewed some of these implications are made explicit.

The Supervisor's Role

The role of the supervisor, as perceived by the supervisor and the principals and teachers with whom the supervisor works, was described and examined in a recent study by Cox and Lott (1). A Q-Sort of 100 behaviors of the supervisor was used to make the descriptions. An analysis was made of these descriptions in terms of the "most liked" and "least liked" behaviors of the ideal supervisor.

Each group of respondents ranked highest those behaviors which relate to belief in people, acceptance of contributions of each child and teacher, and respect for individual differences of teachers. There was, however, a lack of agreement about some of the behaviors ranked high by the different groups. Supervisors indicated with a high rank that cooperative efforts of a group are more effective than efforts of individual members. Principals regarded this behavior as of much less importance, while elementary teachers ranked it even lower. Secondary teachers did not place this behavior among the "most liked" behaviors.

Principals and elementary and secondary teachers placed considerable significance upon the supervisor's "having the know-how and giving it to teachers." The supervisors placed this behavior very high in the "least liked" behaviors. Supervisors considered cooperative formulation of policies and plans as a very significant behavior and the other respondents gave it no place among the "most liked" behaviors.

The behaviors ranked lowest by each group of respondents were stated as follows: "Discusses freely teachers' problems with outsiders"; "points out specific teacher's deficiencies to help another teacher"; "feels that he is fully capable of doing a good job independently of help from others"; "makes the decisions and tells the staff what to do"; and "questions the authority of the principal."

Supervisors placed "having know-how and giving it to teachers" and "saving time by telling the group the right answers" quite high in the "least liked" behaviors. Other

Johnnye V. Cox, Director, Georgia Program for the Education of Supervisors, University of Georgia, Athens

respondents gave these behaviors no place among the "least liked" behaviors. Respondents ranked quite high in "least liked" behaviors the supervisor who always agrees and who feels that he is rejected by the group. The supervisors gave these behaviors no place in the "least liked" behaviors.

The areas of agreement in "most liked" and "least liked" behaviors indicate there is much common ground and much overlapping of basic human values among the groups. With these human values in common, other differences tend to be minimized. The differences in opinion revealed in this study were, for the most part, in terms of specific ways of working. An awareness of the areas of agreement and lack of agreement should be helpful to supervisors in all endeavors of curriculum planning, development, and research.

Services Rendered by Supervisors

To make a study of the services rendered by supervisors to teachers, principals, and superintendents, Manley involved a representative number of persons from each of these four groups (2).

A two-part questionnaire was developed to secure information from the respondents. Part I consisted of 26 statements describing services performed by supervisors. Although not so designated in the questionnaire, the items were selected to represent four categories of supervisory services: (a) Improving teaching methods and techniques; (b) providing leadership services; (c) providing for in-service growth; and (d) fostering good human relationships.

Respondents indicated, on a three-point scale, the extent to which each service had been rendered by the supervisor. In another column the respondents indicated, also on a three-point scale, the benefit derived from the service.

Part II of the questionnaire consisted of two questions: "What services, not included in Part I of the questionnaire, do you think supervisors perform?" "What additional services would you like supervisors to perform?"

The services which supervisors rendered most often, as seen by teachers, principals, and superintendents, fell into two of the four categories of service included in the questionnaire—services which relate to providing for in-service growth and services which foster good human relationships. Each of the three groups gave highest rank to "attending meetings of professional organizations." Each group gave second, third, or fourth place to these items: "Demonstrating a personal interest in the welfare and happiness of all teachers"; "recognizing progress, commending and encouraging teachers"; and "working on committees in professional organizations."

The supervisors placed in the four highest positions items relating to their concern for and work with teachers. The items were: "Recognizing progress, commending and encouraging teachers"; "demonstrating a personal interest in the welfare and happiness of all teachers"; "listening to the comments, opinions, and suggestions of all co-workers"; and "working with teachers in evaluation and selection of instructional materials." Supervisors ranked sixth the service ranked first by teachers, principals, and superintendents.

The four responding groups were in agreement that the most beneficial services rendered by the supervisors were in the area of human relations. They identified these most beneficial services as "recognizing progress, commending and encouraging teachers"; and "demonstrating a personal interest in the welfare and happiness of all teachers." It is significant that although teachers, principals, and superintendents "saw" the supervisor most frequently as attending professional meetings they did not rank this service as very beneficial.

Responses to Part II of the questionnaire supported the services listed in Part I. The respondents wanted more supervisors with more time to do more of the services which they already do. There are implications for the supervisor in that two major categories of supervisory service were not included in services rendered most often and that services in only one area were described as highly beneficial to teachers, principals, and superintendents.

Major Problems of Supervisors

To determine major problems of supervisors and the causes of these problems, Turpin (3) asked 96 supervisors to respond to the following two-part directive: Part I: "List as rapidly as they occur to you *all* the things that bother you about doing your job as a supervisor. Do not evaluate these items, do not try to determine if they are 'acceptable' things to list. Just list them as they come." Part II: "Set aside a time in which to examine the problems that you have listed. Try to reason out why these problems or situations bother you. Write out your reasons or hunches about each problem."

Turpin classified the problems stated in Part I into 21 categories. For purposes of this report some of the categories are combined. This regrouping indicates that supervisors' problems may be classified as follows (the number in parentheses refers to frequency of response expressed in percent):

Insufficient time to render all supervisory services in a satisfactory manner (20%); unfavorable attitudes of teachers and principals toward change (16%); insufficient money for travel, study, and materials (15%); insecurity due to lack of role clarification and scope of the job (14%); inability of the supervisor to organize himself and others for most effective work (9%); inadequate clerical assistance and work space in office (9%); communication difficulties with general public, the State University, State Department of Education and the local board of education (8%); miscellaneous (9%).

It might appear from the statement in Part I of Turpin's directive that respondents would include problems of little significance in their lists. However, the responses of Part II of the directive did not support this hunch. In general the supervisors were very deliberate in their own hunches about the problems.

Supervisors state that the causes of their problems are interrelated. The supervisor's role is not clear to himself or to those with whom he works. The scope of the job is large, the responsibilities are numerous, and there is insufficient time to accomplish all tasks involved in the job. Funds for clerical assistance are limited and supervisors must take time from professional tasks to perform clerical tasks. Frustration and feelings of guilt occur when supervisors are unable to provide as much help to individual teachers or school faculties as they desire. These conditions present a picture which is a vicious circle and demands the attention and study of administrators and others in local and state programs of administration and supervision.

Self-Evaluation of the Supervisor

The procedures and activities which a beginning supervisor used to record and evaluate her own experiences have been adapted and developed into an instrument for the use of beginning supervisors (4).

During her first year as a supervisor, Brannen kept a diary of each day's activities. She recorded the activities engaged in, described her feelings about these activities, and summarized and evaluated these activities by recording the time spent in each major supervisory function. She used a report form entitled, "How I Spend My Time," for the daily summary. She attached to the diary copies of all communications to principals, consultants, and others which related to her work as supervisor. She kept communications and proceedings of committee meetings, grade meetings, and local, district, and state conferences.

Once each quarter she prepared descriptive and evaluative materials for study at a conference with other beginning supervisors. At the end of the year she made a self-evaluation of her competencies in supervision. As a basis for this evaluation she used an instrument entitled, "Guide for Determining Status of the Supervisor."

A final evaluative activity was the preparation of a summary of the year's activities. The summary was made available to all teachers, principals, and other school personnel. Accompanying the report was a questionnaire for evaluating the work of the supervisor.

The "Instrument for the Use of the Beginning Supervisor" is actually a guidebook. It includes excerpts from the diary, descriptions of the many activities in which the supervisor engaged, and a comprehensive evaluation of the supervisory procedures. The instrument or guidebook could be used as resource material by any supervisor or curriculum worker for descriptions of supervisory procedures that have been tested and found to be effective. □

References

1. Johnnye V. Cox and Jurelle G. Lott. "A Study of the Perceptions of the Supervisor's Role." Unpublished study, 1961.

2. Jo Ann Seagraves Manley. "A Study of the Services Rendered by Supervisors of Instruction in Georgia." Unpublished Master's Degree Study, 1958.

3. Henry Russell Turpin. "Determining the Causes of Major Problems Encountered by Instructional Supervisors in Georgia." Unpublished Master's Degree Study, 1960.

4. Jeanne Floy Brannen. "Developing an Instrument for the Use of Beginning Supervisors of Instruction." Unpublished Master's Degree Study, 1958.

Other Studies

1. Thomas Landry. Louisiana State University. "Louisiana Supervisors Examine Their Practices."

2. James R. Ogletree. University of Kentucky. "A Person-Centered Approach to Educating Supervisors."

3. Ohio ASCD and State Department of Education, Columbus. "The Supervisor at Work."

4. Norman Ziff. "Role of the General Secondary School Consultant." *Educational Leadership* 16 (8): 500-502, 516; May 1959.

EL 20 (3): 211-17; December 1962
© 1962 ASCD

Instructional Improvement: Considerations for Supervision

WILLIAM H. LUCIO

IN THE past few years many of the current forces affecting schooling have been described or defined in numerous publications (2, 4, 12, 15). Those persons accountable for instructional improvement are actively aware of the new and powerful ideas and forces requiring their attention. Increasingly, it is evident that the kind and

William H. Lucio, Professor of Education, Graduate School of Education, University of California, Los Angeles

quality of instructional improvement will depend in large measure upon the extent to which these new ideas are grasped and put to use, hypotheses tested, and results evaluated in schools throughout the country (1:5-24; 7:17).

Presently the focus appears to be on: (a) examination of the nature and structure of knowledge in the disciplines (3, 5, 9, 16, 17, 18); (b) better operational definitions of the objectives of learning and teaching and proposals for more precise ways of evaluating outcomes—both stemming, in part, from research in programmed learning and automated teaching (6, 11, 14, 21); (c) a redefining of the essential tasks of schooling (3, 13, 15, 17); and (d) new strategies and tactics for effecting instructional change—proposals growing out of the studies of organizational behavior (10, 13, 20).

A brief analysis of the development of modern supervision may help to place present practices in perspective and pinpoint some requirements for supervisory action (13). Since the turn of the century various patterns of thought have characterized general supervisory practices in instructional improvement. These practices have not always been effective in achieving the objectives of the school. Shaftel (19) has noted the long-existent hiatus between the school's stated objectives and its practices, attributing the gap, in part, to the lack of a systematic theory of action.

In the first quarter of the century a classical view of man and institutions dominated school supervision. Generally teachers were closely directed and required to carry out practices determined by administrative personnel. Though "technical specialists" began to appear, as new subjects were added to the curriculum, supervisory responsibility for instructional improvement continued to be viewed as an arm of administration primarily concerned with holding teachers to certain standards of performance. Later, influenced in part by the scientific management movement, "scientific supervision" developed, and emphasis was placed on measurement, testing, and the setting of standards to be attained by pupils and teachers. The task of supervisors in this view was to discover "laws" of teaching and learning and require teachers to apply these laws under direction.

Starting with the 1930's, attention was given to human relations or group process techniques as a way of influencing personnel toward instructional change. Manipulative techniques were more often emphasized than theoretical constructs in working with groups and individuals. Supervisors found themselves depending upon personalized approaches, using various techniques, prescriptions, and maxims to persuade, influence, or direct others toward the school's goals. While the use of human relations techniques in working with groups and individuals did take into account the feelings and motives of teachers and supervisors and was probably appropriate to some areas of action, not enough attention was given to individuals' properties as reasoning human beings and the application of rational thought to problems requiring intellectual attack (10:50; 13).

Further, because the supervisory process was not always well-defined, many supervisors engaged in tasks primarily the responsibility of other organizational agents. As Skinner (21:377) has noted, solutions to problems revolving around questions of better salaries, improved physical plant, updating textbooks and teaching materials, and ability grouping may often be accomplished without much knowledge about teaching or learning. "In short there is a general neglect of educational method" (21:378). Supervisors served more as technicians ministering to the equilibrium of an organization than as leaders with vision and ability to predict and test the consequences of their proposals (13:vi).

A current view would hold that the main task of supervision is to answer the question of who shall make decisions determining the kind of knowledge, skills, and attitudes to be fostered in schools (13:11-12). Supervisory action requires a more inclusive or supplementary approach, recognizing the importance of *both* mechanism and morale, yet taking into account the importance of cognition and the application of rational and practical intelligence in effecting improvement in schools (13). New analyses and interpretations of the structure of knowledge and contributions from learning theory (5, 16, 17, 18, 22) require that instructional efforts be directed toward new ends. Supervisors and teachers will need to develop the intellectual content of their tasks and to acquire the necessary theories with which to relate particular consequences to the conditions which produce these consequences (5, 13). Instructional improvement is a global endeavor requiring *all* persons responsible for change to make rational choices. Supervision can thus be considered a dimension of behavior in *many* positions and involves: (a) "the determination of ends to be sought, (b) the design of procedures for effecting the ends, and (c) the assessment of results" (13:46). Supervisory roles at any level require: "a clear perspective of the school's goals, awareness of its resources and qualities, and the ability to help others contribute to this vision and to perceive and act in accordance with it" (13:46).

Contemporary theories of organization indicate that individual members of organizations have limits placed on their knowledge and capacities to analyze and solve problems, since no one individual can envision *all* the consequences of any particular task. "To the extent that these limits are removed, the administrative organization approaches its goal of high efficiency. . . . administrative theory must be interested in the factors that will determine with what skills, values, and knowledge the organization member undertakes his work" (20:39).

It is incumbent upon those accountable for instructional improvement to develop "the ability to see the enterprise as a whole" (8:68) and provide the kind of direction which helps teachers toward behavior reflecting and implementing the mission of the school.

Supervisory techniques for making teacher behavior more rational, that is, *more consistent with the schools' goals,* have been proposed (13:15):

1. Divide essential work among teachers, thus focusing their efforts on immediate tasks.

2. Establish standardized practices which relieve the teacher of having to make minor choices remote from or indirectly related to instructional goals.

3. Provide expert help from many sources, yet center the decision-making function in one person when conflicts must be resolved.

4. Utilize "influence systems" such as inservice education programs, seminars, or study groups for developing teachers' commitments to the objectives of the school. Place emphasis on dedication to the overall mission of the school rather than to a teacher's subject field or to a particular service. Communicate exactly how the instructional objectives of the school relate and contribute to each teacher's own professional goals.

5. Recognize that changes are more readily accepted when programs are altered gradually and systematically, thus enabling individuals to see more clearly their own roles in innovation.

6. Make school objectives so explicit, definite, and operational that exact assessments of their attainment are possible.

This last proposition deserves some amplification. More precise ways of specifying behavioral objectives for learning are growing out of the research on programmed learning (6, 14). Viable techniques for describing intended outcomes of learning, systematically ordering learning opportunities, programming the explicit and sequential behaviors required, and assessing the degree of terminal behavior are now available for application to instructional problems (6). Because research in programmed learning provides the theories and techniques to examine *what* is to be taught, *how* it will be taught, and to *assess* predicted effects, instruction should benefit.

The persistent questions regarding the value of one instructional practice or process over another may be answered better by testing hypotheses developed from systematic theories than by dependence upon blind faith in a particular practice. "No enterprise can improve itself very effectively without examining its basic processes" (21:378). Widespread experimentation in the laboratory of the school to test theories, propositions, and techniques should focus attention on, and provide better answers for, the generic problems of instruction. Skinner, in discussing the study of teaching machines, indicated the importance of applying the findings of basic science to instructional problems:

... more than half a century of the self-conscious examination of instructional processes had worked only moderate changes in educational practices. The laboratory study of learning provided the confidence, if not all the knowledge needed for a successful instrumental attack on the *status quo*. Traditional views may not have been actually wrong, but they were vague and were not entertained with sufficient commitment to work substantial technological changes (21: 398).

The responsible roles for persons engaged in the improvement of instruction have been competently examined in the 1960 ASCD Yearbook. A quotation from this source may serve as a conclusion:

... if teachers, principals, supervisors, curriculum workers, and other educational leaders are not, at least in some phases of their operations, out in front testing ideas, discovering new relationships, and exploring the unknown, how can new practical or theoretical knowledge in education emerge?

... educational leadership is responsible for discovering ways to help people feel secure and accepted in their being different, in their individual searchings for ideas and ways of behaving, in their efforts to fulfill their potentialities (1:22). ☐

References

1. Association for Supervision and Curriculum Development. *Leadership for Improving Instruction,* 1960 Yearbook. Washington, D.C.: the Association, 1960.

2. Association for Supervision and Curriculum Development. *What Shall the High Schools Teach?* 1956 Yearbook. Washington, D.C.: the Association, 1956.

3. Harry S. Broudy. *Building a Philosophy of Education,* revised edition. Englewood Cliffs, N.J.: Prentice-Hall, Inc., 1961.

4. Jerome S. Bruner. "The Functions of Teaching." *Readings in Educational Psychology.* William C. Morse and G. Max Wingo, editors. Chicago: Scott, Foresman and Company, 1962. pp. 162-69.

5. Jerome S. Bruner. *The Process of Education.* Cambridge: Harvard University Press, 1961.

6. John E. Coulson, editor. *Programmed Learning and Computer-Based Instruction.* New York: John Wiley and Sons, Inc., 1962.

7. Stephen M. Corey. "Education and the Current Crises." *Frontiers of Secondary Education III.* Syracuse, New York: Syracuse University Press, 1958.

8. Daniel R. Davies and Laurence Iannaccone. "Ferment in the Study of Organization." *Teachers College Record,* Vol. 60, No. 2, November 1958.

9. Arthur W. Foshay. "A Modest Proposal for the Improvement of Education." *What Are the Sources of the Curriculum? A Symposium.* Washington, D.C.: Association for Supervision and Curriculum Development, 1962.

10. Vincent J. Glennon. "Updating the Theory of Supervision." *Frontiers of Elementary Education VII.* Syracuse, New York: Syracuse University Press, 1961.

11. Edward J. Green. *The Learning Process*

and Programmed Instruction. New York: Holt, Rinehart and Winston, Inc., 1962.

12. Stephen P. Hencley. "Forces Shaping the New Perspectives." *Preparing Administrators: New Perspectives.* Jack A. Culbertson and Stephen P. Hencley, editors. Columbus, Ohio: University Council for Educational Administration, 1962. pp. 1-8.

13. William H. Lucio and John D. McNeil. *Supervision: A Synthesis of Thought and Action.* (Second Edition.) New York: McGraw-Hill Book Company, Inc., 1969.

14. Robert F. Mager. *Preparing Objectives for Programmed Instruction.* 828 Valencia Street, San Francisco, California: Fearon Publishers, Inc., 1962.

15. Earl J. McGrath. Needed: A Balanced Educational Policy." *Journal of the American Association of University Women,* Part I, Vol. 52, No. 2, January 1959 and Part II, Vol. 52, No. 3, March 1959.

16. Philip H. Phenix. "Key Concepts and the Crises in Learning." *Teachers College Record,* Vol. 58, No. 3, December 1956.

17. Philip H. Phenix. *Philosophy of Education.* New York: Holt, Rinehart and Winston, 1958.

18. Mina Rees. "The Nature of Mathematics." *Science,* Vol. 138, No. 3536, October 5, 1962.

19. Fannie R. Shaftel. "Evaluation—for Today and for the Future." *Educational Leadership* 14 (5): 292-98; February 1957.

20. Herbert A. Simon. *Administrative Behavior: A Study of Decision-making Processes in Administrative Organization.* New York: The Macmillan Company, 1957.

21. B. F. Skinner. "Why We Need Teaching Machines." *Harvard Educational Review,* Vol. 31, No. 4, Fall 1961.

22. Percival Symonds. *What Education Has To Learn from Psychology,* Second edition. New York: Bureau of Publications, Teachers College, Columbia University, 1959.

EL 21 (2): 107-11; November 1963
© 1963 ASCD

Personalities, Teachers, and Curriculum Change

RONALD URICK
JACK R. FRYMIER

THE prospect of the 1960s is one of great significance for American education. Psychological research into the cognitive processes is beginning to bear fruit in broadening and deepening our understanding of the learning process. A resurgence of public awareness of education and insistence on improvement in its quality is bringing about a reexamination of the organization and content of the school curriculum. In recent years national committees of eminent scientists have developed high school science and mathematics programs which have been widely adopted in the schools. More recently, national committees in the social sciences and humanities have begun work of a similar nature.

On the "firing line" in the public schools, teachers and administrators are faced with the problem of conserving the

Ronald Urick, Associate Professor of Education, Wayne State University, Detroit, Michigan. In 1963, Dr. Urick was Instructor, College of Education, The Ohio State University, Columbus; and Jack R. Frymier, Chairman, Curriculum and Foundations Faculty, The Ohio State University, Columbus

best of the "old" while adopting the best of the "new" within the context of increasing public pressure for "excellence." While it is desirable that outstanding scholars in the various disciplines play an important part in the development of instructional materials for the secondary schools, such programs will not in and of themselves bring improved instruction. An ineffective teacher will not suddenly become effective with the adoption of new curricular materials. If instruction is to be improved, it must be through developments within each school district, in each building, and within each classroom.

Evidence of the crucial nature of local influence on curriculum changes was reported in a recent study by the NEA.[1] Elementary and secondary principals listed local school officials and faculty members as the two most important groups in bringing changes in instructional practices. There is evidence, however, that it is among these same groups that the major barriers to change are found.[2] Noda indicates that the most important "blocks" to curriculum change arise out of the attitudes of teachers as well as out of the nature of their relationships with administrators, supervisors, and students.[3] In another study, Coon found that teachers were more likely to resist significant curriculum change than either administrators, students, or parents.[4]

[1] *The Principals Look at the Schools: A Status Study of Selected Instructional Practices.* Washington, D.C.: National Education Association Project on Instruction, 1962. pp. 28-29.

[2] Harold B. Alberty and Elsie J. Alberty. *Reorganizing the High School Curriculum.* New York: The Macmillan Company, 1962. pp. 18-19.

[3] Daniel S. Noda. "A Study of Successful Practices Used To Remove the Major Blocks to Curriculum Improvement in the Secondary School." Unpublished doctoral dissertation, The Ohio State University, 1952. p. 78.

[4] Herbert Coon. "A Study of the Attitudes of Teachers and Administrators Toward High School Curriculum Reorganization." Unpublished doctoral dissertation, The Ohio State University, 1951. pp. 298, 305.

Resistance to Change

The question immediately arises: How can one account for this apparently widespread resistance to change which is found among teachers in our schools? Several factors should be taken into consideration in any attempt to answer this question.

First, the formal institutional patterns and organizational arrangements of the school may exert a negative influence on teachers' attitudes with regard to change. Administrative failure to initiate opportunity or provide organizational structure for the consideration of change may create a climate in which change itself is actually considered to be inappropriate.

Second, the existence of ill-defined relationships among teachers, administrators, and supervisors and of conflicting perceptions of the role each sees himself and others playing may combine to inhibit the consideration of change, and may, therefore, have a negative effect on teachers' attitudes. If teachers see the principal as the leader in bringing about changes while the principal sees the stimulus for change as needing to originate among the faculty, there will likely be a "built-in" resistance to change.

Finally, inasmuch as a teacher's attitudes are a part of his total personality, there may be certain configurations of personality structures of individual teachers which lead them to be receptive or resistant to a consideration of change. Combs and Snygg describe the "adequate personality" as one who sees himself in essentially positive ways, is capable of acceptance of self and others, and sees himself as closely identified with other persons.[5] The "inadequate personality" is characterized by the reverse of these characteristics. Thus a teacher who

[5] Arthur W. Combs and Donald Snygg. *Individual Behavior: A Perceptual Approach to Behavior.* New York: Harper and Brothers, 1959. p. 248.

sees himself in a basically negative manner and who has difficulty in relating to those around him is likely to react in a highly defensive and resistant way to any suggestions for the consideration of curriculum changes.

Personality Structure

The crucial nature of personality structure in fostering or hindering social change has been discussed by Hagen in another context. In searching for an explanation for the inconsistency of technological progress among different underdeveloped nations, all of which possessed the economic, technological, and educational prerequisites, Hagen concluded that the significant element in those countries undergoing rapid change was the existence of a large number of individuals exhibiting what he calls the "innovational personality."[6] On the other hand, in those countries characterized by a remarkable lack of change, the preponderant personality characteristics were those which Hagen classified as "authoritarian." Briefly, among the qualities which characterize the innovational personality are an openness to experience, a confidence in one's own evaluations, a satisfaction in facing and resolving confusion or ambiguity, and a feeling that the world is orderly, and that the phenomenon of life can be understood and explained.[7] Conversely, the authoritarian is characterized by a fear of using his initiative, an uncertainty concerning the quality of his own judgment, a tendency to avoid frustration and anxiety, an uneasiness in facing unresolved situations, and a tendency to see the world as arbitrary and capricious.[8]

Moreover, personality structure or "perceptual organization" is apparently a determining factor in the effectiveness of counselors. According to Combs and Soper, it is possible to distinguish effective counselors from ineffective ones on the basis of how they view themselves, their tasks, their clients, and their clients' purposes.[9] The perceptual organization of effective counselors, as classified by these researchers, follows closely the personality types outlined previously as "innovational" or "adequate."

Finally, Myers and Torrance studied the personality characteristics of teachers who were resistant to change.[10] Among the characteristics which they identified were authoritarianism, defensiveness, insensitivity to pupil needs, preoccupation with information-giving functions, intellectual inertness, disinterest in promoting initiative in pupils, and preoccupation with discipline.

Within the context of this discussion, the following questions might be raised: To what extent can the rigidity of public schools with regard to curriculum change be attributed to teachers with authoritarian or inadequate personalities? Is it possible that persons who possess personality characteristics which lead to resistance to change are attracted to careers in education, or is it possible that such characteristics may arise out of the experiences which the teachers encounter in the profession? Can teachers who *are* willing to consider curriculum changes be distinguished from those who are unwilling to do so in any reliable way prior to actual involvement in curriculum development?

A study conducted by a graduate class at Ohio State University was concerned with the relationship of teachers' personality structures to their willingness or unwilling-

---

[6] Everett E. Hagen. *On the Theory of Social Change.* Homewood, Illinois: The Dorsey Press, Inc., 1962.

[7] *Ibid.*, pp. 88-89.

[8] *Ibid.*, pp. 97-98.

[9] Arthur W. Combs and Daniel W. Soper. "Perceptual Organization of Effective Counselors." Unpublished report of a study conducted during the 1961-1962 academic year at the University of Florida. pp. 1, 8.

[10] R. E. Myers and E. Paul Torrance. "Can Teachers Encourage Creative Thinking?" *Educational Leadership* 19 (3): 156-59; December 1961.

ness to consider curriculum change. Fifty-four small city and suburban school districts in Ohio which were similar in size, tax valuation, and expenditure per pupil were identified.

The principal of each high school was asked to select the two teachers on his staff whom he considered to be the *most* willing to consider curriculum change and the two teachers whom he considered to be the *least* willing to consider change. He was provided with a series of 11 paired criteria to use as a basis for his selections. For example, included among the criteria for the identification of teachers most willing to consider change were the use of a variety of teaching materials, experimentation in the classroom, the ability for realistic self-evaluation, the viewing of others as capable of making contributions, and the toleration of uncertainty until knowledgeable judgment can be made. On the other hand, criteria for the identification of teachers least willing to consider change included the use of a narrow range of teaching materials, the following of routine procedures in the classroom, defensive self-evaluation, the viewing of others' contributions on the basis of status, and the making of quick judgments to avoid uncertainty.

Each teacher selected was supplied a packet of materials including a personal data sheet and a 100 item questionnaire composed of items from the Dogmatism Scale, the F-Scale, the Junior Index of Motivation, and the GNC Educational Philosophy Scale. An indirect approach was used in that each teacher was asked to respond to each item as he thought an "ideal teacher" would respond.

Of the original group of 216 questionnaires mailed (four to each of the fifty-four selected schools), 137 were returned: 70 from teachers identified as most willing to consider curriculum change and 67 from those identified as least willing. The personal data (sex, marital status, teaching area, educational preparation, etc.) from the returned questionnaires were analyzed and the scores for the Junior Index of Motivation and Dogmatism scales were determined. Further, an item analysis was carried out on the questionnaire, in each case comparing those teachers who were classified as most willing to consider curriculum change with those who were classified as least willing to do so.

With respect to the personal data, there were two factors which discriminated significantly between the two groups of teachers beyond the .05 level of confidence. First, 56 percent of the teachers in the group identified as most willing to consider curriculum change held master's degrees as compared with 40 percent of those in the least willing group. Second, among the married teachers, there were more in the group least willing to consider curriculum change with no children (21 percent) than there were in the most willing group (7 percent).

When the motivation scores and the dogmatism scores for the two groups were compared, no significant differences were found.

The item analysis uncovered four items in the questionnaire which discriminated between the two groups beyond the .05 level of confidence. Considering the fact that 100 items were included in the questionnaire, at least five would have been expected to differentiate between the two groups strictly by chance, so no significance can be attributed to these four items.

For all practical purposes, no significant differences were observed in the way these two groups responded to these various items. Indeed, the general pattern of responses for the two groups was in fact quite similar. With minor exceptions, teachers who were identified by their principals as most willing and least willing to consider curriculum change agreed on the way they thought an "ideal" teacher would respond to most of the 100 items included in this study.

This observation raises certain basic

questions. Are teachers learning, in their college preparation or in-service education programs, what they "ought to do" or what they "ought to say"? If we can assume that principals were fairly accurate in identifying those teachers whose behaviors were distinctly different, does the fact that these divergent groups say the same thing on pencil and paper tests mean that what teachers say and what they do are entirely different? If this is true, attempting to assess teachers' attitudes or effectiveness or philosophical outlooks by means of conventional instruments may be completely unrealistic. If teachers have learned to "say the right things" to the point that even they are not aware of the discrepancies between their stated sensations and their actual behaviors, the problems involved in helping teachers see where they are in relationship to where they want to go are formidable indeed. This problem should be explored much more deeply and with more elaborate design and procedures in future studies.

In this study the data were collected from teachers in communities which were selected according to certain criteria and which, therefore, were quite similar in some respects. It may be that such communities attract teachers with similar attitudes toward curriculum change. Or, it may be that the communities mold teachers' attitudes to such an extent that significant differences (of the sort examined in this study) cannot be isolated. The relationship between teachers' attitudes toward curriculum change and the type of community in which they are teaching would appear to be a fruitful area for examination.

There may also be a real question whether or not principals can identify teachers as most willing or least willing to consider curriculum change on the basis of the criteria employed in this study. On the other hand, it may be that some principals are actually much more accurate than others in classifying teachers according to these criteria.

This study was singularly unsuccessful in its attempt to isolate some differences between teachers who are willing to consider curriculum change and those who are unwilling to do so. It is hoped that this lack of success will not discourage others from studies in what may be a very fruitful area. It may very well be that the dynamics of curriculum development can only be understood by probing deeply into the personal factors involved in acceptance of or resistance to the notion of change. □

Need for Research on Instructional Supervision

BEN M. HARRIS

RESEARCH on instructional supervision has been undertaken in greater or lesser amounts in recent years depending upon the way one defines the term "supervision." Teaching methods have been fairly extensively, and occasionally even rather intensively, researched. Organizational arrangements for instruction—ungraded pri-

Ben M. Harris, Professor, Department of Educational Administration, The University of Texas, Austin

mary, ability grouping, core curriculum, team teaching, etc.—have all consumed enough time and energy of researchers to provide some guidelines for educational practice.

When we consider supervision at its central core as the *tasks* and *processes* of *instructional improvement,* we find, however, that little research of high quality has been undertaken. Most of what is currently known about instructional supervision from this point of view is based upon "folk wisdom" or ideas borrowed from other disciplines (2, 6, 13). This is not to say that practices warranted by and borrowed from these sources are not reasonably useful for instructional supervision. Each sub-profession borrows from others, relies on "folk wisdom" where research is lacking, and extracts the relevant findings from research in related fields. Yet each profession which grows to maturity as an applied science does so partly because of the efforts of the members of that group to promote and employ researches which are *directly related* to the unique problems and circumstances of that sub-profession.

Instructional supervision is practiced as one of the oldest sub-professions in education. Its attainment of maturity through research is, for the most part, yet to be realized! The effectiveness of various supervisory activities and programs applied to influence persons and situations toward better instruction needs to be thoroughly researched. The personal characteristics of instructional supervisors and the relationships between these characteristics and educational change need a great deal of study. The rigorous study of forces making for and resisting educational change needs analysis beyond research undertakings to date. A few notes on specific research studies of these kinds which are most needed are offered in the following paragraphs. Some of these studies can and should be undertaken as action research by practitioners.

Other studies will need more elaborate designs.

Several decades of organized, specialized, supervisory practice in school situations have produced an array of supervisory activities. Such activities as classroom observation, teacher-supervisor interviews, demonstration teaching, lecturing, and group discussions are all well known and widely used. The *usefulness* of these activities is not seriously questioned, yet little is known about the *effectiveness* of these and other activities in different situations, with different problems, and different personalities involved. Rogers (16) is among those who have suggested, through research, the value of nondirective interview techniques for therapeutic counseling purposes. There is good reason to believe that this same approach is valuable in supervisory interviewing, but validating evidence is needed. Hughes (11) and Ryans (17) are only two of several who have recently provided new information on approaches to classroom observations. Their studies relate, however, to the problem of *describing* teacher behavior; they are not helpful in answering questions about the use of observation activities for *improving* teacher behavior.

The study by Hill (10) has emphasized some unique values in both lectures and group discussions in voluntary, adult education study groups. Whether these same results apply to not-so-voluntary adult teacher in-service groups is an open question! Furthermore, Hill's study compared the results from skilled lecturing with unskilled discussion leading. This leaves many unanswered questions about the effectiveness of discussion activities under the leadership of professionals (4).

One of the most important steps toward improving supervisory practice and placing it on a truly professional level could come from a large-scale program of research on activity effectiveness. The known supervisory activities need to be precisely tested for relative effectiveness in a series of situations, directed toward various problems, with diverse personalities involved. This is a large order, one worthy of being sponsored by an organization like ASCD, provided financial support might be secured from agencies or foundations also interested in excellence in education.

Research on Program Effectiveness

Exacting studies of supervision programs as distinguished from specific activities or isolated supervisory endeavors are almost nonexistent. Programs of curriculum development often lack sufficient specificity of purpose to permit adequate evaluation of outcomes. Yet even carefully designed programs, such as MPATI, the Texas Media project, and the Catskill and Rocky Mountain small school projects tend, because of their initial construction, to contribute little to our knowledge of supervision program design. The reasons are various.

1. Programs worthy of study in depth are often large, complex undertakings which make related research difficult.

2. A problem is found in lack of resources. Research on action programs is much more demanding of staff, funds, and time than is old-fashioned, campus-centered educational research.

3. Sponsoring agencies tend to want to advertise the success of a supervisory program before the data are in. This discourages the kind of follow-up studies that are often essential in researching programs or projects.

4. Program research tends to focus attention upon outcomes rather than processes.

Underlying these difficulties hampering program research is a basic problem. To date we lack conceptual models to guide supervisors in designing supervision programs. Theories of learning have not generally been applied to the design of in-service programs for teachers. Concepts of the dynamics of planned change (13) are now emerging with sufficient clarity to serve in designing curriculum development programs. Models for conceptualizing institutional dynamics might well apply to projects, schools, and districts. As these theories and models are used in designing programs of supervision, it will become feasible to research such programs so as to gain new insights into the impact upon people and situations, and the dynamics involved.

Characteristics of Supervisory Personnel

Characteristics of the school principal and the superintendent of schools have been much more fully researched than those of supervisors. We know relatively little about people in such positions as assistant superintendent, curriculum director, general supervisor, coordinator, or consultant. Leadership studies (18) have provided some new insights into the nature of effective leadership for people in administrative positions, but these findings may not apply to supervisory leadership. Ryans' (17) study of teacher characteristics may provide a point of departure for assessing the characteristics of supervisors. The distinguishing "patterns" of teacher behavior which were determined in this classic study were sufficiently *fundamental* as to offer promise as a framework for studying supervisory behavior.

It is curious indeed that we have little reliable evidence even on the fundamental nature of the work of "supervision." Job analyses have rarely been undertaken. Like the teacher, the supervisor often works alone and only fragments of his behavior are readily observable. Unlike the teacher, or the principal, the supervisor usually has no single location in which he or she works, hence, analysis of the job is made still more difficult.

Despite these difficulties, simple descriptions of supervisory behavior and sophisticated analyses of these descriptive data for a variety of persons, positions, and situations could be most illuminating to the profession. Such descriptive studies need to be undertaken before more precise research designs are forthcoming.

The preceding paragraphs have emphasized the supervisor as an individual. This tends to ignore another important aspect of supervision which is worthy of research. Most supervisory endeavors which seem to be productive are *team undertakings;* a variety of people are involved in several supervisory positions. Herein lies the need for study of supervisory staffs and their working relationships. We need to know more about functional relationships betweeen principals, supervisors, and other staff members.

Communication patterns within a staff and the barriers to effective communication have been fruitfully researched in other institutional settings. Role conflicts between principals and supervisors are a reality which needs to be better understood via research (8). How value, interest, and personality structures of supervisory personnel influence their behavior patterns may well provide an important key to help solve the mystery of modern education—*why schools don't change much*! Equally important in this respect may be the findings from studies of the power structure of the social milieu of the school as it influences the curriculum and instructional processes (3).

Problem of Research Publication

No discussion of needs for research in instructional supervision would be in proper perspective without some comment on the problem of dissemination. Just as well tested teaching practices find great difficulty in being disseminated, so research in supervision—limited as it is—is often not available to those who might use it. *Educational Leadership* is rare among nationally circulated periodicals in being devoted primarily to supervision and curriculum development. Yet even this journal publishes few articles on supervision *per se* and few in supervision research. Other journals do, of course, publish manuscripts on supervision topics, but they are limited and research articles are rare. Listings in *Education Index* for the past ten years number only 36 per year on the average under the heading, "Supervision and Supervisors." In none of these years was more than a single article listed as supervision research. Research in the field of supervision is going on, if only in the form of doctoral dissertations. Phi Delta Kappa reported 20 dissertations on supervision completed in 1961 in over 100 colleges. Thirty-seven such dissertations were reported under way or completed in 1962.

One of the needs relating to research in supervision is the publication of studies. The journal *Educational Administration and Supervision* used to meet this need. It is no longer being published and an old problem is made worse. A plain fact that must be faced is this—one important stimulant to research production is research consumption. Supervision research tends not to be consumed because its findings are not published. This is a vicious spiral which might be broken by the establishment of a single journal of supervision research. Perhaps this would be an important step toward more and better research which in turn would mark the emergence of supervision as a genuine profession! □

References

1. K. D. Benne and B. Muntyan. *Human Relations in Curriculum Change.* New York: The Dryden Press, 1951.

2. W. G. Bennis *et al.*, editors. *The Planning*

of Change. New York: Holt, Rinehart and Winston, 1961.

3. Henry M. Brickell. *Organizing New York State for Education Change.* Albany, N.Y.: University of the State of New York, State Education Department; December 1961.

4. Nathaniel Cantor. *Learning Through Discussion.* Buffalo, N.Y.: Human Relations for Industry, 1951.

5. S. M. Corey. *Action Research To Improve School Practices.* New York: Bureau of Publications, Teachers College, Columbia University, 1953.

6. D. Cartwright and A. Zander, editors. *Group Dynamics—Research and Theory.* Evanston, Ill.: Row, Peterson and Co., 1953.

7. J. W. Getzels and Herbert A. Thelen. "The Classroom as a Unique Social System." *The Dynamics of Instructional Groups.* Part II, 59th Yearbook, National Society for the Study of Education. Chicago: University of Chicago Press, 1960.

8. Ben M. Harris. "Contrasting Perceptions of the Instructional Supervisor's Job." Unpublished paper, 1963.

9. Ben M. Harris. *Supervisory Behavior in Education.* Chapter 3. Englewood Cliffs, N.J.: Prentice-Hall, Inc., 1963.

10. Richard J. Hill. *A Comparative Study of Lecture and Discussion Methods.* New York: The Fund for Adult Education, 1960.

11. Marie Hughes et al. *A Research Report—Assessment of the Quality of Teaching in Elementary Schools.* Provo, Utah: University of Utah, 1955. (Mimeographed.)

12. Marie Jahoda et al. *Research Methods in Social Relations,* Part I. New York: Holt, Rinehart and Winston, 1951.

13. Ronald Lippitt et al. *The Dynamics of Planned Change.* New York: Harcourt, Brace and World, Inc., 1958.

14. N. R. F. Maier and A. R. Salem. "The Contribution of Discussion Leader to the Quality of Group Thinking: The Effective Use of Minority Opinions." *Human Relations* 5: 277-88; 1952.

15. D. M. Medley and H. E. Mitzel. "A Technique for Measuring Classroom Behavior." *Journal of Educational Psychology* 49: 86-92; April 1958.

16. Carl Rogers. *Client-Centered Therapy.* New York: Houghton Mifflin Co., 1951.

17. D. G. Ryans. *Characteristics of Teachers.* Washington, D.C.: American Council on Education, 1960.

18. R. M. Stogdill and C. L. Shortle. *Methods in the Study of Administrative Leadership.* Columbus, Ohio: The Ohio State University, 1955.

19. V. H. Vroom. "The Effects of Attitudes on Perception of Organizational Goals." *Human Relations* 13: 3; August 1960.

20. C. Washburne and L. M. Heil. "What Characteristics of Teachers Affect Children's Growth." *The School Review* 68: 420-28; Winter 1960.

EL 21 (5): 297-300, 339; February 1964
© 1964 ASCD

Supervision and Action Research

Mary Columbro Rodgers

EDUCATIONAL organization with its rigidity, its complexity of duty, its monotony of routine, and its tradition of conformity can easily stifle the creative spirit of the dedicated teacher. When this occurs tragedy results, for, since true education is fundamentally a creative process, the teacher who cannot function creatively cannot teach effectively.

There are two resources in the educa-

Mary Columbro Rodgers, Associate Professor of English, District of Columbia Teachers College, Washington, D.C. In 1964, Instructor in Education, Supervisor of Student Teachers in English, and a Doctoral Candidate, The Ohio State University, Columbus

tional set-up which, if used properly, safeguard and develop that individual creative talent which is the essence of effective teaching. Supervision and action research are the two indispensable guardians of teacher growth.

Teacher Attitudes Toward Personal Growth

The supervisor's efforts to help teachers grow is not as difficult as it might seem, for all men are self-oriented. This fact gives sound psychological support to the whole teacher improvement program. To be true to himself a teacher needs and welcomes motivation that is fundamentally intrinsic to personality growth. If a man's yen for self-realization has died, it is foolish to believe that he can effect any growth in others.[1] The teacher then is more apt to respond to supervisory suggestions that espouse his own development than those which point to some general educational objective.

Teachers frequently resist in-service education programs because these programs often ignore personal needs for growth and emphasize subtly but coldly the teacher's value as a useful unit in the accomplishment of the school's aims. Denied recognition of their intrinsic worth, teachers naturally feel inclined to sabotage organized group effort.[2] Teachers, like children, tend to be and become themselves sooner and more consistently than they tend to interact with others.[3] Unless individual needs are recognized it is useless to talk about group effort.

Certainly the supervisor should not limit himself exclusively to a concern for the teacher's individual needs. Paradoxically enough, one of our basic human needs is the need to interact with others. The challenge of maintaining harmonious interpersonal relationships fosters positive personal development. Conversation is itself a highly creative act. The teacher, then, if he is to be truly helped to grow, must be given opportunities to deal with others in significant relationships. Burnham and King make a realistic summary of the importance of people in school organization:

Schools consist primarily of people, and the goals of the school are accomplished through the efforts of people, singly and in groups. The activity of individuals involved does not occur in isolation, but in relation to the actions of all the others engaged in the process of education. The behavior of each person is influenced, stimulated, supported, hindered, blocked, extended, approved, ignored, disapproved by others with whom he is interacting in the organization.[4]

Part of the supervisor's job, then, is to help teachers grow through more meaningful group interaction. This experience, in addition to exercise in personal self-competency, will provide a wholesome program of teacher growth. As the supervisor assesses his concept of a well-organized program, he might ask himself if he has understood and communicated his understanding of the following points:

1. Being and becoming oneself is the great aim of education, and indeed of life itself.

2. Teachers are entitled to grow through their work.

3. Self-improvement is creative action.

4. Teachers who are conscious of self-growth stimulate similar creativity in their students.

5. Teaching cannot improve unless teachers improve.

---

[1] Arthur T. Jersild. *When Teachers Face Themselves.* New York: Bureau of Publications. Teachers College, Columbia University, 1955. pp. 130-31.

[2] *Ibid.*, p. 115.

[3] Lorrene Love Ort. *A Matter of Fences.* Washington, D.C.: Association for Supervision and Curriculum Development, 1963. p. 22.

[4] Reba M. Burnham and Martha L. King. *Supervision in Action.* Washington, D.C.: Association for Supervision and Curriculum Development, 1961. p. 38.

6. Creativity is the criterion of quality teaching.

7. "Creative teaching is the end goal of modern supervision." [5]

8. Supervisory action must include provision for both individual and group growth projects.

9. Uniqueness of teachers is a prior and more fundamental value than social competency.

10. "Valuing the uniqueness of each person is basic to a release of creativity." [6]

If these understandings are functional parts of the supervisor's conceptual theory, he is well-equipped to act as an instrumental cause of teacher growth.

The Supervisor and Action Research

The role of the supervisor in making action research an integral part of the teacher growth effort resolves itself into a number of specific tasks.

Preproject Tasks

The best way to involve teachers in the satisfying process of action research is to demonstrate that this is a means of personal growth. Supervisors who have themselves participated in a variety of projects should use this information in numerous anecdotal ways to communicate both the process and the values of action research.

Professional literature on action research is another means of informing teachers about the method. The following materials, for example, discuss a whole program of individualizing reading and teachers should be supplied with personal copies if they are expected to launch a similar study:

Walter B. Barbe. *Educator's Guide to Personalized Reading Instruction*. New Jersey: Prentice-Hall, Inc., 1961.

Marcella K. Draper and Louise H. Schwietert. *A Practical Guide to Individualized Reading*. Bureau of Educational Research, City of New York, 1960.

Alice Miel, editor. *Individualizing Reading Practices*. New York: Bureau of Publications, Teachers College, Columbia University, 1958.

As these materials are read and then discussed in informal ways for a long period of time, the supervisor should continually point up the personal meaning in experiment and research. Unless teachers understand that the results will change their day-to-day behavior in the classroom, the challenge of personal improvement has been lost. Stephen Corey makes this point:

The study must be undertaken by those who may have to change the way they do things as a result of the studies. Singly and in groups they must use their imagination creatively and constructively to identify the practices that must be changed, courageously try out those practices that give better promise, and methodically and systematically gather evidence to test their worth.[7]

In "selling" action research to the uninitiated, the supervisor must emphasize the fact that the teacher is the *actor* and hence, research has expanded its historical intent of simply adding to knowledge. Action research is a new and integrated approach to knowledge, an approach that recognizes the objective scientific process of research and

[5] Muriel Crosby. *Supervision as Co-operative Action*. New York: Appleton-Century-Crofts, 1957. p. 118.

[6] Association for Supervision and Curriculum Development. *Perceiving, Behaving, Becoming*. Washington, D.C.: the Association, 1962. p. 151.

[7] Stephen Corey. *Action Research To Improve School Practices*. New York: Bureau of Publications, Teachers College, Columbia University, 1953. p. 8.

the subjective inner experiences of the researcher.[8]

We want a way of holding assumptions about research which makes it possible to integrate the pursuit of science and research with the acceptance and fruitful development of one's self.[9]

If the supervisor can demonstrate the personal values of action research, he has already facilitated his next task, that of creating a climate conducive to open-ended thinking and experimentation. The threat implicit in all untried enterprise can be removed if the supervisor stresses process rather than product, method rather than result. Negative results as well as positive ones should be cherished as important outcomes of a project. So, too, individual projects should receive proportionately as much attention as group efforts. Ronald Doll suggests trying to build a feeling that it is all right to have problems.[10] A final injunction might be for the supervisor to create a climate of unhurried professional effort, one in which teachers are not pressured for results.

Problems that are genuinely valuable to teachers are usually deep-seated, and it is realistic to think they will take time to solve. The supervisor should not "legislate" research investigations; rather he should assist in assessing teachers' suggestions and in helping them find a problem that matches the researcher's insight, the needs of the situation, and the amount of time available.

Post-research Tasks

The best thing a supervisor can do in terms of evaluating action research is to evaluate himself. The following checklist is suggestive rather than comprehensive:

1. Have I continually supplied materials essential to the success of this project?

2. Have I supplied reliable moral support throughout its development?

3. Have I been available for consultation on problems that arose during this study?

4. Did I take enough time to interpret results and to discuss ways in which this new information can be implemented in everyday teaching?

5. Did I provide opportunities for the individual or the group to be recognized for worthwhile action?

6. Did I provide opportunities for the results of the action research project to be shared by other members of the profession?

7. Have I myself recognized how this information will modify present curriculum guides in the school, and have I taken positive steps toward the necessary revision?

8. Have I helped to make teachers aware of personal growth through this action research?

9. Have I continually stressed values of the process rather than the product?

10. Have I used the present success to stimulate new research enterprise?

The supervisor's use of action research is thus seen to be a challenging and continuous activity. In the final analysis it is the teacher who adjusts the school curriculum to the *de facto* needs of his students. If teachers are not taught and assisted in doing action research, there is danger, for example, that the guides and syllabi remain sterile compendia of objectives never trans-

---

[8] Abraham Shumsky. "Learning About Learning from Action Research." *Learning and the Teacher*. Washington, D.C.: Association for Supervision and Curriculum Development, 1959. p. 187.

[9] Ross L. Mooney. "The Researcher Himself." *Research for Curriculum Improvement*. Washington, D.C.: Association for Supervision and Curriculum Development, 1957. p. 166.

[10] Ronald C. Doll. "Freedom for Research." *Research for Curriculum Improvement*. Washington, D.C.: Association for Supervision and Curriculum Development, 1957. p. 260.

lated into those specific teaching points that make learning meaningful to both teacher and student.

If supervisors can help teachers to acquire the breadth of viewpoint inherent in intellectual inquiry, they themselves will become instrumental in initiating change. As Stephen Corey states, "Most of the study of what should be kept in the schools, what should go, and what should be added must be done in hundreds and thousands of classrooms in thousands of American communities." [11]

Hilda Taba, curriculum and evaluation specialist, calls for curriculum development through practical action research over and above general educational research:

> Principles derived from general research need to be reexamined in the light of their application in a particular practical situation to be of real value to solve curriculum problems and to make changes in curriculum. For example, while a good deal is known about the general nature of developmental tasks and their bearing on learning, little is known about the variation of these tasks by socioeconomic class culture, by ethnic or racial backgrounds or by variations in social learning introduced by family styles. Hence, if this concept is to bear fruit in curriculum and teaching, its application needs to be studied in many different practical situations.[12]

Teachers, then, are at the heart of the educational setup. Their growth is vital to the improvement of the entire enterprise. When supervisors can promote action research and self-development as one integrative action, they make an outstanding personal contribution to the improvement of education. When supervisors free teachers to be themselves and to function creatively in school circumstances they are, at the same time, liberating the creative potential of the students. Jane Franseth makes the self-realization of students largely dependent on the dynamic growth of teachers:

> Freeing children to create and to become their best is in large measure dependent on the extent to which the adults closest to children are themselves free to make the best of their own potential.[13]

The supervisor who dedicates himself to teacher growth and to action research as an instrument of self-actualization for teachers brings genuine meaning into education. His is the laurel of creative achievement for having made the business of education and the business of living one coherent enterprise. □

References

Association for Supervision and Curriculum Development. *Perceiving, Behaving, Becoming.* Washington, D.C.: the Association, 1962.

Reba M. Burnham and Martha L. King. *Supervision in Action.* Washington, D.C.: Association for Supervision and Curriculum Development, 1961.

Stephen Corey. *Action Research To Improve School Practices.* New York: Bureau of Publications, Teachers College, Columbia University, 1953.

Muriel Crosby. *Supervision as Co-operative Action.* New York: Appleton-Century-Crofts, 1957.

Ronald C. Doll. "Freedom for Research." *Research for Curriculum Improvement.* Washington, D.C.: Association for Supervision and Curriculum Development, 1957.

Jane Franseth. "Freeing Capacity To Be Creative." *New Insights and the Curriculum.* Washington, D.C.: Association for Supervision and Curriculum Development, 1963.

Arthur T. Jersild. *When Teachers Face Themselves.* New York: Bureau of Publications, Teachers College, Columbia University, 1955.

Ross L. Mooney. "The Researcher Himself."

---

[11] Stephen Corey, *op. cit.*, p. 8.

[12] Hilda Taba. "Problem Identification." *Research for Curriculum Improvement.* Washington, D.C.: Association for Supervision and Curriculum Development, 1957. p. 42.

[13] Jane Franseth. "Freeing Capacity To Be Creative." *New Insights and the Curriculum.* Washington, D.C.: Association for Supervision and Curriculum Development, 1963. p. 316.

Research for Curriculum Improvement. Washington, D.C.: Association for Supervision and Curriculum Development, 1957.

Lorrene Love Ort. *A Matter of Fences*. Washington, D.C.: Association for Supervision and Curriculum Development, 1963.

Abraham Shumsky. "Learning About Learning from Action Research." *Learning and the Teacher*. Washington, D.C.: Association for Supervision and Curriculum Development, 1959.

Hilda Taba. "Problem Identification." *Research for Curriculum Improvement*. Washington, D.C.: Association for Supervision and Curriculum Development, 1957.

EL 22 (7): 494-96, 513; April 1965
© 1965 ASCD

Emergence of Technical Supervision

BEN M. HARRIS

SUPERVISION, the oldest of the non-teaching specializations in American education, began as simple inspection of teaching. It was oriented toward stability and conformity. The approach was to inspect, to see whether teachers were doing what was expected of them or not, to promote conformity, and to avoid deviations. The era of the progressive education movement in the United States thoroughly destroyed inspection as the basic image of supervision. The concept of inspection for conformity is no longer an acceptable one, and it has not been for many years. On the other hand, during the past years since World War II the supervisory profession has been developing new directions and new definitions of its function. A new professional image is beginning to emerge.

Supervision is developing as a distinctive function of the school operation. Supervisors are increasingly finding it possible to earn recognition for themselves as members of a sub-profession with specialized competencies, with unique responsibilities, and identifiable programs. *Specialized competencies* are required for a sub-profession. Although they are not the unique property of supervisors, certain specialized competencies in supervision have been developed that are uniquely valuable in the school operation. *Unique responsibilities* of the supervisor are gradually beginning to be defined in such a way as to delineate the supervisor's work from that of the principal, the teacher, the superintendent, and others. *Identifiable programs* of supervision are being developed so that the supervisor emerges as a person who gives direct leadership to distinctive programs replacing the more rigidly service-oriented operation of the supervisor of the past.

A Point of Focus

How does this new image of supervision come into focus as we move toward the development of supervisory programs? Let us start with the teacher and other instructional personnel as the central concern of supervision. Let us assume that conditions are appropriate for change in a par-

Ben M. Harris, Professor, Department of Educational Administration, The University of Texas, Austin

ticular direction. With focus upon people, our purposes are essentially those of the in-service education task. We are concerned about changes in behavior in people so that instruction might be improved and pupils might better learn.

We approach the question of the use of supervisory activities from the point of view of *strategies* for change and program development. This is somewhat different from the approaches which have sometimes been used, in that a strategic approach involves three basic considerations as follows:

1. *Diagnosing problems and factors that are involved in a problem area.* This process of diagnosis of problems is an important part of the procedures leading to a strategy to be selected in supervisory program planning.

2. *Designing a supervisory program.* Once the problem has been clearly diagnosed, a strategy can be selected which permits the designing of a program involving careful selection of purposes and appropriate activities.

3. *Implementing a supervisory program.* This involves strong leadership, technical competence, the development of appropriate resources, and cooperative effort.

In a sense, we are referring to a problem-solving process; moving from the diagnosis of the problem, to designing approaches to that problem, to implementing and evaluating. Let us look separately at each of these three aspects of the supervision process.

Diagnosis in Supervision

Systematic classroom observation is essential to diagnosis of teaching. This is only one way to find out about the problems that exist at the classroom level. Yet without systematic, rigorous, skilled observation, we have very little basis for dealing with teachers' problems.

Diagnostic use of standardized test data has also aided in the identification of teaching and program problems. Diagnostic and standardized test results have been used for a variety of purposes. All too often, such results have been ignored in the process of identifying teaching problems. There are some hazards, of course, in using test data in this way, but if these hazards are appropriately avoided, their use can be effective.

The exacting use of evaluative criteria focuses upon problems beyond the scope of tests for individual classroom situations. By this I mean the use of evaluative criteria for diagnostic purposes in contrast with more superficial uses sometimes made of these criteria for accreditation purposes. Several very useful evaluative criteria-type instruments have been developed that might well serve for the diagnosis of school-wide or system-wide problems, if the instruments are used with this intent.

The opinions, feelings, and observations of pupils can provide very valuable clues to problem areas in the school. There is a natural reluctance to use information from pupils for evaluation purposes. Nonetheless, there is no one in our schools who knows what goes on in the classroom better than the learner himself. We must gradually learn, with due caution, of course, how to make use of these opinions, feelings, and observations of pupils to understand better the problem areas in our instructional programs.

The behavior of our graduates and nongraduates alike as they live in a larger society is most significant in discerning the fundamental problems in our program. Follow-up studies can help to provide genuine insight into the strengths and weaknesses of our program as these characteristics are reflected in the kinds of lives our students live.

Finally, teachers themselves can be a source of diagnostic information to guide supervisory program planning. Teacher opinions about problems they face have been widely used and sometimes misused in supervisory planning. More systematic opinion and attitude studies could serve well. Formal testing programs might prove worth while if we had the courage to try these.

Designing a Program

As we diagnose teaching-learning problems, we identify large goals upon which supervision programs must concentrate. These large goals, if truly significant, are too large to deal with *in toto*. It is necessary for such goals to be specified in terms of more limited realizable purposes. Objectives for supervisory programs should be specified in behavioral terms. We need to be able to indicate clearly what behaviors should be promoted; what skills, understandings, knowledges, and attitudes we want to develop as they relate to a diagnosed problem area.

Having specified our purposes, it is possible to select appropriate activities in terms of these purposes. The context of the larger problem should be maintained to enhance the transfer from the supervisory program to the operational situation. Organizational arrangements for implementing activities must be given careful consideration as they involve schedules, assignments, and sequences of events.

There is, finally, a question of resources to consider, both in the implementing and in the planning stages. It is necessary that we seriously consider the time, the material, the staff resources, the facilities, and money that will be required to implement a supervisory program. One of the most serious mistakes we tend to make is to launch upon a program which is highly desirable but impractical in the sense that we cannot muster the necessary resources for implementing it.

Implementation

Many factors, of course, influence the successful implementation of the program. We must give serious consideration to the flow of events. A supervisory program needs coordination in its implementation phases. Distractions need to be avoided. Unpredictable events need to be considered as they arise and influence the planned program. Side effects need to be dissipated.

It is highly unrealistic to expect all things to function smoothly as planned when we are undertaking a supervisory program of significance that really has an impact on people. Side effects and reactions will be real and considerable. They must be anticipated. They must be dealt with in constructive ways.

Of course morale must be maintained throughout the implementation of the program. Supervision programs cannot be programmed for automation. This may be possible in the distant future, but to date, effective implementation involves constant attention to ongoing activities. High-level leadership responsibilities must be exercised for stimulation, coordination, allocation of resources, and dealing with turbulences that arise.

A final point that needs to be considered is the relationship between interest, leadership, and progress toward designated purposes as we move through the phases of a program. As we move into a program in the early stages, participant interest is high, leadership is high, but progress is low. As participants run into problems, leadership may be withdrawn and interest may decline before progress can be attained. At this point there is serious danger of the whole program's collapsing. When problems emerge, if leadership personnel will invest renewed energy, the problems can be overcome, progress will result, and interest will remain high.

It is important to remember that a supervisory program is something that grows out of a careful set of diagnostic procedures which identify problem areas. A supervision program can be designed with careful attention to the kinds of supervisory activities required to accomplish specified purposes. □

Knowledge About Supervision: Rationalization or Rationale?

JAMES B. MACDONALD

WOULD schools be as effective without formal supervision? In what way or ways does supervision contribute to the total educational structure? What are the most effective procedures in supervision? These questions (and many others) are unanswered, at least in terms of research findings today. What do we know about supervision? Where is the research that provides knowledge about the supervision process?

This year the ASCD Research Institutes are focused upon this concern—Research and Development in Supervision. As noble as this theme appears to an organization with a major commitment to supervision, the truth of the matter is disturbing. The institute planners were hard pressed to find research in supervision.

The ASCD 1965 Yearbook, *Role of Supervisor and Curriculum Director in a Climate of Change,* was a special disappointment in this search. One would assume that a yearbook devoted to this topic would refer to and/or note the research on supervision. Little mention was made of research studies or research efforts in the area. This is not to say that the yearbook failed in its specific intent, but rather it indicates dramatically the essential folklore, personal experience, philosophical, and/or psychological derivation of most supervisory practices. The conclusion seems warranted that in comparison with other aspects of educational concern (e.g., teaching and administering) supervision has less basis in fact.

Common sense tells us that teachers need and can use help and/or guidance, perhaps even direction. Research tells almost nothing about how to implement these aims. We are left with the still unanswered question of whether supervision has any value at all.

James B. Macdonald, Professor of Education, Department of Social Foundations, School of Education, University of Wisconsin-Milwaukee

Evidence of Change

From a rational viewpoint one would expect supervisory efforts to result in desired changes in teacher behavior. What evidence is there that these changes take place? Certainly, supervisory or even teacher testimonials, well intended and honest to be sure, do not provide a solid base of evidence.

There is, in fact, little sound evidence that teachers change at all, to say nothing about changing in relation to supervisory efforts. Flanders (2, 3), and Bowers and Soar (1), for example, have reported studies which demonstrate changes in teachers. Still the change was minimal, it was not clearly predictable; and the procedures for promoting change were not the usual types of supervisory activity.

A few short years ago the Wisconsin ASCD Research Committee attempted to develop a study on supervision in the state. The committee hoped to examine the effects of supervision in groups of teachers versus supervision on an individual instruction basis for beginning teachers. The study never was begun, primarily because of the inability to get subjects (supervisors). As one supervisor put it, "We already know that individual classroom visitation is far superior." ... The evidence? "Anyone who has supervised for a long time knows that."

Wings of Wax

It was the writer's definite impression that many supervisors and central administrative personnel were not anxious to research supervisory practices. This is understandable in the sense that supervisors are busy people and overloaded in terms of present day concepts of function. Yet the truth of the matter was that many supervisors did not appear very anxious to find out about their activities.

Supervisors seem to be soaring on ideological wings stuck together with wax, and they may be getting too close to the sun. In many ways the supervisory credo is open to the same criticism that some psychologists make concerning psychoanalysis. Hard-headed psychologists are prone to remark that ⅔'s of the patients improve with psychoanalysis and ⅔'s without.

Further, one finds little discussion of failure in supervisory literature. It is not even clear whether one actually knows when one has failed in the supervisory process. There appear to be no rationales for explaining why goals are not achieved, but primarily after-the-fact explanations of success. Surely there is something to be learned by the error of our ways.

Supervisors, as have many functionaries in education, have moved firmly toward the mental health myth as a rationalization of their practices. This phenomenon should be a clear warning signal.

This is not to say that supervisory personnel should be unconcerned with the mental health of teachers, but is to say that they are not trained to do this and are in danger of sliding over into a comfortable rationale which justifies the lack of specifiable results.

There can be little doubt that there is an "art" of human relationships. Some persons are more capable than others in this respect.

It further makes good sense to have supervisors who are able and comfortable in their human relationships. What is not at all clear is what difference it makes in terms of some clearly defined goals of teacher behavior change.

Why has not anyone brought all the supervisors into a central office for a year or two (and put them to work on curriculum tasks), while they test to see what difference it makes?

There is some partial evidence that automated and/or audio-visual feedback via television, tape recorder, etc., can be a useful agent for teacher change. Why have these procedures not been tested against interpersonal supervisory practices, or in addition to live practices?

What does a supervisor need to know about teachers in order to work effectively? Is observation of teaching the most important source of information for constructive supervisory function?

If teachers may become obsolete in the next fifty years, at least in terms of present conceptions of their function, then perhaps traditionally conceived supervisory activities may also become anachronistic.

Status and Role

How do status and role in the school system affect the achievement of supervisory goals? Are principals with line authority (when they supervise) more effective or less effective than supervisors with staff authority?

Should supervisors be chosen or elected by teachers? Should the role of supervisor be rotational and earned as a symbol of staff acceptance and reward? Would this make any difference in supervisory outcomes? How much is enough supervision? How much is too little? What are the critical incidents in supervisory activity?

Lest there be misunderstanding, let us hurry to add that our research knowledge of most aspects of education is open to considerable improvement. Yet supervision ought to be a central concern of ASCD members, and research knowledge ought to be one solid base for professional activity. At present there is very little evidence that either ASCD or supervisors in general are very much concerned about research knowledge in supervision.

What we need are many more attempts to visualize varieties of supervisory patterns and the necessary trial and error and systematic evaluation of these patterns in operation. Further, although most educational functions, such as supervision, are "long" on goals and "short" on evidence, it would facilitate matters a great deal if the values applied to the supervisory process were clearly identified and related to some kinds of operational criteria that could be evaluated.

If supervisors are to be "product" oriented, then we must clearly specify the changes in teacher behavior and/or teaching conditions that are possible and desirable. If supervisors perform an essentially political function of communication and/or facilitation of school ideology and goals, then these functions ought to be objectified for evaluation purposes. Or, if supervision is essentially a humanistic function providing help and support for humanizing the bureaucratic aspects of schooling, then this should be specified clearly.

It is the hope of the ASCD Research Commission that this year's Research Institutes will serve a useful purpose by helping ASCD members and others involved in supervision to clarify needed knowledge, focus values, and become aware of promising research in the field. ☐

References

1. N. D. Bowers and R. S. Soar. "Studies In Human Relations in the Teaching Learning Process." V Final Report: Cooperative Research Project No. 469, 1961.

2. Ned Flanders *et al.* "Helping Teachers Change Their Behavior." Terminal Contract Report, Title VII, N.D.E.A.

3. Ned Flanders. "Teacher Behavior and In-service Programs." *Educational Leadership* 21 (1): 25-30; October 1963.

Supervision: Focus on Thinking

MARY LOU USERY WHITE
MURIEL RADTKE
LOUISE M. BERMAN

The rational powers of the human mind . . . are central to individual dignity, human progress, and national survival (6).

FUNDAMENTAL to man's humanness and effectiveness is the development of his rational powers. Traditionally the school, as an agent of society, has accepted the development of these powers as one of its key functions. To supervisors has fallen the task of mediating between teachers and society's goals.

Conscientious supervisors are aware of current trends in thinking. At the present time, however, resources to assist supervisors in working with teachers in developing rational processes are somewhat scant. With this dearth of resources in mind, the intent of the writers of this article is to assist the supervisor who wishes to work in more detail on developing the cognitive skills.

One basic assumption permeates this article. A relationship is suggested between a teacher's awareness and awakening of his own thought processes and the comparative attention he gives to the development of such processes in students.

Building upon this assumption the writers have attempted to do the following: (a) to describe briefly thought processes as commonly discussed in the literature, and (b) to sketch a program for supervisors desiring to help teachers improve their thinking skills.

One Conception of Thinking

Thinking [1] has been described as a process that has a beginning point and an end product. What comes between these points is speculative. Bartlett states, "The process moves from the start to its finish with a kind of necessity" (2). Russell says, "Thinking is a process rather than a fixed state. It involves a sequence of ideas moving from some beginning, through some sort of pattern of relationships, to some goal or conclusion" (10).

In discussing what transpires when a person thinks, psychologists and educators agree that thinking can take many forms. Following are nine thinking processes and brief descriptions of each.

[1] In this article the terms *thought processes, thinking skills, thinking behaviors, rational powers,* and related words are used interchangeably.

Mary Lou Usery White, Assistant Professor of Education, University of Maine, Orono. In 1965, Mrs. White was Doctoral Intern, College of Education, The Ohio State University, Columbus; Muriel Radtke, Assistant Professor, Newark State College, Union, New Jersey; and Louise M. Berman, Professor of Education, University of Maryland, College Park. In 1965, Dr. Berman was Associate Secretary, ASCD

Perceiving is the act of noticing or selecting stimuli from the individual's total environment. The process may operate at different levels moving from seeing only the obvious to seeing the unusual as well as the obvious.

Imagining involves the ability to invent new or original ideas. These ideas may not necessarily be new to the outside world but are new to the individual and are characterized by freshness and newness.

Analyzing is concerned with taking apart the elements of a situation and studying the singular parts.

Patterning is the process of putting together elements of a situation that have some relation to each other. The process may operate at different levels, moving from simple classification of items into categories to a totally new complex of ideas at a foundational level.

Redefining involves the finding of new or uncommon uses for a given idea or object. Flexibility is inherent in the process.

Predicting involves projecting ideas. The process can move in a logical pattern from known facts to probable outcomes, or it can involve a creative leap beyond known facts.

Judging is the process of weighing evidence and forming opinions. Depending upon the nature of what is to be evaluated, the individual bases his judgments on a collection of data, intuitive insights, or a combination of both.

Developing fluency involves the ability to express many ideas in rapid succession without immediate consideration of the worth of each idea. This process is associated with freedom, looseness, and flow of thought.

Elaborating involves embroidering or restating the old. Newness is not as essential here as refinement, clarification, and extension of a previously formulated concept.

Improving Thinking Skills

One means by which a supervisor might work with teachers both individually and in groups is through a workshop designed to help teachers develop their thinking processes during their planning for teaching. Planning involves the pre-thinking prior to what transpires in the classroom. What actually happens during the lesson is a combination of the pre-thinking plus the on-the-spot thinking that the teacher does. For this workshop we are concerned only with the pre-thinking. Elements concerning the organization of a workshop such as timing, items related to credit or non-credit, membership, and facilities are not central to this article and, therefore, are not included in the discussion.

The crux of the workshop is the awakening of the teacher's awareness of his ability (a) to develop his thinking behaviors and (b) to expand his thought processes used in planning. The supervisor assists the teacher in the introductory stage of the workshop through the use of a planned interview designed to make an impact on the teacher concerning the status of his own thinking behavior. Prior to the interview the teacher plans a lesson that will be used as the focal point during the interview. A tape recording is made of the entire interview so that future use can be made of the teacher's responses.

The questions in the *Interview Guide* are used in order to elicit responses about the nine thinking processes that were described earlier.

Interview Guide

Perceiving
—What observations prompted you to plan this lesson?
—Describe vividly several characteristics of your classroom.

Imagining
—What exciting ideas for new materials, methods, or resources did you consider while planning this lesson?
—What was the most important idea new to you in this lesson?

Analyzing
—What did you consider that might influence the direction of the lesson?
—What factors made a difference in this lesson?

Patterning
—What means did you use to bring about an understanding of the relationship between the various parts of the lesson?
—How did you plan to relate this lesson to previous and future lessons?

Redefining
—What alternatives did you consider for use if the plans were unsuccessful?
—What materials, methods, or resources did you use in a new or different way?

Predicting
—What did you plan as possible outcomes of this lesson?

Judging
—How did you decide what changes could be brought about through this lesson?
—What criteria did you use to determine that your plan was complete and that your purposes could be accomplished?

Developing Fluency
—What sources would you suggest for a teacher to get help in planning a lesson?
—How many alternative ways can you list for developing the lesson?

Elaborating
—If you had the time, how would you further develop this lesson?
—If you taught a similar lesson before, how does this plan differ?

Individual Focus on Thinking

After the teacher responds to the items on the *Interview Guide,* the teacher and supervisor listen to the recording in order to become aware of various modes of thinking used by the teacher. To assist in sharpened listening, the *Inventory of Thinking Behaviors* has been developed. The behaviors listed in this instrument parallel the thinking processes discussed earlier. A workable plan is to place check marks beside the behaviors listed in the instrument when responses from the interview refer to the behaviors. Key phrases from the responses might be jotted down on the instrument as a reminder of the behaviors.

After the listening experience, the supervisor might find the following instrument helpful in analyzing the conversation:

Inventory of Thinking Behaviors

Perceiving
—Describes the degree of rapport he has achieved with his students.
—States the academic, social, and emotional needs of his students.

Imagining
—Shows originality and curiosity in the use of materials, methods, and resources beyond those found in the classroom.
—Brings freshness and originality to the lesson plan.

Analyzing
—Looks at assignments individually in order to personalize the lesson.
—Shows evidence of having studied his students' total background to find areas that are manageable, important, and most open to change.

Patterning
—Regards this lesson as one part of his students' total learning experiences.
—Provides opportunities for students to translate subject matter into meaningful patterns.
—Prizes a lack of planned order when the concept of order is unnecessary.

Redefining
—Displays willingness to shift focus of the lesson at pupil suggestion.
—Finds new and original uses for materials, methods, and resources.

Predicting
—Projects possible outcomes from the lesson plan.

—Considers possibilities for future lesson development from this plan.
—Predicts changed behavior as a result of planning for change.

Judging
—Verbalizes criteria for selection of materials, methods, and resources.
—Compares and contrasts outcomes of the lesson with groups and individuals.
—Uses information from more than one source.

Developing Fluency
—Gives many responses to open-ended questions.
—Produces a variety of ideas for initiating and developing the lesson.

Elaborating
—Provides for refining ideas so that they are easily managed by pupils.
—Establishes techniques for clarifying concepts that are difficult to understand.

Group Focus on Thinking

Both parties are now ready to move into a small group stage of the workshop. A few activities are suggested from which the supervisor can select those most appropriate to the members of his group. Activities can be centered around

Readings and discussions

Techniques and devices

Adaptations of instruments originally designed for studying the verbal behavior of teachers

Group analysis of planning processes

Preparation of cycles of goal-setting, experimentation, and analysis of outcomes

Extensions and modifications of the *Inventory of Thinking Behaviors.*

Elaboration on a few of these activities might suggest usable ideas for the reader.

Readings and Discussions

Selected readings by writers such as Bloom (3), Ennis (7), and Russell (10) in the area of critical thinking and those of Bruner (4), Getzels and Jackson (9), and Torrance (12) in the area of creative thinking are easily available and provide ideas that could generate discussions.

Techniques and Devices

A variety of techniques and devices can be used throughout the workshop to develop thinking skills. Some of these activities can be carried on throughout the workshop and others can serve a particular need at certain points. Supervisors may want to adapt some of the following suggestions.

Perceiving might be pointed up by the use of motion pictures. Films can be projected without sound, or films produced especially for developing perceptual skills (5) can be used. Both might be followed by discussions of what was perceived. To help teachers perceive more richly, they can be invited to observe a street corner scene and jot down all the uncommon sights and sounds.

Analyzing can be further developed by the use of advertising techniques. Over a period of time, teachers' attention can be directed to advertising techniques employed on billboards, television, radio, magazines, and newspapers. Teachers can study copy for examples of slanted statements, poor logic, and half-truths.

Patterning can be encouraged by using games such as *Wff 'N Proof* (1) in which the play of the game depends on following predetermined patterns. More open-ended types of patterning can be stimulated through the use of activities involving free association. In one such activity each teacher is given four to six unrelated words on a slip of paper and asked to synthesize the words in any way he sees fit. Outcomes might include poems, drawings, stories, musical numbers, etc.

Predicting might be stimulated by the display of a sealed box of unknown contents.

Teachers are informed of items in the room in which the box was packed; the box is weighed, and teachers are asked to guess the box's contents.

Other techniques can be adapted from games such as "Password" (word association) and mathematical puzzles, such as the "Magic Number Square," from creative uses of objects such as kaleidoscopes and photographs of cloud shapes, and from activities such as brainstorming.

Adaptations of Instruments

Instruments originally developed for describing the verbal behavior of teachers might be adapted for use in noting change in thinking behaviors. For example, adaptations might be made of Flanders' framework, which describes classroom interaction (8), and the "Stanford Teacher Competence Appraisal Guide" (11), which is designed to assess and improve levels of competence in teaching.

Group Analysis of Planning Processes

Members of the group can analyze in two ways procedures used in planning: (a) the procedures used by an individual in planning a lesson can be analyzed by the group; (b) processes used by the total group in planning a sample lesson can be analyzed.

Preparation of Planning Cycles

Group members can set up short-term cycles on planning during which they work on hunches about developing thinking behaviors—setting goals, experimenting with ideas, and analyzing the outcomes of the total experience. The cycles can be established by individuals or by the group.

Extensions of the Inventory

The *Inventory of Thinking Behaviors* was developed with the intent that it would be further refined and extended. Persons may elect to take a portion of the instrument, develop it further, test it out, and report any modifications or clarifications to the group. The instrument can also be used for a group analysis of one teacher's interview. With the teacher's agreement, the entire group can listen to the tape recording to note thinking behaviors. Information gleaned from the use of the instrument can be used to raise questions and stimulate discussion.

The workshop can be arranged so that comprehensive study is given to thinking in general. Another way of organizing might be to study in detail two or three dimensions of thinking.

Continuous evaluation of group and individual progress might be an insightful way of viewing personal growth. As teachers gain fuller understanding of the thinking processes and greater awareness of their own thinking behaviors, they may wish to extend their efforts by developing these processes through more personalized supervision. Teachers might consider ways in which they can assist pupils in developing their thinking behaviors. This theme and others might provide topics for future workshops that focus on education's role in developing man's rational processes.

The supervisor is in a key position to provide stimulation and setting for the teacher's self-improvement of his cognitive processes. In this way the supervisor also contributes indirectly to the enhancement of children's thinking. Teachers who are aware of and prize the development of rational powers within themselves are more apt to foster the thinking skills in children because what a person prizes and cherishes is often what he covets for others. Several suggestions have been made as to ways the supervisor can help teachers to use their thought processes more intelligently, particularly in planning for instruction.

The strength of this proposal resides not in assurance of a methodology which will elicit certain thinking skills in teachers. Rather the dynamics of the proposal reside in:

The questions it raises about how to teach teachers to utilize fully their thought processes;

The challenge it presents to the task of the supervisor; and

The concern for the relationship of man's rational powers to other peculiarly human functions that the thoughtful reader will seek to understand. . . . ☐

References

1. Layman E. Allen. *Wff 'N Proof: The Game of Modern Logic*. New Haven: Yale University Press, 1962.

2. Sir Frederick Bartlett. *Thinking: An Experimental and Social Study*. New York: Basic Books, Inc., 1958. p. 76.

3. Benjamin S. Bloom, editor. *Taxonomy of Educational Objectives, Handbook I: Cognitive Domain*. New York: Longmans, Green and Company, 1956.

4. Jerome S. Bruner. "The Conditions of Creativity." *Contemporary Approaches to Creative Thinking*. Howard E. Gruber, Glenn Terrell, and Michael Wertheimer, editors. New York: Atherton Press, 1962. pp. 1-30.

5. *Demonstrations in Perception*. Washington, D.C.: U.S. Department of the Navy, 1951.

6. Educational Policies Commission. *The Central Purpose of American Education*. Washington, D.C.: National Education Association and American Association of School Administrators, 1961. p. 11.

7. Robert H. Ennis. "A Concept of Critical Thinking." *Harvard Educational Review* 32: 81-111; Winter 1962.

8. Ned A. Flanders. "Intent, Action, and Feedback: A Preparation for Teaching." *Journal of Teacher Education* 14: 251-60; September 1963.

9. Jacob W. Getzels and Philip W. Jackson. *Creativity and Intelligence; Explorations with Gifted Students*. New York: John Wiley & Sons, Inc., 1962.

10. David H. Russell. *Children's Thinking*. Boston: Ginn and Company, 1956. p. 27.

11. Stanford University School of Education. *Stanford Teacher Competence Appraisal Guide*. Palo Alto, California: Stanford University.

12. E. Paul Torrance. *Guiding Creative Thinking*. Englewood Cliffs, New Jersey: Prentice-Hall, Inc., 1962.

EL 26 (8): 754-57; May 1969
© 1969 ASCD

Supervision: An Attempt To Modify Behavior

JOHN J. KORAN, JR.

SUPERVISION has as its goal the modification of behavior. Few elementary or secondary school administrators or college professors of teacher education, however, think of supervision in this way, or at least wish to admit it if they do. Nevertheless, as a result of supervision the pre- or in-service trainee is expected to do or say something differently than he did prior to supervision.

John J. Koran, Jr., Assistant Professor of Curriculum and Instruction, Science Education Center, University of Texas, Austin

A common problem with this expectation in practice is the failure of public school and university supervisors to identify specific behaviors to be influenced and then to attempt to influence these behaviors in ways which are suggested by contemporary research. This article will describe a theoretical orientation and research results which have substantial implications for the supervision of teachers for behavior change.

A General Theory

The use of modeling procedures as a means of influencing human behavior has been well documented.[1,2] This research suggests that new social responses may be acquired or characteristics of existing responses changed as a function of observing the behavior of others and the consequences of their responses, without the observer himself performing any responses or receiving any direct reinforcement during the acquisition. A study by Bandura and McDonald[3] indicated that imitation, under certain circumstances, was more more effective than operant conditioning procedures and that the provision of a model alone was as effective as the combination of modeling and reinforcement for initial learning. Bandura, Ross, and Ross[4] have also gathered evidence that indicates that film-mediated models are as effective in producing behavior change as are live models.

A recent group of studies conducted with both secondary teachers[5] and elementary science teachers[6] tend to support the use of imitation in teacher training. The first of these studies sought to train teachers to ask analytical questions of the type suggested by the Bloom's *Taxonomy*[7] categories of analysis. Trainees were exposed to a video-tape model of the behavior to be acquired, a written description of the desired behavior, or a placebo. The treatment groups viewing the film-mediated model or reading the written model produced significantly higher frequency and quality of questions asked than did the control group. The latter study attempted to teach prospective elementary science teachers to ask observation and classification questions of the type suggested by Gagné[8] in the AAAS curriculum *Science—A Process Approach*. The treatment group viewing a video-tape model asking the desired types of questions generated a significantly greater frequency of these questions than did a control group.

Feedback is an equally well-documented means of influencing behavior. McDonald and Allen,[9] in a series of studies done with secondary teacher trainees, have found that reinforcement and discrimination training

[1] Albert Bandura and R. Walters. *Social Learning and Personality Development*. Chicago: Holt, Rinehart & Winston, Inc., 1963.

[2] Albert Bandura. "Social Learning Through Imitation." In: M. R. Jones, editor. *Nebraska Symposium on Motivation*. Lincoln: University of Nebraska Press, 1962. pp. 11-269.

[3] Albert Bandura and F. J. McDonald. "The Influence of Social Reinforcement and the Behavior of Models in Shaping Children's Moral Judgments." *Journal of Abnormal and Social Psychology* 67: 274-81; 1963.

[4] A. Bandura, D. Ross, and S. Ross. "Imitation of Film-Mediated Aggressive Models." *Journal of Abnormal and Social Psychology* 6: 3-11; 1963.

[5] Mary Lou Koran. "The Effects of Individual Differences on Observational Learning in the Acquisition of a Teaching Skill." A paper presented to the American Educational Research Association, Los Angeles, February 1969.

[6] John J. Koran, Jr. "The Relative Effects of Classroom Instruction and Subsequent Observational Learning on the Acquisition of Questioning Behavior by Preservice Elementary Science Teachers." Summary of Research #1, Mimeographed Paper, The Science Education Center, University of Texas at Austin, 1968.

[7] Benjamin S. Bloom. *Taxonomy of Educational Objectives; Handbook I, Cognitive Domain*. New York: Longmans, Green & Co., Inc., 1956.

[8] Robert M. Gagné. "The Psychological Basis of *Science—A Process Approach*." Washington, D.C.: American Association for the Advancement of Science, 1965.

[9] F. J. McDonald and D. W. Allen. "Training Effects of Feedback and Modeling Procedures on Teacher Performance." USOE, 6-10-078. Stanford University: School of Education, 1967.

administered by the experimenter were effective methods of producing behavior changes in teachers (video-tape playbacks of teachers' performance were used while reinforcing). A similar study by Claus [10] with elementary teachers tended to confirm the McDonald-Allen results but with a different type of sample (elementary teachers instead of secondary) and a different dependent variable (questioning behavior instead of verbal and nonverbal reinforcers).

Informal results of supervisor attempts to influence teacher behavior during the microteaching clinic at Stanford University (Summer 1968) by using video-tape models, feedback, and reinforcement as a part of the supervisor's strategies have also appeared to produce change in teacher behavior. These studies contribute to a sizable body of literature which suggests specific strategies that may be of practical value to both the school supervisor and the professor or supervisor in teacher education.

A Practical Application

The implication of the above line of research, and of the methods which were used, for supervision in the schools is great. First, it is essential that a supervisor have clearly in mind the behavior he wishes to influence so that his feedback can be specific and so that the supervisee will know what or how to change as a result of supervision. The component parts of the behavior must be clearly communicated to the supervisee. This can be done by showing the supervisee a video tape which highlights the desired behavior in the context of a lesson or by presenting a written description of the behavior to the trainee.

Both the video-tape model and the written description of a behavior have been found to be effective in producing initial acquisition of certain behaviors. Once the trainee has been exposed to the behavior by one of the above methods and has had time to acquire the behavior, an opportunity to use the behavior in the classroom should be provided.

In university teacher education situations "microteaching" provides an excellent context in which the trainee can practice. After a microteaching session, the supervisor can provide specific feedback regarding the extent to which the skill has been acquired as well as reinforcement for correct responses. Suppose that the skill to be acquired by elementary teachers is that of asking observation and classification questions. The supervisor would first have to specify clearly the components of the behavior:

ASKING OBSERVATION-CLASSIFICATION QUESTIONS

Definition of *Observation Questions:* Questions which elicit from students observations when one or more physical characteristics of the objects observed vary as detectable by sight, touch, taste, hearing, or smell.

Teacher asks the following types of questions:

1. Questions requiring students to identify objects according to color

2. Questions requiring students to identify objects according to shape

3. Questions requiring students to identify objects according to size

4. Questions requiring students to identify objects according to texture

5. Questions requiring students to identify objects according to taste

6. Questions requiring students to identify objects according to smell.

Definition of *Classification Questions:* Questions which elicit from students categorization behavior of objects by single or multiple dimensions such as color, shape, size, texture, taste, similarities, or differences.

---

[10] Karen Claus. "The Effects of Cueing During Modeling Procedures on the Learning of a Teaching Skill." Stanford: Stanford Center for Research and Development in Teaching, 1968.

Teacher asks the following types of questions:

1. Questions requiring students to place objects into student-devised groups or categories

2. Questions requiring students to identify whether objects are the same or different

3. Questions requiring students to place objects into teacher-stated categories.

The supervisory sequence which would employ the preceding performance specification in a microteaching situation is shown in Figure 1.

In the schools an administrator might release beginning teachers for short periods of time to observe a veteran teacher who does or says a specific thing well. If this is done, it is vital that the "model" be told what behavior to perform and how to perform it, and the observer be told what to look for. Again, the specification of the behavior is critical and the provision of a written or video-tape model for the live model to imitate is essential.

Once the supervisee is aware of the behaviors to be acquired and has observed these behaviors on video tape or in person, a practice session should occur. This can take place in the classroom and might be thought of as being equivalent to "microteaching." At the end of a practice session the trainee would receive specific feedback and reinforcement contingent on the approximation of the skills in the performance specification.

The model for this sequence would be similar to that previously described except that the "microteaching" would be "macroteaching" in the classroom, and the model could very well be a colleague "live" in the schools, or a video-tape or written model of this colleague.

Either of the approaches described can be recorded on video or audio tape to help in recalling specific situations about which to provide the teacher with feedback. Regardless of the setting and technology, the supervisor's job is to use feedback and reinforcement to shape the trainee's behaviors to approximate a specific performance standard. During supervisory sessions of this type, a useful approach is to focus on one or two behaviors, at the most, and to provide specific information (feedback) to the trainee about these.

Supervisor	Microteaching-Supervisory Context	Trainee
1. Introduction of the skill	Introduction of behavior by video-tape model or written model	1. Acquisition
2. Observation of performance	Microteaching I	2. Practice
3. Provision of feedback, reinforcement discrimination training	Supervision I	3. Receive feedback, reinforcement
4. Help in planning, observation of performance	Microteaching II	4. Replan, practice
5. Provision of feedback, reinforcement discrimination training	Supervision II	5. Receive feedback, reinforcement

Figure 1. Supervisory Sequence in a Microteaching Situation

When supervising in the schools, frequent visits of short duration by the supervisor rather than long visits spaced some distance apart seem to be satisfactory. In this regard the supervisor may observe in school for 10-15 minutes at a time or have the trainee video- or audiotape a specific performance for short supervisory sessions after school.

Once a behavior has been acquired and demonstrated by the supervisee to an acceptable level of proficiency, it is time to introduce another behavior. The same procedure may be used over again depending on the facilities and equipment available. As the trainee's behavior repertoire begins to show signs of expanding, supervisory strategies should be used, and conditions arranged so that the supervisee begins to see that certain behaviors can be arranged in chains in order to facilitate retention of older behaviors and a flexibility of the response repertoire in actual instructional situations.

In conclusion, the success of the supervisor can only be measured directly by the magnitude of change, in clearly specified behaviors, that he produces in the supervisee. Indirect measures of supervisory effectiveness are the extent to which the students of a supervisee do or say things differently, in a desirable direction, as a result of the teacher's acquiring and using specific skills.

Contemporary research shows that teacher behavior can indeed be influenced under both laboratory and school conditions. Supervisors must clearly define what they want teachers to do or say differently in order to know what to provide feedback on, and reinforcement for, during a supervisory session.

The instructional design which the supervisor employs utilizes social learning theory in the form of video- or audio-taped, written, or live modeling procedures to introduce behaviors to the trainee for acquisition; and operant conditioning techniques, feedback, and reinforcement to secure performance of the behaviors. Finally, the use of performance specifications of the type described permit the supervisor to do a pre- and post-type of analysis of a teacher's performance to provide information about his own supervisory behavior and, of course, information about the teacher's growth.

The methods discussed and the literature described suggest ways and means of going about supervision for behavior change and also a theoretical foundation for these supervisory strategies. These proposals should be considered hypotheses rather than solutions and should be tested under a variety of conditions and with a multitude of skills and trainee populations, with the final hope that they will contribute to the emergence of a theory of supervision.

PART IV

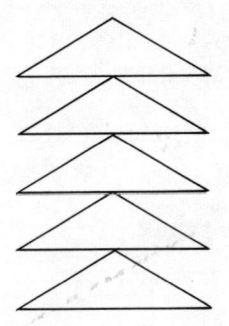

The Supervisor at Work

Coordinating a Supervisory Program

MURIEL CROSBY

WHEN we speak of organizing a complete supervisory program we must ask ourselves first, "What are we organizing for?" Then we must ask, "What is a complete supervisory program?"

It is asserted that the chief function of supervision is to make it possible to help teachers help themselves become more skilled in the processes of fostering children's learning. To achieve this goal, teachers need to look at children with new and fresh vision, to become like the poet Elizabeth Barrett Browning defines in her lines:

> The poet has the child's sight in his breast
> And sees all new.
> What oftenest he has viewed,
> He views with the first glory.

To the extent that this goal is achieved, a school or school system may determine the "completeness" of its supervisory program.

In helping teachers help themselves, supervisors seek ways and means to make it possible for teachers to discover for themselves what "works" for them, ways that successfully interpret their knowledge of children and the learning process in creating a climate in school which encourages children's self-discovery, experimentation, interpretation of experience, and realization that learning in school can be dynamic and exciting because it has use value in living.

When we begin to plan to coordinate the work of the staff toward the achievement of a complete supervisory program, we are reaching toward certain goals. Our objective is to try to help each staff member to discover the challenge of continuously seeking ways of improving the quality of learning, and of finding and using the opportunities available for stimulating children's motivation to learn.

All staff members who have a responsibility for teaching and learning have equally significant roles to play. Teachers, administrators, supervisors, and other service personnel are peers in the fulfillment of the learning process. A breakdown in the functioning of any member of the team presents blocks and frustrations which inhibit the full fruition of the exciting adventure of teaching and learning.

Signs of the Times

Today, more than ever, the schools are challenged by children's out-of-school learning. A single illustration may serve to emphasize this challenge. During a recent airflight, the writer had a four-hour stopover at a large modern airport in the South. The comfortable waiting room was filled with travelers waiting out a sudden storm. Most were deeply buried in newspapers or paperbacks.

In a far corner of the waiting room three boys, approximately twelve, ten, and "going on seven," were quietly seated. On the wall, over their heads, was a "homemade" sign:

Muriel Crosby, Consultant on Urban Education, Wilmington, Delaware. In 1961, Associate Superintendent of Educational Programs, Wilmington Public Schools, Wilmington, Delaware

SHOE	SHIN
STAND	
.15¢	.15¢

After a brief huddle the youngest boy was sent around the room to recruit customers. All he approached refused the service, many with warm smiles but a few "growlingly."

Here was a prime learning situation. What were the boys learning?

1. They apparently had learned appropriate behavior for a waiting room situation—orderliness, respect for the comfort of others, no "horseplay."

2. They were learning the psychology of "selling." No potential customers would be hardy enough to take a pair of newly shined shoes on an airfield that had turned into a stormy lake.

3. They were learning what makes people tick and how they responded differently on a face to face basis. All potential customers refused the service. The boys were learning variety in rejection, however. Most rejections were of the idea, not of the boys. But some rejections were of both. Human relations are learned and these boys were learning.

What of the schools these boys attend, the schools that can only share in the education of boys who already feel at home in the dynamic environment of a modern airport?

1. Were these boys of whom teachers sometimes say, "They are not interested in anything"; "My boys have no motivation to learn"?

2. Were these boys who all too often must accept the conforming, restrictive quiet of too many classrooms in place of the exciting world of reality?

3. Did these boys attend schools in which teachers are told by administrators and supervisors that they *must* use prescribed texts; they *must* cover a certain amount of content in each subject; they *must* use common methods of teaching?

4. Did these boys have teachers who refused to accept the freedom to teach in unique ways, to draw upon many resources for learning, to create curricula with children which are appropriate for them, because the plodding of well-established, known paths is less demanding?

Today, more than ever, the conception of supervision as a service function demands administrators who fulfill their role of leadership by working with the staff, not for the staff. It demands supervisors and other service personnel who render service of leadership, provide spurs to teachers' self-direction, and share in the solution of problems in learning. It demands teachers whose conception of themselves is that of professional peers who find the fruition of their capabilities through working cooperatively with other staff members in the most exciting adventure of learning.

Where this conception of supervision, and of the functions of various staff members in implementing it, prevails, administration as the coordinating medium becomes a potent force. Some examples of administration at work in its function of coordinating supervision may be helpful.

An Administrator Reports

Two problems face central administrators whose pressure of duties often blocks close contacts with the staff. One of these problems centers in communication and the other in establishing between the staff and the central administration a base for professional relationships. Such a base must foster recognition of professional peer status among members of a staff carrying different primary responsibilities, teaching, administration, supervision, or other functions of education.

In one school system in a city of some 100,000 population, the director of elementary education was concerned with these problems. Previous experiences had convinced the director that teachers want to be informed, that they need to know factors underlying administrative decisions, that they want to have a part in decision making and that cooperative decision making demands knowledge of pertinent facts.

One year the director initiated a series of monthly "Reports to the Staff," a two or three page mimeographed bulletin, a copy of which was distributed to each staff member. There was no attempt to "pattern" these reports either in content or form. The primary focus was on establishing an informal style in reporting events or giving information similar to that found in correspondence between professional friends.

The first of these reports contained interesting information related to the opening of school, why some classes were so large and what was being done about it. It commented on current pressures on kindergarten teachers for formalizing kindergarten education and suggested several current magazine articles to fortify kindergarten teachers and principals in resisting unwise demands. It reprinted a choice "story" provided by a local kindergarten teacher in winning the support of a questioning parent. And, finally, it informed the staff of the recognition won by some of the curriculum bulletins produced by the staff.

Subsequent reports dealt with similar current interests of the staff. Often they carried items of encouragement, particularly during times of the school year when the going was rough. The first tangible bit of evidence that the reports were being read and were of value came one cold February day when the director and a beginning teacher happened to meet. The teacher's first impulsive words were, "How did you know that *I* was so discouraged? It helped a lot to know I was not alone."

But one, or even a dozen, positive reactions do not make a base for a generalization. And so the director solicited anonymous evaluations of the "Reports to the Staff." Forty-five percent of the staff replied and the responses were enthusiastic. This group made 52 suggestions for the content of future reports, with priorities being given to items of "current news in education, specific information about local schools, help for evaluating children's growth and development, for self-evaluation by teachers, and community developments having implications for the schools."

Other Coordinating Activities

The thumbnail sketches that follow may reveal myriad opportunities for administrators and supervisors who are committed to a supervisory program rooted in cooperative action:

1. When teachers expressed concern about the availability of needed books for use in a project on human relations education, the director, the supervisor of libraries, and the general supervisors joined forces to produce monthly bulletins on "Growing Up with Books." These bulletins provided annotated references related to human relations concepts which were obtainable from the schools' well stocked children's libraries. One issue was contributed by the elementary librarians and another by one elementary librarian who had become interested enough to explore his school's library more comprehensively than had been done in the initial bulletins.

2. Each spring, the teachers of one school system elect faculty representatives from each school to meet with the director and supervisors as a planning committee for a Fall Workshop. Representatives discuss possible themes, activities, consultants, and participants with individual faculties. They then come to the first committee meeting fully prepared to present the needs and recommendations of the faculties. This is

an important matter to faculties, for each year the central, city-wide Fall Workshop establishes the base for further exploration by individual school workshops under the leadership of principals during the week prior to the official opening of schools. After all recommendations are considered by the planning committee, possible action is agreed upon and the representatives report to their faculties, seeking consensus and additional suggestions and assistance in developing the workshop. By the close of school or shortly thereafter, principals inform their staffs of the final program developed for the city-wide workshop and plan with faculty committees for the building workshops which follow. There are no surprises and no guesswork. Faculties are ready to roll from the moment a new school year starts.

3. The director of elementary education in one city school system believes there is no more justification for central administration to hide behind the demands of business management than there is for a principal to retire to the office with busy work which keeps him from fulfilling his job as professional leader in creating educational programs of merit.

When circumstances reveal a demand for professional help which the director is capable of giving, he frequently provides this through bulletins distributed to the staff. Among the bulletins was a series on problems in the teaching of reading. The staff rated this series the single most valuable supervisory service rendered during the year. This reaction was obtained through an anonymous survey of teachers' opinions regarding problems in the teaching of reading and recommended ways of meeting the problems.

In planning for a complete supervisory program, there is no more critical issue than the role of the central administrator. In an entirely different context, Benjamin Spock has expressed a hazard that administrators may take to heart, when he says that creeping behind a technique or professional attitude may lead to the danger of trying to keep people away from us in order to manage them in a more arms-length kind of way.

Blocks and dodges in relationships among administrators, supervisors, and teachers have no place in good supervision. Only a team, working together, can develop a supervisory program. ☐

EL *19* (2): *107-10; November 1961*
© 1961 ASCD

The Supervisor Reports

H. LEROY SELMEIER

LEADERSHIP is an ability which every supervisor must possess in some degree that is satisfying to the school organization with which he is affiliated. The communicating of information and a sense of direction is an essential characteristic of his job. Without talent in communication his opportunities for service will recede rapidly.

Clyde Hill once described a leader as one who is so close to the crowd that they

H. Leroy Selmeier, Administrative Assistant, The Christian Science Publishing Society, Boston, Massachusetts. In 1961, Assistant Superintendent for Instruction, Grosse Pointe Public School System, Grosse Pointe, Michigan

are forever seeming to step on his heels, yet never so far ahead that they will appear to be throwing rocks at him. A good supervisor is thus the communicator who maintains a close relationship with both his professional associates and the citizen interests of his community. His talents must be directed to the development and expansion of their understandings of the curriculum.

The personal status of the good supervisor is never a matter of primary concern. His bulletins, publications, and public appearances are only aspects of his work as a communicator. He is concerned that his reporting not only relates the facts accurately, but also interprets the trends. Moreover he perceives that the full responsibilities of his role involve a reporting to the general public of his school area even as it does to his immediate professional associates.

Most school systems have an administrative council or staff meeting at which the director of instruction may regularly report on curricular changes which have occurred. Such meetings frequently involve a personal type of reporting that is often lacking in the larger communities that must necessarily rely on bulletins of notes and special items.

In many school systems in which a curriculum council is still expanding its area of usefulness, the annual reports of a director of instruction or supervision in some special area may become one of the major vehicles for passing along information. The interchange of these reports among other members of the staff is often one of the most neglected opportunities for informed communication. Smaller communities wherein there is less of a formal organization have often given a specific period of time in their preschool and post-school workshops to the reporting on curricular developments under way in that community. It is now the supervisor's responsibility to provide the time and the occasion for the exchange of information lest those at home be among the last to learn what is so widely appreciated.

Reporting

Effective reporting requires interpretation rather than a mere relating of the assembled facts. Moreover frank discussion is often necessary before firm and final conclusions are possible. An excellent practice has developed in the Dearborn schools in what has been called the Citizens Advisory Committee. Meeting informally with the superintendent and his staff approximately once each month, the group provides ready reactions to programs as they are developing. In this way a unified arts program and also a continual progress plan were evolved satisfactorily on the basis of understandings developed through the reports and interpretations given by the supervisory staff.

Such developments only come as a supervisor maintains himself as a leader among his peers. Appropriate interaction then comes most often through indirect rather than direct supervisory activity. Citizen committees and neighborhood discussion groups for the public, and administrative or teacher group meetings for staff discussions, become not so much the telling off of some lesser person but rather the occasion for a proper reception and fertilization of the instructional leader's ideas.

However great they may be, these ideas will seem impoverished unless they are assimilated by the supervisor's professional associates and the general public. Even as good teachers, the effective director of instruction must recognize how people learn and so apply these principles to the learning situation which he is directing.

For example, teachers place great importance on the matter of readiness. Where readiness is seemingly absent, the professional educator either waits for the necessary maturity or he strives to build a satisfactory readiness. The instructional leader can and should use this readiness in working with his special groups. Certainly the remarks made to parents at kindergarten round-ups are made with a view to the readiness which these parents and their offspring have for the forthcoming educational experience. Moreover such meetings, as well as those conferences of parents and teachers which are spreading as a more acceptable form of exchanging information on pupil progress, can be used to develop a citizen interest and readiness for new curricular patterns.

Discovery

Consistent also with the knowledge of the learning process which as a good teacher he would use in the classroom, the supervisor ought to use the discovery principle in unrolling curriculum developments with his associates. The excitement of which Jerome S. Bruner speaks in *The Process of Education*[1] is something for all of us as teachers even as it is for our boys and girls in science, mathematics, and history. The supervisor's role ought no more to be confined to telling than that of the classroom teacher is limited to listening. As an in-instructional leader he may help his associates to learn best by his guidance and direction in which the discovery and the decision making are actually functions of the staff.

Local curriculum developments may thus come to a school system through discussion and analysis rather than by administrative blueprint and edict. Jefferson County (Kentucky) schools thus evolved their own concept of an ungraded school. This grew out of staff discussions of various problems and concerns that led to an investigation of various primary or nongraded schemes. This was a reversal of the operation by administrative decree or the traditional approach of imitating the curriculum developments of others simply because they are new and different.

[1] Jerome Seymour Bruner. *The Process of Education*. Cambridge: Harvard University Press, 1960. pp. 20-22.

Moreover coming to a practice because they have discovered its value seems to cause many people to become most ardent missionaries for this practice. Some of the most devoted advocates of the self-contained classroom are those who feel that they discovered the practice and adopted it because they believed they recognized merit in it.

Another phase of the learning process which the supervisor should recognize in his reporting is the degree to which we all learn from differences. While one may like similarities for the security they bring, one seldom learns more by simply repeating what he has already discovered.

Thus a good supervisor will report developments that have many similarities to practices that are already being followed yet in which the differences will challenge one to evaluate his own thinking and time-honored decision.

Many good educators utilize this learning principle when talking with the parents of a special grade or classroom about the curricular practices in that area of common interest. Whether the major objective be the initiation of a new approach or the explanation to the parents of a well-accepted practice which they have misjudged from the limits of a memory as to what was one time considered best, similarities can establish only a favorable climate in which the real learning will come as new differences are apparent.

Audio-Visual Means

Again the supervisor needs to recognize that audio-visual devices can improve the speed and clarity of the reporting. A filmstrip or even a set of kodachrome slides, accompanied by a tape recording or by a human interpreter, can help the parent of a prospective kindergartner to have a keener appreciation of the forthcoming experience which his child is to have.

In Grosse Pointe a concern for improving the use of classroom bulletin boards saw little progress result from the proposals of a committee of administrators. However, when an audio-visual specialist started making a collection of the pictures of the bulletin boards that were better than average, many teachers began to be interested. Then, when the art consultant recorded on tape an explanation of the principles that made some bulletin boards seem better than others, almost all teachers became enthusiastic over a period of time for the improvement of bulletin boards. The newer audio-visual techniques had made converts where staff meetings and mimeographed bulletins had had no effect.

Television and radio are also good means for reporting developments both to the staff and to the community. Admittedly the public has come to expect such usage as being for the purpose of winning an election or a bond issue. Yet these means can also be effective in highlighting curricular developments.

Both South Redford and Dearborn have had experience in producing a television program and then using the kinescope thereof for PTA meetings or discussion groups among the professional staff. For example, a "kine" on how teachers can cooperate and work together has greatly interested the parents of the Stout Junior High and has also been effective with sectional meetings of the staff throughout the community.

However, no principle or device for learning is more important than the involvement of the learner himself. Being consulted about projected practices, knowing that he is a participant in the evolution of a decision, and having some practical sharing in any curricular decision are all procedures which the supervisor should encourage among his co-workers. They make for a receptive partnership in the reporting to his associates.

A story has been told about a nationally known superintendent in an extremely fortunate Midwestern community of several decades ago. A successive series of test results showed his pupils to be decidedly below national norms in spelling. While other evidence indicated that a somewhat more optimum learning situation existed in almost all other respects, the superintendent, nevertheless, decided to do something about the situation. He was a reputable scholar and writer. Therefore, he reasoned, if he only worked out a good spelling program and reported it to the staff, better spelling proficiency ought to follow.

So he studied and wrote. He then reported his findings to the staff. Appreciating his worth as a supervisor, the staff tried to follow his outlines. Yet when spelling was again tested, the results were distinctly below the expectations. Then the teachers asked permission to work out their own approaches on the spelling problem. Realizing that almost any possibility might bring some improvement over the previous situation, the superintendent granted permission. To his amazement, the test results of the next year showed, for the first time in several seasons, the community above the national norm.

Certainly it was not that the teachers had more know-how than did this supervising superintendent. The failure was rather due to the lack of understanding and awareness in a program that was not their own. As they felt a personal involvement in the creation of the lesson design, their perception of learning needs so improved that the evidence of pupil learning climbed to a more satisfactory level.

Similarly, many supervisors have learned that the instructional leader cannot expect that his units will have the same effect on the staff as do those involving representative staff members. Yet such involvement does not absolve the supervisor of the responsibilities of leadership. Creating a sense of direction, involving personnel who are ready to evaluate new ideas, interpreting issues and locating satisfactory assisting personnel are all a part of the supervisor's role. Only when some of those who were formerly critical now turn to praise the new developments can the director of instruction realize how much progress has been made.

The supervisor's role as a reporter of curricular developments is one in which he must think and act with imagination and creativity as opposed to routine and assignment. He needs to utilize the learnings of others rather than anticipate that he may know-it-all himself. As a reporter of curricular developments he views his role as a service to his professional associates, to the citizens of his community, and, above all else, to the boys and girls enrolled in the local schools. ☐

Improving the Skills of Teaching

JOHN PRATER

TEACHING can be improved by an efficient program of supervision. Because they are increasingly aware of this, boards of education and superintendents are appointing directors, special subject supervisors, and consultants to new positions in their school systems. Principals are being encouraged more and more to make improvement of instruction their first responsibility.

The position of this article is that effective supervision is the result of a wise combination of four factors. These factors are:

1. The kind of person who serves as the supervisor

2. The school environment relating to supervision

3. The technical know-how of the supervisor

4. The quality of planning carried on for effective supervision.

The Kind of Person

The most important of these factors is the first. There are at least four characteristics which a good supervisor possesses, and there may be others. Unless the supervisor has a *warmth of personality* that wins teachers, he will find it difficult to establish the rapport that breaks down status barriers and enables the teacher and supervisor to attack instructional problems cooperatively. The good supervisor possesses *ability to communicate* professionally with individual teachers and groups of teachers. He has an *interest in research* and engages in "action type" research activities within his school system and in cooperation with other systems. Finally, the supervisor who leads teachers in the task of improving their own skills must have the *know-how* that includes principles of curriculum development, familiarity

John Prater, Superintendent, Public Schools of District 89, Maywood, Illinois

with supervisory techniques, devices and instruments, and a knowledge of what constitutes good teaching.

The School Environment

The responsibility for creating a positive environment for supervision lies mainly with the administrative leaders of the school system. They set the stage where the play takes place. They must be in accord with the play itself and indicate to the staff their support of it.

Many supervisors accept new positions wondering how strong and sincere the administrative support of the supervisory program will be. It does not take long to find this out. However, if administrators and supervisors work together to develop purposes and plans, there should be no misunderstanding of the role that each group must play to implement them.

The supervisor soon discovers what the teaching staff thinks of supervision. The good supervisor hopes that teachers have been encouraged to accept the attack upon instructional problems as a joint enterprise by the whole educational family. If this attitude exists, supervision becomes something done *with* teachers and not *to* them.

Teachers and supervisors do not always agree that certain services are the most valuable for improving instruction. A recent survey among hundreds of teachers and supervisors by the Illinois ASCD indicates that this is so. There were marked differences of opinion, too, between teachers of different grade levels. This suggests that there is a need for teachers and supervisors to discuss frankly what services are needed and how these can be provided.

The school environment ought to favor the problem solving approach to the study of instructional problems by groups and individual teachers. Are groups allowed to do research which leads to decisions about instructional changes? Are individual teachers encouraged to experiment with different techniques of teaching to test the advantage of one over another?

The professional climate that exists in a school or school system determines how well a good supervisor can serve teachers. The interplay of teachers, supervisors, and administrators is a key condition of a good supervisory program.

The time comes when the supervisor must work with teachers and choose wisely those devices which he believes will help teachers to improve instruction. The supervisor must use his knowledge about each teacher and his understanding of teachers as professional people if he is to be effective. What are some of the means for helping teachers?

Classroom Visits

Classroom visits by the supervisor are not universally popular with teachers. They are necessary, however, as a supervisory technique, and no supervisor can avoid them.

When he visits a classroom, the supervisor observes learning as it happens. He sees the teacher as an active participant in the learning process. By careful analysis of what is happening, he gathers ideas for working with the teacher to improve instruction.

The supervisor should be free to visit a teacher at any time when school is in session. The argument that supervisors should be either on a "call" basis or a scheduled program should not be allowed. If the proper rapport exists, no strain is felt by the teacher or the supervisor whenever a visit is made.

Teachers, however, should never be in doubt as to the purpose of a visit. A conference before the visit can pave the way for the observation. A follow-up conference gives the opportunity to discuss what happened, to analyze reasons for pupil reactions and behavior, and to plan for changes in the techniques of instruction.

Frequent classroom visits to teachers new to the school system or new to the profession help the teachers get off to a good start, which is a real boost toward success. Knowing that the supervisor is willing and ready to help eases the new teacher's natural concern about failure. A teacher wants to know what is expected of him, and he has a right to know how well others think he is doing. Being aware that others care about his service may make the difference between a good teacher and a mediocre one.

Teaching Demonstration

The teaching demonstration is another device that lacks the universal support of teachers. Good teachers often resist giving demonstrations because they fear the criticism of their co-workers. They resent the accusation that they are showing off.

Yet, the teaching demonstration is an excellent device to illustrate specific teaching skills. It can focus attention upon only one skill by excluding other extraneous features of the classroom program.

Suppose the supervisor observes that poetry is not well taught in the literature program of the upper grades. An excellent teacher can demonstrate several valuable ideas and techniques for other teachers. These take-home suggestions soon become the practice in many classrooms.

Teaching demonstrations are more meaningful if they are preceded by briefing sessions with the observers. The purposes of the presentation should be clear. When the demonstration is over, the observers should exchange views with the teacher and the supervisor. Again, the cooperative approach toward seeking improved teaching skills becomes invaluable.

The planned observation of a teacher in action by another is an effective device for helping a person with a specific teaching problem. It is a type of demonstration that is tailored for one teacher.

Suppose the intermediate grade teacher has difficulty with the management of committees in a social studies project. After a discussion with the teacher about the make-up, organization, and purpose of committee work, the supervisor may arrange a visit with another teacher in the school system.

The demonstrating teacher must know what he is to illustrate, and the visiting teacher must know what to look for.

After the lesson has been taught, there should be a careful follow-up. The follow-up may be a discussion between the two teachers, a discussion between the supervisor and the teacher, and a try-out of the techniques with the visiting teacher's own class. The latter should be done under the watchful eye of the supervisor.

The advantage of this technique is that each skill can be more or less pin-pointed for a teacher. The demonstration in a classroom during a regular session proves to him that the techniques or skills in question do work.

The intervisit requires the release of the teacher from his classroom during the time of the observation. Many schools consider the cost of a substitute a wise investment in good instruction. In some cases other teachers in a building care for a class while the teacher is away.

Conference

Conferences are often held in conjunction with other supervisory services. They enable the supervisor to discuss classroom visits, to evaluate a teaching project, to plan a unit, to explain school routine, and to suggest resources for teaching.

Since the conference usually involves

only the supervisor and the teacher, this is the best time to discuss matters that are confidential. There should be a mutual understanding that neither will discuss the conferences with another person. Both the supervisor and the teacher must feel free to talk frankly with each other.

Because personal views are exchanged in the conferences, the teacher can be made to feel that his own integrity as a professional worker is not in jeopardy. He may be reassured of his own personal worth to the school system. The conference is a means of inspiring the teacher to continue his professional growth and to reach for continued improvement of teaching skills.

Group Meetings

Although group meetings are not always popular with teachers, they are essential to the democratic process of administration and supervision. Through group meetings teachers are involved in decision making preceded by discussion, investigation, and research. Teachers should have a share of the responsibility for building philosophy, outlining curriculum objectives, and setting up instructional programs. Actually, the group meeting is a potential morale builder.

In general, group meetings are more meaningful when they are preceded by a bulletin. This bulletin should give an agenda and define the limits of the discussion.

The meeting itself should allow freedom for expression of ideas. The discussion must not stray from the agenda. If new problems are raised, they should be referred to another meeting. No meeting should close without nailing down the decisions or agreements reached by the group.

The workshop technique enables the supervisor to focus attention on problems of interest and concern to teachers. It may be a combination of group meetings and sessions which feature speakers.

Usually, the participants in a workshop meet together for making improvements in the instructional program. Teachers share ideas, examine teaching materials, set goals, and plan units of instruction. A group in one school system developed a unit for teaching about the United Nations. Another explored ways of developing international understandings.

Related to the workshop is a study program often called a "seminar." The theme of the seminar is usually one of the accepted problems or interests of the faculty.

A seminar held in one community dealt with the study of programs for fast-learning children. Time was used for reading, discussion of readings, listening to reports of participants, and listening to outside speakers. The seminar group prepared a short publication which was presented to all teachers and was used as the basis for discussions of the same topic at faculty meetings, workshops, and group meetings.

Participants in the seminar were given credit toward meeting the requirements of an in-service training credit program.

Bulletins

Bulletins serve many purposes. Since they often become substitutes for other supervisory devices in an attempt to save time, they are frequently misused. Like all other supervisory devices, when bulletins are overused they lose their effectiveness.

Many supervisors prepare bulletins to announce and lay the groundwork for group meetings, to summarize the discussion by a group, and to foster an exchange of ideas. They also use the bulletin to suggest references and resources for projects.

One of the most effective uses, however, is that of one supervisor who planned a series of professional bulletins on each of the following themes: "Using Manipulative Materials in Arithmetic"; "Developing

Committee Skills in the Social Studies"; "Strengthening Handwriting Skills in the Intermediate Grades."

Each bulletin was only two pages long and was illustrated. Concrete examples of ideas which teachers might use in their classrooms were given and a notebook was provided for filing bulletins for reference.

The Quality of Planning

At the beginning of this article four factors were enumerated which combine to make good supervision. The last of these must be dealt with briefly.

A strong supervisory program uses the over-all educational objectives of the school system to give direction and assurance to everything the supervisors do for teachers. A program that feels its way day by day, determining from one teacher to another what changes in instruction are needed, is a weak one.

A supervisor must decide each year what he believes he can accomplish and then determine how the job is to be done. His plan should be put into writing for constant reference and an evaluation at the end of the year. It should be formulated with the administrative heads of the school system.

Supervision Strengthens the Teacher

In summary, supervision strengthens the teacher. It has no other reason for existing. Whatever is done to improve supervisory services ought also to improve instruction for boys and girls.

It becomes imperative, therefore, that the choice of supervisory personnel must be carefully made. Supervisors should be professional persons with characteristics and skills that will enable them to weld teachers into working groups for solving problems. The school staff itself must understand and accept the significant role of the supervisors in the constant struggle to attain the educational objectives of the school system.

The New Teacher— and a New Kind of Supervision?

ALEXANDER FRAZIER

DOUBTLESS there are many ways in which we might approach the problem of understanding the new status of teachers and what this may mean for us. Yet if we are to come to a satisfying redefinition of our roles as supervisors and curriculum directors, then perhaps we need to imagine: (a) what the behavior of the teacher as a fully professional person ought to be; (b) what our concept of the curric-

Alexander Frazier, Professor of Education, The Ohio State University, Columbus, and President, ASCD. In 1963, Director, Center for School Experimentation, College of Education, The Ohio State University, Columbus

ulum should be to enable a teacher to function professionally; and (c) what our own program of activities, whatever we may come to call it, ought to encompass to support the development of the kind of curriculum that is enabling to the teacher and also will meet new public expectations.

How do we define a really professional teacher? We can easily enough reject as naive and anachronistic the popular notion that rarity is his chief characteristic.

Indeed, we know that the number of able teachers has greatly increased. Better methods of selection for teacher education programs, better programs of teacher education, more years of education prior to entry into service, more careful selection procedures for initial employment, more supervisory attention in the early years of service, extended programs of in-service education and more consultant help for experienced teachers at work, more opportunities for advanced training, and better salary schedules—all have combined to increase the supply of able teachers. Yet if we were to argue with the lay concept of the "master teacher," we would be missing the point that is to be gained from studying its significance. What it may project is a new level of independence for the teacher. The professional teacher, like any other professional person, is one who is free to test out new knowledge on his own terms and is supported in adding to this as he can. The question we may need to ask is whether we are operating in such way as to make it possible for the teacher to behave as a professional person.

The Professional Teacher

Before turning to this question, however, we may find it useful to spell out what the teacher as a professional person looks like. We may do this by describing the new teacher and for the sake of clearer definition contrasting this picture with the older but still surviving image of the teacher as something less than professional.

The professional teacher, then, is one who has worked through to his own satisfaction the purposes of education and in terms of his convictions has developed a thorough grasp of the understandings, skills, and attitudes that need to be learned by his students. Or, to use a more modern vocabulary, he has well in mind the frameworks or structures of concepts and generalizations that need to be mastered.

With such guidelines in mind, he is free to plan with and for learners from a great range of possible activities and resources. He is emancipated, so to speak, from dependence on any set sequence of learning opportunities or materials, being so well versed in aims that he can follow a great many roads to reach the same ends. He knows that the greatest importance attaches to "the relationship between the teacher, the subject, and the individual student at a given moment." [1]

Thus, he is truly a curriculum expert. The familiar definition of the curriculum that used to be parroted in the early 'fifties, that this was what transpired between teacher and pupils when the door into the classroom had been closed, becomes literally true for the fully professional teacher. His freedom to make choices is limited only by the presence of such agreements as are necessary to ensure order in a school system, the availability of resources, and the exercise of his own imagination.

When we contrast with this the older image of the teacher, we are helped to see how important it may be for us to come clean in our thinking. Just what are we now really willing to accept and support as appropriate behavior for the professional teacher?

In the past, the teacher was too often thought of as generally inadequate. He was

---

[1] *Labels and Fingerprints.* Washington, D.C.: Association for Supervision and Curriculum Development and others. n.d.; unpaged.

perceived as being possibly none too sharp to start with, poorly or at least incompletely trained, and likely to remain in need of continuous official attention. With such an outlook, leadership sometimes saw its task as being not only that of close supervision but the administrative provision of whatever might protect the learner from the teacher. We have had tremendous energies expended on designing perfect classrooms; room size and shape, lighting sources, and the kind of floor covering can become critical matters when the right answers are thought of as compensating for poor teachers. Prodigious efforts have also gone—and indeed are still going—into thinking up ingenious grouping and scheduling schemes that hopefully would make it possible for pupils to learn regardless of who their teacher might be. It is for such an anonymous incompetent that an uneasy superintendent may be led to exalt the textbook and the curriculum guide as freeing the teacher from "the unsuitable responsibility" of deciding what should be taught.[2] How much of our own time has been devoted to pursuit of the same end!

Our task, of course, is to bring our conception of the teacher into line with the facts of advancing education and competence. Then, again, we need to ask whether we ourselves are behaving in such way as to be enabling to the professional teacher. Dare we continue to spend our time chiefly in the induction and orientation of new teachers, the preparation of so-called curriculum guides, and the selection of instructional materials? Indeed, may not some of our present activities actually interfere with the fully professional functioning of teachers? Equally important, can we think through with our teacher colleagues the kind of roles and functions we ought to fulfill that will enable more of them to become independent in the ways we are defining?[3]

Concept of Curriculum

A second task closely allied to clarifying our thoughts on the professional teacher is to think through a modern concept of the curriculum. If the teacher is expected to behave as a professional person, what kind of curriculum does this take? Again, perhaps we can answer this question by contrasting a modern with an older picture.

Today we would probably choose to think of the organizing principles of the instructional program as being derived from larger wholes, from frameworks or structures of concepts and generalizations in relationship. The bases for such structures are several. Sometimes the framework will be derived from a discipline, as in current thinking about mathematics.[4] Sometimes it may come from seeking consistency or order of some kind in a skills area; thus, we speak of a framework of skill development in reading. Or it may come from an area such as social studies and be comprised of those common themes or concerns that would seem to provide a satisfactory way of bringing ideas from several fields into a manageable framework for use in the selection of content, activities, and resources.

In our concept of curriculum, we see this process of selection as mainly a task for the teacher. Many choices could be made that would lead to the desired outcome.

[2] Carl F. Hansen. *The Amidon Elementary School.* Englewood Cliffs, New Jersey: Prentice-Hall, Inc., 1962; p. 159.

[3] See Reba M. Burnham and Martha L. King. *Supervision in Action.* Washington, D.C.: Association for Supervision and Curriculum Development, 1961, pp. 33-64, for list of trends in supervision that would indicate a responsiveness to the new situation.

[4] Jerome S. Bruner. *The Process of Education.* Cambridge, Mass.: Belknap Press, Harvard University Press, 1960.

The teacher is supported in making the relevant curriculum and teaching decisions.

With such a concept of curriculum, learning is thought of as a search. The learner is supported in his discovery of what he has not learned yet, what he needs to learn as we see it and what he wants to learn as he sees it, and of course what he can learn. The emphasis is on the individual's search for sense, satisfaction, and significance, with the expectation that learners will emerge with common understandings but also with each knowing much more than everybody has to learn. A central purpose of education is to support the development of the power to think through learning by discovery.[5]

The growth of learning under such a concept of curriculum is seen as spiral as well as sequential. Many returns will be made to basic concepts and generalizations and the relationships among them as the learner matures. Children's questions are answered now, but mastery comes only with time and perhaps then is never fully achieved.

For contrast, we may recall the older concept of curriculum. Constructing the curriculum was thought of essentially as the careful grading of preselected items. Once so ordered, content was to be incorporated in perfected teaching materials that ideally would be practically self-teaching. Learning was conceived of as mastery of whatever was laid out to be learned. This was never very much, when thought of by the year, but was felt to be enough and was offered as identical for all. Pace was the only dimension of individual differences that really was built into learning.

[5] See Educational Policies Commission. *The Central Purpose of Education.* Washington, D.C.: National Education Association, 1961; also, Jerome S. Bruner. *On Knowing.* Cambridge, Mass.: Belknap Press, Harvard University Press, 1962, especially "The Act of Discovery," pp. 81-96.

Learning was aimed at mastery of the specified content. The practice was to take all learners through the same sequence of items or skills to be mastered with the apparent assumption that if we were successful teachers, everybody would finally come out in the end with the same knowledge of what had been taught. Of course, they never did; when we thought of it, we would concede that they did not all start in even and were widely different in need to know, will to learn, and capacity.

Our Own Program

Perhaps it is not necessary at this point to indicate that the older position on the nature of the curriculum does not fit with the picture of the professional teacher as it is developing—and that we may need to think most earnestly about whether we have kept not only our image of the teacher up to date but also our idea of the instructional program. Through our activities, are we working to make a modern curriculum that supports the teacher as a professional person, or are we living at least part of the time in an older world?

Thus our third task really can only be undertaken as we find that we have a consistent and defensible picture of the professional teacher and a concept of the curriculum that fits with the behavior of this new teacher. How we shall behave depends on what we see as needed for the support and further realization of the teacher in the suitably enriched teaching situation.

Rather than review once again the present uses of our time and whether they fit the current needs, it may be more helpful to project several possibly profitable lines for us to think more about.

One of these is certainly the extent and nature of the agreements we are going to need to maintain institutional unity. It is all very well, we may wish to say, to talk of the independence of the new teacher and the freedom he should and indeed must have to perform professionally. But we do live in an institution. We have many teachers in each grade or subject area. Families move from one part of town to another and in and out of the district. Moreover, we have local needs and wants for our students. And, of course, we must feel a continued responsibility for making sure somehow that what we feel needs to be learned has been taught.

Perhaps this last sentence contains the best clue to further study of the agreements we should work to reach. Too often perhaps we have begun with resources for teaching, textbooks, and the like, and then moved back to the kinds of activities we thought likely to be most successful and then further back yet to the kinds of learnings we were after—and finally, if not exhausted, we may have pushed back all the way to what our purposes were for learning certain concepts and generalizations through selected activities that would require use of the specified materials. What we may need to do is to spend more time reaching agreement on purposes and on content relevant to purposes and less on activities and materials.[6]

Such a possibility may lead us properly to a second area of activity. This is the whole field of keeping professional knowledge of content up to date. The subsidized studies are giving us examples of various ways to approach this question. However these differ, all of them put our own past in-service education efforts to shame in terms of time and resources invested in the reeducation of teachers.

[6] See Gordon Mackenzie for a useful discussion of "determinants" of the curriculum, "Sources and Process in Curriculum Development," especially pp. 78-80, in *What Are the Sources of the Curriculum?* Washington, D.C.: Association for Supervision and Curriculum Development, 1962.

A major problem we face as we attempt to make use of national major curriculum studies is to figure out ways of learning enough about the new programs so that we can evaluate them. This evaluation must be not merely from the standpoint that these studies may be in competition. More fundamentally we must be enabled to choose from various studies the content that we believe will be valuable if added to what we presently hold as being suitable for realizing our local purposes. We have many questions to ask in the reworking of our in-service education programs to bring them up to date.

A third area in which we may need to think through our activities can be related to the problem of learning new content. Many of us lived through the action research movement when we were, perhaps somewhat prematurely, being urged to engage in cooperative research projects aimed at thinking up and trying out new ideas. Now we are caught in the midst of tremendous activity of all kinds that demands some sort of testing out.

The professional does test out new knowledge, not all of it, of course, but whatever promises to help him perform better. We need to exercise our best judgment in choosing the most promising new proposals for testing.

Yet we need also to remember that the professional adds to knowledge as well as he can. The hope for the profession is that more of us will find ways of working with our teacher colleagues on ventures into the unknown that will result in new knowledge of a kind that can genuinely make a difference in the quality of the opportunities we provide for children and youth. These are times when we are confronted and perhaps plagued by many proposals that are plainly nonprofessional and some that are possibly injurious. Unless we can turn some of our own best energies to the search for better answers,[7] we may find ourselves forced by the pressure for improvement into changes that we know ahead of time will be worthless.

The sense of urgency about improvement in instruction comes to us from a broad public context of concern for making more of our capacity in every aspect of national life. As we have tried to respond to the new expectations, we have undergone significant shifts in leadership roles and functions.

The attempt here has been to examine the resulting new status of teachers as it may affect the behavior of supervisors and curriculum workers. It has been contended that the teacher needs to be perceived as newly independent; that the curriculum must be conceived of as open to as much choice-making among specific activities and materials as is possible in light of the institutional nature of the school; and that we must ourselves learn a good many new things if we are to support the teacher in such a setting.

The question may remain as to whether we really need to make the effort to reformulate our roles and functions. Perhaps if we just bide our time, teachers will fade out of the curriculum limelight and superintendents will return to building programs and budgets. It is possible, of course, that a relaxation in public expectations may come about, yet this seems unlikely.

What we might better anticipate is that since curriculum leadership is newly identified with the administrator and curriculum expertness with the teacher, lay forces may begin to wonder at the need for specialized supervisory and curricular services. Indeed, this kind of doubt has already been aroused in several communities and more than one state.

[7] Alexander Frazier. "Our Search for Better Answers." *Educational Leadership* 20: 453-58; April 1963.

Yet more worrisome to us may be that our ineffectiveness may cause the sources of outside curriculum leadership to gain greater influence than they now have. We must learn to relate internally so that we have an adequate local apparatus for assessment and adaptation of proposals from outside and hopefully for development of creative programs inside. Otherwise, we may find that the functions pertaining to curriculum construction and in-service education have been altogether assumed by others. One thoughtful surveyor of present practice concedes that "Properly led, a group of able teachers may design a new type of instructional program even while they operate the old one." However, as he further remarks, "the question is not whether it can happen" but "whether we should depend upon it." [8] His doubt leads Brickell to propose a state program of instructional innovation that would seem to most of us to promise interference with our proper functioning.

Perhaps even more challenging to us should be our own professional response to the pressures recently defined by the Association for Childhood Education International. Can we somehow reinstitute a concern for basic human values as integral to learning at every level and for every purpose? [9]

This would seem to be the ultimate challenge to our professional insight and ingenuity. The perspective we represent and our expertness in defining purpose and clarifying process are essential to the support of of the professional teacher in a soundly based, modern program of instruction. We must maintain both perspective and expertness. Can we do this? The only answer is that we must. ☐

[8] Henry M. Brickell. *Organizing New York State for Educational Change.* Albany: State Education Department, 1961. p. 65.

[9] *Basic Human Values for Childhood Education.* Washington, D.C.: Association for Childhood Education International, 1963.

Strategies for Instructional Leaders

FRANK GERHARDT

"STRATEGY" is a term that may be applied to a broad general approach designed to suggest specific techniques for expanding three basic areas: (a) involvement; (b) decision-making processes; and (c) political sophistication on the part of professional and lay communities.

"Instructional" is an elusive term applied broadly to the application of the findings of the social and behavioral sciences to changing behavior. Instruction of whom, why, and when suggests situational contexts for all who are involved. The contexts may be formal or informal.

"Leadership" is applied to the using of techniques in supporting a broad strategy. This strategy relates to purposeful involvement, to expanding a process whereby leadership is freed to be multi-dimensional as situational needs help determine, and to the bringing to a cognitive level of the political processes involved in who gets what, when, and where. In short, instructional leadership is simply a directed attempt to facilitate the broad strategy—a strategy which we feel to be basic to a cooperative community.

You will notice that neither the strategy nor the instructional leadership is confined to a formal classroom context; they are broadened to include the total system. The basic premise is that we must practice what we teach and this includes uncovering problems, encountering conflict, honoring the problems that promote dissent, and most of all, practicing the skills of inquiry, creativity, and human interaction within task-oriented activities. This is not easy.

The broad strategy for instructional leadership does not seem too startling. If we read the reports from public administration, business, and the social and behavioral sciences, we are attempting little more than to apply the common sense of a practitioner.

What *is* startling (at least for me) is the frequency with which acquaintances from neighboring communities offer unsolicited sympathy about the headlines our system receives in the urban newspapers: "You must be having all kinds of trouble, Frank. Too bad!" or "It's a shame when an educator has to spend his time in crisis management."

I find myself making rejoinders that attempt to reverse the flow of condolence. I sometimes suggest that they might be wise to look for "trouble" or some impending "crisis" in their own community.

A quick reference to some of our headlines might help:

NINTH-GRADE COURSES CAUSE HEIGHTS STIR

BREAK IS SEEN IN HEIGHTS SCHOOL CURRICULUM

HUMAN RELATIONS MEETINGS END IN SHOUT DOWN

TWO HUNDRED ATTEND DEBATE ON SCHOOL CURRICULUM

Frank Gerhardt, Superintendent, Cleveland Heights-University Heights Public Schools, Cleveland, Ohio

TEACHERS AND PARENTS HELP SELECT SCHOOL ADMINISTRATORS

TEACHERS TAKE "PROFESSIONAL STUDY DAY"—INSUFFICIENT LEVY

STUDENTS HELP IN ORIENTATION OF NEW TEACHERS

TEACHERS RECRUIT TEACHERS

FORTY-FOUR CURRICULUM TASK FORCE COMMITTEES FORMED BY TEACHERS

The headlines seem isolated from one another. Yet, as one local reporter perceptively wrote: "A quiet revolution is taking place in the Cleveland Heights-University Heights System." We would like to think that this quiet revolution is designed to move from a verbal allegiance to democratic processes to the *practice* of such processes in a public institution.

A Practical Revolution

The revolution is not one of ideas. Just practices. It is simply an attempt functionally to relate philosophy, policy, and practice—something which the school people say they have been trying for centuries to do in the classroom.

We have been verbally admonishing people (especially our students) to practice democracy. We urge such practice by insisting upon various kinds of incantations. Yet, when have we honestly encouraged teachers, parents, administrators, citizens, and students to get involved in influencing many of the decisions that affect their daily lives? For all our democratic ritual and rites, in most cases the public school has remained a bastion of autocratic practice.

It is not surprising that we have found that it is easier to preach than to practice. Not everyone is willing to make the transition. Not everyone is willing to relinquish a corporative posture for a cooperative one.

We have been fortunate in having at least a precedence for initiating this transition. Former Superintendent O. E. Hill received national recognition over a decade ago for establishing lay committees to study areas of school and community concerns and to make recommendations to the board of education. During the past few years lay committees have been influential in helping the school personnel address such things as: Data Processing, Outdoor Education, Educational TV, Foreign Language Teaching in Elementary Schools, Philosophy of Education, Public and Nonpublic School Relations, Technology Education, Buildings and Grounds, and Human Relations.

In a real sense, a lay committee is a study group. The group is comprised of citizens, teachers, students, and administrators. The citizens may or may not be "experts" in a particular area. The important aspect of these committees is not *only* the study and report made to the board of education. It is also an awareness of the complexities of working with publics and the interacting variables at work in board and administrative decisions. This awareness brings to committee members a greater sophistication as to what it means to be involved.

Reorganizing Leadership

Three years ago our staff raised some serious questions about the organization patterns used to bring about curriculum change. At this time the system had subject matter specialists (K-12) who assumed the responsibility for "leading" in curriculum development. Recognizing a greater extent of teacher competency than is commonly believed, the staff discussed type, kind, and direction of leadership.

How could the system organize in order to allow leadership to emerge from the teachers? How could the system organize in a way which honored the classroom teachers' responsibility *and* ability for instructional improvement? These questions were thrown open to the total faculty and from this came a staff-planned Instructional Leadership Program which brought focus to the processes of change rather than to set ends.

The teachers have been involved. Comparing the two instructional programs we find:

Under the Coordinator Program, the system had 12 steering committees involving 130 teachers—most of whom were appointed by the administration.

Under the Instructional Leadership Program, we had over 400 staff members *volunteering* to work on 44 Task Forces. The Task Force addresses a problem area defined by the staff.

We are not so naive as to assume that quantity implies quality. Yet, Task Force recommendations to the superintendent have indicated more depth and more positive alternatives than have previous attempts at change.

The community is involved through lay committees. The staff is involved through the Instructional Leadership Plan. What mechanics are provided for student involvement? At this point in our development we are still shaping an organization to include such activity. Last year we established a special committee of secondary students, administrators, parents, and teachers to explore this topic in depth. This exploration is not easy. As administrators and supervisors we know the suspicion by members of the teaching staff; the student's suspicion is even more intense.

After the third meeting of the committee, a ninth-grader asserted that his peers had warned him that the superintendent was "up to no good. . . . after all, superintendents are not interested in kids." After the fifth meeting, I was told that students had no need to meet with the superintendent periodically to influence decisions; but, if I had a need to meet with them, "they would be happy to come." Students serve on our Curriculum Advisory Council, several lay committees, and in the past supported a staff Philosophy of Guidance Committee.

Role of the Board

Many elements must be present to make a transition from a traditional school organization climate to one in which all persons associated with the school have opportunities to influence its goals and activities.

An enlightened board of education is essential. The board members must recognize that the democratic experiment and the experiment called "public education" require a sophistication about the processes involved. Board members, along with staff and the public, need to be reminded that, as a public institution becomes responsive to local desires and to the larger social issues, they, as public servants, can, and should, expect a number of complex and difficult issues to emerge for shared consideration by all groups concerned. Each member of these groups is tested as he creates his own views through confronting honest differences in an open and responsible way.

The board, through its superintendent, must assure the appointment of leaders comfortable in the use of the democratic processes. These individuals must be content to see their successes and accomplishments reflected in the successes of teachers and students.

This attitude requires a new breed of supervisor or administrator who does not strike a win-or-lose position when he serves as a learning facilitator for all groups in the school community. He must be willing to risk, to confront, and to trust.

In our district, a special training program has developed from isolated efforts we have made in social inquiry, creative behavior, and human interaction. The effort we made for our youngsters had significant implications for determining the strategy and techniques for encouraging and refining instructional leadership.

The implications became formalized within an adult training program called "Process Training."

Process Training assumes that leadership involves the interaction of: (a) the rational processes of inquiry; (b) the divergence and convergence of creative behavior; and (c) the host of human factors at work in any task-oriented group effort. With intensive, small-group sessions designed to bring to the cognitive level the skills *and* feelings involved in human effort—individual and collective—a greater sophistication is reached.

This greater sophistication is needed if the broad strategy is to become more effective. It is also needed if the system is consciously to strive toward creating a climate conducive to effective extensions of involvement in all types of decision making.

In recent years new curriculum programs and individuals associated with them (particularly administrators) have been attacked publicly by individual citizens. Such attacks, when combined with positive examples by individuals and groups in education, often are perceived as a form of "interference" with "professional" decisions.

Politics of Education

There have been times when supervisors, administrators, and teachers have demanded a professional "shield" from the board of education and from community groups—a shield which denies the need to share in the public arena. This demand sometimes takes the form of a bifurcation between that which is "political" and that which is "educational."

A substantial part of our broad strategy is to break down the myth that public education is apolitical. This is perhaps one of the most difficult problems we face. Political processes are often perceived as negative patterns of human behavior and the term "political" carries negative connotations.

Combine this denial of the politics of education with the mystical missionary zeal which some educators assume in a "win-lose" position in supporting the "rightness" of their cause and one can readily see the difficulties inherent in trying to evolve a democratic strategy that can prove effective.

Perhaps one of the most difficult tasks for the superintendent is to encourage his staff to "keep the faith" in our effort. There is far less insecurity when position and power are welded into an authoritative structure. A good number of personal needs are met through being an "expert." There is far less ambiguity, far less need to be willing to risk. The lack of political sophistication—on *all* of our parts—can be disheartening.

Yet, we must (and do) constantly ask ourselves: What is the alternative? As yet we have not found one that allows personal integrity, social ethics, and democratic processes to function in a public school. So, as Dewey suggested, we "do not shoot because targets exist, but set up targets in order that throwing and shooting may be more effective."

Ends and means constantly modify each other. As we sharpen our ways of addressing and hitting the targets, we may find the need for different kinds, types, and placements of targets.

Our strategy should allow for both ends and means in a process of change. If it does not, we are still hung up at the verbal level. And this is not enough. . . . ☐

Supervisory Visits Locate Teachers' Needs

George C. Kyte

THE supervisory visit requires more time than does any other technique of supervision. This is a finding of many research studies regarding the various supervisory functions and the proportion of time devoted to each one. How this type of supervisory visit is conducted has been well treated in the educational literature. With few exceptions, however, the purposes in using the technique have been based primarily on problems reported by teachers and other personnel. Consequently, symptoms and causes have been intermingled so that the actual needs of teachers usually have not been determined. Only carefully planned and conducted supervisory visits permit the discovery, analysis, and diagnosis of specific classroom problems and needs of teachers and pupils.

One of several research studies was designed to reveal detailed information regarding actual needs located through supervisory observations. Hence the data indicate conditions to be treated by supervisory officers through individual conferences, teachers' meetings, supervisory bulletins, and demonstration lessons planned to improve teaching and learning.

The investigation is based on (a) 30 pairs of tape-recorded classroom sessions by 30 teachers respectively, (b) the tape-recorded supervisory conference between each teacher and the supervisor, the observer of the first lesson in the pair, (c) the latter's own analysis of the help given the teacher, and (d) the critical comparisons of the two classroom sessions in each pair, made by at least ten other trained supervisors. The latter specialists made their evaluations independently of each other, using accurately reproduced transcripts of the two performances. These supervisors were not informed which lesson occurred first. The sets were stapled so that at least five supervisors read the first lesson first and at least five read the second lesson first, in order to control the effect of order of exposure.

In the records are evident excellent teaching, good but improvable teaching, and serious weaknesses. The present investigation is delimited primarily to the various discerned weaknesses requiring supervisory attention. The items included here are not characteristic of all teachers but occur so commonly or so detrimentally that they are noteworthy.

Planning

Inadequate planning by some teachers affected adversely the classroom performances. Evidence of inadequate preplanning included hazy purposes not grasped by children, insufficient preparation of the physical environment, incomplete provision for all

---

George C. Kyte, Professor of Education Emeritus, University of California, Berkeley

essential learning activities, and teacher's lack of fundamental knowledge needed in the teaching-learning activities. The other aspects of weaknesses in planning are presented under other headings because of the obviously direct reference to certain instructional defects.

Grouping

Undesirable conditions in the grouping of pupils occurred in arithmetic, reading, spelling, dramatic play, and social studies. The analyses of children's performances disclosed that individual abilities, needs, and interests were not being met efficiently. The range in some groups was too extensive; bright children were wasting time and weaker ones were obtaining too little help. Some classes were divided into groups which were so much alike that they might have been combined in one group to economize effective instruction.

Lack of needed flexibility in grouping also occurred. Sometimes the effect of grouping was seriously minimized by avoidable distractions caused by faulty seating arrangements and interruptions. Inadequate planning was evident in many weaknesses in grouping.

Audio-Visual Aids

Weaknesses involving audio-visual aids in areas of learning resulted from some teachers' insufficient preplanning or failure to utilize available aids. Opportunities were overlooked to strengthen learning by the use of the blackboard in teaching the Three R's especially. Reading and arithmetic charts were not obtained or prepared, were poorly designed or ineffectually used. Instructional aids included in textbooks or suggested in teachers' guides were either not used or misused.

Illustrations of these weaknesses are: failure to use pictures in readers, omission of essential steps in teaching arithmetic meaningfully, and omission of the use of available maps, globes, and other concrete materials. These weaknesses handicapped pupils' clarification of concepts and relationships. Some visual aids were incorrectly prepared or poorly arranged in the classroom for effective instructional use.

Children's Learning Activities

Both teacher planning and teacher guidance included weaknesses that affected adversely the pupils' learning activities. One quite common omission was that of differentiated activities necessary to meet the specific needs of certain types of children. The most marked kind was the failure to provide for the abilities and interests of bright pupils. Another weakness was the unsatisfactory conduct of class or group discussions. They failed to arouse children's interest or were not pursued until they fixed the desired learning.

Two specific mistakes of some teachers were evident in the discussions. The correct answer given by one child was accepted as being the answer all or most of the pupils would give. Conversely, the answer made by the group was accepted as the answer each child in it had given. These two weaknesses were especially noticeable in the teaching of reading, speech, and arithmetic, and occurred primarily with respect to items requiring individual mastery.

Integrative types of activities were overlooked or unskillfully used. Learning situations requiring dramatization or dramatic play were not included or were conducted ineffectually. Too commonly omitted were field trips which would have provided rich concrete experiences needed by children. Normal and natural units of work were not included or were only partially developed. For example, opportunities to correlate reading and social studies were overlooked, especially in the primary grades. The considerable reading materials and pictures on home and family in the readers were studied in relation to reading but without relating the content to social studies activities. Essential follow-up activities in the unit of work were not planned with the pupils or were inadequately planned.

Readily available out-of-school experiences for the children were not used or were misused. Common experiences in the home and community were not directly related to the vocabulary and concepts included in the children's learning activities. The failure to utilize extensively the pupils' meaningful experiences in arithmetic affected their learning. At times, also, the selection of arithmetical experiences involved inclusion of concepts and efforts at generalizations too advanced for the children's level of development. Analogous conditions were observed in the reading activities.

Teachers' ineffective questioning affected adversely children's learning. Questions improvised offhand were not thought-provoking or they served to evoke unnecessary recall of facts. Some teachers' questions interfered with the desired spontaneity of the pupils. One form of this weakness was questioning by the teacher which should have been done by the children. The natural flow of conversation was impeded or prevented.

Teachers' English Usage

The records of classroom performances disclosed some teachers' oral English requiring supervisory attention. Serious time-consuming and ineffectual speech habits were the most common ones. They included frequent repetitions or poor formulations of questions, directions, and answers. Many teachers also overworked certain words, phrases, or clauses so that the instructional value of these elements was minimized. Some teachers wasted considerable time by repeating habitually the pupils' answers, questions, and oral reading. These various weaknesses will be presented in detail in another article [1] and therefore are only mentioned in the present study.

A second research study includes a number of grammatical errors made by the teachers. Most common were incomplete sentence elements, repetition of words, incorrect omissions, lack of agreement between noun and verb or object, and the use of nouns and pronouns so that the intended reference was difficult to determine or was not discernible.

There are other detracting or poor usages in the English of some teachers requiring self-correction but often needing supervisory attention. The tape recordings disclosed prominently mispronunciations such as "cause" for "because," "gonna," "wanna," "gotta," and "sorta." Similarly detected were misuses of certain modifiers, as in "awfully good," "pretty good," "terrific answer," "how come," "got time," and the not interpretive "sort of" and "or anything."

Slang terms were used by some teachers, the most commonly noted expressions being "uh huh," "huh?" and "O. K." One teacher, for example, frequently used "uh huh" in answering her pupils' questions or approving their answers: "John, 'They have white tails.' Teacher, 'Uh huh.' Jane, 'They are mostly brown.' Teacher, 'Uh huh. Tommy?' Tommy, 'Aren't they lighter brown underneath?' Teacher, 'Yes, uh huh.' . . . Mary, 'But some have big black spots.' Teacher, 'Uh huh. Yes, uh huh. Those are all right answers.' " It was not surprising to hear her pupils using "uh huh" later in the lesson. Another teacher used the extraneous "O. K." 20 times in a ten-minute period with the result that the children were also saying it frequently.

[1] George C. Kyte. "Supervisory Visits to Classrooms Disclose Teachers' Incorrect Speech Habits." *The Educational Forum,* Vol. 25.

Some teachers formed the habit of interjecting "er," "ah," or "uh" very often in their questions, directions, and answers. The interjection was poor classroom practice into which the teachers fell while thinking during a conversational period. Following are illustrations of this fault. "Er, why would that be a good subject?" "The knights had, er, armor made out of iron." "I want someone to, ah, take this strip of paper, ah, I've cut out." "I'll bring it over here, ah, so that you can show the class, ah, how it looks." "When you got to the, uh, store, you said, uh, uh, 'I haven't anything from the dairy.' How did that, uh, happen?" "You, uh, also should read to, er, find out what Dick said."

Class Control

In some cases of beginning teachers, inadequately trained teachers, or weak ones, the recordings uncovered causes and conditions of unsatisfactory class control and the nature of poor disciplinary measures used. The correction or elimination of various other observed conditions discussed here should contribute to improved class control. Some situations, however, were serious ones requiring specifically planned supervisory observations in order to determine the nature of assistance needed by the teacher. One teacher who used, "shush," frequently was an instance.

Teachers who were ambivalent in discipline and class control were in serious difficulties. The teacher who resorted consciously or unconsciously to severe disciplining of individuals before the rest of the class needed helpful consultation in order to avoid this harmful practice.

Having determined through supervisory visits to the classroom the specific strengths and weaknesses of teachers, the supervisor is able to plan insightfully the kind of help to be given. Some needs can be met in teachers' meetings, others in individual conferences, and still others through the demonstration of better procedures. Related to any one technique may be carefully selected pertinent professional reading recommended to the teacher. □

EL 26 (8): 772-77; May 1969
© 1969 ASCD

To Improve Instruction, Supervision, and Evaluation . . .

THOMAS A. PETRIE

RECENT years have witnessed much effort directed at changing education—changes in teaching, changes in organizational patterns, changes in curricula, changes in media. Hopefully, the changes are not in name only but will result in improved instruction. That some fail surprises no one; that some succeed and even surpass expectations is exciting and encouraging. An in-service program of the Educational

Thomas A. Petrie, Research Coordinator, Educational Development Cooperative, Homewood, Illinois

Development Cooperative[1] is one such exciting and encouraging plan for change. The goal is nothing less than improvement of instruction, supervision, and evaluation.

This program seeking simultaneous improvement of instruction, supervision, and evaluation assumes: (a) having explicit goals allows the integration of teaching and supervisory roles; (b) supervising requires ability to describe exactly the competencies needed for teaching; (c) skills can best be acquired as needed; and (d) the evaluation cycle provides a means for ordering the process of supervisory and instructional improvement.

In the paragraphs that follow, the EDC program will be described step by step as it unfolds in an actual in-service training situation.

Development of Skill List

The training program begins when an EDC staff member meets with a district superintendent, assistant superintendent of instruction, and principals to identify goals, objectives, and skills which they believe are important. By doing this the behavior necessary for success in that district can be deduced and described. For example, one district valued and rated teachers on "instructional skill"; but "instructional skill" was undefined. Teachers could not know exactly what teaching skills were valued. Therefore, the group worked to identify what was meant and an aspect of instructional skill was specified: "a lesson plan shall include an explicit objective, teacher-student activities, and desired performance." So a list of specific and desired teacher skills or competencies is formulated.

[1] EDC is an interdistrict organization composed of 62 elementary and secondary school districts in south Cook and north Will Counties, Illinois. It is funded locally and by a Title III ESEA grant.

Workshop Orientation

Then the workshop composed of six to eight teachers plus the teachers' principals and immediate supervisors begins. The list of behaviors necessary for instructional success is reviewed by the group. It is presented as a list of competencies (or behaviors) which teachers in that district must acquire to be considered successful. It specifies skills or ways of managing students, subject matter, time, space, and equipment needed in the repertoire of the teacher, supervisor, or principal. Teachers may, and do, add to the list. When the list is complete, it is apparent that teaching actual lessons, incorporating the described behaviors, is to become the focus of the workshop.

Orientation continues—the steps required for planning a specific lesson to be taught the next day to a regular class are reviewed. As the teacher, supervisor, and principal create the lesson plan, the supervisor and principal will share experiences and make recommendations so that the plan specifies behavioral objectives, teacher activities designed to achieve objectives, complementary student activities, the information necessary to describe the class before, during, and after the lesson, and desired standards.

As the orientation session ends, discussion centers around the nature of supervision and instruction, teachers as decision makers, and the change process.

Planning Cycle

At this point, a teacher, supervisor, and principal actually plan a lesson. The supervisor and principal share their experiences and make recommendations with regard to the lesson, but the teacher decides what to incorporate. Clear understanding of the instructional objectives and of ways to achieve them is sought by the three co-workers.

With clear understandings regarding objectives and teacher-student activities, the sorts of information (feedback) needed to describe what occurs during the teaching of the lesson can be decided. "Feedback" is anticipated; indeed, it is planned for.

As the lesson is planned, the complementary nature of teaching and supervision becomes evident. The planning process requires that the teacher and supervisor exchange ideas, solve problems, and secure mutual understandings about objectives, activities necessary to achieve them, information necessary to describe the class before, during, and after instruction, desired standards, and the relevance of the list of district instructional competencies to the particular lesson.

Teaching and Taping

The next day the teacher teaches the lesson as planned; the supervisor arranges for recording the class on video tape and collecting any other information according to agreement. A critique follows during which the supervisor relays his observations to the teacher. Together they view part or all of the video tape. Then reactions of the workshop group are sought; this in turn leads naturally into planning another lesson and recycling the process.

As a result of the critique, skills needing improvement have been noted by the teacher and supervisor. Usually these are the same desired skills or behaviors listed during the orientation stage of the workshop. Acquiring these is paramount; therefore, use of desired behaviors is planned in subsequent lessons. After planning, teaching, taping, and critiquing, the cycle can be shortened. Planning occurs again but taping and feedback focus on the appropriate five or ten minutes when the selected skill is needed and used in the classroom. In this manner the training program concentrates on increasing instructional competencies one at a time.

The in-service program thus far described concentrates on classroom teaching activities. However, supervisory activities usually require attention, too. To date, supervisors have found that they must learn to gather information skillfully in order to provide the needed feedback to teachers. Sessions to help supervisors accomplish this are incorporated into the workshop.

Is This Evaluation?

Essentially, a process of evaluation has been described. Mutual development of objectives (what we are trying to accomplish), teacher-student activities (treatment, or how it is to be done), data collection (what information we need to collect to describe the state of affairs), instrumentation (how it shall be measured), and standards (is it significant) provide the basis of evaluation. When the cycle is experienced and re-experienced, evaluation occurs and reoccurs. Hopefully, by participating and, in fact, working at it there will be increased understanding of the process of evaluation. Though not simply accomplished, a reasonable process has been described engaging principals, supervisors, and teachers.

Figure 1 exemplifies a lesson plan and the mutual agreements of a teacher, principal, and supervisor. The plan in Figure 1 was developed by the teacher, department chairman, and principal in approximately 30 minutes. The teacher understood and approved the plan. Perhaps the objectives could have been more operational, activities more explicit, and recommendations extended. But to smother the teacher would have been, in essence, to impose upon her the supervisor's plan—a pitfall to avoid.

152 • Supervision: Emerging Profession

Supervisors agreed that to meet their responsibilities, as outlined, they had to increase their competencies in interaction analysis. Sessions were planned to acquaint them with "The CVC System" of behavior classification.[2] Further, it was necessary to decide what noninvolved behavior actually

[2] The CVC System, July 1968, Cooperative Educational Research Laboratory, Inc., Northfield, Illinois.

Objectives
1. To understand eight selected vocabulary words in the story
2. To comprehend the theme in *The Call of the Wild*.

Activities

Teacher Activities	Student Activities
1. Review the story to date.	1. Teacher-student discussion.
2. Introduce the eight story vocabulary words in text.	2. Students define them.
3. Instruct the students to write them in their notebooks.	3. Students write them down.
4. Call attention to the unique spellings in dialect passages.	4. Discuss and relate them to their home or peer talk.
5. Call for student volunteer to read.	5. Student reads.
6. Every two paragraphs, discuss the progress and student reactions to the story.	6. Discuss.
7. Call attention to vocabulary words. Secure student interpretations of words, synonyms, and antonyms.	7. Students define them in their own words and relate to story context.

Teacher's Concerns
1. Tenor of class
2. Involvement of class in the activities.

Recommendations Teacher Accepted
In a discussion, press dialogue with a specific child; state questions in a manner requiring more than a single word response. Elaborate on response.

Agreements Regarding Supervisor's Responsibilities
1. Videotape the class
2. Record incidents of noninvolvement in activities
3. Record classroom responses on CERLI Matrix.* (Particularly concerned about Teacher Seek Thinking and Student Inform Thinking.)

Standards
1. 90 percent involvement of the class in the discussion
2. Teacher questions of 50 percent seek thinking
3. Student responses of 50 percent inform thinking
4. 90 percent student accuracy in interpreting vocabulary words in their context.

* A 4x4 grid used to tally verbal content of students or teachers regarding thinking, recall, management, and feeling according to who informs, seeks, accepts, or rejects.

Figure 1. A Lesson Plan for Ninth Grade English

is. After categories of noninvolved behavior were established, it was agreed that incidents of noninvolvement were to be recorded by the supervisor.

As the teacher taught her ninth grade class, each person attended to the task of observing, teaching, or recording. The supervisor observed the class and recorded the involvement of the children. The principal arranged to have the class videotaped and later reviewed the tape in order to classify classroom interaction.

During the subsequent "feedback" session, the workshop leader reviewed objectives, activities, teacher concerns, information required, and standards. The teacher described her instruction according to her own perceptions. The principal reported the information regarding involvement and vocabulary interpretation. Each piece of information was related to the appropriate objective and activity, and differences regarding other interpretations were listed. Finally, segments of the video-tape recording were reviewed for resolving differences regarding interpretations. The focus was on *the plan as presented*.

Apparently supervisors and principals can develop sufficient skills to sustain the training program described. The program may be modified to minimize observation time and demands for information collection and analysis.

Desired skills or behaviors serve as objectives of the program, and the evaluation process provides the vehicle for improving teaching skills one at a time in the classroom setting.

Other considerations could be raised with respect to instruction, supervision, and evaluation. Underlying the program is the rationale that organizations consist of complementary roles and functions. In an educational organization every role has to some degree administrative, supervisory, instructional, and evaluative functions. These complementary roles and functions need to be understood and experienced as they contribute to institutional goals and individual achievement. In this respect the previously mentioned program attempts to be straightforward regarding the potential that evaluation holds for the improvement of instruction and supervision. ◻

The Supervisor's Part in Educating the New Teacher

Roy A. Edelfelt

THERE is an old assumption that new teachers know how to teach, that they know how to create and use teaching materials, and that they may even know a little more than experienced teachers about new methods, new subject matter, new psychology and sociology.

As a result, we expect the beginners

Roy A. Edelfelt, Executive Secretary, National Commission on Teacher Education and Professional Standards, NEA, Washington, D.C.

to assume the full responsibilities of teaching, treat each as if he could succeed in almost any assignment, expect them to be our equal, and treat them all as if they will stay in teaching for a full career. The new teacher is treated almost the same as the experienced teacher—except for salary and tenure.

We need to take a new look at this old idea. The new teacher today is not the same as his experienced colleague, nor is he one of 200,000 copies of the same model. And he should not be treated as such. All kinds of teachers are in the new crop each year. And despite differences they are similar in only one respect—all are beginners.

Help for the New Teacher

Should the new teacher be expected to start at full steam? I say emphatically *no*. He should not assume the full responsibilities of a regular teacher in his first year, and maybe not even in his second or third, not until he has demonstrated the necessary competence.

I am not recommending less work. Although the new teacher should not have a full teaching load immediately, he needs extensive time to plan, analyze, and evaluate his teaching, to study children and subject matter, to investigate teaching materials—all with the help of highly competent supervisors.

The cost to society for what we are presently doing with and to new teachers is too high. Only about half the teachers who began teaching last fall will be in the classroom three years from now. Supervisors are fatigued and frustrated by the constant orientation and induction of new teachers, but some of this work could be cut if the dropout rate in teaching could be reduced. Many new teachers are too slow in reaching their potential as experts because they are told or they sense that the system is set, the boat cannot be rocked.

Supervisors Can Help

Job No. 1, then, is to find ways to organize a teaching force so that *no* new teacher assumes a full teaching load immediately.

Job No. 2 is to find effective ways and competent people to help the new teacher learn to teach.

Few new teachers want to assume full responsibility on a job, and most will admit they are not ready to.

This leads me to an attack on the myth about the equality of new teachers and experienced teachers. Equals in what? If regarding a new teacher as an equal means treating him as if he were as competent as an experienced teacher, then either we are kidding ourselves or we have some pretty inadequate experienced teachers.

If, however, equality means regarding the new teacher as a colleague, as a person of integrity and responsibility, as a person entitled to protection against capricious attack or dismissal, as another professional who should be guaranteed academic freedom, then we have a defensible concept of equality, and incidentally one which is not adequately championed by people in education.

What the new teacher wants most, perhaps, is not to be treated like a student. The best solution to the destruction of the myth about equality may be to use more precise terms, to make clear what is meant by a colleague relationship and be honest about what a neophyte-senior teacher relationship might be.

Job No. 3, then, is to be sure that the status of the beginning professional is clear. He is not the equal of his seasoned mentor, the experienced teacher, but he is his colleague and he has certain rights and responsibilities which should be recognized.

If the pretenure transition period lasts three or four years, if it involves intensive analyses and evaluation of teaching, independent and group study, graduate work, and activities designed to achieve some clear goals for a "career teacher," it may be that all new teachers will not choose to take this route because it would mean seven or eight years of study (including the undergraduate years) to become a career teacher. The transient teacher might choose not to follow such a plan. Some other teachers might choose less than career status. For such teachers, other aproaches to orientation and induction might be followed.

A career teacher should have a specified level of competence in teaching and more responsibility in the school than a regular or beginning teacher. He should be rewarded on a basis comparable to that of the principal.[1]

Job No. 4. Within existing circumstances, make the pretenure period a screening time. Make clear the desired competencies of teachers who stay, and be sure the school climate supports these expectations.

Job No. 5. Set up some pilot projects to try the idea of career teacher status. Experimentation would provide a chance to involve both teachers and laymen in developing the idea and to test its validity.

A teacher is not clearly a success or a failure because he "makes it" or "flubs it" in one school or one classroom. We treat new teachers as if they can succeed in almost any assignment. Their assignment is often a matter of placing *a person* in a classroom on the basis of preparation for a specified subject at a particular level. If the neophyte fails in that particular assignment, too often we tend to brand him a failure.

We know that teaching styles differ, that different experiential backgrounds and attitudes influence success or failure in a particular situation. We know, too, that when a teacher obviously cannot succeed in his first assignment despite a supervisor's efforts to help, there should be other alternatives than admitting failure.

Transfer to a new assignment, even in the middle of a semester, should be possible. Temporary relief from a teaching post should also be possible. And both without loss of face.

Job No. 6, then, is to be much more careful and deliberate about the initial assignment of teachers and to build more flexibility into the way teacher assignments can be shifted during the school year.

The neophyte in most professions has something to look forward to, there is a visible career pattern. We have this in teaching if the teacher moves into administration, college teaching, or government employment.

Yet the classroom teacher begins about where he ends at retirement, in status, responsibility, and privilege. To keep good teachers in the classroom, to make it possible for them to afford to stay in the classroom, beginners must see opportunity and rewards ahead that can be earned. These might include:

a. Reduced teaching loads for career teachers, who will have other responsibilities—working with student teachers, teacher aides, interns, and beginning teachers; developing ideas for improvement in content and instruction; serving on district, state, and national committees; traveling, study-

---

[1] To explore the concept further, see National Education Association, National Commission on Teacher Education and Professional Standards. *Remaking the World of the Career Teacher.* Report of the 1965-66 Regional TEPS Conferences. Washington, D.C.: the Commission, 1966.

ing, and thinking (the sabbatical leave); working on curriculum committees; consultant work in other buildings; teaching in-service education courses; writing (e.g., grant proposals).

b. Recognition within the district—a status similar to the full professorship in college, being consulted on important district decisions.

c. Added privilege and reward—expenses and salary while attending conferences, secretarial and teacher-aide help, pay on a basis comparable to or above that of principals.

As important is the fact that the roles of teachers are changing and expanding. Teachers are beginning to assume a variety of roles, depending on competence, experience, and training. As differentiated roles are developed there will be even more flexibility in possible career patterns and assignments for those who choose to stay with teaching.

These ideas are illustrative. Perhaps the most important idea is that status should be based on demonstrated competence. But we must believe that competence is important. This means we must know what competence is and be able to recognize it when we see it, which is not the case now.

An Action Program

I wish the Association for Supervision and Curriculum Development and other groups—at state and national levels—would take action on some of these points. It would be feasible to:

1. Communicate what is being done to help beginning teachers, short one-page vignettes describing effective programs.

2. Find school systems which are not doing anything much with new teachers where there might be some interest and willingness to experiment.

3. Establish contact with Research and Development Centers and Regional Laboratories (sponsored under Title IV, P. L. 89-10), to discover what these centers are doing about the beginning teacher and try to influence what they do.

4. Develop some practical suggestions for working with the beginning teacher which will help people deal with situations as they exist—where sweeping changes are not yet appropriate.

5. Develop programs for the retraining of supervisors to establish specialists for dealing with problems of the new teacher, such programs to include new developments of various systems for analysis of the teaching act.

6. Specify some of the unique problems of the beginning teacher, such as getting to know materials, applying child study procedures, study and application of strategies of teaching, and use of evaluative techniques for student growth.

7. Develop a theoretical and philosophical basis for dealing with the beginning teacher—the learning-to-teach phase of career development

Schools will never be any better than the teachers who man them. One of the ways to get better teachers is to make sure the new crop each year get sufficient time, help, and encouragement so that each new teacher has a chance to develop his own teaching style to a high level of perfection. This goal is a primary professional obligation for teachers and supervisors. It deserves more attention than it is getting presently. ☐

Supervision and Continuing Education for Teachers of English

ROBERT F. HOGAN
JAMES R. SQUIRE

NO JOB is less likely to be done than the one which is "everybody's job." Any nation operating on the assumption that "peace is everybody's business" would do well to arm itself. Prior to Social Security legislation and organized social welfare agencies, care for the aged, which was then everybody's responsibility, was deplorable. Similarly, in no period of American education did instruction in English and the language arts suffer more than in the 1940's and early 1950's when every teacher, presumably, was a teacher of English. Unless a job is divided into components, assigned to and accepted by *someone,* no one does it.

During those "every teacher" decades, English in some schools lost virtually all identity as a discipline. School personnel officers, furthermore, interpreted the slogan to mean that anyone could teach English. As a consequence, despite subsequent efforts to raise certification standards, statewide studies such as those in Pennsylvania (1) and California (2) and two nationwide surveys by the National Council of Teachers of English (3, 4) reveal that half the teachers now teaching English in secondary schools across the nation still lack a major in this subject. In fact, nearly a third have neither a major nor a minor in English.

In elementary schools the time devoted to direct instruction in English and the language arts, apart from incidental instruction in the teaching of other subjects, ranges from 40 to 50 percent of the total instructional time (5). Yet after full certification and nine years of in-service requirements, the typical elementary teacher has given eight percent of his total academic and professional education, preservice and in-service, to the content and the teaching of the language arts (4). Elementary teachers devoted eight percent of their preparation to approximately 50 percent of their task.

The argument with the slogan, "Every teacher is a teacher of English," is not with the principle, but with the result. To be sure, marking any piece of student prose is an occasion for teaching English, or reinforcing it, or ignoring it. Except for foreign language teachers who may rely completely on the direct method, any teacher who speaks before a class sets a standard of English expression, good or bad, for his students to emulate. Yet to someone must fall the principal responsibility for initial and sequential instruction in the skills and the arts of language, for teaching the principles of composition, for organizing access to our literary heritage. At least half of

Robert F. Hogan, Executive Secretary, National Council of Teachers of English, Champaign, Illinois; and James R. Squire, Senior Vice President and Editor-in-Chief, Ginn and Company, Boston, Massachusetts. In 1964, Dr. Squire was Executive Secretary, National Council of Teachers of English, and Professor of English, University of Illinois, Urbana

those to whom it falls in secondary schools and many of those to whom it falls in elementary schools are not even minimally prepared to meet this responsibility (3, 4). If the "specialists" themselves have not been adequately trained, on how firm a footing is the program if it simply rests with "everyone"?

Improvement in the long run depends on teachers who insist on better preparation, school systems which both demand it and reward it, colleges which offer it, and a national program of institutes to make additional training available to those now in service. Large-scale improvement in English instruction cannot be realized unless all these individuals and agencies meet their responsibilities. Yet each must meet his own responsibilities; this cannot all be "everybody's job."

Essential Needs in Teaching of English

In May 1964 the National Council of Teachers of English published *The National Interest and the Continuing Education of Teachers of English,* a national survey of the responses of 3,000 elementary teachers and nearly 7,500 secondary teachers of English, dealing with in-service education, both with graduate and professional courses available in colleges and universities and with programs sponsored by school systems. This study pinpoints certain essential needs which will go unmet unless those responsible for supervision and curriculum development take appropriate action. (In the following pages all data not otherwise credited come from this report.)

Refine patterns of requirements for in-service growth. Recommendations of the profession and common sense notwithstanding, fully half those now teaching English in secondary schools have not majored in English. Moreover, only 55 percent of secondary school teachers of English and 45 percent of elementary teachers are employed in schools which have formal requirements for continuing education. That is to say, approximately half of the teachers work in schools which do not have such requirements. These are likely to be the schools accepting substandard preparation in the first place.

Where they exist, blanket requirements for a given number of credits in a specified period of time do virtually nothing to close the gap between preparation and professional responsibility. If a high school English teacher has not taken a course in composition or rhetoric during preservice education, even when it is available, this is the last course he will take to satisfy general requirements for in-service growth. Similarly, the elementary teacher, in a program calling for instruction in grammar and usage from the third grade on, will usually avoid courses in modern English grammar.

The Education of Teachers of English for American Schools and Colleges (7), as well as the earlier report entitled *The National Interest and the Teaching of English* (3), specifies indispensable areas of preparation. Those in charge of in-service education should be familiar with such recommendations and make certain that teachers who offer additional credits in satisfaction of requirements make an effort to compensate for gaps in their preservice education.

Encourage experimentation and the study of research. It is one thing to accept change cautiously. It is another to go on in utter innocence of new developments. Despite all the current discussion about team teaching, ungraded curricula, interage grouping, and lay readers, fewer than 10 percent of secondary teachers of English are in schools that have even begun to experiment with such programs. Their counterparts in the elementary schools have not done much better. Curriculum consultants can do much for in-service growth by encouraging experimentation and study. Local research projects make teachers more intelligent consumers of other research reports. Moreover, they place teachers in the clear position of needing additional information. With the strategic use of invited consultants and additions to the professional library, teachers participating in the study would on their own initiative not only seek to help to shed light on a real problem, but also to fill in gaps in their academic and professional preparation.

Develop professional libraries. In no other profession is the gap as great between what is known and what is practiced as it is in the teaching profession. And in few academic subjects is this gap greater than it is in English. Time and again research has demonstrated, for example, that under certain conditions the teaching of formal grammar not only fails to produce improvement in writing but actually inhibits it (8). No doubt the lag between professional awareness and professional practice explains to a considerable degree why leaders like Ruth Strickland can assert that no major recent change in the language arts curriculum has resulted from research (9).

One reason for the negligible impact of research is that reports of research are so inaccessible. Approximately 50 percent of teachers work in schools or systems without access to a professional library. The other half do not always find accessibility easy. The supervisor or curriculum director who wants to establish and maintain an up-to-date professional library will find help in the minimum professional libraries for elementary and secondary schools in English and language arts listed in the appendix to *The National Interest and the Continuing Education of Teachers of English.*

Reevaluate the function of the teachers institute. Despite occasional moves to substitute other activities for it, the teachers institute remains strongly entrenched. Over 70 percent of secondary school teachers of English and over 80 percent of elementary teachers are employed in schools or districts which hold such institutes regularly, usually once each year. For a majority of teachers, attendance is "expected" or mandatory.

To what extent are such programs aimed at closing one or more of the gaps between preservice education and professional responsibilities? With the scope of their task, the institute for elementary teachers cannot give a preponderant amount of time exclusively to the English language arts. But 56 percent of elementary teachers regularly attend institutes that give less than 25 percent of the time to it. In fact, nearly 50 percent of the secondary school teachers of English attend institutes with equally little concern for their subject.

All teachers should have interests and knowledge outside a particular academic specialty. Yet an elementary teacher with no work in literature for children or a secondary teacher of English whose last composition course was in his senior year in high school has specific and urgent needs that will never be satisfied by the kind of speaker engaged more often than any other for the annual institutes, a speaker from the field of general curriculum.

Few districts can afford to engage annually an outstanding speaker in every subject field. Yet a succession of such speakers over a few years' time would be better than an "all-purpose" speaker each year. Most schools, moreover, have on their teaching and supervisory staff more subject matter strength than they ever utilize sufficiently. The curriculum director responsible for institute planning can use district as well as outside specialists to ensure that teachers have the chance to improve their understanding and teaching of the English language arts.

Encourage participation in the activities of subject matter organizations. The

National Council of Teachers of English holds its annual meeting each fall, bringing to one city for a series of programs several hundred of the national leaders in English and the teaching of English. It sponsors many other conferences, institutes, and workshops each year. The International Reading Association, the other national organization entirely devoted to issues of special interest to teachers of the language arts, holds an annual meeting in the spring. Both organizations have hundreds of local, regional, and state affiliates with their own programs and activities. Both, too, have comprehensive publications programs, including regular periodicals, occasional bulletins, and a variety of books.

Here is an inexhaustible reservoir of in-service growth. To what extent do schools encourage teachers to tap this reservoir? Approximately one third of the teachers of English in secondary schools hold membership in the Secondary Section of NCTE. But for elementary teachers, total memberships in NCTE and IRA constitute less than six percent of the total number of teachers. Despite the fact that for the past several years NCTE has followed a policy of placing its convention within 1000 miles of every teacher at least every fourth year, 82 percent of the secondary teachers of English and 92 percent of the elementary teachers have never attended. NCTE affiliates sponsor each year at least 200 local or regional programs, but 68 percent of the elementary teachers across the country have never attended one.

Many of these meetings are held on weekends or on holidays. With how little effort and at how little expense could schools put teachers into contact with outstanding scholars in English and the teaching of English! Some schools have found that all that is needed is an announcement, some encouragement, an occasional token reimbursement of expenses. By joining such associations, staying informed of their programs, and making it possible for teachers to attend, an alert supervisor or curriculum consultant, for little more than the cost of mileage, can do at least as much for the local English program as he could with several hundred dollars spent to bring speakers into his community.

Know and capitalize on the strengths of present staff members. If half the secondary school teachers of English across the country lack a major in English, an approximately equal number have such a major. Seven percent began their teaching with a master's degree; another 27 percent have earned this degree since beginning teaching. Sixteen percent of elementary teachers have an undergraduate major in English or language arts. An additional one fifth have group or field majors which included English with one or more other subjects.

Although the general picture of teacher preparation in English is grim, across the country are outstanding teachers with academic and professional preparation unparalleled in the history of the profession. Of seven different in-service activities, elementary teachers ranked meeting with other teachers first; secondary teachers ranked meeting with other teachers second only to additional college courses. Yet barely one third of the secondary teachers and one fourth of elementary teachers have frequent opportunities for such meetings. In fact, more than 10 percent of both groups *never* have such an opportunity.

Working with department chairmen, grade level chairmen, or steering committees, the supervisor can set up a sequence of meetings on topics selected by the teachers. In one secondary school, for example, at the invitation of the English teachers, the county consultant in elementary reading led a series of seminars on the teaching of reading. Particularly needed is leadership to bring together elementary teachers and junior and senior high school teachers of English. Again and again teachers identify this need to break down the "professional isolation" of the individual teacher. Yet to whom does the initiative belong?

By studying personnel records and by observing classes, the curriculum specialist can identify teachers with special training and competencies, teachers who might otherwise escape his notice. By similar study and observation, he can identify needed strengths that are nowhere represented on the teaching staff. If no one in a high school English department, for example, has taken advanced work in rhetoric or studied modern English grammar, then the next vacancy reported to the personnel office should so stipulate. By keeping abreast of needs as well as present strengths, supervisors who have responsibilities for interviewing candidates will be in a unique position to make strategic recommendations.

Reevaluate the need for strengthened supervisory resources. In recent years the whole concept of supervision has changed. Dropping a policing function and adopting new procedures and often a new title, the supervisor in recent years has done much to enhance rapport with teachers and to create a climate more conducive to improving instruction. Yet as the supervisor has relied less on classroom observation and more on group process, as his assignment has been based more on geography or on school level, he has had to become a generalist. This is particularly true at the elementary level. There 80 percent of the teachers have at least some opportunity to meet with a general supervisor, but over 40 percent have never had an opportunity to meet with a supervisor trained in English or the language arts. This unavailability of direct supervision, as well as the remoteness of generalized consultant help, no doubt accounts for the low evaluation which teachers in many districts place on supervision. Secondary teachers, for example, rate conferences with supervisors of less help than any other in-service activity except reading research reports. The NCTE report indicates that new approaches to supervision are hardly more effective than the old in promoting curriculum change. Approaches are needed to relate supervision to active classroom instruction.

More recently the trend has been to include subject matter specialization within the larger framework of supervision. Yet in English, as contrasted with other academic subjects, the swing has been slight. In 1963, for example, 15 states provided full or part time supervision in English while 33 states provided 221 supervisors in science, mathematics, and foreign languages. While one cannot reasonably expect every district, large or small, to engage a full time supervisor in English, half the school districts in cities of more than 200,000 did not offer specialized supervision in English, although the supervisory staffs have been substantial.

One indication of the growing importance of specialized supervision in English was a national conference of some 50 English supervisors called in February 1964 by the U.S. Office of Education to develop guidelines for supervision in English. Leaders of NCTE, ASCD, NASSP, and The Modern Language Association participated in this conference. Similarly, in October and November 1964, the National Study of High School English Programs is calling two conferences on the supervisory responsibilities of high school English chairmen.[1]

The issue here is not entirely fiscal. To

---

[1] Director of this project was James R. Squire. A report of both conferences was published: *High School Departments of English: Their Organization, Administration, and Supervision.* Champaign, Illinois: National Council of Teachers of English, 1965.

be sure, federal funds supported supervision in science, mathematics, and foreign languages. Yet awareness of advances in these subjects has led to specialized supervision even without outside help. In English, much of the problem grows from a failure to recognize that here, too, are new scholarship and new techniques. The profession has given up the idea that anyone can *teach* English; in many areas, however, any supervisor can *supervise* the teaching of English.

The demands for strengthened supervision are clearly implied in ASCD's "The Role of the Curriculum Supervisor" (10). This working paper underscores the rapid expansion of knowledge and the need to recognize that "teacher education is a lifelong process.... In-service education by local school districts is essential if the teaching corps is to keep abreast with advances in knowledge...." The paper, furthermore, highlights the central responsibility of curriculum specialists in this process. They "must play major roles in a school district's in-service education program. Both the generalist and the subject-area specialist have important parts to play...."

The need for subject specialization implied in the discussion of changes in the educational scene is reiterated in subsequent discussions of basic assumptions. "It is essential that the supervisor be regarded ... as a helping teacher, a consultant, or a co-teacher...." Finally, it is spelled out in the section dealing with staff organization, which distinguishes between the contributions of general supervisors, who "are primarily concerned with looking at any curriculum proposal or instructional problem in its relation to the students' total educational experience," and the subject matter supervisors, who "are the specialists in the content, methods, and materials of a particular discipline...."

Competing with traditional school grammar are three distinct grammars of English, any one of which improves on the traditional in describing accurately the structure of English. With respect to language learning, Charles Ferguson, Director of the Center for Applied Linguistics, has said that more information has become available in the past five years than in the previous one hundred. Joint efforts of linguists, psychologists, and reading specialists promise to reorganize if not to revolutionize fundamental principles of reading instruction. These are but a few of the changes. Keeping up with the new scholarship and discriminating among suggested changes in procedure and techniques demand full time commitment.

Apart from any steps taken to improve the in-service and continuing education of teachers of English, the implications for the supervisory staff are clear. In the absence of a supervisor trained in the English language arts, schools can and probably should rely more on their best prepared teachers for instructional leadership.

Generalists in supervision can do much to create a climate that releases the energy these teachers can bring to the problem. Yet in the long run if supervisors are to be leaders, as they must be, the continuing education of supervisors themselves and the selection of replacements or additions to the supervisory staff should command at least as much attention as the continuing education and recruitment of teachers of English. ☐

References

1. Department of Public Instruction, Commonwealth of Pennsylvania. *A Pennsylvania Problem: Professionally Prepared Teachers of English.* Harrisburg: the Department, 1964.

2. California State Department of Education. *The English Language Arts in California Public High Schools,* Bulletin No. 7, No. 26. Sacramento: the Department, 1957.

3. Committee on the National Interest. *The National Interest and the Teaching of English.* Champaign: National Council of Teachers of English, 1961.

4. Committee on the National Interest. *The National Interest and the Continuing Education of Teachers of English.* Champaign: National Council of Teachers of English, 1964.

5. National Education Association. "Instructional Time Allotment in Elementary Schools." *NEA Research Memo,* January 1961. Washington, D.C.: the Association, 1961.

6. Francis Keppel. Testimony before the House Committee on Education and Labor, February 1963.

7. Commission on the Curriculum. *The Education of Teachers of English for American Schools and Colleges.* Champaign: National Council of Teachers of English, 1963.

8. Richard Braddock et al. *Research in Written Composition.* Champaign: National Council of Teachers of English, 1964.

9. Ruth Strickland. "Some Important Research Gaps in the Teaching of the Elementary School Language Arts." *Needed Research in the Teaching of English.* Erwin R. Steinberg, editor. Washington, D.C.: U.S. Department of Health, Education, and Welfare, 1963. Curriculum specialists should also familiarize themselves with: David H. Russell, Margaret Early, and Edmund Farrell. *Research Design and the Teaching of English.* Champaign: National Council of Teachers of English, 1964; and with: David H. Russell and Henry R. Fea, "Research in Teaching Reading," and Henry C. Meckel, "Research in Teaching Composition and Literature," in *Handbook of Research on Teaching.* Chicago: Rand McNally & Company, 1963.

10. Association for Supervision and Curriculum Development. "The Role of the Curriculum Supervisor." A tentative working paper studied and discussed in the ASCD 1964 conference.

EL 26 (4): 378-81; January 1969
© 1969 ASCD

Supervisory Techniques with Beginning Mathematics Teachers

SANDRA NOEL SMITH

APPARENTLY many variations exist in the procedures used by supervisors of teachers, especially of beginning teachers, in the field of mathematics. A survey was conducted to determine to what extent the variations in supervisory techniques did exist.

This survey was designed to evaluate the degree of variability of attitudes toward supervisory techniques among beginning teachers of mathematics in the public secondary schools of the Middle Atlantic States. This investigation is an analytical appraisal of the various attitudes as determined from beginning teachers of mathematics with five years or less experience.

Data for this study were obtained through a questionnaire directed to teachers in selected secondary schools accredited by the Middle States Association in the states of Pennsylvania, New York, New Jersey, Maryland, and Delaware. Distribution of the 300 responses to the questionnaire was as follows: Pennsylvania 121; New York 60; New Jersey 82; Maryland 31; and Delaware 6.

The techniques investigated and evaluated by the teachers were: Orientation of New Teachers, Classroom Visitation, Individual Conference, Faculty Meeting, Departmental Meeting, The Workshop, Small Group Activity and Teacher Committees Within the School, Curriculum Development

Sandra Noel Smith, Assistant Professor, Department of Education, Howard University, Washington, D.C.

and Implementation, Demonstration Teaching, In-Service Education and Professional Growth, Instruction in the Use of Audio-Visual Aids, Evaluation, and Research and Experimentation. Each of these 13 categories was subdivided into 74 aspects which were scaled in terms of frequency and value by the responding teachers.

This study has conveyed a brief history of supervision and the attitudes and opinions of the experts in the field of supervision in general, and in mathematics in particular, as they relate to the 13 categories of supervisory techniques as surveyed by the author. An evaluation of the experts' opinions as to the relative worth of these techniques seems to indicate that their main thoughts lie in the theoretical application of these techniques rather than in their practical application, which is desired by a majority of the classroom teachers. These experts did not place a numerical value on the technique, but rather leaned toward the techniques in light of their previous experiences and their proximity to the mathematical supervisory officials.

Throughout the study of the most effective supervisory techniques used with beginning teachers of mathematics, a pattern of similarity existed in the frequency and value of the 13 techniques as utilized and valued with the beginning teachers of mathematics. Therefore, the analysis of the 300 responses is also a true representation of the 5 states on an individual basis.

In each state and in the composite summary, the value of each technique was greater than the frequency of the said technique. In the states of New Jersey, Maryland, Delaware, and in the composite picture of the five states, there were 7 techniques of supervision which had a percentage of value which was greater than or equal to the percentage of frequency of all of the techniques. In Pennsylvania, this number of techniques was 8 and in the state of New York, the number was only 2 techniques. There was little variation in the ranking of the techniques according to frequency and, throughout the states, the techniques of Research and Experimentation, Orientation of New Teachers, Evaluation, Workshop, and Demonstration were among the least utilized techniques.

Mathematical computations were used to reach the recommendations derived from this survey. The author was able to secure a graphic and accurate evaluation of the usage of these techniques by employing the proper statistical procedures commonly used by statisticians in gaining meaningful and useful information from responses such as those received in this survey.

In a final analysis of these data, the author found that there were some areas that were suspect and could be strengthened. These areas have been suggested by teachers whose hopes are that the implementation of methods to improve these weaknesses would be initiated as soon as possible. These recommendations are based on the factual expression by the teachers of the desire for activities which were highly valued by the beginning teachers but not frequently utilized by the supervisory officials.

Recommendations

Consequently, in light of these opinions and statistical results, the author makes the following recommendations that could strengthen the practices of mathematics supervisors and thus improve the quality of instruction in the classroom. Such enhancement would be of great value not only to the students concerned, but to the school system as well.

We will not present here all of the recommendations derived from the evaluation of the responses of the teachers. Only those recommendations of most significance and that promise the most far-reaching effects in changing and improving supervisory techniques in the area of mathematics are listed. These recommendations are as follows:

1. Teachers should receive helpful suggestions on the economic use of time and effort, on useful materials, and on effective ways of grouping pupils.

2. Assistance should be given, within the regular curriculum, in providing for individual differences, special interests, and creativity.

3. Teachers should be visited in their classrooms for purposes of evaluating the teaching-learning situation rather than for inspection or rating.

4. The mathematics supervisor should do continuous research on the new developments in mathematics education and should interpret the new ideas to the teachers.

5. There should be a continuous development of in-service education opportunities that will improve teaching.

6. Guidance in the effective use of available aids in the various units of work should be given to the teacher.

7. Methods and techniques used by the supervisor during the classroom visitation should be adapted to the experience, degree of mastery of subject matter, and personality of the teachers.

8. In-service programs should fulfill the needs of teachers of children of *all* abilities.

9. Suggestions should be offered by the supervisor relative to initiating or carrying through a unit of study.

10. Adequate time should be scheduled for discussion and evaluation of the procedure observed in a demonstration lesson.

The author has been notified by several of the schools which participated in this survey that steps have been taken to incorporate some of these recommendations in the guidelines being prepared by their supervisory personnel. Consequently, the implementation of these recommendations (those listed and others not listed in this article) would improve the effectiveness of the teacher and of the supervisors. The full usage of these recommendations could strengthen the lines of communication between the teacher and supervisor and might erase some of the fears and dislikes that some teachers have toward some supervisors. However, the major accomplishment is that the student's instruction would be greatly strengthened in this aspect of education, on which greater stress is placed than upon any other discipline—mathematics. ☐

Supervision and Team Teaching

WARD SYBOUTS

THERE are indications that many educators are still asking, "What are the advantages of team teaching?" This is apparent when we realize most schools have not adopted the newer techniques of staff utilization.[1] More effective use of skilled teachers for the improvement of instruction

[1] Judson T. Shaplin and Henry F. Olds. *Team Teaching.* New York: Harper & Row, Publishers, Inc., 1964. pp. 323-26.

Ward Sybouts, Professor and Chairman, Department of Secondary Education, Teachers College, University of Nebraska, Lincoln

has been recognized among the several objectives of team teaching. However, Ivins has reported that many principals in schools in which team teaching was being used were overlooking the potential for staff growth and development.[2] Supervision is one of the areas in which team teaching extends an opportunity for improving the quality of education.

Supervision has been defined in many ways. Simply stated, supervision should encompass a major portion of the efforts of the principal and staff to improve instruction. Supervision is not limited to specific acts of visitation, evaluation, or in-service training. Supervision is an educational and social process of high professional character which is essential to the accomplishment of the aims of an educational program.

Historically, supervision has progressed from the level of inspection to the involvement of democratic leadership which focuses attention on the acts of the teacher. Supervisory techniques typically reported in the literature include: (a) in-service training; (b) class visitations; (c) teacher conferences; (d) staff meetings; (e) demonstration classes; (f) intervisitations; (g) supervisory bulletins; (h) professional readings; and (i) summer school attendance.[3,4] By their very nature, most supervisory techniques do not tend to involve the teacher as a participant, but the teacher becomes primarily a recipient. Supervision has typically consisted of a one-directional flow of information.

Professional school administrators have promulgated the hypothesis that supervision is necessary to the effective functioning of a public school staff. Some, who envision teaching as a profession, find existing supervisory philosophy contradictory to their hypothesis that the professional teacher, within the framework of a profession responsible for the competence of its members, is most effective when granted professional autonomy.[5]

Much of the supervisory behavior of administrators has not given adequate consideration to professional changes which have taken place among teachers during recent years. The failure to realize that teachers are in fact changing has been the cause of concern among some educators who focus their attention, and perhaps justly so, upon questions of authority and control. There are those who warn that as democratic administration moves forward teachers will demand an increasing voice in decision making.[6] As educators become more knowledgeable—more professional—there should be a growing respect for demonstrated professional judgment and less concern for the balance of power between administration and staff.

Team teaching extends to educators many opportunities to improve instruction by advancing the level of supervision beyond the limits of communication patterns designed primarily to send information in only one direction. Through the interrelationships afforded by team teaching there is an opportunity for the professional autonomy of teachers to be recognized and harnessed to provide a better quality of education.

Productive Supervision

The various ramifications of team teaching for supervision are too numerous to attempt a complete listing. A few illus-

---

[2] Wilson Ivins. "Team Teaching in Southwestern Secondary Schools." *Bulletin of the National Association of Secondary School Principals* 48: 25-30; March 1964. p. 27.

[3] Paul B. Jacobson, W. C. Reavis, and J. D. Logsdon. *The Effective School Principal.* Second Edition. Englewood Cliffs, New Jersey: Prentice-Hall, Inc., 1963. pp. 97-108.

[4] Stanley W. Williams. *Educational Administration in Secondary Schools.* New York: Holt, Rinehart & Winston, Inc., 1964. pp. 136-40.

[5] John Wilcox. "Another Look at Supervision." *Bulletin of the National Association of Secondary School Principals* 47: 82-94; February 1963. p. 83.

[6] W. A. Wildman. "Implications of Teacher Bargaining for School Administration." *Phi Delta Kappan* 46 (4): 152-58; December 1964.

trations of how the supervisory relationship can be more productive between administration and teacher in a team teaching setting are these: (a) promoting cooperative planning; (b) reducing teacher isolation; (c) providing new teachers with more constant assistance and guidance; (d) promoting peer evaluation of teaching; and (e) relating supervision to staff-identified needs and interests.

Cooperative Planning

Adequate planning is basic to good teaching. Master teachers have consistently facilitated learning through well-planned and well-organized lessons. In contrast, many teachers who fail to reach their potential have limited themselves through poor planning. The administrator, or supervisor, has a golden opportunity to help staff members grow if he can direct some of his supervisory efforts to the planning phase of teaching.

When teachers are working in a team, planning takes on new dimensions. In utilizing the collective abilities, knowledge, and background of staff members, planning is brought out into the open where the judgment and contributions of all team members can be applied. The team can discuss, evaluate, and critique as they work together. Within the procedure of team planning the supervisor has many opportunities to exercise a high level of leadership.

Reduction of Teacher Isolation

The reduction of teacher isolation, which is in part reflected in cooperative team planning, constitutes an important ingredient in the supervisory process. The elimination of teacher isolation initially establishes a new and different working climate.[7] "The teacher, accustomed to the professional isolation of normal classwork, finds he must learn new skills, polish old ones, work for honest harmony with colleagues, assess his own performance, and expect to be judged by his colleagues. . . . "[8] Growth of staff can result from teachers' observing and being observed by their colleagues.

The exchange of ideas among teachers can be a more fruitful experience than traditional "supervisory visits" made by the principal. This is not to imply the principal quits, or even reduces supervisory activities. It does mean he will be involved as one of several observers and be a contributor and resource person with those who are on the team. Supervision of team teachers, to be most effective, requires of the administrator new approaches, such as greater recognition of the professional qualities of his staff, more dynamic leadership, and less commandership.

Supervision of New Teachers

A reduction of isolation can help new teachers overcome their reluctance to ask for help. All teachers, experienced or inexperienced, need to grow in the recognition that one's colleagues are valuable resource persons and there need not be a threat involved in asking for help.

The new teacher, who in the typical school has often received too little assistance, will be able to work with experienced teachers in planning and observing the various phases of teaching. For many years industry has taken the attitude that once the young college graduate comes to an organization he is ready to be trained. A young graduate in business administration may spend a year and a half in a training program. Education must assume a posture which recognizes that a college graduate entering teaching is, like the graduate in business administration, in need of further training. Working with experienced staff members as a team member enables the

---

[7] Medill Blair and Richard G. Woodward. *Team Teaching in Action.* Boston: Houghton Mifflin Company, 1964. p. 61.

[8] Glenn F. Varner. "Team Teaching in Johnson High School, St. Paul, Minnesota." *Bulletin of the National Association of Secondary School Principals* 46: 161-66; January 1962. p. 164.

beginning teacher to receive adequate on-the-job training and supervision.

Development of Peer Evaluation

One of the advantages of team members working together is the change that can occur in the "evaluation" aspect of supervision. In many ways, supervision has been deterred by the inseparable quality of supervision and evaluation of teachers. When team members work with each other to improve instruction, there is little or no threat involved. When team members evaluate what they have done, there is more emphasis placed on improving teaching and less emphasis placed upon evaluation or rating of the teacher.

Relating Supervision to Staff Needs

In a traditional setting the topics dealt with in the supervisory process are usually identified by the supervisor. At the end of a visitation the supervisor lists the strengths and weaknesses, discusses these with the teacher, files the report form, and goes on to other pressing administrative chores.

Team members and a supervisor are able to arrive at a decision about the areas which are satisfactory or which are in need of change or improvement. The areas needing change or improvement can then receive the mutual attention of the members of the team and the supervisor.

The best, in terms of supervision, will not be realized if the principal does not provide adequate leadership. The principal needs to demonstrate more *leadership* and less *commandership* as a means of working *with* people in place of having people work *for* him. As the principal works with teachers, there must be evidence of the fact that he recognizes the worth and professional qualities of each staff member. Changing patterns of instruction and supervision continue to place new demands upon the secondary school principal.

As the principal and his staff develop an understanding of team teaching and see the new supervisory relationship in operation, there will be a growing awareness of the opportunities for supervision through team teaching. ☐

EL 25 (3): 249-55; December 1967
© 1967 ASCD

The Supervisor's Role in Personnel Administration

JAMES E. RUTROUGH

PUBLIC school supervision generally is viewed as a staff function. The role of the public school supervisor has been defined in various ways. During the 1920's his role was much like that of the supervisor in industry. He was viewed as an autocratic superior who was charged with seeing that teachers would "stay in line." Concepts of the role of the educational supervisor have changed over the years as new educational practices have been introduced into the schools.

James E. Rutrough, Associate Professor of Education, Virginia Polytechnic Institute, Blacksburg

Perhaps the basic factor that has affected the emerging role of the public school supervisor has been the rising level of professional preparation of teachers. Today, the supervisor is viewed as being a friend, a co-worker, a consultant, and advisor to teachers. He works with teachers as a team member in providing the best possible program of education for boys and girls.

If the educational program is the focal point of school personnel administration, the superintendent of schools must assume definite responsibility for supplying a certain degree of leadership himself as well as making staff provisions in terms of supplementary leadership for more penetrative development in this particular area.[1] This specialized leadership may be provided through certain administrative and supervisory personnel attached to the staff of the superintendent of schools.

Although the personnel activity may be the major responsibility of the director of personnel, the supervisor and other school employees have important roles to play in this area of school administration. The supervisor is in a key position to make valuable contributions in enhancing the success of personnel administration for the following reasons:

1. He is a professionally trained employee of the local school board.

2. He is a professional charged with developing promising professional relationships with the teachers with whom he works.

3. He is in a position to influence directly the self-confidence, morale, and effectiveness of teachers.

4. In the modern sense, his role is seen as that of being a consultant, a helper, a friend and mutual confidant of the teacher.

5. He is in the position of contributing to the objective that all school employees have the competencies needed for their respective jobs.

[1] James A. Van Zwoll. *School Personnel Administration.* New York: Appleton-Century-Crofts, 1964. Chapter I.

6. His work involves providing instructional leadership to enhance quality education in the school system.

The supervisor appears to be in a position to contribute to many of the functions of school personnel administration.

Emerging Role of the Supervisor

Personnel administration is a relatively new development in the field of school administration. As school districts become larger and more complex, this phase of school administration becomes more important and more specialized. In recent years personnel administration, which was once the exclusive job of the superintendent of schools, has become a partnership arrangement. The assistance of supervisors, principals, committees of teachers, and others is needed to cope with the personnel activity in the modern school complex.

The literature pertaining directly to the role of the supervisor in personnel administration is extremely limited. Apparently, few studies have been completed pertaining to the supervisor's role in this area. It seems evident, from a review of recent literature pertaining to the role of the supervisor in the modern school organization, that many opportunities exist for the supervisor to make worthwhile contributions to the personnel administration field. It appears that many of the functions of personnel administration may be more appropriately carried out with the supervisor as a cooperating team member. The very nature of supervision in the modern school system lends itself to the support of personnel administration in the following areas:

• *Orientation.* Beginning teachers and those new to the school system may find their adaptation and adjustment to the new situation eased as a result of the work of the supervisor. Many preliminary and pre-session orientation programs are inadequate at best. Thus personnel administration, and the school system in general, have an obligation to conduct a continuing program of orientation as the school year proceeds. The supervisor is called upon to play a major role in this continuing program.

Among the activities that may be included in such a program, to which the supervisor can make excellent contributions, are the following:

1. Arranging for new teachers to observe demonstrations and teaching by experienced teachers.

2. Organizing workshops for beginning teachers and for new teachers that will provide for professional growth and the exchange of ideas.

3. Tours of the school system and the school community to enable new teachers to learn more about the community, its school system, its goals, customs, and assets.

4. Arranging social events to provide opportunities for new teachers to get acquainted with colleagues, and to provide for an element of recreation. This is also helpful in gaining the good will and cooperation of the new employees.

5. Helping new teachers to become familiar with the job, and with its problems.

Much of the supervisory program is concerned with continuing orientation activities for both new and experienced personnel.[2]

As a specialist in human relations, the supervisor can smooth the path of human interaction, ease communication, evoke personal devotion, and allay anxiety on the part of new teachers.[3] Thus, valuable contributions are made in enhancing the job performance of new employees, and in improving instruction. The supervisor is a logical supplementary agent in exercising leadership in the development of a stimulating atmosphere free from tension for the new employee.[4] This is an important contribution that relates to several of the principles of personnel administration.

• *In-service education.* Within the school system all supervision of personnel has the function of providing in-service education that relates to the objective of promoting and maintaining competency.[5] This is a basic objective of school personnel administration. In teaching, it is imperative that the teacher keep up with the changes in his teaching field. Regardless of how competent beginning teachers may be, the leadership of the school system has a responsibility to provide opportunities for these teachers to continue their professional growth. This is an objective of an efficiently operating school system. According to Lucio and McNeil,[6] the supervisor is generally responsible for six kinds of duties with reference to in-service education:

1. He plans with individuals and groups to develop policies and programs in various academic fields.

2. He makes decisions, coordinates the work of others, and gives directions.

3. Through conferences and consultations, he seeks to improve the quality of instruction.

4. He participates directly in the formulation of objectives, selection of school experiences, preparation of teaching guides, and in the selection of instructional aids.

5. He gives and arranges for classroom demonstrations of teaching methods, use of aids, and other direct help to classroom teachers.

---

[2] *Ibid.,* pp. 143-49 and 239.

[3] William H. Lucio and John D. McNeil. *Supervision: A Synthesis of Thought and Action.* New York: McGraw-Hill Book Company, Inc., 1962.

[4] Edith S. Greer. "Human Relations in Supervision." *Education* 82: 203-206; December 1961.

[5] Van Zwoll, *op. cit.,* p. 87.

[6] Lucio and McNeil, *op. cit.,* p. 26.

6. Through systematic surveys, experiments, and studies, he explores current conditions and recommends changes in practice.

- *Morale.* The most important single factor in getting the best that a school employee has to offer is how he feels about his job, his associates on the job, and the school system in which he is employed.[7] This is one of the principles of personnel administration that relate to morale. Actually all personnel in the school system play roles in facilitating this process. Morale cannot be created or guaranteed, but the climate which favors its development can be created. Greer [8] states that one of the important elements in supervision is the development of a stimulating atmosphere free from tension. Therefore, the supervisor occupies a strategic position, as the friend and confidant of, as well as consultant to the teacher, in helping to create a climate conducive to development of good morale.

From a personnel administration point of view, it appears that the development and maintenance of morale might be looked upon as developing and maintaining organizational health.[9] In reality this means taking action to improve school employee-job relationships. The supervisor can make excellent use of his relationships with teachers in bringing to the attention of the personnel division those problems, issues, grievances, and injustices that need to be corrected to improve the working situation.

- *Motivation and personal adjustment.* Implicit in the concept of personal adjustment is the fact that the satisfaction of individual needs is a continuous process. Supervision contributes materially to the total administrative effort to satisfy both organization expectations and the physical and psychological needs of personnel. The supervisor can contribute to the achievement of these ends by:

1. Providing assistance to members of the school organization in solving problems with which they are constantly confronted.

2. Helping the organization to decide whether the individual is capable of fulfilling role expectations.

3. Helping the organization to clarify the position requirements and the qualifications necessary for successful performance.

4. Assisting in the selection process.

5. Motivating members of the organization to accept responsibility for self-development and creativity.

6. Dealing with personnel maladjustment, which is expressed in such forms as aggression or regression; thus minimizing the tension and strain within the school system.

7. Motivating the teacher to establish appropriate working relationships with his colleagues, and to enhance his personal and professional development.

8. Recommending changes in work assignments, dealing with unsatisfactory superior-subordinate relationships, and providing assistance to potential retirants.[10]

In summary, personnel administration must increasingly deal with the complexities of human nature and its implications for organizational behavior. The supervisor has an important role to play in assisting the personnel division in coordinating the multiplicity of activities involved in its broad field of operation. The major concerns of the personnel division are also areas of interest to the supervisor. Supervision shares with personnel administration the basic objectives of doing whatever is necessary to make sure that all who work within the school system have the competencies, the

---

[7] Van Zwoll, *op. cit.*, p. 172.

[8] Greer, *op. cit.*, p. 204.

[9] William B. Castetter. *Administering the School Personnel Program.* New York: The Macmillan Company, 1962. p. 80.

[10] *Ibid.*, pp. 65-66.

will, and the working conditions for providing the best program.

It appears that the supervisor can make his most effective contributions to the personnel activity in the areas of orientation, in-service education, morale, and personal adjustment and motivation. Contrary to the views held by some authorities in the field of personnel administration, supervision is a dynamic, growing process that is occupying an increasingly important role in public education. ☐

EL 22 (5): 322-26; February 1965
© 1965 ASCD

Merit Rating:
Have the Issues Changed?

FRANCES R. LINK

IT IS possible to point to school districts, including my own, in which merit rating works. We can devise rating scales and use them. We can devise a team approach to supervise the evaluation of teachers. Within this system we can select our "superior" and our "inferior" teachers with some degree of accuracy; and we can feel reasonably comfortable that careful supervision and the independent judgments of principal and supervisor concur. This is what we mean when we say—"it works."

However, there is an accompanying phenomenon. Teachers begin to perceive themselves, each other, and their supervisors in new ways. As a supervisor, I hear teachers developing a classification system somewhat as follows:

One type says, "Why should I lose money because of a limiting factor? [1] I received 'merit,' so I'm not eligible for three more years—that doesn't make sense. Why can't I get a merit raise every year?" This is the "I want merit every year" teacher. "If I'm good this year," she says, "I'll be the same next year. Why should I lose money because of a limitation factor?"

Another type says, "I did not receive merit; perhaps I should leave the profession." He may add, "I received 'good' supervisory reports. I felt certain I was a merit teacher. Why didn't I get a merit rating? I don't care about the money; I feel I'm a failure." He asks the supervisor, "Do you think I should stay in teaching?" He is not asking how to improve his professional competence; rather, he is feeling failure to the point of considering leaving his chosen career. He asks for advice but he wants ego restoration.

Still another type says, "You don't have to visit my classes, I'm not interested in merit." This teacher has adopted a limited concept of the purposes of supervision. This creates a chain reaction. The supervisor visits his classes feeling unwanted and struggling to know how to help the teacher grow professionally. The teacher, the supervisor feels, has equated improvement of instruction with merit rating. The supervisor wonders whether the teacher really

[1] The Cheltenham plan makes a teacher eligible for a merit increment once every three years. Four hundred dollars is added to the normal increment. As of 1968, the Cheltenham plan has not been functioning. It is under study and is likely to be replaced by a "new" scheme of differentiated staffing.

Frances R. Link, Director of Curriculum and Research; School District of Cheltenham Township, Elkins Park, Pennsylvania. In 1965, Coordinator of Secondary Education, School District of Cheltenham Township

wants to grow professionally and a chain of negative feelings interferes with the supervisory act.

In 1950, the Commission on Teacher Evaluation of the Association for Supervision and Curriculum Development conducted a study that resulted in a pamphlet entitled, *Better Than Rating*.[2] In this most provocative work, edited for the Commission by Robert R. Leeper, new approaches to the appraisal of teaching services are presented. In the section concerned with "How Rating Affects the School Program," the following statement appears:

> The teacher, knowing he has been rated, usually says, "But I can't find any trace of myself or my work in these results!" He feels his work has been compared, almost always unfavorably, with the ideal practices of a teacher who never existed in reality.[3]

The "Elusive Ideal Teacher"

Most school rating schemes have evolved as descriptions of so-called ideal practices which have little or no basis in instructional theory or research. Most merit rating schemes would never have evolved in schools without the pressure from School Boards or some force outside the profession. It is not surprising that the teaching profession and school systems, not ready to develop merit rating, have selected models for rating schemes from outside the profession.

Merit rating models have come, in the main, from business and industry, and the pressure to institute them has come largely from School Board members associated with such merit programs in their own work.

Many school systems have abandoned merit rating programs after several years of trial. In systems where it continues, I am convinced that it "works" only because those who administer it admit to the limitations of the system and that the teachers involved basically trust their supervisors. I am also convinced that school morale is affected by merit rating to a lesser degree than we thought, but that the subtle and persistent pressure felt by some individual teachers serves to inhibit their personal development and their teaching performance.

Better Than Rating makes a strong case for the profession's concern for respect for the individual teacher:

> School people in modern times have come more and more to base the educational program upon the premise of respect for the individual. In order to guide his development, they must start with the individual child, accept him where he is, as he is. Beginning with this acceptance and understanding, they can guide his development in accordance with his own rate of growth. The child is thus not always unfavorably compared with an ideal child who never really existed. His achievements and shortcomings are interpreted, for the most part, in the light of his own rate of growth and development.
>
> This acceptance of the individual person where he is and as he is accords with the basic democratic principle of respect for individual personality. This applies to adults as well as to children.
>
> Teacher-rating plans, whether they rank teachers in a certain arbitrary order, give an overall score or mark on performance, or judge teachers according to a listing of ideal qualities, are administrative plans which do not basically respect individual personality. These plans do not provide for acceptance of the individual as a competent professional person, where he is and as he is. Neither do they encourage an attitude of acceptance on the part of the rater that would cause him to point out any change and growth which may have been achieved by the individual, or what the direction of change should be to further his professional growth.[4]

[2] Association for Supervision and Curriculum Development. *Better Than Rating: New Approaches to Appraisal of Teaching Services.* Washington, D.C.: the Association, 1950. 83 pp.

[3] *Ibid.*, p. 55.

[4] *Ibid.*, pp. 55-56.

Much of what is quoted here is reflected in the feeling of teachers who attempt to exclude the supervisor from the classroom because they are not interested in merit rating. Many supervisors have tried to separate improvement of instruction programs from merit rating. This is possible and perhaps even desirable, for until we can more precisely describe the act of teaching, how can we really place a value judgment on it?

Better Than Rating makes an important statement on rating scales:

> If teachers know that their teaching is going to be judged in certain predetermined ways, it is only natural that they will plan their teaching in such a way that they will show up well in the judging. Educators, for example, have long recognized that if teachers knew in advance that the growth and development of their pupils was to be measured by the use of standard achievement tests or regents or college board examinations, they would plan their teaching so that pupils would have as adequate as possible a mastery of the facts to be measured. In like manner, teachers who know that their efficiency as a teacher is to be judged in terms of predetermined items listed on a rating scale or in a personnel record, will plan their teaching so that they will make as good a showing as possible when the scale is applied to their work.[5]

In practice, this is indeed true. As a matter of experience, the inadequacy of the rating scale looms large as teachers work to fit the scale. We have experienced some difficulty in trying to guide a teacher out of the profession because she or he *can* be rated satisfactorily on most single items on the teacher rating scale. The ASCD Commission on Teacher Evaluation found very few teacher rating scales which provided for weighing the component traits to be rated, and they state that "the impossibility of assigning weights is obvious, since the matrix of factors that makes one teacher eminently successful may not be the same combination of qualities that account for the success of another."[6]

Rethinking the Issues

Firsthand experience with merit rating had led the writer to reexamine the literature and rethink with colleagues the issues involved in merit rating. Four significant issues were identified 14 years ago by the ASCD Commission on Teacher Evaluation in the pamphlet, *Better Than Rating*.

The first of these issues has to do with motives which underlie efforts of individuals toward self-improvement. Does the reward-or-punishment provision implicit in most rating plans help the individual to make his greatest effort toward professional growth? Does fear of demotion or of reduction in pay cause the teacher to strive consciously and intelligently to "mend his ways"—even though he has to go in the direction prescribed by the rating plan or by the person who does the rating? Or has modern psychology not found sounder principles upon which to base a program for encouraging teachers' efforts to accomplish best results in working with children?

A second issue involved in teacher rating has to do more directly with the process of evaluation. What is the purpose of evaluation? If evaluation is part of the means by which people judge and guide the direction of their growth, then this process should be thoroughly understood and participated in by all concerned. The question involved is whether we, in a democracy, want a type of authoritarian evaluation which guides individuals into unquestioning obedience and submissiveness to persons superior in status. On the other hand, is it not preferable to develop a democratic organization in which qualities of cooperative evaluation would be explored, understood, and used continuously, freely, and creatively by all concerned in the process?

[5] *Ibid.*, p. 58.

[6] *Ibid.*, pp. 64-65.

A third issue has to do with the effect of current teacher-rating practices upon professional growth. Just what are the characteristics of the main types of rating plans currently in use? Do these plans actually help the teacher see his "points of weakness," and thus automatically encourage him toward greater efforts to overcome these faults? Or do the plans, because of their very nature, cause greater tension and anxiety, and thus have an undesirable, and sometimes disastrous effect upon the professional development of the individual?

A fourth issue relates to the kind of organization which will best foster and encourage professional growth on the part of individuals and groups. Is the school, or the superintendent, alone concerned in evaluation of the school's program, of results of instruction? Or is evaluation the privilege and responsibility of every person affected by the school's program? An organization is shaped by people, and yet an organization also shapes people. The important thing in evolving an organization to foster professional growth in democratic schools is that it faithfully exemplify the soundest principles of democracy. This will make possible the effective working of cooperative evaluation procedures.

These four issues, *fourteen years later,* are still crucial. An issue which becomes increasingly sensitive as one experiences merit rating is *how an organization is shaped by people and how an organization also shapes people.* A rating scale becomes a shaping device no matter how supportive the supervisor, the principal, or the system may be.

With "merit rating" the classroom visit is "different," no matter what the relationship has been with the supervisors. Staff relationships, which shape the school atmosphere, become difficult to assess—and often guarded. Parents inadvertently shape a new problem by saying to a teacher, "Of course you got a merit raise, didn't you?"

Styles of Teaching

If we could effectively deal with the issues stated above, the issues to be proposed might not be forthcoming. One "new" issue relates to the research and knowledge being developed about the styles of teaching, theories of instruction, the nature of classroom interaction, and the relationship of personal mental health to professional growth. Some educators who have been doing research in the area of teaching and classroom interaction have stated that their work is not to be used to evaluate teachers. Perhaps this should be true in the initial stages of research. The issue seems to be, however, what will be the effect of current research on teacher education, instructional theory, and "styles of teaching" on the evaluation of teacher performance. There is a need to bring together new knowledge and research from a variety of disciplines in order to rethink the nature of teaching and the structure of better teacher evaluation procedures.

Rating or evaluation of one's work as a teacher is not an issue in most school systems today. Whether it be formal or informal, rating exists. Will we be able to resolve old issues and professionalize our task of rating teachers when we use what we know from both experience and research about the phenomena of teaching and learning? This leads to the related issue of the nature of teacher preparation. The work in curriculum development and even school building design for future needs has already surpassed efforts to study and improve teacher preparation. Teacher education has many dimensions, some of which will have a powerful influence on teacher education in the future. These are defined in *The Education of the American Teacher* by James B. Conant and *The Miseducation of American Teachers* by James D. Koerner.

The writings of these men will no doubt have an immediate influence, but whether

176 • Supervision: Emerging Profession

or not their recommendations will improve the quality of teaching is central to the issue of teacher performance and ultimately teacher evaluation. My hunch is that we will find more effective guides for understanding teaching in the research on teacher education conducted at San Francisco State College by Fred Wilhelms and others and in the work of Ned Flanders, N. A. Fattu, Arno Bellack, B. O. Smith, Hilda Taba, Elizabeth S. Maccia, and others who have been engaged in developing "models" of instructional theory and classroom interaction. Once we know *who* should teach and *what* teachers *do* that results in learning, then we will begin to know what to value and reward in teaching. ☐

References and Readings

Association for Supervision and Curriculum Development. *Better Than Rating: New Approaches to Appraisal of Teaching Services.* Washington, D.C.: the Association, 1950.

Arno A. Bellack, Joel R. Davitz, in collaboration with Herbert M. Kliebard and Ronald T. Hyman. *The Language of the Classroom: Meanings Communicated in High School Teaching.* New York: Institute of Psychological Research, Teachers College, Columbia University, 1963. (The research was supported through The Cooperative Research Program of the Office of Education, U.S. Department of Health, Education, and Welfare. Cooperative Research Project No. 1497.)

Harry S. Broudy, B. Othanel Smith and Joe R. Burnett. *Democracy and Excellence in American Secondary Education: A Study in Curriculum Theory.* Chicago, Illinois: Rand McNally & Company, Education Division, Box 7600, 1964.

David G. Ryans. "Assessment of Teacher Behavior and Instruction." *Review of Educational Research* 33: 415-41; October 1963. Washington, D.C.: American Educational Research Association, 1201 Sixteenth Street, N.W.

David G. Ryans. *Characteristics of Teachers, Their Description, Comparison and Appraisal: A Research Study.* Washington, D.C.: American Council on Education, 1960.

B. Othanel Smith. "Toward a Theory of Teaching." *Theory and Research in Teaching.* Arno A. Bellack, editor. New York: Bureau of Publications, Teachers College, Columbia University, 1963.

Hilda Taba. "Teaching Strategy and Learning." *The California Journal for Instructional Improvement.* Burlingame, California: California Association for Supervision and Curriculum Development, 1705 Murchison Drive. December 1963.

Asahel D. Woodruff. "The Use of Concepts in Teaching and Learning." *The Journal of Teacher Education.* Washington, D.C.: National Commission on Teacher Education and Professional Standards. March 1964.

EL 23 (8): 652-55; May 1966
© 1966 ASCD

Supervisor: Coordinator of Multiple Consultations

PAT W. WEAR

A SUPERVISORY function of growing importance is that of coordinating the contributions of the many and varied consultants who are now available to assist the school in improving its staff and program. Such consultants may include leaders in the system, teachers with special skills and competencies, college personnel, state

Pat W. Wear, Chairman, Department of Education, Berea College, Berea, Kentucky

department representatives, members of professional groups and organizations, representatives of state or federal governments, lay citizens with special skills and knowledges, textbook company consultants, reading specialists, psychological service specialists, guidance counselors, speech therapists, librarians, music and art specialists, physical education specialists, school nurses, and the like.

The bringing of on-the-job assistance to teachers is rapidly becoming recognized as a central function of local supervisory personnel. The utilization of multiple consultative services will, without doubt, become more prevalent in the years ahead because our rapidly changing society demands almost unlimited resources to help solve constantly emerging educational programs in the local school situation.

The development of a more complex society, the explosion of knowledge, the increasing school enrollments of more diverse students in the schools, the development of a technical approach to learning, and the development of school faculties that include well-prepared teachers from varied backgrounds of training and experience demand an in-service program that is aimed directly at the practicing staff extending its own professional knowledge, refining its old or developing new professional skills, and focusing on the modifications of its own professional behavior. In-service education depends on the nature and quality of the changes that are produced. The intelligent use of consultative service that includes not just one or two consultants but many individuals who contribute, share, and interact cooperatively with school staff through careful and artistic coordination by the supervisor will be an imperative change-factor of the future.

The supervisor's effectiveness as a coordinator of multiple consultation is based on an understanding of and an ability to function within a number of socially complex situations which exist in a school or school system. A description of some of the more important conditions follows.

Supervisory Coordination

The supervisor must possess a basic understanding of the school as a social institution within a community that varies in its structure and that holds different role expectancies for consultants who may be used with the staff. The role expected by the faculty for the consultant must be lived up to, initially, or the resulting threat will make impossible the acceptance of the consultant and his contribution, or certainly will markedly reduce such acceptance.

The supervisor must possess a broad comprehension of the total school program and of the role each individual staff member has in the school's functioning, evaluation, and further development. The absence of such understanding limits the clarity of the purposes held for the establishment of consultative acts that will contribute meaningfully to both the development of the overall program and the individuals involved.

The supervisor through well-planned evaluative efforts must have arrived at a point that he feels he has identified growth behaviors needed within the staff in order to move the program ahead in a positive and progressive manner. These judgments must be arrived at by cooperative assessments made in the day-to-day relationships with staff over an extended period of time and must, in reality, stem from the mutual concerns, interests, and needs expressed by staff. The outcomes emerging from and within the coordinated consultative acts would also be assessed for directional cues for future action and activities within the staff.

There must be developed an institutional climate in which the individual growth of the staff member is as important as that of the individual student in the classroom of the school. Such an environment for growth is vital to the full development and utilization of the creative potential of each individual on the faculty. The supervisor has a key place in the development of this type of working environment by the way he behaves as he seeks to work with the staff in the improvement of the teaching-learning situation. The modern supervisor must be keenly alert to the process of change as well as the end product sought through the process.

The awareness by faculty members of the process in which they are engaged, in many instances, is as important as reaching the desired goal. Constant analysis and interpretation of the consultative act in process often determine its final effectiveness.

The accurate identification and clarification of problems or situations in the school that are vital to staff members, and for which there is a need for experience that cannot be provided from within the immediate group, dictate a setting in which a consultant or many consultants may be needed. The suggestion that consultative help may be used at this point does not preclude the use of consultants in aiding faculty in understanding the school as an institution in the community, the development of new understandings and insights regarding school programs, the development of appropriate working climates, and the like.

The role of the supervisor, once there has been a recognition that the knowledge, skill, or competency needed is not available, becomes one of the selecting, out of the breadth of his own experiential contacts, the consultant or consultants who may be matched to the needs of the situation. This suggestion implies the need by the supervisor to have almost unlimited contacts with individuals and groups who may be called on either to furnish the needed person and service or who may be a resource to seek out the needed personnel. Once the person or persons have been identified, a relationship of some depth must be developed between the supervisor and the consultant. This relationship is one of the more important aspects of being able to appropriately coordinate consultations that will have full meaning for all those involved.

The supervisor must work within a leadership complex that includes the school superintendent, principals, subject supervisors, group leaders, and many others. There must be an orientation period in which the gradual involvement of the consultant in the school situation takes place. The consultant must be aware of the purposes of the group. The role expectancy must be defined for the consultant as accurately as possible. If there is more than one consultant, then there must be developed the kinds of relationships that will permit this group to function and interrelate as a team.

There might be a few situations in which a consultant may be brought in to provide a special ingredient without the long period of orientation and involvement suggested here. However, to bring about important changes in behavior within a school staff, an intimate and continuous effort over an extended period of time is demanded.

A word of caution is needed in regard to the selection of outside consultants. There are many cases in which the consultant needed is actually a member of the local staff. Called for here is a refocusing on the resources that lie within a staff as well as those that may be brought in from outside. The supervisor as a coordinator of multiple consultations is as vitally needed, if not more so, in the identification and use of in-staff consultants as in the case of out-of-staff personnel.

The competency of the supervisor to coordinate multiple consultations is obviously based on a number of vital personal relationships. These relationships are with the school as an institution within a community, the individuals who implement the program, the specific group involved in problem identification and clarification, and the consultant.

The supervisor must also provide for the development of appropriate relationships and understandings between and among the consultants, and the consultants and the group to be worked with. Appropriate relationships must also be maintained between the consultants and the administrative leadership of the school.

The choice and assignment of consultants are as vital as the assignment of the teacher to the appropriate classroom. The supervisor must be open to and respond to feedback emanating from administration, teaching staff, consultants, and ultimately to the reaction of the student to a changed program or curricular experiences. The supervisor must recognize that the constant examination of his own behavior in these social-education complexes is a vital necessity. The improvement of his own skills and competence as a person who seeks to act as a coordinating agent between a group with expressed needs and the provision of experiences that fulfill such needs is dependent on accurate self-perceptions. The consultants' consultations may be as valuable to the growth of the supervisor as to the group involved.

The supervisor's changing role includes not alone an understanding of the technical aspects of institutional improvement or curriculum building. This role also includes the ability to participate effectively in action research, where appropriate human relationships have been formed. The job of curriculum improvement has become one of more than making adjustments in organizational structure, modifying instructional materials, remodeling school facilities, and building courses of study. There is an increasing awareness that instruction cannot be fundamentally changed unless the staff itself changes its own understandings, attitudes, concepts, and ideas through having experiences that are provided at the right time and when there is a state of readiness for such activity.

Preparation for Coordinating Multiple Consultations

A supervisor may be better equipped to carry out the coordination of multiple consultations, as described, if he has had preparatory experiences similar to those in internship programs. This type of program provides actual contact with a school staff and the intern is faced daily with the actual need to work in consultative situations. The guidance offered by both local school district and college personnel may be invaluable in such on-the-job situations.

The preparatory experiences should consist of opportunities for the supervisor-intern to gain: knowledge and understanding of the school as a social institution and its role in present day society; knowledge and understanding of the curriculum, of its development, and of current curriculum research; knowledge and understanding of human growth and learning; knowledge and understanding of teaching and leadership methods and techniques which include the function of the staff on the job; knowledge and understanding of instructional materials and resources and their utilization in the teaching-learning process; skill in communicating effectively with individuals and groups through written, oral, and overall behavior; skills in helping others identify, clarify, and develop procedures for arriving at solutions, problems, and concerns; skills in problem solving using the methods of intelligence; and skill in group processes related to working with people to more appropriately utilize resources and develop solutions to problems and meet needs adequately. □

Supervising Supervisors in an Urban School District

HARVEY GRANITE

RECENT writers on the problems of urban schools seem to insist that most supervisors and administrators are irrelevant and often obstructive in the process of education. Such major theoreticians of public education as Conant, Bruner, Keppel, and Clarke hint strongly that the Age of Reformation in education, particularly urban education, is in danger of foundering upon the rock of administrative hierarchy.

A fair question to be answered, then, in investigating the relationships between a supervisor and his subordinates in the central administrative hierarchy, is why *are* supervisors necessary? One would hope that it is not, as most of the stereotypes of the supervisor imply, to serve as inspector of a generally poorly trained and incompetent teaching staff—the chief duty of supervision in the late nineteenth century, and apparently still their chief duty in the sclerotic bureaucracies remaining in some of the major metropolises today.

It is not that the supervisor is the "specialist," possessing all that is worth knowing about his subject and feeding it in nourishing mouthfuls to the infantry in the classroom, although a good supervisor must continue to be recognized as one of the outstanding teachers of his subject to be found anywhere. Nor can the supervisor any longer be the manipulator of teachers, cajoling them into discovering goals and methods which have already been set for them by top administration.

Instead, the most important words found in recent descriptions of the supervisor's function are "help," "aid," "stimulate," and "lead." McKean and Mills, for example, see the supervisor as a facilitator, helping each school, each teacher, to develop the goals and methods appropriate to the particular educational climate within that school. For the central office consultant in the large school district, McKean and Mills are specific in delineating the limitations imposed upon him by the very nature of his job:

> The central office consultant is limited in his contributions because he necessarily must spread his energies and resources among many schools in the system. He probably lacks intimate insight into the nature of the individual school's student population, the strengths and weaknesses of the faculty, close and continuing acquaintance with the building and equipment, evolving local modes of operation, shifting patterns of interrelationships among the staff, and prevalent feelings and attitudes toward change.
>
> At the same time, he is apt to have a broad view of the total program of the school system. He can safeguard the individual school from excessive provincialism. His function may be to bring new perspective to local problems, to suggest different points of view, to help broaden the vision of building personnel, and to indicate new possibilities.
>
> Ideally, the central office consultant works

Harvey Granite, Chief Consultant for English, Reading Improvement, and Libraries, City School District, Rochester, New York

in a staff capacity. He has little or no administrative authority. For example, his services are better received and evaluated if he is not required to rate teachers. He ordinarily does not visit classes unless invited. As a supervisory consultant he must convince teachers of the worth of his suggestions. The special art of supervision is the ability to help teachers discover better approaches to instruction, rather than directing or requiring them to use different methods or teaching materials.[1]

If supervisors in urban school districts could work within the definition set down by McKean and Mills, they would be welcomed into the classroom rather than dreaded, as apparently they are in some systems. Nevertheless, in many urban districts, central office consultants continue to rate teachers, often on the basis of a single observation. There may be some value in this central office observation, in that it obliges the supervisor doing the rating to visit probationers regularly if he is to perform this function honestly. The disadvantage, aside from the strong possibility that the evaluation is based on skimpy evidence, is that rating inevitably raises a barrier between the supervisor and all but the most secure or the most indifferent of teachers, a barrier which interferes with the primary job of the consultant—to help, to stimulate, to lead.

In a large school system only two basic approaches to central supervision can be possible. One is to hold the entire system to a single approved approach to all instructional problems. The other is to maintain a flexible and varied curriculum by helping individual schools and even individual teachers to make the fullest use of their own talents and resources, and without ignoring individual liabilities. The second approach, despite the difficulties it poses for the central office supervisor, is the direction of the future. The supervisor in education will continue to exist only if his role changes from that of the "overseer" to that of stimulator and colleague.

There are disadvantages to democracy, even in education. For one thing, it takes longer to come to a decision, and in these impatient times for the cities, when federal funds come trailing hundreds of strings—guidelines, deadlines—it is often difficult to give up time to democratic planning, when to the experts the solutions already seem so obvious.

Teachers themselves are often unwilling to give up the time for joint planning, but perhaps this is because their contributions to planning have had to be made on their own time. Districts must provide meeting time for teachers if they expect joint planning efforts to work. The involvement of principal and teachers in determining for their school the best use of the services of a reading specialist means that the reading specialist will receive stronger staff support than if his job description were determined centrally. The decision of an individual school to adopt structural linguistics, transformational grammar, a multitext or eclectic approach, or no text at all, as the best way to develop sensitivity to and precision in the use of English in communication, is the best way to ensure that teachers *want* to make a method work. Whether it be Hawthorne effect, professional pride, or just plain stubbornness, teachers when challenged will make their own methods work—when, somehow, other methods fail.

Of course, as supervisors, the members of our staff often find themselves in disagreement with the teachers and administrators they are trying to help. Often the director will find himself in disagreement with his supervisors. Yet if he were consistently to overrule their decisions (sometimes it may be necessary) in recommending a particular teacher for transfer or a particular textbook for adoption, he would be communicating his lack of faith in their

---

[1] Robert C. McKean and H. H. Mills. *The Supervisor.* Washington, D.C.: Center for Applied Research in Education, Inc., 1964. p. 40.

judgment as specialists in their particular field. On the other hand, if he can convince his colleagues through reason, through his ability to win respect and confidence, even enthusiasm for a point of view not originally their own, then he has made his point as a professional rather than as an authoritarian. In the same way he and his staff members try to direct their efforts in working with principals, department heads, teachers, and librarians, to promote their enthusiasms, their feelings of adequacy and personal worth, their originality, toward the goal of helping children to learn.

Preparation of Supervisors

Martin Haberman describes teacher education as "a process whereby each individual is offered numerous personal choices as he lives through a variety of experiences."[2] The education of supervisors does not differ markedly in terms of goals and objectives from the education of teachers. McKean and Mills' list of personal characteristics necessary for the successful supervisor are much the same as those for the successful teacher:

- Ability to win respect and confidence
- Empathy and sensitivity
- Enthusiasm
- Feeling of adequacy
- Originality
- Sense of humor
- Sense of relative value
- Resourcefulness.[3]

Another writer describes the successful supervisor as one who is democratic, "people-oriented," able to see situations as others do, well-informed, and so forth,[4] again undeniably the qualities of the successful teacher. The important difference is that the supervisor works with adults, with professionals, with intellectual equals, with teachers often more gifted than himself. Insofar as the supervisor is a model, a leader, a teacher of teachers, he must exemplify all that is best in contemporary teaching by stimulating professional growth among the teachers with whom he is working.

As head of a large department in the instructional division of my school district, I am charged with curriculum and staff development in English, reading improvement, and libraries. My department, because of its strategic importance in the education of disadvantaged children, has mushroomed during the last three years, as a result of the wider availability of federal and state funds. By the fall of 1968 Rochester schools had employed 160 English teachers, 60 or more reading improvement teachers, and 30 librarians. To accomplish any change in language instruction, in library utilization, or reading improvement, I must rely upon the supervisors reporting to me to maintain an efficient and coordinated program.

Nine of the supervisors are English department heads in secondary schools, who are responsible chiefly to their schools. We meet together regularly on a city-wide basis to discuss materials, methods, and curriculum; we meet individually to discuss specific school problems of personnel, class load, and innovation. Three of the supervisors—a teacher on special assignment in English, a supervisor of reading improvement, and a supervisor of libraries—work directly with me. Although their responsibilities are great, they have a more immediate knowledge than I of the teachers and students with whom

[2] Martin Haberman. "The Professional Sequence for Preparing Teachers: A Proposal." Mimeographed working paper for the Teacher Education Conference, University of Rochester, Rochester, New York, January 6, 1966.

[3] McKean and Mills, *op. cit.,* pp. 42-44.

[4] Jane Franseth. *Supervision as Leadership.* New York: Harper and Row, Publishers, Inc., 1961. pp. 59-71.

they work. In working with these supervisors I have found it necessary to delegate increasing amounts of authority as my own responsibilities have increased. This delegation in turn has placed obligations on me to help the supervisors meet these new responsibilities.

In an article discussing the relationship of administrators to their staffs, Chester Ingils probes the motivations of administrators who hesitate in their obligations to staff development.

> Many administrators . . . follow practices that indicate a lack of recognition that they have any part in the developmental process of subordinates. Some follow practices that show signs of actions that would impede (if not prevent) a subordinate from progressing in his development. They withhold from a subordinate knowledge of the organization or the environment in which the unit operates.[5]

Ingils sees the delegation of authority as "an absolute necessity for the successful operation of an organization. Without delegation, growth and development of the organization is limited to the capacity of one man."[6] He suggests that an inability to delegate grows out of fear by an administrator or leader that he will be superseded by a more successful or more dynamic subordinate—the same kind of fear, one might propose, that makes it difficult for authoritarian supervisors to give teachers the initiative.

An administrator's feelings toward delegation are often mixed. The leader has attained success and often believes that this success is truly a result of his own ability and efforts. This feeling becomes a psychological block that impedes him from delegating responsibility and authority. . . . Because of the competitive environment in which he has worked and progressed through the ranks, he often is concerned about the competition he will experience from subordinates. A latent fear of this competition causes him to be afraid that his subordinates will do the work as well as he can—or maybe better.[7]

Although Ingils published his article in an educational journal, he could actually be discussing any organization with an administrative hierarchy. And although he is discussing the relationship of an administrator to subordinates within the hierarchy, his comments are equally pertinent to the relationship of the supervisor to the teacher. Human awareness, "empathy" McKean and Mills call it, is key to any supervisory relationship.

Staff Responsibility

What Ingils means is that, having participated in the choice of staff, the administrator is obligated to make it possible for staff members to do their job. The nature of the work must be clearly defined, as well as the sources of information necessary to accomplish it. In reflecting on this point recently, I discovered that it was much easier for me to define responsibilities for the supervisors of reading and of libraries, areas in which I have less training, than in English. Perhaps this was because I was reluctant to share these responsibilities, even though the growth of my own job made such delegation necessary.

As the subordinate becomes familiar with his new responsibility he should be assigned increasing authority and responsibility that in part was previously held by the administrator. The administrator should retain the prerogative of evaluation of the work that is performed and the privilege to redefine the subordinate's responsibility. At the same time, he should guard against interference with how the work is accomplished.[8]

Guarding against interference includes

---

[5] Chester Ingils. "Advice to Administrators: Clues for Success." *The Clearing House* 42 (1): 15; September 1967.

[6] *Ibid.*, p. 16.

[7] *Ibid.*

[8] *Ibid.* See also: Amitai Etzioni. *Modern Organizations.* Englewood Cliffs, New Jersey: Prentice-Hall, Inc., 1964. pp. 51-54.

concern for the conditions under which the supervisor must work. The leader must also be concerned for the morale of his subordinates. He must be sure that their status and salary are commensurate with their responsibilities relative to the organization. He must help them obtain the office space and clerical assistance necessary to their positions. He must help them to define the limits of their individual responsibilities so that they do not attempt more than their capabilities at a given time will allow and so that they can work to their fullest capacities without fatigue and without frustration. When necessary he may have to intervene in support of his subordinates when additional assignments from elsewhere in the organization threaten accomplishment of their regularly defined tasks. A leader who is insensitive to these needs may unconsciously but deliberately be contributing to the lack of success of his subordinates, just as a supervisor who is unconcerned about the work-load or free time of the teachers with whom he is working may in effect become an obstacle to education.

For supervisors and for leaders of supervisors, the possibilities in a democratic organization always exist that (a) the subordinate may accomplish a particular task more successfully than the administrator and (b) the subordinate might make a mistake. Here, I feel, lie the greatest challenges of all to the ego of the democratic administrator-supervisor. For he must be willing to recognize publicly a job well done (even when it is done differently from the way he would have done it) and, paradoxically, to share without rancor the responsibility for mistakes.

Many administrators find it difficult to do this. . . . They do not have faith in their subordinates, and instead are prone to elaborate and dwell on the error. Such an approach does not correct the mistake, aid the employee in improved decision-making, build his confidence, or aid in the growth of the organization.[9]

When the leader has selected competent subordinates and has provided them with problems clearly defined and with sufficient information and sufficient time to act upon the problem, the problem will probably be solved. "If these elements do not exist," says Ingils, "it is the failure of the administrator." [10] It is a point worth pondering.

American education is undergoing a dramatic change in organization. Within a relatively short time teacher councils, through collective bargaining, will assume many of the functions in decision making now performed almost exclusively by top administration. It would be unfortunate if this shift is based upon power relationships rather than on consideration of what is best for the children in the schools.

In 1961, Henry Brickell could still say pragmatically that the moment the teacher steps outside of his classroom he exerts little force for change.[11] By 1968 it has become clear that in large school districts, and ultimately in all districts, teachers and administrators will shortly become either colleagues or rivals in educational leadership. A central office organization can prepare for this likelihood by developing "collegiality" within its own ranks as it continues at the same time to involve teachers in educational leadership.

Authority for appropriate decisions would rest, not with an official leader, but with the staff as a whole. Leadership would be by consent—delegated to the emergent leader who would be elected by the staff itself. Decision-making would be broadly based, a product of wide involvement.

[9] *Ibid.*, pp. 17-18.
[10] *Ibid.*
[11] Henry M. Brickell. *Organizing New York State for Educational Change.* Albany: New York State Department of Education, 1961. p. 23.

One might well ask, "What will this do to the profession of school administration?" It seems clear that an administrator is no less a professional if he participates as a member of the staff rather than as the official leader of the staff! [12]

There is still need for individual leadership in education. The first task of that leadership is to remove the obstacles that have prevented teachers from sharing in the decisions affecting their work. The second is to join with teachers in a common concern for education as a profession. ☐

References

Henry M. Brickell. *Organizing New York State for Educational Change*. Albany: New York State Department of Education, 1961.

Amitai Etzioni. *Modern Organizations*. Englewood Cliffs, New Jersey: Prentice-Hall, Inc., 1964.

Glen G. Eye and Lanore A. Netzer. *Supervision of Instruction: A Phase of Administration*. New York: Harper and Row, Publishers, Inc., 1965.

Jane Franseth. *Supervision as Leadership*. New York: Harper and Row, Publishers, Inc., 1961.

John I. Goodlad. *School, Curriculum, and the Individual*. Waltham, Massachusetts: Blaisdell Publishing Company, Inc., 1966.

Paul Goodman. "Mini-Schools: A Prescription for the Reading Problem." *The New York Review of Books*, January 4, 1968. pp. 16-18.

[12] Robert C. McKean. "Decision-Making: The Administrator Needs a New Outlook." *The Clearing House* 41 (5): 287; January 1967.

Mary Frances Greene and Orletta Ryan. *The Schoolchildren: Growing Up in the Slums*. New York: Pantheon Books, 1966.

J. Minor Gwynn. *Theory and Practice of Supervision*. New York: Dodd Mead & Company, 1961.

Martin Haberman. "The Professional Sequence for Preparing Teachers: A Proposal." Mimeographed working paper for the Teacher Education Conference, University of Rochester, Rochester, New York, January 6, 1966.

Ben M. Harris. *Supervisory Behavior in Education*. Englewood Cliffs, New Jersey: Prentice-Hall, Inc., 1963.

Chester Ingils. "Advice to Administrators: Clues for Success." *The Clearing House* 42 (1): 15-18; September 1967.

Ralph B. Kimbrough and Eugene A. Todd. "Bureaucratic Organization and Educational Change." *Educational Leadership* 25 (3): 220-24; December 1967.

Jonathan Kozol. *Death at an Early Age: The Destruction of the Hearts and Minds of Negro Children in the Boston Public Schools*. Boston: Houghton Mifflin Company, 1967.

Daniel U. Levine. "Training Administrators for Inner-City Schools." *National Elementary Principal* 46 (3): 17-19; January 1967.

William H. Lucio and John D. McNeil. *Supervision: A Synthesis of Thought and Action*. New York: McGraw-Hill Book Company, Inc., 1962.

Robert C. McKean. "Decision-Making: The Administrator Needs a New Outlook." *The Clearing House* 41 (5): 285-87; January 1967.

Robert C. McKean and H. H. Mills. *The Supervisor*. Washington, D.C.: Center for Applied Research in Education, 1964.

Richard F. Neville. "The Supervisor We Need." *Educational Leadership* 23 (8): 634-40; May 1966.

PART V

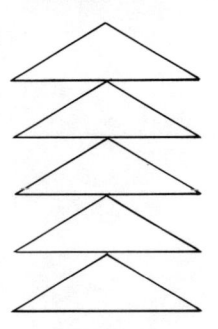

Supervision: Its Potential

New Frontiers for Supervision

(An Editorial)

MARCELLA R. LAWLER

PROBABLY never in the history of American education have so many exciting frontiers been developing simultaneously. In fact, never in world history has any nation had so much to build on educationally—thousands of highly trained, professionally motivated persons, an interested citizenry believing in the importance of education, and a rich tradition of continuous, thoughtful study to improve the quality of educational opportunity for all children and youth.

Historically the supervision role has encompassed two functions: (a) providing leadership for developing, improving, and maintaining effective learning opportunities for children and youth—which means giving attention to content selection, teaching methods, materials, and evaluation, both inside and outside the classroom; and (b) providing leadership in designing effective ways of working with teachers and other members of the school staff to achieve the first function.

Emerging Curriculum Developments

Changing and intensifying emphases for a changing society: The central purpose of education in the United States of America has always been to develop children and youth able to function at a high level as citizens of our society. This has involved developing people intellectually but at the same time giving much attention to personal-emotional-social development so that individuals could operate as high level human beings in the best tradition of our society.

Exciting frontiers are opening for consideration in both the planning for what to teach and the planning for the human beings we teach.

Expanding emphases in our cultural heritage: In line with our expanding national purposes, which indicate a new role for us as leaders in a world society, we are attempting to work with children and youth so they will better understand the peoples of the world as well as the general world scene. Knowledge and understanding of religions, literature, music, international economics, and languages of nations around the world are widening the horizons of American students. Depth study of our unique American purposes, ideals, and contributions to civilization, along with study leading to new insights into the world scene, is causing many American students to assume a new stance in their considerations of social and political world problems. Education for our national purposes demands that our programs be thus extended and deepened.

We still have much upward mobility in our population. In a society whose democratic origins have sometimes been indicated by the saying, "A poor boy from an unknown family may become President," we need to be very careful in schools that we do not label groups and then deny them rich educational opportunity. Havighurst

---

Marcella R. Lawler, Professor of Education, Teachers College, Columbia University, New York

reports that in 1920, twenty percent of our population was identified as lower-lower class. In 1920 and 1940, zero percent of that population entered college. However, in 1948, six percent of the males entered college; in 1958 six percent males, zero percent females; in 1960, ten percent males and five percent females. Of the forty percent of the population in the upper-lower class, in 1920, two percent entered college; 1940, five percent; 1948, males, fifteen percent; 1958, twenty percent males, seventeen percent females; 1960, ten percent males and five percent females.[1]

Changing emphases in subject-matter disciplines: The explosion of knowledge has caused scholars in each subject-matter discipline to explore new approaches to the organization of the discipline in an effort to discover improved ways of knowing. Scholars of the disciplines and educators are striving to find ways to teach students the tools of the disciplines. This exciting adventure not only opens up new considerations for the purposes of teaching the disciplines but also provides the possibility of releasing school people to select content beyond the usual stereotypes.

Much of the exploration under way is reflected in the work of major national committees in mathematics, science, foreign languages, English, and the social studies. Each committee is making major recommendations relative to what to teach from its discipline in the school program, how to teach it, and in many cases at what point in the child's life he is able to develop these understandings. Because of NDEA funds and private foundation grants, reports, courses of study, and text materials have been prepared by the various groups at work and are now available to schools. Text-book development is already being influenced.

Changing and extending emphases in foreign languages: Research drastically affecting the teaching of foreign languages has made a marked impact on language programs in the schools. Students are excited about language and are gaining competence in the use of languages which heretofore have not been available. Many language teachers seem to feel that while language laboratories admittedly introduce problems such as housing, expense, teacher time for supervision, the preparation of material, initial installation, they also do much to move the individual student ahead.

Extending the time of introduction of a foreign language into the elementary school is causing intensification of interest in language. This trend also is forcing us to rethink the secondary school language program. In many school systems language is for the first time becoming a kindergarten-through-high-school subject for study.

Coordinating the arts: While the scholars and educators in such fields as mathematics, science, and linguistics have been working to identify concepts which might help students learn the structure of their disciplines, some artists and teachers have moved ahead in identifying concepts such as line, form, and rhythm common to all art forms. Following careful and detailed planning, specialists in each of the arts areas have pioneered in team teaching efforts. Advanced class enrollments in these situations have increased greatly with the result that many students are going on to college to major in the arts areas.

Testing new media for instruction: Technological development has provided the American public with television for entertainment, and the American school with television for teaching. It has also provided

---

[1] National Society for the Study of Education. *Social Forces Influencing American Education.* Chicago: University of Chicago Press, 1961. Chapter 5, p. 123.

business with programmed billing, and education with programmed teaching. Utilization of these media is very much in the experimental stage. While teaching by television has been used in some schools for a period of time, significant research on what may best be taught through this medium still remains undone. An interesting question raised by one leader in the field is, "How can we use students on camera?" Outstanding and exciting shows in the teaching of ballads were produced in one school system, using high school juniors and seniors.

Teaching by machines is an area needing much research. Just how and how long children will relate to and be motivated by a machine are unanswered questions.

Research in psychology: Many of the questions to be raised by educators concerning the exciting possible frontiers in the refocusing of teaching in the disciplines, the experimentation in the teaching of foreign languages, the use of the new media for instruction must be answered in terms of research being carried on in psychology. Scholars in this area are insistently calling to the attention of educators the limitations of the I.Q. as an index of ability as we now measure it and of giftedness, and the impact of lack of opportunity and low motivation in causing underdeveloped capacity to learn.

Psychologists are also developing theory and reporting researches which hold tremendous promise for teaching in such areas as perception and the development of human potentialities. As we learn more about how to detect and to build upon the learner's perceptions we will be able to make startling strides in selection and organization of content as well as teaching methods, in terms of our purposes for teaching. As we learn more about the uniqueness of human potential and ways of developing it, we will unlock among human beings many resources which are now imprisoned.

Programs for Engineering Curriculum Changes

Developing personal potential: As indicated earlier, the primary purpose of supervision is to improve the educational opportunities for boys and girls; this means that the quality of teaching must be developed to its limits. Opportunities through which professional staff members may broaden horizons, develop new interests, deepen insights must be encouraged and, whenever possible, be planned for as an integral part of the professional development program of the school. This will result in richer and more varied opportunities for learners. Deliberately creating an atmosphere in which intellectual and cultural development is valued is an important aspect of supervision.

Developing professional potential: Professional and personal potential are, of course, inextricably related. However, they are deliberately separated here for purposes of this discussion. This is well, for an extensive retooling job lies ahead for thousands of American elementary and secondary teachers as new formulations are developed relative to the teaching of several of the subject matter areas. This retooling will require teachers and curriculum leaders to work with educators and scholars in the disciplines. Programs of supervision in the immediate future will necessarily include intensive workshop opportunities, possibilities for on-campus as well as in-service courses in the subject matter areas. Many excellent summer workshops and fine academic year scholarships for retraining personnel have been developed under the NDEA and foundation grants. Supervisors should become familiar with these many opportunities so that they can encourage staff participation.

It likewise is of critical importance that teachers and curriculum workers have systematic opportunities within the program of supervision to become familiar with new research frontiers in psychology, sociology, anthropology, and philosophy. The supervisory program should be so designed that much opportunity will be provided school staffs, not just to listen to lectures in these areas, but to have systematic opportunity to explore what the meanings are for curriculum and teaching in new formulations, theories, and research. Decisions relative to content, grouping, organization of the school day must be made with recognition of the research in these areas.

Developing research studies for curriculum: It seems important to recognize that much of the thinking and planning being done, many of the proposals being made in the subject-matter areas and in the utilization of machines and television in teaching are untested. For example, staffs of some school systems located in uniformly high socioeconomic areas are already reporting that the "new mathematics program" is only good for the upper two-thirds of their students. What does this mean for the other one-third of the students in these areas, most of whom would expect to go on to college? Does this indicate that the content is inappropriate for the majority of the high school youth; that the organization of the content is not well conceived; or that the methods of presentation have not been good even though the teachers have had and are continuing to have training in the teaching of the content and in the use of the materials?

In addition to these considerations another factor deserves attention. There are several "new mathematics programs." While the proposals are alike in some respects they are quite unalike in others. Differences are found in vocabulary, in the timing of presentation of some key concepts, and in organization. At a time when much work is being done internationally in many fields, when many professional workers are meeting in international conferences, it seems questionable that there should not be agreement on at least the language of mathematics—and of other disciplines as well.

These facts are presented only to emphasize that all curriculum innovations should be carried on within a research framework. This applies not only to the content and methods employed in teaching the subject matter areas, but also to grouping, testing programs, unmotivated learners, and gifted learners. Bench marks should be established, hypotheses developed in terms of anticipated outcomes and systematic observation, testing, and reporting.

If supervisors are not trained in designing and carrying out research studies, this is an area of competency they should develop. While that competency is being learned, assistance in designing and executing studies is available from colleges, universities, and state departments of education.

It is also hoped that ASCD's Research Commission will give leadership to the development of some nationwide research endeavors in which many individuals and school systems over the country can participate. Much curriculum work must become research oriented.

What are some of the frequently stressed principles to which supervisors must continuously give attention as they work for curriculum development, improvement, and maintenance? Some helpful principles are these: (a) Planning for activities should be done with those who participate. (b) Development of plans for coordination should be done with the staff; developing and maintaining open lines of communication throughout the individual school and school systems are essential for successful curriculum work. (c) Providing opportunities for parents and other lay citizens to discuss their hopes and expectations for their children, for the school program is essential. (d) Providing continuous information about education and the educational program of the community increases not only understanding of but also support for the program.

Working toward a theory of supervision: A plea has been made in this statement for supervisors to take leadership in placing their curriculum development work in a research setting.

A further plea is made that supervisors and other curriculum workers shall proceed in developing a theory of supervision and curriculum in order that activities in this area of leadership may be more effectively analyzed and researched. At present we do not have sufficient descriptive data as to how curriculum change takes place, the factors that seem to facilitate and to block. Systematic efforts in theory building for this leadership function need to be undertaken. ☐

EL 23 (8): 615-17; May 1966
© 1966 ASCD

What Should Be the Crux of Supervision?

(An Editorial)

LOUISE M. BERMAN

THE Association for Supervision and Curriculum Development is committed to the professional welfare and development of all persons who perform supervisory functions within the educational milieu. The Association has concerned itself with age-old questions, continuously begging for new and more persuasive answers.

Some of these questions have been: How can a supervisor simultaneously play a helping and an evaluative role? What are the tasks of the principal in the process of supervision? What types of cooperative arrangements should be developed between the supervisor and principal to ensure adequate help to teachers?

Although these questions still need to be asked, the current nature of schooling is such that finding answers only to the old questions will not meet today's educational challenges. New priorities and emphases demand that the field of supervision rearrange its boundaries and reconsider its central foci.

Shifts on the horizon such as the following are necessitating a new look at the concept of supervision:

Preschool programs in which professionals and semiprofessionals are expected to collaborate to build sturdy programs for the young child

Cooperative teaching in which teams of teachers must adapt to new types of hierarchial and horizontal arrangements among themselves

---

Louise M. Berman, Professor of Education, University of Maryland, College Park. In 1966, Associate Secretary, ASCD

in order to provide more "meaty" programs for children and youth

New plans of school organization, such as the middle school and the extended secondary school, in which new kinds of administrative and supervisory arrangements provide the setting for exciting innovations in line-staff relationships

Cooperative arrangements among public schools and universities in which persons are needed who can mediate between the two institutions in order to utilize most fruitfully the unique and common features of each institution

Research emphases in the public schools necessitating additional staff or reeducating old staff in order to help make the educational undertakings more precise.

These trends are cited merely to indicate that principals, supervisors, and curriculum coordinators are no longer the primary persons fulfilling supervisory functions within the school. New and revitalized studies need to be made concerning the tasks of directors of research, department chairmen, master teachers, teacher leaders, coordinators, cooperating teachers, and numerous other persons who have significant supervisory roles in today's schools.

The increasingly complex and proliferated nature of supervision demands the profession's rethinking the issues to which it will address itself. The questions need to be pervasive and penetrating. One good question can often be of such strength that a myriad of insignificant queries no longer need to be asked.

The Facilitating Process

One question related to the function of supervision which appears to get at the crux of the problem is: *What is the nature of the facilitating process?* Inherent in the dictionary definition of facilitating is the notion of making easy or less difficult and of freeing from impediments. If supervising is considered as facilitating or making the work of others easier, those persons who are responsible for helping teachers see their tasks with less difficulty and more clarity need to reassess their modes of providing service and to ascertain how this work is perceived by others.

In considering the facilitating process we might consider it from the stance of the behaviors the facilitator exhibits or the perception of the facilitator's behavior by others. The latter stance seems the more profitable.

Among the qualities which the facilitator is seen as possessing is acuity and accuracy of perception. Visual and psychological perception is seen as being keen both in viewing the reality of persons and the abstractions of ideas. The facilitator is perceived as being aware of himself and others to the extent that he realizes the levels of awareness and the types of blind spots he and others bring to a situation. That persons are simultaneously strangers and intimates to themselves is evident in practice.

The facilitator is considered as being more interested in the internalized organizational schemes and plans of the teachers with whom he works than in external organizational patterns which are precise on paper but dissatisfying to those who must "fit in." He is seen as prizing the models, patterns, and plans which the individual teacher develops to help explain his intent and actions to the magic models designed by "experts." The model of the expert serves only as a source of guidance for more personalized models. No rational plan of organization offers consolation when the person operating within it has been dichotomized so that his inner self is slave to an outer organizational plan.

The facilitator is seen by others as possessing reality-centered excitement. Such excitement demands discernment in reaction to ideas. When the ends of a project are even dimly discernible, he may appear to react with greater caution than when ends are clearly visible. He is perceived as doing more than giving support, although this commodity is generous when appropriate. At other times, however, he is perceived as asking the prickly, barbed questions which sharpen the issues of a dilemma. He is seen as knowing the difference between decisions that are made because of current fads or pressures, and those that are based upon the promise of long-term and far-reaching consequences.

The facilitator is perceived as respecting the integrity of others and caring for their well-being. Because of his staunch enthusiasm for what persons are and can become, he is not seen primarily as an "authority" but rather as a person who is willing to throw his considered judgments into the arena of ideas. Others have the opportunity to react honestly without fear of recrimination. Teachers are aware that his proposals are subject to the same type of discussion, decision making, and evaluation as their own. At the same time he is seen as establishing the setting so that others have equal opportunity for a hearing. Insofar as possible, the group is utilized in making decisions but various responsibilities in the decision making process and who performs them are clearly visible.

Although the facilitator is genuinely interested in others, he is *not* perceived as having a continuous "open door policy." Even as teachers are expected to build into their days time for increasing their knowledge and for making considered judgments, so he practices his policy of allowing for intake as well as outgo of ideas. He formulates "maps," schemes, and *Weltanschauungs* which enable him in the long run to be a better facilitator.

Because of his integrity, his relative freedom from game and role playing, and his ability to place himself in the position of others, he is perceived to be a caring, human individual. In brief, he is a person capable of the total range of human behaviors. He earns the respect of his colleagues primarily through his total being as a person rather than through his title or status.

If the many new jobs demanding competency in facilitation are to be adequately filled, then the profession needs to give increased attention to this important process. The basis of initial and continuing preparation should be reexamined and additional insights should be sought from other fields and disciplines which focus upon the helping relationship—theology, psychology, psychiatry, social work, and the like. Attention should be given to including in the preparation of all persons who have responsibility for facilitating the work of others, intern-type opportunities for experience which focus directly upon the competencies needed to enhance the professional activity of another. Such preparation would enable instructors to understand better the motivations of persons seeking to become educational facilitators and to establish criteria for selection of those who should do this type of work.

If supervision is to enlarge its borders to take in those persons who will be facilitators as a result of newly created jobs and if supervision is to address itself to more powerful questions, then the nature of facilitation should be studied as the crux of supervision.

The field of supervision has some "mighty men." Oftentimes through random experiences these persons have become great facilitators. Our task now is to explicate more fully the task of educational facilitation so that more "mighty men" will emerge. ☐

The "Guese" of Supervision

BERNARD J. LONSDALE

SPEAKERS and writers frequently refer to the language peculiar to a trade or profession as the "guese"; for example, the language of educators is referred to as "pedaguese." If the butcher, the baker, the candlestick maker can afford the luxury of a "guese"—why cannot the educator have his pedaguese?

The blocks to communication and the threats to wholesome human relations in our society are not the "guese" but the failure of the in-group to interpret language to the out-group. One's social graces should dictate when a particular "guese" is proper and when it is improper. If a person has some money to invest with a banker or at the track, he goes out of his way to learn the "guese" of the banker or of the racing expert. If individuals have an interest in education, they will go out of their way to find the meanings of the terms frequently used.

Many Voices—Many Languages

The writer has difficulty in recalling any glossary of educational terms prepared for public consumption which might improve communication between the school and the community. Those glossaries which have come out are directed to educators and most of them are attempts to lampoon terms used by fellow educators. It might pay dividends if every school district were to prepare a glossary which would be ready for each child to take home after his first day at school. The programs of parent organizations and other civic groups might be planned around the glossary, using a variety of techniques to enhance communication between the school and the community.

It is difficult to talk or write about the language of supervision apart from the many interrelated languages that affect educational programs—the language of the child, the language of the mother and father, to say nothing of the languages of the other members of the family, the language of the teacher, the principal, the superintendent, the school nurse, the psychologist, the school board—not to mention the languages of the power group and the various minority groups in the community.

True, democracy is made up of many voices and each voice has the right to be heard again and again. However, there are certain principles unique to the processes of democracy which make it possible to determine whether the voices ring true and whether the language expressed is in harmony with the principles of democratic living. Sometimes we hear the voices of the fakers riding on bandwagons who speak and write glibly about serving society and protecting the welfare of children. At other times we hear the dedicated educators who see the perpetuation and improvement of democracy as being realized through an education program custom-built for each individual so he will meet his needs and reach his highest potential.

Supervision in education has moved

Bernard J. Lonsdale, Education Consultant, Sacramento, California. In 1963, Visiting Professor in Education, University of Maryland, College Park

from the time when it meant demonstration and inspection. This function has become, in effect, a many-splendored thing set in a matrix of understandings, skills, and values related to the growth of individuals as participating members of a democratic society. In earlier days supervision was a simple operation when it meant that someone from "downtown" or the "county seat" walked up and down the aisles of a classroom making notes in a little black book and then went back to the office to fill in a form, a copy of which was sent to the teacher, which answered, with *Yes* or *No,* such questions as:

Was the lesson socialized?

Did the children stand to recite?

Were the decorations in the room seasonal?

Franseth adds new dimensions to supervision in the statement:

Today supervision is generally seen as leadership that encourages a continuous involvement of all school personnel in a cooperative attempt to achieve the most effective school program.[1]

In a summary statement Franseth suggests four ways in which supervision is most effective in realizing these new dimensions:

(1) When it contributes significantly to the accomplishment of goals considered important by the teachers as well as by the supervisors; (2) When the teachers are meaningfully involved in making and carrying out plans that affect them, with a part in determining what the supervisory service should be; (3) When supervision provides an atmosphere of acceptance, support and understanding, and helps people experience feelings of worth; and (4) When supervision helps people make sound judgments and act on the basis of careful study of adequate and accurate information.[2]

[1] Jane Franseth. *Supervision as Leadership.* Evanston, Ill.: Row, Peterson Company, 1961. p. 19.

[2] *Ibid.*, p. 29.

The Supervisor's Language

As supervision moves to encompass new dimensions, the language of supervision talks about such things as:

The Goals of Education: The emphasis is on a statement of goals or a set of beliefs which is built school by school, district by district, with everyone affected by it participating in its preparation. The answers to the question of appropriate opportunities for children and youth will be found in a clearly defined statement in harmony with the principles of education in a democratic society. Such statements should provide the platform upon which to build programs suited to the needs of our times.

A publication of the California State Department of Education suggests the following questions as the basis for evaluating statements of goals:

1. Is the statement of the objectives available to all interested persons?

2. Is the statement in accord with the broad purposes of democracy?

3. Have legal requirements as established by the Legislature and the State Board of Education been met?

4. Is the statement based on the requirements of the course of study as established by the governing board of the school district or the office of the county superintendent of schools?

5. Is the statement in harmony with well-substantiated research in child growth and development?

6. Is the statement in harmony with well-substantiated research in mental health?

7. Are school practices consistent with the established goals?

8. Does the school have an organized plan to evaluate progress toward the fulfillment of the goals?

9. Do school personnel and members of the community refer to the goals when making decisions?

10. Are the goals reviewed and revised from time to time as the situation changes? [3]

Numerous statements of the purposes or goals of education in a democratic society have been prepared by committees of national repute. Accepting these statements for a particular school by a local committee or an administrator is one thing. Having them used for study purposes as a basis for working out statements that will fit their peculiar needs is quite another thing. The people whose nervous systems are most deeply affected by statements of goals or purposes are those who participated in their preparation.

Individual Differences in People: The stress is placed upon the differences— physical, social, and intellectual—that characterize human beings. Each individual is recognized as a unique personality. Each has the right to develop to his fullest potential. Each is entitled to feel that he counts. Too often in our society some individuals feel that if everybody is somebody then nobody is anybody. The talk turns to "keeping certain people in their place." The question asked in supervision is, "How can the differences that characterize an individual be turned into assets for the good of the whole group?"

The Basic Human Needs That Individuals Must Satisfy: Unless an individual has opportunity to satisfy his basic needs which come out of the structure of his organism, the social context in which he develops, and his personal growth, he may be frustrated and spend his life in fruitless searching which often ends in despair and personality damage. Stress in the language of supervision is placed upon the need to sense the extent to which the basic needs of individuals are being met and as one meets his own needs to help others to meet theirs. The help to others may be shown in a warm smile, an invitation to coffee, a willingness to listen.

The Need To Know Children and Youth: Emphasis is placed upon a knowledge of the characteristics of growth and development of children and youth. These characteristics also apply to adult development. Each one goes through the same pattern but each goes through at a rate peculiar to himself. Each one comes through as a custom built job—some with more assets than others, some with more liabilities than others—but each with his own pocket full of stars. Stress in the language of supervision is placed upon the need for skill in the techniques of observing, studying, and interpreting human behavior. Understanding that all behavior is caused and that the causes are many and interrelated is an important dimension in human relations. It may not be possible in many instances to know the cause, but to know that there is a cause contributes to better working relations.

Effective Teaching Methods: The language of supervision has stopped saying, through the use of directives, "This is the way to do it." Good supervisors realize that any change that might come from a directive can only be of the narrow routine type. The big changes, the really important ones, are those that come out of the teacher's changed behavior. Extensive research pertaining to effective methods of teaching has been done.

Many of these research studies have set boundaries as to the most and the least effective ways of working. There is need for studies which will extend the boundaries set by this research. There is further need for research done by teachers who will be identified with the findings and who will put them into practice.

What evidence is there that certain

---

[3] Bernard J. Lonsdale and Afton D. Nance. *Evaluating the Elementary School*, Revised. Bulletin of the California State Department of Education, Vol. 30, No. 3. Sacramento: California State Department of Education, 1961. p. 29.

methods of instruction are more effective than others? Could a particular method yield more learnings than another? Why does a child fail in one situation and succeed in another? How does one way of learning interrelate and support another? These questions are merely illustrative of the myriad questions teachers ask every day. The language of supervision suggests that teachers carry on research of significance to themselves.

After they have defined a problem, they can state a hypothesis that will indicate the procedure to be followed and the outcomes to be expected. With this as a basis for starting, they have a laboratory in the classroom in which to collect and to evaluate data, and to test the hypothesis. The emphasis in the language of supervision should be of the kind that will help teachers to create the design for the research, develop instruments needed for securing the necessary data, and interpret the records.

Use of Instructional Materials: Emphasis is placed upon the use of a variety of materials of instruction. As new insights are gained regarding the learning process, it becomes obvious that materials that have appeal to all the senses should be made available in classrooms. Each day, it seems, new materials come on the market which have learning value or which facilitate learning. Teachers are encouraged to experiment with these new materials and to use them in their research patterns. Too often new materials are condemned and passed over before they are even tried. Community resources are of immeasurable value as materials of instruction. People, places, and things outside the classroom can contribute significantly to learning situations.

Creativity: A high premium is placed on the potential for creativity which is innate in each individual. The time has passed when creativity was thought to belong only to a chosen few. Kelley and Rasey say:

Whenever an individual takes a set of known answers and contrives a new response, concept, or artifact he is creative. It is the process of taking the things we now have or now know and putting these together in such a way that something new emerges.[4]

This concept of creativity is furthered by Russell when he says:

In one sense, all a child's learning is creative in that he arrives at what is, for him, new solutions. Some writers prefer to limit the more routine school and community learnings to the process of discovery and to describe by the term *creative thinking* only those processes which result in some product or solution of an original sort. Children's learnings may be described on a scale ranging from routine associative learnings through rather stereotyped problem-solving processes to highly original creative thinking resulting in new solutions for the individual and his subculture.[5]

The language of supervision urges an atmosphere in which teachers are encouraged to express themselves creatively. As teachers are motivated to develop their own creative abilities they in turn provide creative opportunities for children.

The creative personality does not develop under an autocratic regime. The language of supervision places a heavy stress upon the democratic processes because they hold most promise for freeing individuals to make their fullest contribution to the welfare of the individual and the group.

In part of the response to the question, "Is America Neglecting Her Creative Minority?" Toynbee says:

Potential creative ability can be stifled, stunted, and stultified by the prevalence in society of adverse attitudes of mind and habits of behavior. . . . When creative ability is

---

[4] E. C. Kelley and M. I. Rasey. *Education and the Nature of Man.* New York: Harper and Brothers, 1962. p. 116.

[5] David H. Russell. *Children's Thinking.* Boston: Ginn and Company, 1959. pp. 326-27.

thwarted, it will not be extinguished; it is more likely to be given an antisocial turn.[6]

The challenge today in education is for everyone to think creatively. No one group of individuals in our society has an option on creative living. The satisfactions which are the by-products of creativity are available to all.

All of this supervision talk implies the need for continuous education, not only for teachers but for everyone responsible for planning educational programs. The language of supervision has a chance to be heard and understood by the types of in-service education programs developed cooperatively with the people who will profit from them.

The language of supervision will continue to talk about the goals of education, individual differences in people, the basic human needs that individuals must satisfy, the need to know children and youth, effective teaching methods, the use of instructional materials, and creativity.

It is evident that supervision means differt things to different people. Many of the concepts held by the different individuals are inadequate as guides to the improvement of instruction. As a result, the language of supervision becomes a voice crying in the wilderness.

Supervision will never go back to inspection and demonstration. Through the thinking, action, and language, both spoken and silent, of dedicated educators its new role has emerged. Supervision will continue to improve instruction. The future greatness of our country will be built through the quality of education made available to every individual who is a part of this nation.

[6] Arnold Toynbee. "Is America Neglecting Her Creative Minority?" *Mills Quarterly* 44: 5-6; May 1962.

EL 25 (1): 54-61; October 1967
© 1967 ASCD

"Osmosis"—The New Supervision?

WILLIAM C. JORDAN

IF ONE reviews the college, graduate-level textbooks on organization, administration, and supervision which have been published in the past 25 to 30 years, he will find that the major instrument of instructional change is a "committee." Almost without exception, author after author, the present writer included, points out that supervision, the improvement of instruction, is teacher oriented at the grass roots level and that the "participatory process" is the one insurance policy that guarantees progress.

Invariably we administrators are told to gather about us a group of "interested teachers," define and delimit a problem, set up a hypothesis, attack the problem, determine alternatives, choose a solution, and arrive(!) at a conclusion—be it a new method, report card, a new course of study, a recommendation about noontime supervision, or adoption of a textbook. The advocates of this type of supervisory operation contend that the end product is not the important outcome but that the major con-

William C. Jordan, Assistant Superintendent, Educational Services, Napa County, California. In 1967, Acting Superintendent, San Rafael City Schools, San Rafael, California

tribution lies "in transit." The true goal, they say, is in the intragroup, interpersonal relationships that mold teacher opinion as the group progresses, and teachers, seeing the reasons and need for revision, actually accept, for themselves, change which is put into action upon their return to the classroom.

Such committees, fortified by gallons of coffee—and possibly doughnuts—are clothed with such presently pertinent phrases as "democratic practices, involvement, communication systems, participation, group dynamics, feeling of belonging, and purposeful activity." When you strip all the verbiage away, the educational administrator, supervisor, or principal is saying, "We want the teachers to do what we want them to do, but they must think it is their own idea!" Imagine! Another famous administrator indicates that he "gets teachers to do what he wants but entirely without friction"—again imagine!

One of the reasons that the educative process changes so slowly is that too many supervisors feel that teachers fall for this line of fluff. Teachers are not stupid! They are aware of the literature, they know that change is necessary; they patiently observe the rules of the game as played by some administrators and go stoically through the motions of meetings and coffee and committee caravans as part of the price they must pay for membership in a fine and rewarding profession.

More deadly than the above questionable and limiting experience is the "group therapy" approach to supervision. Here we find the administrator-executive "curing" teachers by repealing the past. Little by little, step by step, he leads his staff out of the gloom of confusion into the bloom of professional profusion—*as he sees it!* This is the administrator who, in advance, knows what he wants, picks his own committee, and tells it where he wants the group to go! And, what's more, gets there by leading his tethered teachers down the path of least resistance.

Again when one realizes that this process has been functioning for years under the cloak of democracy, one understands the lag of educational advancement. Teachers justifiably resent this type of nonsense as beneath their dignity. One will find thousands of courses of study, arrived at through such chicanery covered with dust, unnoticed by the teacher, in a stack on his desk or in his book cupboard. So much for "supervision" in its traditional form.

Let us now turn our attention to another chapter of progress. The words, *obligated boundary maintenance,* should have special meaning to the supervisor who truly is interested in change. *Obligated boundary maintenance* indicates the reaction and resistance of a group to a suggestion of change. Even if the people (teachers) involved know that change is necessary, even though they know that new ideas, methods, materials, or techniques are profitable, the group feels "obliged" to join hands and, with bowed heads, shout, "No!"

To change, you see, is tantamount to admitting that what one has been doing in the past is not "quite right"—and there are too few people in the world who are secure enough to admit that there might be a better way or that they are or have been wrong. We, all of us, therefore, deny progress by saying, "My kids are different; we did this before and it doesn't work; parents won't stand for it; my principal is against it; takes too much time," and on and on. There are hundreds of ways to scuttle a new idea.

A New Method

How, then, does one who wants to innovate, lead, create, or simply supervise, organize for progress? The writer would like to offer a new method which for want of a better term I call "Osmosis," the gentle movement of liquid through a barrier.

To begin this "Osmosis" process, the supervisor-administrator searches through his own staff for teachers with adventurous souls. They are not hard to find. You take one teacher by the hand and say, "Come with me." With this one teacher, the supervisor works as a partner to develop a new teaching technique, explore a new method of organizing a classroom, experiment with a unique unit, build new methods of presentation of material, or construct a continuing self-evaluation system for the students. One is limited here only by the ingenuity and creativity of the two educators involved.

While the "Osmosis" process is attractive and exciting, it should be obvious to any educational administrator that this operation can be "fraught." The process requires great delicacy; one must be extremely sensitive to the feelings of other teachers when a specific member of the staff may be given a surplus of notoriety and publicity. Professional jealousy is difficult to handle and administratively requires tact. We all know that the truly great teachers, the artists in the classroom, are usually dramatic classroom actors and the fact that someone else is a recipient of a great deal of applause and attention can breed dissatisfaction within the staff. It is obvious, then, that as the project goes on, the rest of the staff needs to feel secure. This is why the writer stresses continuously, "I like what you (the others) are doing, please don't change."

In essence the supervisor stops talking and starts doing. You quit telling teachers what and how they should be doing and start showing them. This is, then, the basic difference. Suddenly the supervisor becomes an enthusiastic partner in a teaching-learning situation. He becomes less a supervisor and more a co-worker in the vineyards of the profession. The management-labor aspect is completely eliminated as the leader leads because he earns it and deserves it through enthusiasm, drive, and creative initiative, not because he is appointed. The difference of this "Osmosis" approach is, of course, quite obvious and from any standpoint pays premium dividends not only in improved instruction but, what is more encouraging, in improved staff morale.

There are only two criteria to be observed here: First, it must be fun for the teacher and the children, and second, it must be productive educationally.

When other teachers inquire about the new activity, you say, "We're not sure the process works as yet." Every teacher, then, is positive he can make it work better! However, we are seldom in a hurry! To all teachers the writer says and means it, "You are wonderful just the way you are; you don't need to change; I like what you are doing right now. I could care less whether you change or not." When teachers feel that no one is trying to force them to change, no one is trying to slip something over on them, no one is going to "chew them out" for not changing, when they feel secure enough to try, *they will* try!

When the supervisor says, "Come with me, I will help you; I will show you," that one teacher will move forward confidently, secure in his or her guide. Moreover, when pressure and fear are removed and the pseudo-democratic drapery is eliminated, teachers move forward rapidly, happy at last to be treated as intelligent adults.

Change in Attitude

The writer had the opportunity and advantage of experimenting with this type of activity only briefly in the midwest, but has been able to bring the process to full fruition in San Rafael, California. Progress has been startling. On the wings of one or two exciting and excited teachers, ideas and techniques have spread through our small (225 teachers) school system with great rapidity.

However, and more important than the progress that has been made, is the change in attitude that one notices in teachers and administrators alike. Now that change is pleasant, it must be fun, and, since change is individual, no one is submerged in a group. Ideas spring from the staff with surprising and satisfying regularity. Not all of these ideas are productive but this is not important. What truly counts is the growing ability of some of our teachers, with such encouragement, to stand back from their activities and look at the total teaching-learning process with an objective professional eye, all the while saying, "Now, how can I do it better—or differently?"

As ideas pop up from the teachers and administrators we take them from school to school and teacher to teacher saying, "Who wants to take a look at this one?" It does not take long now, after two years, to find teachers who are anxious to share ideas, experiment, innovate. Now that invention is fun, nearly everyone wants to get into the process. We are at the point now at which, when we say, "Who wants to try to . . ." we seldom are able to finish the sentence. Everyone volunteers; no one wants to be left out. Teachers are saying, "How come I didn't get to try that first?"

No one is naïve enough to think that every individual teacher is wild about every idea or technique. Some teachers are always fearful of progress for the reasons already mentioned. Some will forever retreat into the past and sigh longingly for the good old days and for the "committee" operation wherein they can be submerged unnoticed in the group. This is not to be critical but to recognize people as they are. The height of absolute zero is a report card committee which after three years brings forth a report card that only half the staff approves when it is finally adopted.

While there is still a place, quite small in the writer's estimation, for a group meeting in education, the modern, dynamic professional leader will today find the "Osmosis" method (if given the right treatment) far superior to the traditional "committee and coffee caravan" of the past. We urge educational leaders to take off in high gear in a new direction with a new method. As a technique may we suggest "show" instead of "tell," individual instead of group, personal commitment instead of professional detachment as we work with teachers to lift "our" level of instruction. The results will be amazing! □

A Challenge to the Supervisor

Doris G. Phipps

WITHOUT realizing it, most teachers possess enough unused potential to make themselves two or three times more effective in their jobs. Self-motivation is the key that unlocks such potential. What can the supervisor do to spark a self-motivating attitude in teachers?

Many teachers believe that instructional materials are only the vehicles for teaching and learning. Nevertheless these same teach-

Doris G. Phipps, Curriculum Consultant, C.E.S.A. #10, Sheboygan County, Sheboygan Falls, Wisconsin ers place important emphasis on the first grader who was "first" to read in a "hard covered" book or on the symbol "five" on a math book needed to help a slow seventh grader. Similarly, few teachers will argue against the fact that greater learning evolves from student-oriented participation in social studies. Yet one finds many such teachers assuming the role of "purveyor of the facts," while bored class members listen only for the bell.

Some English teachers frankly admit that hanging words on hooks or slanting them in brackets does nothing to improve the written communication skills. Yet these same teachers would not think of omitting that one-third of the text which deals laboriously with the minute details of "diagramming sentences."

Need for Supervision

Almost all teachers will recognize that there are differences among their students, but these same teachers will literally slave to get all students to be alike. It would be very difficult to find even one instructor who would try to refute the fact that success is closely related to good mental health; yet every time he prepares report card data, the the same students who failed last time fail again.

One could exhaust pages in enumerating the gaps that exist between what is known by teachers about the growth patterns and problems of the children and youth they teach and what is practiced by the same teachers in the process of instruction. Does the difference between the thinking and doing reflect a lack of understanding the skills necessary to accomplish the task? Does it indicate that to escape from an overburdened work load and pressures, one pursues an "easier" path? Do the teachers see their administrative personnel lost in administrative detail with no time to help—hence a feeling, "no one cares what is done"?

Whatever this lost horizon means to the reader, it is an alarm giving rise to a need for the warmhearted, undivided attention of a person called a supervisor. Eye and Netzer in their recent book, *Supervision of Instruction: A Phase of Administration*,[1] indicate that a "supervisory program is a program of persons, behaviors, and situations" and it could not be more succinctly described.

How does the supervisor proceed to bridge the gap between the thinking and the doing? By working in a person-to-person relationship and in small group in-service meetings.

. . . it is a widely accepted psychological fact that human beings tend to find time for and learn to do those things which they understand, believe in, and value as important. The task of the supervisor, then, is to assist teachers in the examination of their present beliefs and of the values they hold, and to assist them in modifying those beliefs and values in light of the changing needs of children and society and the findings of research in child growth, development, motivation, and learning.[2]

Techniques and Process

It is refreshing to note in the recent literature on supervision an emphasis on the importance of classroom visitation. The writer is convinced that this is a vital technique and one which promises the most hope for instructional improvement. The technique is not easily described because there is no one single procedure. The teacher visited, the purpose of the visit, the type of activity observed, determine the procedure one uses. Classroom observation is a complex professional skill. It implies that the observer must have a "basic familiarity with

[1] Glen G. Eye and Lanore A. Netzer. *Supervision of Instruction: A Phase of Administration.* Evanston, Illinois: Harper & Row, Publishers, Inc., 1965.

[2] Ross L. Neagley and N. Dean Evans. *Handbook for Effective Supervision of Instruction.* Englewood Cliffs, New Jersey: Prentice-Hall, Inc., 1964. p. 115.

teaching, children, subject matter, and their relationships." [3]

Conferences must precede and/or follow a classroom visit. "If ideas are to have effect, it is usually through persons. Ideas are mediated by people." [4] In the person-to-person relationship, the supervisor is better able to stimulate change because the teacher has confidence to experiment when he knows someone is being supportive. Not only are ideas of change communicated in the conference, but the behavior problems of children are analyzed, new materials are found, school policies are interpreted, and the burden of a personal problem has been shared.

For the beginning teacher, a conference prior to the opening of school can not only dispel the fears of the neophyte but it can give the supervisor an understanding of the creativeness and attitudes of the new staff member.

In conducting the conference with the beginner as well as in other conferences, the writer makes it a practice to have the names and recent test data of the children assigned to the staff member. This list helps to focus the discussion on specific needs for the particular classroom.

The individual conference-classroom observation approach is a slow, time-consuming process. Nevertheless, until teachers feel supported in their venture of experimentation, are helped to understand the changing behavior of children and youth, are assisted in finding and evaluating materials, are encouraged and shown how to use a conceptual framework, they will continue to "fact find" and "cover material."

Closely related to the person-to-person working relationship is the small group in-service conference which the writer believes is more effective for change than a total-faculty approach.

In the small group conference, the design for action research is established when the members concern themselves with a specific hypothesis; cooperatively study, experiment, and solve that problem; and evaluate the results in terms of their needs. The literature of Corey, Shumsky, Taba, Franseth, and other proponents of Action Research reflects the value of this process.

The writer has found the Action Research method most effective in curriculum innovation. To develop a conceptual approach to the social studies in the intermediate grades, the teachers from one small district met to determine their problem, namely, what to teach in the social studies and how to teach this more effectively. A division of tasks, review of the research, defining a scope and sequence, planning a conceptual framework, and putting their ideas into writing required numerous meetings. Each time, the supervisor served as a supporting, reinforcing, and interpreting agent. This type of curriculum revision becomes meaningful to the individuals concerned. Teachers also develop respect for each other by working together; and their classrooms come to reflect more experimentation.

After some experience with Action Research in working with teachers, the same idea may be transferred by teachers into the classroom, where teachers may obtain most interesting results in using this technique. Davison [5] concludes:

If there is to be a revolution in educational research, it should come from the classroom teacher and the curriculum specialist. There are several reasons for this. The professional personnel have the basic tools for research: the children, the materials, and a large accumula-

---

[3] Ben M. Harris. *Supervisory Behavior in Education*. Englewood Cliffs, New Jersey: Prentice-Hall, Inc., 1963. p. 157.

[4] Mildred E. Swearingen. *Supervision of Instruction*. Boston: Allyn and Bacon, Inc., 1962. p. 268.

[5] Hugh M. Davison. From address to Department of Supervision and Curriculum Development, Pennsylvania State Education Association, November 1961.

tion of experience with children in a school setting.

The techniques already discussed are only two of the many which one can use. Yet they do represent some of the promising practices for change. Other supervisory practices which have merit at particular times include the sharing of bulletins or specific material with a teacher at a psychological time, conducting workshops of various kinds, or large group meetings such as a convention or conference, and using visual aids in demonstrations. Choice of the technique is determined by the time and need.

The supervisor's function is to generate improvements in instruction, motivate teacher growth, and promote curriculum development in a changing world. All of these are time-consuming tasks and the teachers' workdays offer little time for cooperative work with the supervisor. Perhaps more thought should be given to providing time for teachers to grow on the job. The colleges and universities are unable to prepare the graduates for all the work load they assume as they enter our schools to teach. Those entering the profession as well as those on the job need to be involved in continuing in-service education. This cannot all be done after so-called school hours. Perhaps those concerned with supervisory tasks should research the fruits of their labors so that findings could be presented to prove the need. ☐

EL 21 (7): 433-35, 455; April 1964
© 1964 ASCD

A Supervision Experiment with the Disadvantaged

GERTRUDE L. DOWNING

IN THE junior high schools of New York City are many thousands of children who apparently live outside the cultural mainstream and who stand in need of highly specialized and skillful instruction. Our problem is compounded by the critical shortage of teachers prepared specifically to meet these extraordinary demands. To staff the special service schools, there is urgent need for teachers who are competent, creative, adaptable, sympathetic, and emotionally secure, and who can feel a strong commitment to the urgent work at hand.

A large proportion of the instructors in these special schools must be recruited from the ranks of beginning teachers newly graduated from college. Because the teacher education institutions have placed increased emphasis on the overwhelming need, recent graduates have volunteered in growing numbers for service in the special schools. Yet, although the problem of teacher recruitment is abating somewhat, that of teacher retention is still crucial.

For the most part, our new teachers have had excellent preparation both in col-

Gertrude L. Downing, Assistant Professor of Education, Queens College of the City University of New York, New York. In 1964, Coordinator of BRIDGE: A Teacher Education Project, Queens College

lege and in the schools as student teachers. Usually, they are fired with idealism and enthusiasm for the work they face. Yet during their first days as full fledged teachers they are dismayed by the dismal reality which confronts them.

These novices, usually with a sheltered middle class background, often find themselves incapable of understanding the behavior and the motivations of the underprivileged children they meet in the classroom. In many cases, experiential disadvantage has produced youngsters who, quite literally, do not speak the teacher's language. The teacher's "good" motives and idealism are misunderstood by the pupils. Kindness is misinterpreted as weakness. Without the support of a cooperating teacher, the classroom routines and controls of student teaching experience seem to vanish. The methodology which was so successful with more fortunate adolescents results in chaos here.

The teacher is rendered impotent by unrealistic courses of study and inappropriate instructional materials. His subject matter competence gained through years of college study is ridiculed by teen-agers who have no standards by which to judge its value. And when he turns to his colleagues for support, frequently he faces the cynicism of those who have already run this gauntlet and who now take refuge in the self-justification that these pupils are "unteachable." By the end of the first year of teaching, all too often, recruits either leave the depressed area schools for more congenial surroundings or join the ranks of the cynics.

A Living Laboratory

It was to prepare teacher candidates more realistically for their vital role and to study the needs of beginning teachers in slum ghetto junior high schools that the BRIDGE project was initiated. In a representative school, ninety randomly selected pupils were assigned to classes taught by three recent Queens College graduates. With the assistance of a coordinator, these teachers will guide the selected pupils through their entire three year junior high school experience. In our "school within a school" we are scrutinizing the instructional needs of the children and the supervisory needs of the teachers.

During the early months of our first year of work, the multiplicity of problems which characterizes such a school mounted a relentless seige about our classrooms. We had three classes of disadvantaged children who, in the main, were unconvinced of the importance of learning, burdened by years of school failure, and mistrustful of authority figures. We had to meet the difficulties of adapting curriculum, adjusting methodology and securing materials on appropriate levels. Concurrently, we had to experiment with various approaches to classroom management, routines, and controls while keeping pace with the required intricacies of administrative paper work for the school. Finally, we were committed to the maintenance of a classroom atmosphere designed for long range development of verbal fluency, intellectual curiosity, and individual responsibility in our pupils. Therefore, it was necessary to reconcile this with the much more rigid controls outside our classrooms which were deemed necessary for the management of the school as a whole.

To meet the many and varied needs of our ninety deprived children and our three beginning teachers, the supervisory structure has radiated at many angles from an unprepossessing hub known as Room 400. This haven was made attractive with the addition of simple curtains, pictures, posters, plants, and books. It is here that the coordinator engages in the continuing struggles with curriculum, planning, ordering, and reporting. Here, too, the teachers confer, plan, consult curriculum resources, type plans, ditto materials, have coffee together, and give vent to the frustrations and successes, the pathos and humor of the day. It is here, also, that the children receive the initial guidance, discipline, and encouragement of which they stand in such desperate need. It is here that parents come and reveal glimpses of seemingly unendurable burdens and intricately snarled human relationships.

Structure of Supervision

Conferences

We have found it well to organize the many ramifications of our work around a framework of weekly conferences. Each Monday, we have a case study conference attended by all our teachers and the coordinator as well as the project psychologist and the school guidance counselor.[1] During each meeting, which is carefully structured and is based on previously and independently written reports by each of the participants, one child is studied in detail. The meeting culminates in the formulation of practical recommendations for action in the classroom by the teachers as well as for follow-up by medical and social agencies where necessary.

Our second meeting of the week is a group conference devoted to such matters as general administrative directives, common curriculum problems, and correlation of instruction in the various subject areas. In addition, difficulties in interpersonal relationships are aired and are mended here before pressures wear the fabric too thin.

The final general meeting each week is devoted to a discussion of reading instruction. At this time, pupil needs are examined and pupil progress is evaluated. Specific aims are set up for developmental instruction during the following week. Means are devised for reinforcing reading skills in various subject areas by all teachers, and appropriate instructional materials are suggested.

In addition to our three group conferences, each teacher is scheduled for an individual conference with the coordinator. To utilize time effectively, these periods are organized to include a review of the teacher's work of the past week as indicated by his written plans and by his observed classroom activities. This is followed by cooperative planning of his projected work, both immediate and long range. The hour is terminated by a consultation on specific teacher problems.

Although all these conferences are indispensable to our work, many of the most important revelations and enduring decisions are made during the daily incidental conferences which grow out of our "team" relationship. In Room 400, while running the ditto machine or munching a cookie or making a chart, we can share the most urgent problems before they have lost their immediacy and can arrive at group unanimity in informal and open exchange.

Classroom Participation

A large part of the coordinator's time has been spent in the classrooms, not as an observer but as a participant. At the outset of our work it was essential to provide the maximum support and assistance to our teachers. In order to do this, the coordinator deliberately defined her role, in part, as that of an auxiliary teacher in the classrooms. She participated in group discussions, shared instructional duties with the teacher when procedures needed bolstering, and occasionally taught entire lessons for demonstration. The pupils grew accustomed quickly to the coordinator's perambulations and accepted her as a natural part of the school organization.

From time to time, we have engaged in our own interpretation of team teaching, with the coordinator (a reading specialist)

---

[1] During the first two years of the project demonstration, the development of these conferences has been promoted greatly by the participation of the College Committee: Leonard Kornberg, Director; Robert Edgar, Albert Harris, and Helen Storen.

handling the general presentation of a lesson and the aspects requiring reading skills, and the teacher providing instruction in all learnings related specifically to his content area specialization.

This aspect of in-service education has met with gratifying success, for although coordinator demonstration and intervention were frequent during the first months of the project, they have decreased steadily as teacher security and competence have grown. This writer believes that three factors have contributed to this success. First, there is no substitute for actual demonstration of methodology in its natural context and at an appropriate time. Second, it was found possible to provide this instruction in a manner which did not diminish the professional stature of the teacher. Finally, the relationship of the coordinator to the teachers was supportive rather than threatening, since she has an evaluative rather than a rating function. Her role, in large part, is one of leading the teacher to examine his own successes and failures and to strive for higher professional competence.

Observed Results

We have now passed the halfway mark of our project. Our teachers are no longer raw recruits, but are tried veterans of an exhausting campaign. They have shown impressive growth in their understanding of disadvantaged adolescents. They have become increasingly proficient in teaching techniques, skilled at the adaptation of subject matter, and creative in finding and in developing materials of instruction. Because, in the inevitable moments of exhaustion and frustration, the members of the team have relied constantly upon each other for support and for understanding, group loyalty, and solidarity have developed steadily. The long range relationship with our pupils and awareness of their tremendous needs have produced in our teachers a strong devotion to the children.

Of course, the true measure of our work will be made in the future. Only then will we learn whether, as a concomitant to building professional competence, we have succeeded in developing commitment to this vital teaching task. □

EL 24 (5): 393-98; February 1967
© 1967 ASCD

Supervising Teachers of the Disadvantaged

MARCIA R. CONLIN
MARTIN HABERMAN

AUTHOR'S NOTE: *During the Summer of 1966 Bank Street College of Education conducted an NDEA Institute for 29 supervisors and leadership personnel from New York City, Washington, D.C., San Juan, Puerto Rico, and Milwaukee, Wisconsin. We lived in Manhattan and worked in several of the Harlem Schools. Our goal was to develop strategies for changing*

Marcia R. Conlin, Assistant Editor for Research Services, Phi Delta Kappa, Bloomington, Indiana; and Martin Haberman, Professor of Education and Chairman, Department of Curriculum and Instruction, Rutgers University, New Brunswick, New Jersey. In 1967, Dr. Haberman was Associate Professor of Administration and Supervision, School of Education, University of Wisconsin-Milwaukee ourselves, our colleagues, and our schools in order to better serve the disadvantaged.

The fact that this staff, its consultants, and the participants were the most able we have ever worked with became a source of gut-grinding discouragement: We realized that unless we could come to grips with some of the realities of supervision in urban areas, there was even less chance that others would. In only six weeks we made some heartwarming progress by using our racially integrated staff and participants to encounter and feel each other as people. But we failed—perhaps because of time—to confront each other with some of the racial problems of supervision in the schools. We were defensive about ourselves and our schools, ashamed of our participation in discriminatory activities, and reluctant to discuss our feelings of helplessness.

The issues selected for this article are merely a few of many which must be openly discussed. There has now been a cooling-off period of several months to determine whether feelings would somehow become more objective and less intense once we were all back in our own comfortable situations. They haven't.

—MRC and MH.

OPERATIONALLY, the disadvantaged are those whose teachers perceive them as disadvantaged. So we begin with occupational tunnel vision. The vernacular of pedaguese derivatives from eviscerated concepts and results in near-miss approximations labeled "objectivity," so this circuitous definition does not reveal anything about the nature of these children. But it does focus on the most powerful determinant of children's achievement: their teachers' assessment of their potential. Methodology, curriculum, school organization, and materials are all launched from this teacher perception.

How can supervisors help teachers surrender the distortions of these negative expectations? A beginning might be an injection of reality into what supervisors study, work on, and talk about.

The paucity of supervisory strategy is often attributed to the newness of our field; bogus cries are raised for a theory of supervision, more research, and firmer value commitments.

But what would such theory describe and predict? Which variables could be researched? And how might we strengthen our values? Finally, why would any of these exercises influence our daily practices or the social system of the school?

These "supposed" needs are merely smoke screens of a flight syndrome; the real problems are a little too real. For example, supervisors must develop coping behaviors and action strategies which are germane to urban schools serving the disadvantaged.

Reluctant Teachers

The supervisor's basic problem is like that of the Boy Scout helping reluctant little old ladies to cross streets when they would rather stay on corners. We Americans are socialized to believe we should be able to solve life problems independently. A welter of guilt results when we soon discover our need for friends and family, to borrow money, and to use hospitals. Overlay this fantasy-like moral prescription with a teacher education that portrays instructional problems as teacher or pupil faults, rather than as opportunities and we can see that an impossible role perception has been conveyed to teachers. As "normal" adult Americans, they do not want "help," and as teachers, they cannot admit to needs.

As if this were not bad enough, the supervisor is perceived as someone who cannot "help" with reality problems. Just as the disadvantaged pupils perceive their teachers as powerless to help with any real problems (e.g., Can he get me a job? a decent place to live? police protection? a loving home? sexual gratification? equal opportunity?), so the supervisor is perceived as powerless to help with problems the teachers perceive as real. (Can he give me a smaller class? more supporting and psychological services? fewer emotionally disturbed pupils? effective methods and techniques for my instructional problems?)

Teachers' Dislike for Children

It is unpleasant, almost impolite, to mention our pretense that teachers like their pupils. Many do, but supervising others—particularly in schools serving the disadvantaged, who discriminate against poor youngsters of various ethnic backgrounds—is analogous to helping children learn subjects they hate. Without positive teacher regard, little beyond drill, rote, or mechanical teaching occurs. Youngsters might escape irreparable damage from the hands of a bigoted coach or bandmaster, but the positive regard of one's teacher is too powerful, too essential to their growth, to be completely washed out by even the most technical subject matter.

Teachers (certified in their states, tenured in their systems and paid-up members of professional associations) who dislike their youngsters have a natural reluctance to discuss their feelings, while we, their leaders, are often prejudiced and unaware ourselves. When this round robin of unawareness is revealed, we find we lack the know-how to change the behaviors from which prejudiced perceptions develop.

The most grinding, debilitating aspect of their deprived subculture is its failure to offer these children any choices. When their teachers perceive their potential with equally negative expectations, their classroom experience concurs with and reinforces this demoralization. The positive regard of his teacher may be a deprived child's only hope.

Since the most powerful determinant of teacher effectiveness is his perception of pupils' potential growth, this effectiveness cannot help but be affected negatively by tendencies to stereotype, or to remain closed to the talents, divergencies, and strengths of individuals of different backgrounds.

Supervisors of Resentful Whites

The status gap between teachers and supervisors is a real one; but teachers are often wiser about recognizing its validity than supervisors who attempt a strategy of co-worker, helpmate, team-member, colleague, etc. Overlaying these basic distinctions in role are age and sex differences; supervisors who are younger than teachers; women attempting to help men. These differences which deepen the natural gulf between them are compounded when we add the difficulties of Negroes who supervise whites.

Symptoms of the "racial problem" between Negro supervisors and white teachers usually occur in integrated or predominantly Negro schools—where one is most likely to find non-white supervisors. We find this constellation:

• Teachers who are fearful their supervisor will no longer back them up in situations involving corporal punishment of a Negro pupil

• Teachers who are reluctant to discuss their perceptions of "disadvantaged" problems because they do not want to appear prejudiced

• Teachers who over-react, love everyone, and have absolutely no problems

• Supervisors who become overly oriented to academic progress and avoid recognizing emotional problems of pupils. The remedial reading syndrome is a common phonemonon among supervisors bent on "proving" success

• Supervisors who solidify in the belief that only a Negro can understand the problems of educational disadvantagement—even a middle class Negro living in the suburbs

- Supervisors who become more concerned with their own advancement and play militant for the community and Uncle Tom for the system.

The interaction of mutual prejudice and fear between white teachers and Negro supervisors is understandable. After understanding, however, behavioral techniques are required to help supervisors who are struggling for an identity of their own to establish functional relationships. The problem is not unlike the fearful teacher forced to work with resentful, hostile youngsters at a time in life when self definition may be *his* greatest need.

One of the most difficult forms of pupil rejection occurs in schools serving urban Negroes. It is the lowest form of reverse prejudice which fails to recognize the wide range of abilities, attitudes, and effectiveness amongst middle-class, well educated Negroes assigned as teachers in urban schools. Typical placement procedures which assign Negro teachers to schools serving the disadvantaged fail to recognize the personal needs and class level of different individuals. Many Negroes merely respond to the white "they all look alike to me" syndrome which lumps all Negroes together. As a result, some Negro teachers try to "prove" they are in no way related to or identified with these youngsters. Others respond with an intensified need to demonstrate masculinity, and they often try to dominate rather than relate to their pupils.

Many Negro colleges guide the least able into teaching; better students are advised to enter business or the more prestigious professions in order to more influentially "represent" their group.

Although these problems all have causes which invariably derive from centuries of discrimination in which whites have brutalized Negroes, the fact remains that important problems are now at home roosting. Supervisors need courage to risk accusations of discrimination and reverse discrimination. More important, white leadership needs to open up all white schools to those Negro faculty members who work best with middle class students.

Most supervision is directed toward helping beginning teachers, although the evidence indicates that they do as well or better than experienced teachers. We assume (erroneously) that beginners are more amenable to change than experienced teachers. (This usually means "susceptible to directive influences." What are beginners changing from?) In reality much supervisory practice is the imposition of unwanted assistance, and beginners are less able to resist than the securely-tenured, more confident teachers. Another explanation is logistical; there isn't enough time to help all, and supervisory effort must be expended where it will do the most good. This is a dangerous rationalization, since most beginners work less than a year and merely pass through the profession, while the experienced "older" teacher with twenty years of experience is overlooked in spite of the fact that he may have another twenty to go.

Changing Experienced, "Model" Teachers

Unfortunately, many experienced teachers are perceived as having "connections" and as informal leaders in their schools and neighborhoods. Supervisors, particularly newly appointed ones, are reluctant to risk "rocking the boat" with such teachers under their egis. An experienced, informal teacher-leader has immeasurable power to control by merely threatening to request transfer. As a result, much supervision mollifies the strong and over-supervises the weak. In schools serving the disadvantaged, where turnover is high or requests for in-transfer infrequent, supervisors often practice the realistic but unprofessional philosophy of "leaving well enough alone." In reality, conservation of an inadequate status quo is preservation of failure.

The ignorant may become educated, the disaffected involved, and the prejudiced more open; but strategies to release the potentialities of the fearful teacher are as yet unexplored. We might begin with the recognition that many (perhaps most) supervisors, principals, and teachers are fearful. But fearful of what? The sources of fear may be in both the nature of the person who becomes a teacher and in the nature of a "disadvantaged" classroom where many pupils need to feel some power. Demonstrations of fear are natural responses to feelings of powerlessness.

Fearful Teachers

Do teachers fear change? Behind all the rationalizations (e.g., My principal won't let me. My fellow teachers will be upset. The children need structure.) is fear of the new, the unfamiliar, the unpredictable.

Do teachers fear expression of emotions—aggression, love, bursting joy? It is clear that schools are not the best settings for natural behavior. The current cardinal operating principle of American schools is "keep the lid on feelings." We were nearly run down on the sidewalk outside a junior high school recently by exuberant, naturally expressive adolescents whose apathetic, glazed-over responses in the classroom we had observed only five minutes earlier.

Fear of all three factors—supervisors, change, and emotions—are present to some degree. Also, these fears are all interrelated and derive from one basic fear: a fear of inadequacy. In their professional lives, teachers lack the ability to predict the multiplicity of problems with which they may be instantly and continuously confronted and they lack the more complete predictability present in other professional roles. They lack power.

To assume that fear is *not* a factor, or should not be, is unsound and unrealistic. By recognizing teachers' feelings of inadequacy, we can consider possible causes, and connect them with the teacher's perception of power. Since our own perceptions of fear and power are also involved, the problem is now more complex and emotionally charged. Power, personal and professional, is not given but taken. The usual discussion of how to *give* teachers more power is sterile; we need to identify situational elements and to structure conditions in which fearful teachers can learn to take power.

When teachers and supervisors independently arrive at the same objectives for changing themselves, we have an optimum condition for supervision. In practice, such convergence rarely occurs. Supervisors perceive their major raison d'etre as changing teachers' attitudes; teachers perceive their biggest problems as large classes, individual problem-students, and rigid curricula. Operationally then, supervision becomes a search for means to detour around teacher-perceived problems, and attempts to shift the locus of teacher concern from the children and the curriculum to themselves.

The democratic ethic, principles of learning, and our own needs for approval prevent us from overtly imposing our ideas through directive supervision. Yet, we are powerless to deal with the structural and basic problems perceived by teachers—even when these perceptions may be accurate and we recognize that their perceptions must be the starting point for supervisory practice.

The situation is not unlike the teacher who asks his class, "What are you interested in?" When they respond, "Girls, money, fame," he replies, "No, no. I mean like any of your after-school hobbies that might help me to relate your life experiences to the acid and base weights of the chemical elements."

Meanwhile, ask teachers to describe their basic concerns; they tell about classes that are too large to differentiate assignments, the need to cover prescribed material with children who cannot read, and the difficulty of managing a group situation with several emotionally disturbed youngsters. To which the supervisor replies, "No, no. I mean what are you doing that will help me to relate your problems to the workshop I offer Thursday afternoons on 'Creativity in Written Expression'!"

This article has raised issues and ignored canons. Our questions imply that what we have been doing is not good enough; yet no concrete suggestions have been made. (That's cynicism!) We have implied that opening up tough issues in urban schools may change supervisors personally and professionally, as well as teachers. (That's derogation!) One might infer that teachers and supervisors frequently perceive each others' services as somewhat less than useful; we need, first, to recognize that supervisory reality begins with teachers' perceptions—not supervisors' needs and interests. (That's insulting!)

Finally, the stress on disadvantagement has been underplayed; we believe that supervision, like teaching, is basically the same in all situations, but pupils in "disadvantaged" schools are less likely to learn in spite of their teachers, and their teachers are less likely to succeed without realistic help. (That's devious!) Right answers only result from the right questions: What are teachers' *real* problems? The right supervisory objectives will develop in the light of those needs. ☐

EL 25 (5): 393-96; February 1968
© 1968 ASCD

The Powerlessness of Irrelevancy

LARRY CUBAN [1]

I HAD some reservations about writing this article mainly due to my lack of formal training in supervision and curriculum development. In other words, I did not want to reveal my ignorance. Whatever I have learned about either has been through performing both functions for a number of years, reading and relying—more than I like to admit—on instinct. I decided, however, to run that risk because—from where I stand—supervision and curriculum development, especially for the disadvantaged and their teachers, are irrelevant to their needs and problems.

The current critical self-examination that supervisors and curriculum workers are indulging in reveals bleakly how little the frontiers of knowledge about both crafts have advanced.

Some researchers and practitioners admit candidly that the role of the supervisor

[1] Former Director of the Cardozo Project in Urban Teaching, District of Columbia Public Schools, Washington, D.C.

Larry Cuban, Teacher, Director, Staff Development, District of Columbia Public Schools, Washington, D.C.

confused and results are murky. In the words of one researcher:

> There is, in fact, little sound evidence that teachers change at all, to say nothing about change in relation to supervisory efforts.[2]

Similarly, some curriculum workers speak with little confidence when roles and results are discussed. In effect, the profession is at that primitive stage of relying on personal observation, intuition, and "feeling."

Now there is nothing to be ashamed of in admitting that the role of the supervisor has yet to be carved out with precision, or that a solid theory and practice of supervision have yet to be created; English and social studies education, for example, share similar problems and, for that matter, so does education in general.

What is deeply irritating and even arrogant, however, is the assumption that supervisors should and can be "agents of change" in the present order of things. Or as one professor profiled the supervisor urgently needed in the public schools:

> He is responsible for identifying instructional problems and for providing leadership in their resolution. He is an authority on teaching, a resource person, an expert in group dynamics, and more recently is conceived of as a catalyst or an agent of change.[3]

Rhetoric and Reality

When I think of how large urban school systems are organized, the circumscribed staff function of supervisors and curriculum people, and what teachers of the disadvantaged are most concerned about, and match all of these against the rhetoric,

[2] James B. Macdonald. "Knowledge About Supervision: Rationalization or Rationale?" *Educational Leadership* 23 (2): 161-63; November 1965.

[3] Richard F. Neville. "The Supervisor We Need." *Educational Leadership* 23 (8): 634-40; May 1966.

I almost laugh at the absurdity of it all. Yet I do not laugh, because irrelevancy is intolerable at a time when teaching is at its lowest ebb and youngsters continue to die a slow death in too many inner-city classrooms.

Supervisors are powerless to deal effectively with the concerns of teachers. What teachers need—smaller classes, time to plan and think, opportunities to analyze with others what happens in a classroom, freedom to experiment, and support for that experimentation—supervisors cannot provide.

Indeed, what does a supervisor do? While my observation of large city operations may be narrow, I gather that he collects and distributes materials; he visits classrooms sporadically, usually those of first year teachers, convinces teachers that they should review textbooks, checks lesson plans occasionally, and presides at meetings with teachers, etc. In short, the supervisor is irrelevant and is powerless to cope with the needs and concerns of teachers.

And his colleagues across the hall share the same fate. After all, what do curriculum workers do? Preparing curriculum guides, compiling reading lists, bringing together teachers to list materials and activities in teaching a particular unit, introducing in selected schools some recently developed materials from a curriculum reform program pinpoint their functions.

Curriculum workers in the central office will crank out course guides and syllabi and send them to teachers. The teachers stack them neatly on the shelf next to the last batch of materials that were sent out. Knowing full well what happens to their products, the staff can only bemoan the low-level intelligence of teachers and their inability to use effectively the abundant instructional materials the central office provides.

Again, what do teachers of the disadtaged need? They need diverse materials

from which to choose what works with their kids, not just the most recent textbook. They need assistance and support to learn how to use these materials. They need time and facilities to prepare lessons and units that are not commercially available. As with supervisors' needs, teachers' needs and concerns slide past noiselessly the services offered by those who are supposed to help teachers perform their job effectively.

To charge that supervisory and curriculum staff are powerless and irrelevant does not raise a new issue. Talking to teachers reveals that they know quite well the rituals and charades carried on between themselves and supervisors and curriculum people.

The fact of the matter is that teachers see such staff as highly paid agents of the system—not as free-wheeling entrepreneurs of change. Staff people who visit schools or send directives have responsibility but little authority; they can be easily dealt with by teachers who nod their heads, "yes sirring" each statement, and waving goodbye.

Now the question is whether supervisors and curriculum workers can become relevant to teachers in inner-city schools and link up the social ferment occurring in the community with the school. Yes, they can. Will they? I doubt it.

Suggestions from a Skeptic

Enough writers have sketched out the knowledge, skills, and attitudes supervisors and curriculum workers must have to be effective. Suggestions range from more familiarity with current research on the teacher-learner process to equipping these professionals with the skills of working with people. I would add three to the list: (a) specific knowledge of the community—its diversity, crises, and politics; (b) actual classroom teaching; and (c) more face-to-face contact with teachers.

For supervisors and curriculum workers to be especially knowledgeable about the city, urbane if you will, is the first step toward making school staff relevant to the community. They could provide support and expertise to teachers who encourage student involvement in the community; they could assist teachers in creating units and courses on the city.

That civics courses, for example, in most large school systems remain pristine in their imbecilic innocence of urban reality is shocking. The failure of social studies supervisors and curriculum workers to drag these courses into the 20th century and deal with metropolitan America speaks of their powerlessness and lack of personal involvement with the city. Supervisory and curriculum staff must be conversant with the promise of and threat to urban life.

So, too, must they continue to keep one foot in the classroom door. A high correlation seems to exist between flatulent rhetoric and distance from youngsters. Too little information exists on what happens in the classroom to permit a supervisor to be promoted out of teaching and thereafter see only the backs of students' heads. A supervisor who teaches and maintains an open-door policy for colleagues is solid evidence to everyone in the school that the act of teaching has an intrinsic value; that he wants to retain honesty and perspective in his advice to individual teachers.

None of what I suggest is new. It has been included in any number of recommendations by well qualified persons. Gestures toward implementation have been made in various parts of the country, with clinical professors being the ones who come most readily to mind. Paper recommendations are plentiful; implementation is scarce.

And the reason is simple enough. Implementing these suggestions would require a fundamental overhauling of staff and line organization, a closer examination and ultimate revision of graduate courses leading toward certification in these fields, and a decentralization of supervisory and curriculum staff and activities. The enormity of what has to be done paralyzes even the young and energetic.

Let me multiply the enormity by spelling out briefly the changes that would follow upon decentralization.

To get more supervisors into the field to teach and work with faculty, centers of teacher education would have to be established at various schools. Each of these centers would have a staff that teaches, supervises, and develops curriculum materials. Thus, an action center for instruction and development of materials would be physically closer to teachers and the community.

These centers, of course, could easily provide training for new and experienced teachers.

Many additional staff members would have to be recruited and, while costly, such recruitment would pointedly demonstrate to all teachers that there is a career open to those who want to stay in the classroom.

Certainly this would be costly, perhaps duplicative and, worst of all, such a scheme may not even attack the issues that trouble teachers. Yet if not decentralization, then another plan is essential that will eliminate the charades that teachers and supervisors play with one another.

Will anything happen? I doubt it. Supervisors and curriculum workers are part of a system that is monopolistic and, I believe, almost incapable of generating the energy necessary to reform the traditional relationships and procedures that have accumulated over the years. Consider how cumbersome it is to initiate curriculum changes in most school systems. Or note the inspector-general attitude of many supervisors toward teachers departing from established conventions. And if this is a myth, it is one that continues to shape teacher behavior.

What I had always thought was an apocryphal story turned into reality when I heard a supervisor lambast, in my presence, a teacher for the unorthodox letters and colors used on her bulletin board. I thought the supervisor was imitating a stereotyped version of a supervisor until I realized she was serious.

The situation is deplorable and sad. I do not know how to energize a school system into revitalizing itself and in the process retool the supervisory and curriculum roles. That the pressure must come from outside the system is evident to me. One hopeful sign is the anti-poverty money that has poured into most inner-city schools. That money has produced many exciting programs, involving a great number of teachers in supervising, in developing curriculum materials, and in creating in some schools intellectual ferment. Some of that ferment has already begun to percolate upwards and to challenge existing relationships and procedures. This is all to the good.

Whether the results will shake up people and programs remains to be seen. More to the point is whether anything short of eliminating the conventional supervisory apparatus will bring into line the disparity between teacher needs and problems and the services proffered by supervisory and curriculum professionals.

And when that disparity disappears, then we can begin to examine with more precision exactly what supervisors can do to bridge the gap between school and community. Until then, no real dialogue on supervisory and curriculum worker effectiveness can take place. ◻

Beyond the Status Quo:
A Reappraisal of Instructional Supervision

DAVID T. TURNEY

INSTRUCTIONAL supervision as presently employed in the United States is not a definable area of specialization. The kinds of duties performed by supervisors vary widely from one school system to the next and collections of job descriptions reflect this basic variability in the duties described by Neagley and Evans (1965). As a further complication, the functions that are most often performed by supervisors are distributed over a wide range of educational specialties which have been assigned other identifications.

Administrators supervise and so at times do classroom teachers. Lucio and McNeil (1962) note that, "We believe that supervision is a distributive function, a common dimension in the expected role behavior of those who hold various positions in the school system." What we actually find in practice is that there are a number of functions thus distributed; and as a consequence, we are likely to find teacher, curriculum coordinator, supervisor, or superintendent all, at one time or another, engaged in supervisory activities, coordinating activities, developing leadership, and the host of other functions that may be found listed in the professional literature.

Harris (1963) further reinforces the notion that supervision is a distributive function in his theoretical analysis of the relationship of supervision to the major functions of school operation. He describes a two dimensional model that includes the functions of teaching, supervision, management, special services, and general administration. For Harris, these functional areas are not mutually exclusive but tend to overlap.

Such observations about the nature of supervision by these authors are most helpful in clarifying the role of the supervisor as it is presently defined by school systems. These observations, however, still do not provide us with a clearly defined direction for the further development of supervision as an educational specialty. As long as we continue to see supervision as a multi-functional task that may be accomplished by a wide variety of specialists we will continue to experience difficulty in developing effective programs of preservice education and in-service development for this educational specialty.

Earlier writings on supervision are even less helpful in this respect. Moreover, we find on inspection an even greater lack of unanimity as to what supervisory functions really are.

Wiles (1955) lists five major functions having to do with skills in leadership, human relations, group process, personnel administration, and evaluation. Swearingen (1962) discusses eight functions beginning with "coordination of efforts," and ending with "integrating of goals and energy building."

One could identify as many other

David T. Turney, Dean, School of Education, Indiana State University, Terre Haute. In 1966, Director of the University School, Kent State University

diverse viewpoints as there are books on supervision.

One result of this multi-functioned conception of supervision and the accompanying diffusion of role has been the reduction of the supervisor's position to that of a sort of educational, utility infielder whose responsibilities are likely to shift from time to time depending on the nature of current emergencies or the need of superiors to unload some time-consuming and unrewarding task that has drifted their way.

A second result of this global definition of supervision has been an excessive duplication of teaching about these functions in most graduate professional courses. Since everyone from administrator to classroom teacher may on occasion supervise, instructors feel obliged to devote some portion of their classes in these areas of study to a consideration of supervisory functions. Instructors in supervision courses, because of the scope of the field, feel obliged to include in their presentations work on administration, personnel, curriculum development, and a liberal sampling of the rest of the functions identified at one time or another as a part of supervision.

A Proposal for Delimitation

As a way out of this miasma of conflicting, overlapping, and intertwining responsibilities, it is proposed that supervision be redefined as including those services that *contribute directly to the improvement of classroom instruction*. It is further proposed that curriculum development work and administration be specifically excluded from this definition.

Obviously current staffing practice will not change rapidly as a result of the acceptance of such a definition, but until we are able to specify reasonably discrete areas for supervisory specialization, the supervisor will remain a sort of educational chameleon. More immediate improvements could be realized if programs of graduate professional preparation were reorganized into the discrete and clearly defined areas of study toward which this definition leads.

Since the supervision and curriculum development specialties are already partially separated in practice from administration by the "line and staff" form of organization, we may expect comparatively little objection to this formulation from administrators since no real change in this pattern is involved. Changes in the ways that curriculum specialists and supervisors are used within the pattern would be involved. Curriculum specialists, on the other hand, may be expected to object to this proposal on the grounds that effective supervision is generally a consequence of curriculum development work and therefore may not be thus readily separated from its counterpart. Let us therefore examine this probable objection.

Improvement of Instruction

It has been assumed that involvement in curriculum development programs, action research projects, human relations workshops, and other educational problem solving endeavors will automatically result in improved teaching competence. To assume this is to base the program of instructional improvement on the fortuitous operation of concomitant learning. Without question such learning does take place and many teachers have profited from their involvement in these diverse activities. It is, however, highly doubtful if rapid and continuous professional growth can be adequately supported by learning processes whose outcomes are so generally unpredictable.

An assessment of what is presently known about teaching, as described in the many research studies so ably reviewed in *The Handbook of Research on Teaching* (Gage *et al.,* 1962), leads one to the conclusion that teachers fail to work effectively with their classes for very specific reasons.

In order to improve their professional competence, teachers need to be engaged in carefully devised programs of serious study which are aimed at the development of substantive understandings, methodological skill, or knowledge about the availability and uses of learning resources.

For example, current experiences with National Science Foundation summer and full-year institutes clearly indicate that mastery of new content areas and the procedures needed for teaching them requires a kind of instruction, a degree of concentrated study, and large blocks of time that we have not heretofore dealt with in school in-service programs.

Substantive learning about the content of a discipline, the growth and development of children, and the theoretical principles of learning requires a disciplined approach by the learner and a quality of teaching rarely encountered in an in-service setting. In general, on campus, advanced degree programs seldom provide adequate backgrounds of this type for a variety of reasons, one of which is the heavy emphasis on training for administrative or other specialty positions in such programs. Undergraduate programs of instruction generally offer a brief overview of these areas, but usually fail to get past the superficial aspects.

It is difficult to see how any great advances in the improvement of teaching methodology can be achieved without recourse to laboratory experiences in which teachers can try out new ways of working and receive dependable feedback on the consequences of their efforts. The possible usefulness for such instruction of sound films, closed-circuit television coupled with video-taping, and simulation exercises is only beginning to be explored. Empirical studies by Bowers and Soar (1961) and Flanders (1962) are examples of the laboratory approach to the improvement of teaching methodology. Comments by Broudy (1964) on the laboratory aspects of the preservice education of teachers also reinforce this point of view.

With regard to the problem of helping teachers learn the function and uses of the wide variety of materials and media available to them, it must be pointed out that present preservice and in-service preparation programs do not generally make a very great contribution to this part of the teacher's professional equipment.

For example, it is not very likely that a high school English teacher will be very effective in guiding the reading of pupils unless the teacher has an exhaustive knowledge of the literature that is most appropriate to the age group he is teaching. Furthermore, it is not enough to know the materials that exist, but one must also know which of these materials may be found in the local setting. Preservice preparation courses rarely deal with this problem, and in-service time devoted to a thorough exploration of the school library is indeed a rarity.

A basic prerequisite to the individualization of instruction is a teacher who will know what to try once the individual learning need has been identified.

Curriculum plans and the accessibility of learning materials may be viewed as limiting or facilitating factors in teaching effectiveness; however, it is what the teacher is able to do with the plans and materials that must be the supervisor's central concern. Materials and plans are not necessarily useful because the teacher has constructed them himself; rather they will be helpful to the degree that they are appropriate to a given learning task or a specific learning problem of an individual. While the teacher must be a skilled diagnostician of learning difficulties, he need not compound his own prescriptions for the remediation of learning deficits. What the teacher does need is an exhaustive knowledge of the media that may be employed to accomplish specific teaching goals. This is, in a sense, the pharmacology of the profession, and its dimensions are presently expanding at a staggering rate of speed.

Without deprecating the importance of curriculum problems, we believe that the most critical area for concentration of supervisory effort is on the professional development of the teacher and not on the instructional program to be employed. In the final analysis the teacher must make the specific curriculum decisions that make the difference for the individual pupils in his charge. In difficult cases, consultation may be desirable, but the critical decisions will always be a responsibility of the teacher.

The supervisor's major objective should be to help the teacher *master the substantive content he may not understand, attain competency in teaching techniques he may not know, and catalog, classify, and test the countless resources that may be brought to bear on the specific learning problems he may encounter.* With such skills as these at his command, the teacher will be in a position to create that rare blend of professional competence and personal understanding which results in the fine and sensitive decisions vital to the development of superior programs of classroom instruction.

If the arguments presented in the preceding sections of this paper are valid, then some special areas of competency for the supervisor are clearly implied.

Refining the Supervisory Specialty

First of all, the supervisor needs to be a person highly skilled in the analysis of the teaching act. He should be knowledgeable about and able to employ in his work a variety of the research techniques now available for the objective study of classroom teaching. In order to improve his work, the teacher should have available a continual feedback of reliable data on the characteristics of his own performance. The supervisor should be the specialist who is able to collect and present such information to the classroom teacher. The studies listed in the pamphlet recently published by AACTE entitled *A Proposal for the Revision of the Pre-Service Professional Component of a Program of Teacher Education* (1964) would constitute a nucleus of substantive content for instruction in this area.

Second, the supervisor should be able to employ effectively techniques of individual and group counseling with members of the professional staff he proposes to help. If supervision is a teaching speciality, the need for such skills is paramount. If individualization of instruction is an important educational goal, then supervisory efforts should provide for the classroom teacher a model of such teaching methodology worth emulating. Real gains in teaching effectiveness are more likely to be produced in the context of the face to face interaction between the teacher and supervisor and among the members of small groups that include the supervisor as an instructional leader than in the large group, inspirational address approach usually employed in in-service work.

It also follows that the supervisor should be highly skilled in the use of instructional media. His own instructional work with teachers should exemplify the wise and deliberate selection of media of instruction and his knowledge of this field of study should be comprehensive enough so that he will be able to guide teachers in their own use of such instructional tools.

Since the structure of knowledge in the several disciplines appears to be so closely related to the teaching methodology essential to their adequate presentation, it will be necessary for the supervisor to have a considerable depth of understanding in at least one of the instructional areas common to the public school curriculum. In addition to his own special area of accomplishment, he will need a thorough understanding of and sensitivity to the critical differences among the different curricular areas and the implications of these differences for modification in teaching strategy and methodology.

These four areas of study—*the analysis of teaching, individual and group counseling techniques, instructional media, and the structure of knowledge in the content areas*—should constitute the major emphasis in the preparation program, both preservice and in-service, for the instructional supervisor.

Depending on native ability and background of previous training and experience, additional work will be necessary in differing degrees for specific individuals in communication skills, administrative and management techniques, and principles of curriculum construction. Beyond these specialized studies, it is assumed that the common elements of a good graduate program in education would supply the broad understandings of the nature of public education in the United States, and the philosophical, social, and psychological bases upon which it rests.

It is believed that a major shift in emphasis toward the basic functions described herein would make possible the development of a supervisor who will be able to provide the educational guidance essential for the classroom teacher's continuous professional growth and achievement.

In summary, the notion that the supervisor is essentially a teacher of teachers is not a new one. This function, however, has not been viewed as the central role around which the preparation and work of the supervisor should be developed. Supervisors do have a responsibility for curriculum development, but the curriculum that should concern them most is the program of learning for the teachers they supervise.

Supervisors also have a responsibility for administration, but their major concern in this area should be with the elements that are directly related to the instructional programs they develop for professional improvement of the teachers they supervise.

Supervision viewed as a logical extension of college and university professional instruction carried on within a school system will have a unique and crucial role to fulfill. The continuous educational growth of classroom teachers has been an ideal long recommended. Effective supervision properly conceived and executed can move us rapidly toward the achievement of this goal. ☐

References

American Educational Research Association. *Handbook of Research on Teaching*. N. L. Gage, editor. Chicago: Rand McNally and Company, 1963.

Norman D. Bowers and Robert S. Soar. *V Final Report: Evaluation of Laboratory Human Relations Training for Classroom Teachers*. Chapel Hill: University of North Carolina, 1961. U.S. Office of Education, Cooperative Research Project No. 8143. (Mimeographed.)

Harry S. Broudy. "Laboratory, Clinical and Internship Experience in the Professional Preparation of Teachers." *Ideas Educational*. Kent, Ohio: Kent State University School 2 (2): 5-14; Spring 1964.

Ned A. Flanders. *Teacher Influence, Pupil Attitudes and Achievement*. Minneapolis: University of Minnesota, 1960. U.S. Office of Education, Cooperative Research Project No. 397. (Mimeographed.)

Ben M. Harris. *Supervisory Behavior in Education*. Englewood Cliffs, New Jersey: Prentice-Hall, Inc., 1963. pp. 7-11.

Herbert F. LaGrone. *A Proposal for the Revision of the Pre-Service Professional Component of a Program of Teacher Preparation*. Washington, D.C.: Teacher Education and Media Project, The American Association of Colleges for Teacher Education, 1964.

William H. Lucio and John D. McNeil. *Supervision: A Synthesis of Thought and Action*. New York: McGraw-Hill Book Company, Inc., 1962. p. 46.

Ross L. Neagley and N. Dean Evans. *Handbook for Effective Supervision of Instruction*. Englewood Cliffs, New Jersey: Prentice-Hall, Inc., 1964.

Kimball Wiles. *Supervision for Better Schools*. Englewood Cliffs, New Jersey: Prentice-Hall, Inc., 1955. pp. 18-26.

Supervisors: A Vanishing Breed?

MAURICE J. EASH

THE supervisor's role, which has always been afflicted by vicissitudes in its halting progress toward professionalization, now conceivably faces extinction. This could result from two new trends in the educational scene: teacher organizations' negotiations and the commercial production of the packaged curriculum. There is a certain quality of irony in the appearance of these threats to the supervisor's existence at a time of considerable ferment and heightened interest in the theoretical analysis and practical application of supervision. However, there is cause to believe that some of the current emphasis in supervisory practice and preparatory programs may be a prime contributor to the role obsolescence of the supervisor.

In the historical development of supervision, the role of the supervisor has become synonymous with the effort to improve instruction. Parallel with the acceptance of improvement of instruction as the *raison d'être* of supervision is the formation of an accompanying professional mandate: those acting in a supervisory capacity must work in close relationship with the personnel most directly connected with the teaching-learning act, the classroom practitioner. Acting upon this mandate, the college preparatory programs and the ideal role behavior of supervisors as found in the literature have in the past two decades emphasized interpersonal relations as the principal route of instructional improvement. Consequently, the role of the supervisor is not infrequently equated with being a human relations expert with a strong commitment to humanistic values in the instructional program and in professional relationships.

A New Era

There is indeed reason to question whether the supervisor's role, as it has been defined, can be maintained in the face of the twin emergent forces—the teaching profession's new militancy in negotiating with school boards, and the extensive introduction of the prepared packaged curriculum as the major approach to curriculum development.

Consequently, supervision predicated upon human relations techniques emphasizing good intentions and mellow feelings toward classroom practitioners is not likely to eventuate in professional practices which can be effective in the face of these formidable countervailing forces. And although prophecy always entails a degree of risk to the prophet, it would not seem terribly presumptuous upon the examination of the data on trends in the operation of teachers' professional organizations, and the designing and preparation of curriculum, to predict that supervision is entering a new era where the old pattern of direct teacher-supervisor transactions will disappear.

Supervision, as we have known it, may be a dying role. The possible demise of supervision, like the personal confrontation with the inexorable destiny of each indi-

Maurice J. Eash, Associate Professor of Education, The City University of New York, Hunter College, New York

vidual, is not viewed with pleasure by the supervisory ranks. A perusal of the literature and activities of supervisors reveals that in the main, as a professional group, they have simply denied the existence of this unpleasant though highly probable eventuality.

Supervision is brought to this confrontation by the intersection of two movements, both taking place outside the traditional sphere of the supervisor, but having wide ramifications for his operation. In the new realignment of political power, the classroom teaching staff negotiates directly with school boards on items and areas which were once the province of the supervisor. These negotiations have expanded the areas of determination for the teachers and eroded the functions of the supervisor. Space does not permit a point-by-point analysis of negotiated agreements between school boards and teachers. Yet the realignment of traditional relationships of classroom teacher and supervisor is extensive and indicates that the hallowed practice of direct face-to-face operation with classroom teachers is on the wane.

The traditional techniques of supervision which involved a defined relationship of superior and subordinate, the required classroom visits and conferences, the detailed supervisory report, and the requirement of attendance at supervisor organized meetings, are constrained and circumscribed through contracts drawn up between school boards and classroom teachers. Furthermore, the areas of authority that are not restricted in the contract are frequently inhibited by the psychological climate that prevails, especially if a supervisor works for a politically hypersensitive superintendent who prefers dealing with handcuffed supervisors rather than aggressive teacher grievance committees.

The second combination of forces restricting the supervisor's role are the current approaches to curriculum development which again take place largely outside the school system. Prepackaged programs of instructional materials bypass the supervisor and are directly implemented through the teacher. The teacher receives the packaged program of instruction and in some cases is trained by an outside-the-school system agent.

Present developments would suggest that future instructional designs will elaborate the closed system of prepackaged materials even further, locking the supervisor out as effectively as the teacher is locked in. Thus the supervisor's position and role are drastically altered and can be eliminated, if he is adamant in persisting in operating in the conventional, traditional mode. And many of the "live" issues forming the substance of supervision theory classes (line *vs.* staff positions, authoritarian *vs.* democratic supervision) are obsolete for projecting the future role of supervisors.

Unfortunately, the practice of the past and accumulated research evidence on supervision do not hold much promise of assistance in mapping the future position of the supervisor. Despite the broad general agreements that have historically evolved (the stress on instructional improvement through interpersonal relations), an examination of university graduate programs of preparation and state certification requirements underscores the confusion and limited agreement on the theoretical basis and conceptional definition of the task function.[1]

The supervisor's work can only be handicapped by this lack of professional role clarity. When the field of supervision is viewed in practice, the task function seems to be governed by a practical pragmatism, i.e., a person is needed to tidy up unfinished tasks and shore up obvious instructional weaknesses, and the role behavior is guided by a store of conventional

[1] H. Irene Hallberg. "Certification Requirements for General Supervisors and for Curriculum Workers Today—Tomorrow." *Educational Leadership* 23 (8): 623-24; May 1966.

wisdom. In a professional world where technical competence is increasingly mandated by the complex nature of professional tasks, and consistent with this general trend, the research on learning and instruction and human organizations systematically exposes greater subtlety and more profound complexities, supervisors are by training ill-equipped.

A Relevant Program

What then is a relevant program of preparation for the supervisors if they are to carve out a role which will make a meaningful contribution to curricular practice?

First, it is imperative that if a supervisor is to have a role in the newly emerging patterns of curriculum and instruction, he will be required to have an understanding of, and the technical ability to cope with the realities of the new social system of the school where authority relationships and power balances are being radically restructured. Essential to the ability to understand and cope with the new power balances is the competency in assessment of social systems: defining their boundaries, identifying the norms of behavior governing their participants, gauging the influence of power forces, and projections of consequences of the system as it shapes curriculum and student behavior.

In a sense the supervisor requires the skills of a systems analyst with special concern for the total effects of the social system on the curriculum. This, then, is the unique function that a supervisor can fulfill—*designing the curriculum in a comprehensive sense.*

Where the curriculum is moving into the negotiation-bargaining arena, outcomes are being shaped by other criteria than have been used in the past. The classic approach of proceeding to curriculum construction through an initial statement of objectives is being redefined by the negotiations at the bargaining table.[2] In this process one of the major contributions of the supervisor can be a preservation of concern and a gathering of evidence on instruction and its outcomes within the school system during the present power conflicts. Moreover, if curriculum construction is to advance to a stage where it receives its rightful primacy, new skills for resolution of conflicts and cooperative procedures for program development will need to be supplied. While research data on the technical competence needed is scarce in education, a considerable body of literature is accumulating in related behavioral sciences which suggests how human organizations can be moved from confrontation and conflict to mutuality in determination of goals and objectives.[3]

As for the second cluster of forces, the packaged curriculum programs bypassing the supervisor as a curriculum development specialist, there exists a great unmet need in putting these programs into a total design. These programs developed independently of each other are only fragments of the total

[2] Howard G. Foster. "Dispute Settlement in Teacher Negotiations." *ILR Research* 3 (3): 13; February 1967.

In an analysis of teacher negotiations, Foster recommends: "Scope of bargaining should be defined as clearly as possible. School districts should be encouraged but not required to bargain over issues of broad educational policy as curricula and textbooks" (p. 12). Nevertheless, the National School Boards Association has listed one area of bargaining as the curriculum, and many of the negotiated contracts have specifics written in which very clearly and directly affect the curriculum: class size, number of hours of instruction, assignment of personnel, and even definite programs of instruction.

[3] See: Chris Argyris. *Understanding Organizational Behavior.* Homewood, Illinois: The Dorsey Press, Inc., 1960; and Rensis Likert. *The Human Organization: Its Management and Value.* New York: McGraw-Hill Book Company, Inc., 1967.

These are only two examples of a growing body of behavioral science literature which offers very solid evidence on the organizational approaches needed for productive use of human resources.

experience of the learner in the school. Therefore, the supervisor as a specialist taking the outcomes of the total curriculum as his province must deal with the *macro* or total design of the curriculum, concentrating on the configuration of the separate curriculum programs and their impact on the students. Scant attention, indeed, has been paid to the total effect of the present separate micro-centered curriculum on the learner.

In brief, some macro-curriculum design problems[4] that can be readily identified are:

1. Curriculum dissonance: contradictions, incompatibilities in teaching methods and subject matter in separate subject areas, experiences which produce conflict at a level to cause students to reject the curriculum

2. Coordination: concern for commonalities as well as duplications with emphasis on wholeness in the curricular experiences for the student as he pursues the various subject areas

3. Balance: concern for relationships of general education to special education, vicarious and firsthand experiences, product and process learnings

4. Hypertrophy of areas of experience: overexpansion of curricular offerings, excessive commitment of students' time in premature specialization, exploitation of students in areas of experiences for purposes other than personal growth

5. Continuity: preserving and expanding threads of experiences from grade level to grade level and lower school to upper school, observing principles of learning in concept presentation allowing for structural development of fields of inquiry

6. Application of analogous developments in separate subject fields: for example, "learning by discovery" techniques developed with mathematics applied to health education or natural science

7. Evaluation of total curriculum design: gathering data on the total influence of the school experience, investigation of dysfunctioning in general or special education areas, desirability of adding or terminating curricular offerings on the basis of contribution to the total design

8. Assessment of internal and external pressures to effect change in parts of the curriculum and the impact on the total curriculum design.

Problems of this range are not receiving attention in present curriculum development efforts, and preparatory programs for supervisors are needed to develop the technical competencies which will be required to study *macro* curriculum design. An analysis of preparatory programs finds that few give major attention to preparation along these lines.

The research evidence supporting the contribution of supervision to the improvement of instruction is negligible.[5] However, the function of supervision has wide acceptance and there is a demand for and employment of supervisory personnel which appears to be rising at a slightly faster rate than the employment of classroom teachers.[6] These figures may be deceptive if interpreted as forecasting an unusually bright future for the supervisor and, correspondingly, overlooking some of the other trends which will temper if not dramatically change the supervisory function.

Supervisors can play a viable role, but the technical ability needed to pursue the future role as it is being shaped by powerful

---

[4] With some modification, these are drawn from a previous article by the author which appeared in "Guidelines for Preparatory Programs for Supervisors and Curriculum Workers." *Toward Professional Maturity of Supervisors and Curriculum Workers.* Washington, D.C.: Association for Supervision and Curriculum Development, 1967. pp. 21-22.

[5] See: Kimball Wiles. "Supervision." *Encyclopedia of Educational Research.* Third Edition. Chester Harris, editor. New York: The Macmillan Company, 1960. pp. 1444-45.

[6] *The Estimates of School Statistics, 1966-67,* Research Division, NEA, Research Report 1966-R20, lists a five percent increase in principals and supervisors from 1965-66 to 1966-67. This compares with slightly over three percent increase in classroom teachers.

forces is far different than most supervisory personnel have at their command at this time. Whether supervisors can gain command of these technical abilities and contribute to the design of the curriculum may mean the difference between survival or disappearance of the supervisor's role, and more importantly, the emergence of a more meaningful curriculum design than now exists. ☐

EL 26 (5): 482-89; February 1969
© 1969 ASCD

Is Systems Analysis for Supervisors?

MAURICE J. EASH

SUPERVISION in education is an applied discipline whose professional ranks are chiefly made up of field practitioners. As a consequence, the theory and knowledge that have fueled practice have been chiefly developed through analogy from the research in allied behavioral sciences. Thus we see in the past three decades major contributions to supervisory practice developed from learning theory, role theory, group dynamics; and, more recently, from sensitivity training, teacher behavior research, classroom interaction analysis,[1] and organizational theory.[2]

Among the latest newly emerging analogous developments holding potential for supervisory practice is *systems analysis*. The definition of systems analysis as used in this article encompasses the term in its broadest sense: "... any orderly analytic study designed to help a decision maker identify a preferred course of action from among possible alternatives. . . ."[3] There are other more restricted, and purportedly more precise, definitions of systems analysis, which specify use of mathematical models and cost effectiveness procedures in weighing and selecting alternatives. However, these approaches, popularized by former Secretary of Defense Robert S. McNamara, which emphasize techniques of cost accounting and mathematics, can ignore or distort other variables which are not specifically quantifiable.

Other systems experts have documented the severe limitations of the mathematical model systems approach when applied to situations that have emergent (variables are unclear and changing), and not established, qualities. Supervisors are much more likely to be involved in situations composed of variables which are unstable and in many cases unknown; consequently, assignment

[1] One comprehensive statement with many pertinent suggestions for applications of the research on teacher behavior to supervision is: Louise M. Berman and Mary Lou Usery. *Personalized Supervision: Sources and Insights.* Washington, D.C.: Association for Supervision and Curriculum Development, 1966. 64 pp.

[2] For an example of the use of developments in organizational theory and research as analogies for supervisory practice see: William H. Lucio. "The Supervisory Functions: Overview, Analysis, Propositions." In: *Supervision: Perspectives and Propositions.* William H. Lucio, editor. Washington, D.C.: Association for Supervision and Curriculum Development, 1967. pp. 1-11.

[3] E. S. Quade. "Systems Analysis Techniques for Planning-Programming-Budgeting." Santa Monica, California: The RAND Corporation, March 1966. p. 1.

Maurice J. Eash, Associate Professor of Education, The City University of New York, Hunter College, New York

of specific quantities to these variables can be a delusion.[4]

As curriculum and instruction advance in complexity, supervisors have felt the need for more sophisticated skills to cope with demands made on the professional role. As in the past, when supervision has selected from allied behavioral science research aspects which assist in meeting specific problems, selected techniques of systems analysis offer promise of upgrading supervisors' technical skills to deal with the problems which confront the supervisor in new developments in curriculum and instruction.

Systems analysis *in toto* is far too comprehensive a field for treatment in a short article. It is the author's purpose here, however, to propose concepts and techniques of this approach which appear to have special significance for the supervisor.

A Total Systems Emphasis

At the heart of systems analysis theory is a conceptualization, which can serve as an important foundation for delineating the role of the general supervisor; the total system is the unit to be used in analysis and planning. A total system in the case of the general supervisor could be the total curriculum design and its influence upon the student.

It must be recognized that the total system approach runs counter to the recent dominant trend, supervision by separate subject areas, and to the movement from general supervision over several subject areas to specialized supervision in one subject area. Moreover, the movement for specialized supervision from the standpoint of a total system approach falls heir to the negative criticism directed at the excessive fragmentation of curriculum. Among the net effects of fragmentation of curriculum on students are these: further competition for their learning time, a tendency to teach techniques and processes in isolation from social applications, and a reductionism of instructional goals to simple accumulation of more subject matter. Furthermore, if we really wish to measure the long-range impact of educational institutions and their curriculum on students, there is some hint that the total influence of the system may be a better predictor than the more finite measures of achievement in each separate subject.[5]

The total impact of the curriculum and the interrelationships of the various components of the curriculum necessitates the viewing of a curriculum as a total system, and has received minimal attention. Certainly, there is a badly needed role to be fulfilled if one merely begins to catalog the problems that are prevalent and attributable to the inadequate consideration given to designing the curriculum as a total system. A sample cataloging of some of the problems in curriculum design that result from approaching curriculum and attendant supervision on a piecemeal basis rather than as a total system follows:

1. Curriculum dissonance: contradiction, incompatibilities in teaching methods in subject areas, experiences which produce destructive conflict at a level to cause students to reject the curriculum.

2. Coordination: concern for commonalities as well as duplications with emphasis on unity in the curricular experiences for the student as he pursues the various subject areas.

[4] A clear definition of established and emergent situations and a trenchant criticism of the error in applying approaches designed for established-to-emergent situations is contained in: Robert Boguslaw. *The New Utopians*. Englewood Cliffs, New Jersey: Prentice-Hall, Inc., 1965. pp. 7-9. For a recent criticism of the closed-ended approach of systems analysis which is particularly applicable to education, see: Victor A. Thompson. "How Scientific Management Thwarts Innovation." *Trans-action*, June 1968. pp. 51-55.

[5] For an example of the types of questions under investigation on overall impact of educational institutions and their curriculum, see: Martin Trow. "The Meaning of Impact." Proceedings of the 1966 Invitational Conference on Testing Problems, Educational Testing Service, 1966. pp. 25-33.

3. Balance: concern for relationships of general education to special education, vicarious and firsthand experiences, product and process learning, pupil-directed and teacher-directed learning activities.

4. Excessive complexity of areas of experience: overexpansion of curricular offerings, excessive commitment of students' time in special areas, exploitation of students in areas of experience for purposes other than personal growth.

5. Continuity: preserving and expanding threads of experiences from grade level to grade level and one school to another, observing principles of learning in concept presentation enabling structural development of fields of inquiry.

6. Application of analogous development in separate subject fields: for example, "learning by discovery" techniques developed in science applied to health or mathematics, and the development of organizing principles for masses of data.

7. Evaluation of total curriculum design: gathering data on the total influence of the school experience, investigation of dysfunctioning in general or special education areas, desirability of adding or terminating curricular offerings depending on contribution to the total design.

8. Assessment of internal and external efforts to effect change in parts of the curriculum and the impact on the curriculum design.[6]

An appropriate analogy to the necessity of supervisors' viewing curriculum design as a total system is the recent turn toward a comprehensive approach to urban planning. There it was found that urban reconstruction must be viewed as a total system having economic, political, business, educational and organizational variables as contrasted with an earlier simplistic approach of razing deteriorated buildings in order to provide warm, efficient, rat-free housing for the poor.

The failure of supervisors and administrators in education to treat curriculum design as a total system and the continued emphasis on the piecemeal approach are equally as disastrous. As Alfred North Whitehead insightfully observed so many years ago, educational objectives, especially in a broad sense, cannot be met by fragmenting life experience into discrete separate subjects. The resultant of a less than total system view is seen in some of the current "new" separate subject curricula, in which significant social problems are ignored for abstract technical and "scholarly" objectives.

While there are hopeful signs that the profession is becoming more interested in a total operating unit approach, which conceives the designing of the curriculum as a total system, there is a major need for serious scholarly study by supervisors and curriculum workers of the more specific techniques that systems analysis has developed for approaching complex problems.

Models

When a systems approach to a problem is used, large quantities of data are generated, and a multitude of variables are encountered. One procedure which has been employed by systems analysis to organize and reduce variables and data to manageable proportions has been that of *models*. Models, according to one philosopher of science, are the *sine qua non* of science, for they are the primary mechanism for systematically abstracting, organizing, and relating complex variables.[7]

Kenneth Boulding recently characterized the chief purpose of models as the

---

[6] Maurice J. Eash. "Guidelines for Preparatory Programs for Supervisors and Curriculum Workers." In: *Toward Professional Maturity of Supervisors and Curriculum Workers.* Roy Patrick Wahle, editor. Washington, D.C.: Association for Supervision and Curriculum Development, 1967. pp. 21-22.

[7] Abraham Kaplan. *The Conduct of Inquiry.* San Francisco, California: Chandler Publishing Company, 1964. p. 258.

"doing violence to complexity." He cited as a prime exemplar the model used by economists, "Gross National Product." So acceptable has this model become that the initials GNP have become part of the conventional wisdom. When one reflects on the violence that such a model does to complexity (the figure GNP includes *all* goods and services nationally produced), supervisors should not be reticent to try model building in curriculum and instruction, since the complexity in these fields cannot be greater. Further encouragement to undertake model building in curriculum and instruction is given when one reflects on the boon that the GNP model has been to economic analysis and forecasting.

Supervision has been lacking in models with a clear-cut design of activities directed to instructional improvement. The cost effectiveness of instructional improvement efforts in particular has been neglected. Models which are directed to identifying the critical variables, positing the relationships, manipulating these relationships, and evaluating outcomes do assist in superimposing control over otherwise uncontrolled and previously indeterminate outcomes.

Let me be more specific. A recent in-service education project in which the author has acted as a consultant is developing a model directed to retaining and improving the effectiveness of beginning teachers. The postulates on which the model is based are drawn from research on organizational behavior and sensitivity training. Using research from these areas, definite objectives for the in-service education of new teachers were established, a planned series of transactions was organized, internal and external evaluation of the program was planned. A cost effectiveness procedure is being built into the model.

There is evidence that retention of a teacher saves the school system approximately $800 in recruitment of a replacement. Proceeding on the assumption that experienced teachers are more effective than inexperienced teachers, a procedure of assigning weights to increased teacher effectiveness as the result of experience is being tested. In this model, a cost effectiveness criterion on retention and increased teacher effectiveness is being devised. If the model is viable, then it will be used to guide other in-service programs and extended to in-service programs for more experienced teachers. This is only one example of the importance of model building to guide a common supervisory activity; others might be described in building instructional units and in similar supervisory problems.

For supervisors' use, the most significant contribution of systems analysis may be iteration. Model building becomes an essential process of iteration in moving from the talk to the action stage. Iteration contains ten steps: selecting objectives, designing alternatives, collecting data, building models, weighing cost against effectiveness, testing for sensitivity, questioning assumptions, reexamining objectives, opening new alternatives, formulating the problem.[8] Thus, model building is placed in the cycling of a problem. Although the tool of iteration does not guarantee a solution, it does offer far more protection against mis-identification of a problem or being seduced by one's own built-in biases.

Specific Approaches to Models

Systems analysis has pioneered specific techniques which are used in model building where one faces many uncertain parameters and a number of alternatives. To experienced supervisors who have been recipients of "mustang" reactions in human organizations, when what were thought to be mild uncontroversial proposals were made, there is scarcely need to dwell on a definition of uncertain parameters.

Most of the problems in supervision do

[8] E. S. Quade, *op. cit.*, pp. 8-11.

not lend themselves at this time to precise mathematical formulation. Therefore, there is a basic need to rely on models and techniques which do permit more rigor than the usual way of playing it by hunches, but do not mislead with a pretense of precision that is unobtainable.

Operational gaming is a laboratory simulation approach in which a group of experts are gathered together and asked to simulate the attitudes and consequent decisions of their real-life counterparts. Rules governing the options, constraints, and actions are provided by experts with a knowledge of the real-life counterpart. From the interaction, hopefully, the participants will gain insight into the predictions of actions and reactions which result within the gaming model and indirectly the real world which it represents. In-service programs and curriculum design approaches might all be tested out by supervisors through operational gaming techniques.

Scenario writing is a model building technique that has been used by military systems analysts to show how, starting with the present state of affairs, a future state of affairs might evolve through following a reasonable course of action.[9] When several individuals produce scenarios, many alternatives are developed and factors influencing future events are laid bare. Thus this series of primitive models shows how the future may be determined by present factors and suggests options and intervention strategies.

In a very rough sense, scenarios of curriculum are available in the evaluation data which are gathered for accreditation purposes in many high schools. A recent study of the longitudinal influence of the accreditation process on curriculum change found it to be very limited, principally due to lack of follow-up, accreditation in this study coming only every 10 years. A further handicap was the presentation of recommendations by the evaluators, which were subsequently rejected by the high school staffs as too expensive, too time consuming, or otherwise too impractical to implement.[10] If both evaluators and the evaluated understood the basic elements of scenario writing, accreditation visits could produce models to guide systematically further curriculum study.

A third method in model building is one that appeals to long-suffering participants in committees, and is directed toward dispensing with conventional committee meetings. The *Delphi method*[11] exchanges committee confrontation for an interchange of expert opinion through a carefully designed sequence of questionnaires by a third party. After the initial data from the first questionnaire are collected and compiled by the third party, a second document containing information on positions is exchanged and interrogation is begun on assumptions and data supporting positions. The process can be continued until consensus is achieved or conflicting positions are carefully documented.

The obvious advantage of obtaining experts' opinions without the necessity of convening them is perhaps not as significant as the circumventing of many of the psychological shortcomings which stymie committee meetings. The Delphi method merits considerable field investigation in supervision in which committee work has been the heart of practice. It could also test the hypothesis of whether group interaction is necessary to obtain follow-through on the part of participants, a hallowed rubric of supervision.

[10] Vynce A. Hines and William M. Alexander. "High School Self-Evaluation and Curriculum Change." Paper presented at the American Educational Research Association Annual Meeting, 1968.

[11] Norman Dalkey and Olaf Helmer. "An Experimental Application of the Delphi Method to the Use of Experts." *Management Sciences* 9 (3): 458-67; April 1963.

[9] As an illustration of a use of scenarios in a problem with many indeterminancies, and in this respect, not totally unlike those supervisors meet, see: Gilbert Burch. "How Big a Peace Dividend?" *Fortune* 77 (6): 86-89 ff.; June 1, 1968.

In sum, what systems analysis has to contribute to supervision are precisely those tools and techniques which the supervisor has lacked. These tools and techniques are a conceptual framework to view curriculum improvement; a procedure to select, refine, and delineate objectives; systematic comparison of alternatives; and use of a logical sequence of procedures in cycling problems that can be replicated and validated by others.

For several reasons, supervisors have been concerned about their lack of role definition and even the viability of their role in the organizational scheme of education. The lack of rigorous training and technical skills has handicapped supervisors' efforts to tackle significant problems in curriculum design and instruction. Supervisors knowledgeable in the technical skills of systems analysis, a few of which have been outlined here, will be ready to furnish leadership in the improvement of instruction. Supervisors so equipped will not be required to struggle for role definition; a functional role awaits them in every school system. ☐

EL 26 (1): 41-45; October 1968
© 1968 ASCD

Supervising Computerized Instruction [1]

WILLIAM VAN TIL

ADMITTEDLY, computer-aided instruction is in its infancy. To date, most supervisors have encountered the computer as a force in the curriculum only through the printed word, typified by a special section on computer-assisted instruction in *Phi Delta Kappan,* in April 1968, or the issue on instructional technology of *Educational Leadership,* in May 1968. Few supervisors have yet had the experience of carrying out their roles as supervisors in systems in which computer-aided instruction makes a major contribution to the curriculum.

Yet infants have a way of growing up. It is not too early to speculate on alternatives concerning their craft which will confront supervisors as computer-aided instruction develops. It is better to begin reflecting now on alternative models for supervising computer-aided instruction rather than realize belatedly that it is later than we thought as technology moves swiftly on.

A natural caution rightly impels us to ask whether we are dealing with a likely eventuality when we raise the question of alternative models for computer-aided instruction. So far as we can judge, what is the probable impact of the computer upon American society and American education in the years ahead? Though the gods give no guarantees, there are thoughtful scholars who are willing to speculate on the future. There is agreement among them that the impact of the computer will be powerful upon the American scene and American living patterns.

[1] This article is based upon a presentation by William Van Til to the session on supervising computer-aided instruction, Association for Supervision and Curriculum Development Conference, Atlantic City, New Jersey, March 1968.

William Van Til, Coffman Distinguished Professor in Education, Indiana State University, Terre Haute

Scholars who speculate on the future foresee substantial use of computer-aided instruction in the school and in the home. For instance, Kahn and Wiener say:

> Computers will also presumably be used as teaching aids, with one computer giving simultaneous individual instruction to hundreds of students, each at his own console and topic, at any level from kindergarten to graduate school; eventually the system will probably be designed to maximize the individuality of the learning process.... Individual computers (or at least consoles or other remote input devices) will become essential equipment for school, home, business, and profession, and the ability to use a computer skillfully and flexibly may become more widespread than the ability to play bridge or drive a car (and presumably much easier).[2]

The computer is likely to become a powerful force in American society. Computer-aided instruction will apparently become an important factor in the multiple media used in education through schools and homes.

Present Models in Supervision

How about supervision of computer-aided instruction? On this matter, it is too early for expertise. As we have said, supervision of computerized instruction is only in its infancy. The best we can do at this stage is to speculate on possible models, partially derived from the work of ASCD's Commission on Supervision Theory,[3] and on their possible relationship to computerized instruction.

The first model, as reported by ASCD's Commission, is derived from the pattern of supervision which prevailed in industry and education from 1910 to 1935 and which still persists to a degree today. This is the scientific management model, so named for the classic book by Frederick W. Taylor. Key concepts are efficiency, hard-nosed scientific standards, depersonalization, chain of command, clear communication up and down, specialization in jobs, and impersonal measurement. Resultant supervision stresses close direction by supervisors, teacher implementation of tasks determined by their superiors, specific performance standards required of teachers and of students, rating by supervisors, guiding ideas derived from administrators and not from teachers or students.

The scientific management model as applied to computerized instruction would involve determination of a pattern of laws of learning by psychologists (probably those of the school of thought of Skinner and his fellow behaviorists), determination by curriculum experts of exactly what is to be taught, and translation of content and psychology by computer experts into computer technology. The general or specialized supervisor, operating on the next rung down in the managerial hierarchy, would see to it that the teacher prescribed the correct computer technology for children and carried through classroom instruction efficiently, impersonally, and accurately.

The supervisor would direct closely, communicate clearly, and carry out without deviation the mandates of the experts above in the hierarchy. The supervisor would hold the teacher to defined teaching tasks, demand high performance standards, evaluate results closely, and rate the teacher on performance. In turn, the teacher would hold the students to their defined learning tasks, require high performance standards, examine extensively, and grade the students. We might quote Miranda, with a despairing inflection, "O brave new world that has such people in't."

The second model is derived from the pattern of supervision which influenced in-

---

[2] Herman Kahn and Anthony J. Wiener. *The Year 2000: A Framework for Speculation on the Next Thirty-Three Years.* New York: The Macmillan Company, 1967. pp. 90-91.

[3] William H. Lucio, editor. *Supervision: Perspectives and Propositions.* Washington, D.C.: Association for Supervision and Curriculum Development, 1967.

dustry and education in the period from about 1935 on and which is still heavily influential in education today. This is the human relations model which cites the classical experimentation at the Hawthorne plant of Western Electric and which reflects the work of such theorists as Elton Mayo and Fritz J. Roethlisberger. Lippitt, Benne, Bradford, Cartwright, and Zander are among the names associated with the educational aspect of the human relations emphasis. Bethel, Maine, may be regarded as the spiritual capital of this approach.

Key concepts of the human relations approach are the importance of the individual and his satisfactions, drives, needs; the importance of informal groups rather than exclusive primacy of the formal structure; participation by all in decision making; concern for high morale. Resultant supervision stresses warmth, personalization, individualization, equality relationships, reduction of status roles, recognition of individual and informal group purposes, participation by teachers in curriculum making, partnership assumption, and avoidance of rating by supervisors.

The human relations processes model as applied to computerized instruction would probably involve advice and consultation to school systems, individual schools, and individual classes by psychologists (possibly of the perceptual viewpoint typified by Arthur Combs, Earl Kelley, Abraham Maslow, Carl Rogers), by curriculum leaders, and by computer technologists. The work of the supervisor would be to harmonize the know-how of the psychological, curricular, and computer consultants with the computer programming for individual students requested by the classroom teacher. The teacher would be regarded as a highly educated and well-trained professional who utilizes a variety of old and new media, including computer-aided instruction, and who is a decision maker and a creative force.

The teacher would be conceived of as the person best equipped to foster learning experiences for the individuals whom he knows best. The teacher would describe the needs of his students. The supervisor would act as a partner, facilitator, and middleman in attempting to implement through technology what the teacher perceives as needed. The teacher would be the single most important participant in the determination of the particular content of the computer technology used in the classroom. We might quote Miranda again, but with a somewhat incredulous inflection, "O brave new world that has such people in't."

These are the two classic and polar models of supervision which have influenced educational practice. In addition, some, including William H. Lucio, have described a revisionist model intended "to consider both individual and organizational goals in their proper perspective," and "to eliminate the unrealistic aspects of the human relationist approach without sacrificing the advantages of its departures from the viewpoint of scientific management." [4]

Without necessarily subscribing to the revisionist view (which aspires to but may not be able to achieve a reconciliation of those ancient antagonists—individual needs and organizational demands), I would like to suggest that supervision of computerized instruction may result in and follow a model somewhat different from both classic models.

Is a New Model Needed?

The different model may conceive psychologists, curriculum specialists, and computer technologists not as all-knowing authorities, yet as more than consultants. It may conceive teachers not as completely autonomous, yet as far more than robots. It may conceive supervisors not as taskmasters, yet as more than just facilitators.

We must guard against the possibilities of psychologists, curriculum specialists, and

[4] *Ibid.*, p. 8.

technologists becoming the arrogant masters implied in the scientific management computerized model. Yet let us recognize also that the psychologists, curriculum specialists, and technologists may have to achieve a more independent role than simply consultation if computer-aided instruction is to be widely used.

Perhaps they will become the creators of a great and a highly varied library or bank of materials from which educators may selectively choose.

We must work so that the teacher does not become the mere mechanic and puppet envisioned in the scientific management computer model. But let us recognize also that the teacher in a highly specialized world cannot build computer technology with bare hands or through round-table discussion and must instead utilize selectively the product of specialists.

Let us devoutly hope, and indeed let us make sure, that the supervisor does not become a Prussian drillmaster serving narrowly the prescription of a master race of experts and presiding over a subordinate race of humble teachers, as envisioned in the scientific management computer model. But let us recognize also that a supervisor is more than a facilitator or a yea-sayer. The supervisor should have a leadership role in solving problems, in injecting ideas, and in humanizing and enriching the process of education both in relationship to teachers and to developers of the new technology.

This may involve a different model for supervising computerized instruction. If so, let us move toward its construction. □

EL 23 (8): 656-59; May 1966
© 1966 ASCD

The Supervisor and Media

ELWOOD E. MILLER
DELAYNE HUDSPETH

MANY persons in education today seem to believe that in the teaching-learning situation of tomorrow the student will relate only to machines and that the teacher will become as important as the horse in today's modern transportation system.

There can be little doubt in the minds of those involved in education that the impact of educational technology is growing. While the dangers of an impersonalized, dehumanized teaching-learning process are unmistakably present, it is our position that the teacher does have a role, an important one, in any modern system of education. Furthermore, it is the supervisor who can help the teacher maintain and redefine his role as educational media become increasingly significant in education.

Media in the Schools

First, let us define what we mean by "educational media." In this article we are including any and all materials and equip-

Elwood E. Miller, Associate Professor of Education and Director, E.P.D.A. Institutes, Michigan State University, East Lansing; and DeLayne Hudspeth, Assistant Professor, Instructional Development, Center for Instructional Communications, Syracuse University, Syracuse, New York. In 1966, Dr. Hudspeth was Media Coordinator, Learning Systems Institute, Michigan State University, East Lansing

ment which communicate ideas and facts to students. Further, we are talking about using these in a man-machine-materials *system* with components in proper relation with one another so that optimal learning will take place with students of varied interests and aptitudes. It is in the development of such a system that the supervisor has a large and very important role.

We perceive the supervisor's role in the development of these systems to be that of a catalyst. That is, the supervisor can improve the teaching-learning situation by supplying ideas, inspiration, and guidance which will cause a reaction when the right mixture of students, teacher, and materials is brought together.

But what do we mean by "ideas, inspiration, and guidance" in relation to media? Or to put it another way, why are these especially important in fostering intelligent use of media?

It obviously is impossible to spread new ideas unless one keeps up with new ideas. In a very real, tedious sense, this means that the supervisor has to keep abreast of new methods and new materials. To some, this will sound like absurd advice. We read countless pieces of mail, visit endless numbers of booths at conventions, and take time to talk with salesmen. While this does not provide a lot of worthwhile information it is still one way of learning about what is new. Actually there should be no need for such a cumbersome way to collect materials. The technology is available so that a person could walk to the phone, "dial" his question to a materials center, and receive a packet of materials in the mail the next day. The cost to the school of such a telephone unit has been estimated at approximately $4.00 a month plus the cost of the call.

Of value also is the kind of visitation program all too often discouraged for lack of travel funds and staff time. If possible, the supervisor should find where the newer materials are being tried nearby and obtain an evaluation from the users as to the effectiveness of their particular program. We should keep in mind that personalities, both of individuals and of schools, vary considerably and that what may be good for Brown is not good for Green. Nonetheless, personal observation still remains one of the best ways to spread ideas.

Art of Inspiring

We use the word "art" at this point because we simply have little concrete knowledge about how one can take an idea, transmit it to a teacher, and create the kind of atmosphere in which new ideas are welcome and subsequently tried. What little we do know suggests that the variables are exponential to the number of people and ideas involved.

However difficult the problem, few deny the need in most of our school systems for that kind of atmosphere wherein people are excited enough to tackle the problems of tomorrow (and if we do not, those *outside* of education will) and still do the work of today. What is the best bridge between inspiration and the problem? We suggest it to be research and development.

Few other sectors of our society spend so little on research and development as does education. The cry used to be that there "is not enough money for research, we have a job to do." With the advent of greatly increased federal funds, plus the willingness of industry to test materials, there is little excuse left in the financial arena. Supervisors need to become familiar with the guidelines set by the U.S. Office of Education and to urge faculty members to apply for small research grants.

Other kinds of media research can result through university affiliation. Of considerable concern to many persons in higher education is the lack of communication between the "ivory tower" and the "firing line." We suggest that the distance between the public school and the university needs desperately to be reduced—by both academicians and practitioners. Furthermore, the practitioners have as much or more responsibility for generating testable ideas as do the theoreticians. What this will mean is an attitude of critical analysis toward some sacred cows as well as a willingness to experiment with new tools of education.

What this also means is that the supervisor must guide faculty into thinking more deeply about what is actually going on in the teaching-learning process. We do *not* mean we should tell the teacher what he or she is doing is wrong, which is apt to lead to alienation. Rather we must develop a climate in which the supervisor feels free to suggest new ideas, new materials, and new systems. The supervisor and the teacher can then work together to see if the idea has merit.

Primary Technology

As our society becomes more complex we rely on what might be termed primary technology. In our house this means that we have electricity, gas, sewage services, etc.

We believe that education is one of the most backward and underdeveloped segments of society when it comes to primary technology. We have little excuse not to rectify this.

For example, let us automate the routine procedures in pupil accounting, in test scores, in all of the multifarious types of housekeeping details faced to a degree by every classroom teacher. Data processing equipment is a part of the administrative patterns of most school districts and these machines could well be used to eliminate a considerable share of teacher paperwork.

There is also a primary technology of teaching-learning materials. There is a need for adequate, easily retrieved materials, sufficient and easily run machines, and classrooms that are designed to allow for more than talk, talk, talk, to take place.

Let us be done with the notion that the teacher's role is to present information. The teacher's role is to *organize opportunities for learning experiences*. It is at this point that the supervisor can be of considerable help in working with the teacher to utilize the kinds of primary technology that should be available in every school. If this primary technology does not exist, then the supervisor will need to work with administrators, librarians, audiovisual specialists, and others who are involved in developing the necessary learning systems.

Again, let us state that we perceive the supervisor to be in a catalytic position regarding the use of mediated instruction. We have indicated that the supervisor must bring to the teacher the pertinent ideas, in an atmosphere of inspiration, and help guide the change process that occurs.

What must emerge from this interaction, and this growing sophistication with the use of teaching-learning tools, is an ability to look objectively at the process of education and to be able to say: (a) This is what this material will do for the student; (b) this is where it fits (for this group, and time, and place); and (c) this has accomplished what it set out to accomplish.

We urge that teachers view all of instruction in a "programmed" manner. That is, as a series of steps leading to some identified objective, with each step scrutinized for its effectiveness in leading from the past step to the next step. We are not suggesting that this is easy, but we do maintain that it is necessary.

Encourage and Aid Innovation

How can the supervisor encourage and develop innovation in the school setting? First, he can single out several teachers who are willing to try new ways of instructing. Administrators are usually willing to battle for improved services, once the need for these services has been demonstrated. Second, by urging both teachers and administrators to visit schools that are trying new methods, and who are effectively demonstrating the use of media. Third, by developing a need for the use of media based on a critical analysis of those present patterns of instruction which can be viewed as wasteful of the time and talents of administrators, teachers, *and* students.

Real instructional leadership is needed to take full advantage of the technological advances that are becoming more and more available to teachers of the future. The simple fact is that technology is capable of assuming responsibility for large sections of the educational effort, though teachers must learn how to manage and use it with judgment and skill.

If curriculum leaders and planners develop this judgment and skill in fostering the use of educational media, educational techniques can change, and change rapidly, without a depersonalization and dehumanization of the learning process. Technology can then solve many of the problems we face, and at the same time can create conditions for truly effective, efficient learning in the schools. □

Curriculum Negotiations: Present Status – Future Trends

WILLIAM F. YOUNG

EDUCATION and educational personnel have commanded more news media time and space in recent years than during any period in the history of education in this country. The development within the profession mainly responsible for the recent wave of notoriety is negotiations. Whether the process is labeled professional negotiation or collective bargaining is immaterial. It is the nature of the process and the impact of the process that we must analyze and respond to in a constructive manner.

The practice of labor groups organizing for collective action—a practice that is now accepted as a basic factor in our economic system—has a very long history, nationally and internationally. The trade guilds in Europe during the Medieval Period were probably the forerunners of labor unions as we know them today. However, collective action by teachers in education is a recent development which has marked the beginning of a new era within the profession.

The New Force

State laws authorizing negotiation for teacher organizations are becoming quite common across the nation. In many states the laws on negotiaton pertain exclusively to public school personnel, while in other

William F. Young, Deputy Superintendent, Dearborn Public Schools, Dearborn, Michigan. Formerly Director for Administration and Communication, Michigan-Ohio Regional Educational Laboratory, Detroit, Michigan

states the laws apply to all public employees. This development was prompted by, and is now accompanied by, militant behavior on the part of teachers.

Teacher associations and teacher unions, at the local and national levels, have been organizing for the purpose of pursuing their interests vigorously at the bargaining table. In many instances, when bargaining has failed, strikes and walkouts have resulted. Regardless of the terminology used, the collective bargaining process and collective bargaining behavior reflect what is happening in most school districts where negotiations are taking place.

Realities of Negotiations

The power struggle within the profession is between teachers on the one hand and boards of education and administration on the other. Operationally, the laws and organizational behavior have tended to follow the labor-management adversary relationship patterns found in business and industry. The collective bargaining model has been tried and tested in business and industry. The utilization of this model by school personnel has resulted in a pattern of employee demands, management counterproposals, heated bargaining sessions, the use of labor attorneys, the use of management attorneys, the use of outside professional organizers and negotiators, the struggles for control between teacher organizations, alienation of relationships, and general adoption of "we-they" attitudes. In some instances, curriculum workers and supervisors have been put in the position of "taking sides."

Impact on People

The new force in education represented by teacher power through negotiation is long overdue. Our problems are not the new force and the rightful involvement of teachers in matters that affect them. The problems are the procedures and tactics being employed in the process by teachers and administrators; and the nature of the items that are being placed on the bargaining table. There is evidence indicating that teacher organizations regard curriculum as part of wages, hours, and conditions of employment. The wording of legislation, some judicial interpretations, and practice support the fact that curriculum and curriculum-related items are negotiable.

Negotiation in education is in its infancy stage and many of the attendant problems have resulted from naïveté, inexperience, and the fact that alternative models are not available. The most perplexing problem of our profession is that we have not learned how to negotiate on a coprofessional basis. Many issues rightfully belonging to professional settlement have been settled in the context of adversary relationships accompanied by antagonistic confrontations. Curriculum matters are being caught up in this process. The resultant alienation of individuals and groups poses a challenge to all of us.

The effects of collective bargaining behavior in general, and curriculum negotiation in particular, have been observable. Within the profession there has been a new type of hostility between teachers and administrators; there has been a new type of hostility between and among teachers, an increase in work stoppages, decreased feeling of responsibility in each group for the welfare of the other group; communication between administrators and teachers has been adversely affected; and professional staff members have spent tremendous amounts of time, energy, and talent in bargaining sessions and planning for negotiation at the expense of other primary professional functions.

Outcomes within the community of the labor-management game in education are also observable. People, community organizations, and newspapers choose sides. Emotions run high. In some communities, it will take years to rebuild the image and restore the level of respect that teachers and administrators deserve. Gaining increased financial support will become even more difficult.

Impact on children and youth of the adoption of collective bargaining behavior on the part of teachers and administrators is probably less predictable at this time but perhaps more serious. It might be said that we are exhibiting behavior that is a direct contradiction of the stated goals of our instructional program related to proper attitudes and values basic to our democratic way of life. In some school districts the actions taken in violation of the laws of a state pose an even more serious problem. It is difficult to understand how we can expect young people to abide by school rules, develop as good citizens, and support law and order when we flout these traditional values and the law. Young people lose valuable instruction time in some instances. Curriculum negotiations also affect the instructional program.

Impact on the Instructional Program

Down through the years educators have advocated the development of curriculum through teamwork and a co-professional approach. This position is now in jeopardy. The climate of labor-management bargaining not only has had a negative impact on working relationships among professional staff members but has also had a negative impact on the instructional program and curriculum development activities.

Many master contracts contain provisions that are curricular in nature. They also include some provisions that are closely related to curriculum. Examples of such items are: textbook selection procedures; teaching assignments; restrictions on classroom visitations; teaching hours; transfer policies; released time; clock length of class periods; length of school day; curriculum committee selection procedures; class size averages; length of the school year; number of weekly teaching periods; preparation periods for elementary teachers during art, music, and physical education instructional time; procedures for selection of instructional equipment and materials; pupil-teacher ratios; and class size maximums. All of these items are curricular in nature or have serious curricular implications. They are related to quantity of instruction, quality of instruction, quality of instructional materials, staffing, and school organizational patterns.

At this point in time it is difficult to appraise results of curriculum negotiations from a positive standpoint. The collective bargaining approach in the curriculum area appears to be a self-defeating process for teachers and administrators (including supervisors and curriculum workers). The education profession faces a major challenge in the next few years, since negotiations are here to stay.

Our present dilemma in the curriculum area perhaps can be attributed to inexperience of school people with a new force, to negative attitudes, and to the striving for some goals that are divisive. In spite of current problems, the long-range effects of the negotiation development will be positive. The new power base has the potential of improving education for the young people of our society and of significantly advancing our profession. The challenge is to learn to live effectively with this new force.

We can ill afford to have the human resources within our profession divided into two camps. A unified profession is essential. As a first step toward the evolvement of more mature behavior and a more appropriate model for negotiating, we should start with new approaches to curriculum negotiation.

Critical Year Ahead

Negotiation approaches that seem appropriate, at this time, for welfare matters are not appropriate for curriculum matters. Optimum conditions for productive curriculum development work require a high degree of mutual faith, trust, and respect among professional staff members. Collective bargaining behavior has not promoted these conditions.

It would be helpful if agreement were reached on the point that it is unwise to negotiate specific curriculum development activities and curriculum content. Activities and content should evolve as teachers and administrators work together on a co-professional basis in an effort to improve the instructional program.

Hopefully, continuing experience with curriculum negotiation will also result in limiting the process to consideration of organizational patterns for curriculum work, teacher representation in curriculum development activities, and structure for curriculum decision making. Curriculum development work is a growth and study process that evolves as a result of interaction between teachers and administrators. The end products of curriculum study must continually change as the study process progresses.

These changes are possible if members of the profession agree that the present negotiation approaches in regard to curriculum matters are inappropriate. These changes would make it possible, within the law, for professionals to live and work cooperatively in this new power relationship. New approaches can provide the vehicle for making significant breakthroughs in education by providing opportunities for a co-professional approach toward the achievement of common goals in a rational and responsible manner. ☐

Negotiations: Inevitable Consequence of Bureaucracy?

ROBERT L. SAUNDERS
JOHN T. LOVELL

PERHAPS no current movement in education poses more questions about the organization and structure of educational administration and the role of the administrator than does the emergence of professional negotiations. By the same token, probably no other movement in education has offered as much potential for establishing a new role for the teacher in policy formulation in public schools. Professional negotiations and their accompanying ramifications have moved to the forefront of public attention.

The movement has all the ingredients for controversy, emotionalism, and front page space; it is also critically important to

Robert L. Saunders, Associate Dean of Education and Professor of Educational Administration, Auburn University, Auburn, Alabama; and John T. Lovell, Dean of Education, University of Bridgeport, Bridgeport, Connecticut

the future of education and to the teaching profession.

The authors believe that the emergence of some form of negotiating machinery between the power structure representative of teacher interest and the power structure representative of management interest was inevitable, primarily because of two sets of factors. These two factors are: (a) changes in teachers and their behavior, and (b) the nature of the organizational structure of public education.

A "New Breed"

Many of today's teachers are pictured as a "new breed," having been produced out of the larger context of man's continuing desire to improve himself and from the observation that objectives often can be achieved more readily through aggressive behavior. Increased mobility of the American people has resulted in an increased number of "cosmopolitan" teachers as compared to "locals." Teachers are now better prepared than ever before; more of them are working in big school systems brought about by school consolidation and urbanization. Also, teachers more and more are aware of society's increased expectation of public education and the unprecedented demand for excellence. NEA President Elizabeth Koontz is probably correct when she says that today's teacher is

. . . sufficiently frustrated and actively dedicated enough to do something about the many problems that stand in the way of successful efforts, be they problems of working conditions, staff relationships, or welfare of teachers.[1]

The authors, as school administrators and professors of school administration,

[1] Elizabeth Koontz. "Why Teachers Are Militant." Paper read at seminar on "Who Controls American Education?" Joint Committee of National Education Association and Magazine Publishers Association, New York, New York, December 7, 1967.

agree that the new breed of teacher is on the scene, but we are inclined to believe that many of our schools and institutions are headed by a "not so new" breed of school administrator. Despite statements to the contrary, many administrators do not really view the teacher as being at the apex of the profession. The so-called advantages administrators enjoy over teachers are not as basic to the problem as is the fact that only administrators have legitimate authority to make decisions. This factor, in all likelihood, is the major reason that teachers in approximately 1,500 school systems in the United States have considered it necessary to develop formal procedures for negotiations in order to have a voice in the development of educational policies.

We believe that this situation developed, not so much because administrators want it this way, but because administrative behavior in educational organizations is primarily a function of the nature of the organizational structure within which it takes place. More specifically, the organizational structure of education is basically bureaucratic and has not provided a formal and legitimatized basis for teacher participation in the development of educational policy.

The Bureaucratic Model

Close observers such as Abbott,[2] Miles,[3] and Moeller[4] have concluded that there is a close and positive correlation between the ideal bureaucratic model proposed by Weber

[2] Max G. Abbott and John T. Lovell, editors. *Change Perspectives in Educational Administration*. Auburn, Alabama: Auburn University, 1965.

[3] Matthew B. Miles. "Education and Innovation: The Organization as Context." In: *Change Perspectives in Educational Administration*. Max G. Abbott and John T. Lovell, editors. Auburn, Alabama: Auburn University, 1965.

[4] Gerald H. Moeller. "The Relationship Between Bureaucracy in School Organizations and Teachers' Sense of Power." Unpublished Ed.D. dissertation. St. Louis, Missouri: Graduate Institute of Education, Washington University, 1967.

and the structure of educational organizations. But the point is that there is a legal basis for authority in educational organizations which has constitutional and statutory foundations and is vested in boards of education and superintendents of education. There is, also, an ordered system, actually a mandated one, of subordination and superordination which is achieved through administrative offices. Administrators have the necessary authority to make and implement the decisions required to achieve the goals for which the organization is responsible. There is not, however, a formal, legitimatized structure through which teachers can make policy decisions and be held responsible for those decisions.

The literature is rather complete with various suggestions regarding new and desirable administrative practices which have been advanced in light of the fact that professional negotiations are here, that teachers are more militant, and that their expectations are different from those of a decade ago. There is every reason to believe that this trend will continue, at least in the foreseeable future. We believe that it is regrettable that the negotiating machinery has been based on the industrial model, although this was clearly predictable inasmuch as the educational organization itself has been modeled along the industrial line.

A New Model Is Needed

We are concerned, also, about the dichotomy that is developing between teachers and administrators and believe that, although this is an inevitable consequence of negotiations between two competing power structures, it need not continue. Accordingly, we believe that a formal structure is needed which will provide for legitimatized teacher participation in policy development. This, it seems to us, is the basic question and one to which we now give attention.

What kind of structure will alleviate the problems outlined here and provide for the legitimatized involvement of the teacher in the achievement of organizational goals? Clearly no model has been offered, but the beginning of one may be on the scene. The literature contains some theoretical formulations which might be helpful as concerned educators move toward the establishment of a structure. For example, the principles offered by Saunders, Phillips, and Johnson, who summarized much research on educational leadership and developed a set of guides for effective leadership, might serve as an adequate base upon which some new conceptualization of structure might be developed.[5] A major tenet of these principles is that the nature of leadership behavior in any organization is at least partly dependent upon the organization's functions and should operate within a structure which releases and invokes the leadership capability of the total group.

Miles talks about a similar proposition when he proposes an alternative model for educational organizations in which he formulates the idea of "organizational health." He develops a definition of a "healthy" organization and also defines a set of interpersonal process norms which support the idea of organizational health. He goes on to identify these norms as openness, trust, inquiry, collaboration, consensus, and individuality and shows that they are interdependent with role specifications and performance.[6]

Argyris, who also recognizes the need for a new organizational model, hypothesizes that formal and informal dimensions of organizational activities may be studied and understood by using a model that incorporates such properties as the following:

[5] Robert L. Saunders, Ray Phillips, and Harold Johnson. *Theory of Educational Leadership*. Columbus, Ohio: Charles E. Merrill Books, Inc., 1966.

[6] Matthew B. Miles, *op. cit.*

1. The organization is a pattern of parts.

2. The parts maintain the whole through their interrelatedness.

3. The parts change their interrelationships to cope with, and adapt to, new stimuli threatening the organization.

4. The whole is able to control the environment up to the point that is necessary for maintenance of itself.[7]

From this rationale Argyris develops a tentative model for understanding the organizational mix, including in the model such dimensions as awareness, control, internal influence, problem solving, external influence, time perspective, and organizational objectives. He makes no claim that a complete theory has been developed, saying instead that, although one is needed, no such formulation is now available.[8]

Other examples of promising formulations could be mentioned, but the above summaries substantiate the point that a beginning is visible and that there is a reason for optimism.

In summary, the emergence of professional negotiations is a part of a much larger movement. Teachers also yearn for a better lot in life and a major part of their yearning deals with their professional careers.

The increased success by groups employing aggressive behavior has been apparent to teachers, who have adopted this pattern of operation on pragmatic grounds.

It is our contention that the education profession should initiate action immediately to change the legal structure within which schools now operate so as to permit the legitimatized involvement of teachers. It is possible, it seems to us, that objectives being sought through structured, industrial-type negotiations may be achieved through a different model of educational administration which would generate greater efficiency in goal attainment, better policies, higher levels of teacher satisfaction, and less confrontation, unrest, and militancy. ☐

[7] Chris Argyris. "Organizational Leadership." *Leadership and Interpersonal Behavior*. Luigi Petrullo and Bernard M. Bass, editors. New York: Holt, Rinehart and Winston, Inc., 1967. p. 341.

[8] *Ibid.*

The Supervisor We Need

RICHARD F. NEVILLE

WE NEED a supervisor who makes a difference; one who acts directly and effectively to improve the instructional program. Most of us would agree with such an assertion and recognize it as being consistent with contemporary theory in educational supervision. Such theory holds to the primacy of the supervisor in working to improve teaching.

In activating this perspective, the supervisor functions as an analyst of the teaching process, creating the conditions whereby

Richard F. Neville, Associate Professor of Education, University of Maryland, College Park

teachers can study their instructional behavior. He is responsible for identifying instructional problems and for providing leadership in their resolution. He is an authority on teaching, a resource person, an expert in group dynamics, and more recently is conceived of as a catalyst or an agent of change. This constitutes a general statement of the supervisor we need.

Supervisory Theory

In attempting to achieve this state of supervision we have tended to espouse practices based upon the principles of sound human relationships. Drawing upon social psychology, group dynamics, and sociological research, supervisory leaders constructed an interpretation of supervision. If practices stood as reliable exponents of effective human relationships, hewn from the behavioral and social sciences, instructional growth was thought to be assured.

Here the sanctity and respect of each staff member was crucial. The ideas of the individual, his strengths as a teacher and partner in the consideration of professional concerns were accented. The consistency of this motif with our creed as a nation made such a theme suitable—even rational. Its supporters grew and diminished as the fortunes of American education were buffeted by the mainstream of social-cultural change.

The human relations theory of supervision has never been presented as the easy, all's well, interpretation of supervision. Marshaling the resources of variant individuals while providing for their growth and consequently the growth of the instructional program is recognized as a complex undertaking. Where this approach has been applied with understanding, based upon careful analysis and the construction of a conceptual framework to guide it, the results have been most exciting and beneficial.

In too many instances, however, the conceptual framework has not accompanied the development of supervisory programs. That is, a vaguely conceived format of process, roles, and responsibilities can be easily dismissed and replaced by little more than good intentions. Often disillusionment and frustration appear as the power of a lost idea or the momentum for change passes. Old patterns become extremely attractive in such circumstances. Thus an ideal of productivity, growth, and change, through the application of sound human relationships, is subsumed by the need to maintain the system. The symbols, the phrases, the committees, and communication system are retained—more as an expression of hope than reality.

This description of the course of supervisory theory as applied in action programs is not meant to deny the importance of the human relations emphasis in supervision. It is not a comprehensive explanation of supervisory developments. Its purpose is to emphasize that the full power of supervisory programs, utilizing the principles of human relations and the school as a social system, has seldom materialized.

In the judgment of the writer, teachers see this interpretation of supervision as relatively nonexistent, yet one which they desire; also that the major reasons for this discrepancy are the lack of skills attendant to this conception of supervision, and the absence of any real struggle to define the "root" meanings of the theory upon which it is based. In the latter case we have been too ready to accept the generalizations—and acceptance which is devoid of thoughtful study is apt to produce the dissemination of a definition in contrast to an operational design extracted from tenets which have been carefully weighed and measured.

What is needed are supervisors who can transform principles of human relations into substantive programs of action. Making people feel comfortable, creating lines of communication, fostering security, all such concerns are basic but valid only as they contribute to the study of teaching. At a given time disequilibrium may be the appropriate condition for instructional growth. To make operational decisions in these areas supervisors must study formal organization, role theory, communication, decision making, personality theory, the change process, and other areas significant to the human relations perspective of supervision. Offering pronouncements about the power of the group and "working together" does not represent a supervisory program.

If we can give pause to the incantation and realistically assess our approach to improved instruction, needed changes in supervisory behavior may be identified. In particular, the relationship of theory and practice must be reviewed. Where supervision is effective it stands the test of internal consistency; a theory, operational principles, and supervisory procedures hold together. Simultaneously the analysis and research of supervision along with the interpretation of curriculum it breeds must exist. Together, the theory, the operational design, and the constant redefinition as new data are added constitute dynamic supervision.

Analyst of the Teaching Process

The supervisor we need is a skillful diagnostician of the "matter" of his position. The matter in mind here is the teaching act. It is generally assumed that the supervisor, among other things, is a master teacher. He is capable of viewing the teaching process from a variety of dimensions. He is perceptive to the interaction of variables as they operate within a given class or school. As the process is viewed by the supervisor he sees the teacher as a pivotal factor; his strengths and abilities are being applied to the presentation of ideas; the students are engaged in building their conceptual power and hopefully testing and constructing value patterns which will have meaning for them.

To improve teaching, the supervisor must have an intrinsic grasp of the dynamics of teaching and a number of methods for analyzing the process. Does effective teaching behavior have certain logical qualities? (Meux and Smith [6]); is teaching best studied as problem solving or coping behavior? (Turner [9]); how do teachers having particular characteristics, properties, or behaviors affect the behavior of pupils? (Ryans [8]); can teaching be conceived of as interaction? (Flanders [4]).

Research on teaching as identified above can provide the supervisor with a number of alternatives in analyzing the work of teachers. In no sense are the findings of these researchers intended to "wrap up" the problem. They represent, however, systematic, sophisticated approaches to the analysis of teaching and as such they point to valid concerns for the supervisory program.

The supervisor extends his perceptivity of teaching by studying the implications of such research. It aids the multi-dimensional interpretation and should enable the supervisor to refine his conceptualization of the process. This is an imperative. It does not imply that the supervisor's view will become the singular good but rather that it will support the development of supervisory practices and procedures that make *teaching* the core concern. It also promotes depth thinking about the teaching process.

As such thinking prevails, problems and issues begin to assume a priority relationship—even to the point of suggesting that the dress of the teacher and the neatness of the room are relatively subordinate concerns for professional centering on learning and its illusive facets. The supervisor we need is a student of the teaching process who functions to transpose a presentation into a transaction of significance for both teacher and students.

How Do Teachers View Supervision?

Where the intent of my actions is clear to me but held suspect by others the results of our professional relationship will be limited. If I am aware of the disparity between my intentions and the "reality" with which they are perceived, it may be possible to take steps to mediate the difference and slowly build the trust and mutual respect so necessary for instructional improvement. Since teachers are either the recipients of or partners in the supervisory process, what they perceive supervision to be is important data in building a sound program.

In 1961 Carolyn Guss (5) reported on the Indiana ASCD supervision study. She summarized the reactions of teachers concerning supervision as follows:

> They tended to want to avoid being the object of supervision. Some of them considered supervision an attack upon them personally. Others thought of supervision as a program dealing with materials, ideas, and schedules rather than with the teaching-learning situation as it affects personal relationships.

Subsequent studies and numerous prior investigations support the meaning of this reaction. In essence all of these combined attempts to analyze the condition and nature of supervision point directly to the following:

1. Teachers *do not* see supervision as focusing on the improvement of instruction.

2. Teachers *do not* see supervision as having a strong "human relations" base.

3. Teachers *do not* see supervisors as being prepared to help them in the study of teaching.

4. Teachers *want* supervision that will help them attack instructional problems.

It is possible to substantiate these generalizations with numerous research findings that go back to the 1920's. The trend continues to the present day. As the change in supervisory philosophy was made, it was evidently conceived as a statement of intent, while supervision in fact showed a contradictory posture within the school organization.

Teachers continue to recognize a contradiction and express strong ambivalence about the place and function of supervisory services. Keep in mind—they may be wrong! Supervisors, in fact, may be instruction centered; they may be human-relations oriented; they may have the skills to help teachers study the process of teaching—but if so we have not measurably communicated these facts to those who stand to profit from our services.

What Do Teachers Want in Supervision?

In 1960 Lloyd Dull (3)[1] developed at Ohio State University a comprehensive set of criteria for the evaluation of supervisory programs. In many ways this study constituted a breakthrough. Most instruments of this type prior to Dull's study were "homegrown" lists drawn from the experience of local supervisors and teachers. In this case, one hundred and twenty national leaders in educational supervision lent their talents to the verification of Dull's criteria. To some extent the concern of validity of the criteria was accommodated. Dull subsequently showed that he could apply the criteria to determine effective programs of supervision.

---

[1] This study is a most comprehensive statement of criteria for supervisory programs in education. It would serve as a good beginning point for school systems interested in studying their programs of supervision. Individual items are not overpowering in meaning but the total instrument provides a means of delineating the present state and needs in supervision. Again, it is a starting point. As mentioned in this article our problem is to make these ideas operational, not simply to recognize their present level of use. Dull's criteria are consistent with an operational definition of human relations approach to supervision.

Neville (7) (1963)[2] applied a modified form of Dull's criteria to ascertain the views of teachers regarding supervision.

Based upon this study, and recognizing the limitations imposed by geography and criteria selection, the following practices, procedures, and conditions are specified as being very important, as perceived by teachers, in the development of supervisory programs which will make a difference in the quality of instruction:

The supervisory program provides for cooperative development of both immediate and long range curriculum plans.

Opportunity is provided for teachers to study in groups on problems of concern to them.

There is continuous evaluation of the instructional program.

Teachers are encouraged to assume leadership positions.

Job expectations and relationships are understood by professional staff.

Organization of staff for instructional improvement is democratically arranged.

Committees of teachers are organized for the improvement of teaching resources (community, school equipment, personnel, and instructional materials).

There exists a coordinated attack upon pupil personnel problems and the diagnosis of learning difficulties.

The organization of the supervisory function is changed as the needs of the situation are modified.

Facilities and resources to strengthen the development of the curriculum are given priority consideration.

Supervisors are "master teachers."

The plan for evaluation of teachers is cooperatively evolved.

[2] The 1963 study was conducted in Connecticut. Recently another study has been completed in Maryland.

The evaluation system reflects the spirit of in-service development and not that of inspection.

The evaluation plan is a guidance procedure, directed at helping the teacher help himself teach more effectively.

The focus for curriculum development is the needs of the individual school.

Teachers are involved in curriculum development on the basis of their interests and needs of the school.

A curriculum materials center is maintained in the building (or school system).

An adequate library of professional materials is available to teachers.

Records are kept of the work and meetings of the staff as they consider their instructional problems.

Meetings are convened and adjourned promptly at the time set.

Agenda are sent to the staff well in advance of the meeting.

Teachers participate in the planning and organization of their meetings.

A major portion of staff meetings is reserved for dealing with the improvement of instruction.

The principal is with teachers and pupils often enough to be accepted as a peer on the instructional teams.

Demonstration teaching is arranged to show methods, procedures, and instructional devices.

Demonstrations are followed by constructive group discussions.

Arrangements for intervisitation of teachers are available to all.

Granted that we have long been aware of the need for such conditions, and that, as discrete items, these criteria do not dramatically add new dimensions to supervision. By applying them, however, it has been possible to accept tentatively the hypothesis that teachers do not see supervision as being "cooperative action on instructional issues." It is not enough to describe the present status of supervision, as important as this may be.

More important is the development of supervisory programs which are relevant to the study and planned improvement of teaching. Programs which activate the intent of the above criteria would be recognized by supervisory leaders as contributing to instruction based supervision; teachers confirm their importance while reporting their notable absence in any concerted fashion in supervisory programs.

Building a Program

In conclusion, building a supervisory program which will release the power of teachers in the advancement of education is not a matter of applying criteria. Developing criteria and applying them is only a point of departure. As we continue to study the teaching process, and the organizational and social systems within which we operate, a more rigorous guide to supervisory behavior may result.

There is ample evidence that we have lacked either the understanding or the skills necessary for supervision that improves instruction. Clearly this is no easy task and one which can not be formularized. It requires imagination, leadership, and a conceptual framework for the teaching process and human relations. If humanizing instruction, that is the release of human potential, is a universal goal of our educational system, then its existence is as much a concern for the supervisor who nurtures instruction as it is for the teacher.

There are many supervisors and school systems who have made a commitment, stated and operational, to instruction centered supervision. Their effectiveness and the vitality of the programs which result are testimony to the significance of the undertaking. The expenditure of energy and resources required are patently justified. If education for social invention (1), or for the open society, is to develop, there is great need for teachers who are sensitive to their power to cause the release of insight and rationality in others, and to recognize how to use it. *This is the kind of supervision we need: that which causes teachers to go beyond routinized, ritualistic instruction, as an expression of their own personal struggle for fulfillment.*

Lawrence Cremin (2) states the challenge:

Now, there is no denying that teachers must be technically competent, and the reformers have not only the right but the obligation to produce careful and detailed strategies for the use of their materials. (N. L. Gage has even put forth the intriguing suggestion that we develop a standard "choreography" for noting pedagogical prescriptions.) But education is too significant and dynamic an enterprise to be left to mere technicians; and we might as well begin now the prodigious task of preparing men and women who understand not only the substance of what they are teaching but also the theories behind the particular strategies they employ to convey that substance. A society committed to the continuing intellectual, aesthetic, and moral growth of all its members can ill afford less on the part of those who undertake to teach. □

References

1. Jerome Bruner. "Education as Social Invention." *Saturday Review*, February 19, 1965.

2. Lawrence Cremin. *The Genius of American Education.* Horace Mann Lecture. Pittsburgh: University of Pittsburgh Press, 1965. p. 59. By permission of Random House, Inc.

3. Lloyd Dull. "Criteria for Evaluating the Supervision Program in School Systems." Unpublished Doctoral Dissertation. Columbus: Ohio State University, 1960.

4. Ned A. Flanders. "Diagnosing and Utilizing Social Structure in Classroom Learning." National Society for the Study of Education. 59th

Yearbook, Part II. Chicago: University of Chicago Press, 1960.

5. Carolyn Guss. "How Is Supervision Perceived?" *Educational Leadership* 19 (2): 99-102; November 1961.

6. Milton Meux and B. Othanel Smith. "Logical Dimensions of Teaching Behavior." Research supported by the U.S. Office of Education, Project No. 258(7257).

7. Richard F. Neville. "The Supervisory Function of the Elementary School Principal as Perceived by Teachers." Unpublished Doctoral Dissertation. Storrs: University of Connecticut, 1963.

8. David G. Ryans. *Characteristics of Teachers: Their Description, Comparison and Appraisal.* Washington, D.C.: American Council on Education, 1960.

9. R. L. Turner. "Teaching as Problem Solving Behavior." *Contemporary Research on Teacher Effectiveness.* Biddle and Ellena, editors. American Association of School Administrators. New York: Holt, Rinehart and Winston, Incorporated, 1964.

EL 25 (5): 414-17; February 1968
© 1968 ASCD

A Necessary Frame of Reference

JOHN T. MALLAN
FRANK CREASON

CURRENTLY, we are greatly concerned with scope and sequence, with having a cognitive set of teacher and student objectives, with the struggle for a rationale for public education in general, and with the implications for supervision. This concern is fundamentally a warning for those of us in education to assess our frame of reference—to identify what we should be doing and to note why we have made such an identification.

Basic to this call for an operational frame of reference is the assumption that a rational process is one in which there is some kind of relationship between ends and means.

We in education are not alone in this concern. When one reviews the current literature he cannot help but note a pervasive interest in being aware of a major social frame of reference. This is not surprising as the multitude of recent "changes" place the public school in the matrix of all transition.

This awkward placement is compounded in complexity when we realize that the traditional nature of the school has been conservative. This is true in the sense that public education has justified its expensive role in the economy by the implied assumption that it was socializing the young in terms of those values which the major society considered important enough to be preserved.

The transition which we are experiencing has challenged some of the traditional values and hence has perhaps challenged the role of the public school.

John T. Mallan, Assistant to the Superintendent, Warrenville Heights City School District, Warrenville, Ohio. In 1963, Dr. Mallan was Assistant to the Superintendent, Cleveland Heights-University Heights City School System, Cleveland Heights, Ohio; and Frank Creason, Educational Consultant, Arnold Newbanks Company, Syracuse Mission, Kansas. In 1968, Dr. Creason was Associate Director, Southern Central Region Educational Laboratory, Little Rock, Arkansas

Key Social Agent

In dealing with objectives, scope, sequence, content, methodology, and evaluation (all of concern to the supervisor), we come to a realization that the public school itself is a key social agent. Its problem and, consequently, our problem, is one of being enmeshed in a complex web of interaction and action.

Role expectations cast us into the script as practitioners who must select from the theoretical, apply what is selected, justify the selection, and somehow objectively justify our position. In the process we become bogged with communication: communication between specialists and communication with a paying public which is not always aware of the theoretical, let alone the application. Human interrelatedness becomes a paramount concern.

We are faced with countless alternatives. And we are faced with the realization that there is no one "set" answer to our problem. We also recognize that choices must be made or else we muddle in an irrational way, being pushed from corner to corner by the whims of the moment.

As a social servant, the supervisor is forced by the public to be concerned with many types of interaction. For example, the supervisor must be aware of change and the process of change, decision making and the process of making decisions, communication and the process of communication, knowledge and the process of knowing, bureaucratic institutions and the structured protection of cultural lag, values and the sources of values, major social problems and their operation as a total educational environment in interaction with the formal school—things such as economic changes, mass communication, and foreign affairs.

The more complex a social situation becomes, the more tempting is an immediate, sure-cure answer. In a time of threat or fear the pressure mounts to accept the answer being proposed. In such times the answer appears to be one of having the school exist to train the intellect, and the key substance of all school activity is intellectual. We are not sure what the term "intellectual" means. It does, however, connote a view that the mind is a container to be filled by a basic body of knowledge and that a student, so filled, will somehow equate knowing good with being good, knowledge with wisdom, information with use in terms of behavior. Resulting from this view of the purpose of education is the inference that there is agreement on the basic body of knowledge to be given and that a listing of such content automatically designates the aims and objectives of education.

The educator finds bodies of knowledge offered to him which are sequential and ordered. Evaluation becomes less a problem because the concern is with the mastery of content. All this leads to a good deal of security. The teacher can be evaluated in a much less complex manner. So it is with the students, with the school, and with the state or the nation.

For example, we can tell how "good" our schools are in comparison with another country simply by giving the same content examination to respective students of the same age and educational experience. If the aim of education is this type of mastery, comparative education of the described nature is possible.

Aims of Schooling

Yet we are told that different countries and different ideologies have different aims and that the respective educational establishments thus have different functions which cannot be evaluated by similar criteria. If this is so, it suggests an implicit *use* of a body of knowledge which takes primacy and that the body of knowledge is a means to a sometimes unstated purpose.

Those pushing for a "body of knowledge" type of curriculum would probably find a common agreement with their opponents in that the vision is one of having the school's graduate a rational, well-adjusted human being, who recognizes certain areas of independence and self-reliance while recognizing other areas of social dependency. The argument would probably ensue over such things as the meaning of "rational" and "well-adjusted," as well as concern over the meaning of independence. As was indicated earlier, the term rational involves a relationship between means and ends.

Is the "end" already established toward which we consciously guide the young? If so, is the "end" of a society based on intellectual dedication or behavioral patterns? What is the relationship between the two?

If the "end" of society is not already established but rather a part of all-encompassing change, does not the term "well-adjusted" suggest being able to cope with change and the choices which change implies? The meaning of independence may well strike at the root of the differences of opinion. Is "individual" the term for a physical organism? Is the individual personality—its desires, hopes, fears, and motivation—environmentally conditioned? How independent, how "free" is the individual organism? Supervisors live with such questions.

Some of the people who question the intellectual role of the public school would replace the term with "intellectualizing." This is not a question of semantics. One is a given while the other is a process. They do not view the question as an "either/or" when it comes to a body of information. Emphasis is given to the *use* of information. Evaluation is thus more complex than just the mastery of information. There is no promise of security for those who are willing to recognize the complex factors involved.

It would seem that we are at the point of asking the school, the administrator, the teacher, and perhaps the student to identify respective frames of reference. We are asking those involved in public education to question why they are doing what they are. For example, to ask a supervisor why he expects a teacher to teach about the colonies and have him answer: "A student *has* to know this," is to beg the question.

Why does a student have to learn about the Fertile Crescent, the Renaissance, the date 1066? If the learning of such material is a means to an end and not an end in and of itself, is it asking too much to identify the end in view? And is it asking too much to note alternative approaches which might better, more effectively, and more efficiently arrive at the "end" which is now cognitive?

Whatever thinking is, it is not easy and sometimes not at all reassuring. Yet, do we abolish the problem by the refusal to recognize it? To what extent are we rational and to what extent are we rationalizing? It is rather disconcerting to recognize that the social science area is no less immune from the ostrich posture so readily recognized among the teacher's colleagues.

Are we, in fact, saying to the students that when one studies the interaction of man and his social and physical environments, the first thing to do is to deny the existence of major problems because we are not able to cope with them? Play it safe, students ... love the object of desire from afar but forsake hell and do not get involved!

Aims of Supervision

It is suggested that the fundamental aim of the supervisor might be to have a teacher assess what he is, who he is, what he knows, and the types of evidence he accepts for knowing; to assess what it means to be a social being and to so recognize that a world interaction necessitates identifying what other people think they are, who they are, what they know, and the evidence the other fellow accepts for knowing.

A supervisor must assess sources of values, and the difficulties and promises in communication.

A supervisor must understand types of decision making, the implications of compromise.

A supervisor must be able to dissect problems and to construct alternatives for resolving these problems.

A supervisor must recognize that "answers" are often situational and that to rationally appraise the situation is to consult our oracle.

A supervisor must identify the relationship between means and ends which justifies the rights of a minority and of individuals.

A supervisor must struggle with the meaning of the relationship between individual and social freedom.

A supervisor must learn to ask questions.

A supervisor must study all forms of social living—political, economic, and social—in order to better know himself.

And it is to know that all the above is meaningless, unless he acts and lives acaccoording to his meanings as to what living implies.

If these then become the objectives of supervision, let us welcome the opportunity. Let us relate *our* ends and means. Yet we are often told that the teachers are not qualified to pursue such a program. This is true if we maintain that the teacher stands as a sage upon a pedestal offering the answers which he, himself, has been given.

It is not true if the teacher is perceived (and evaluated) in terms of his also being a student, actively looking, guiding, and asking in a terrain which he has scouted to a greater degree than have his students. ☐

EL 25 (5): 387-90; February 1968
© 1968 ASCD

Social Planning and Social Change

(An Editorial)

FRANCES R. LINK

"Let the great world spin forever down the ringing grooves of change."—Tennyson

UNDERLYING the exhibitionist rebellion of the hippies and the flower people is a more subtle and more important change in the great majority of people born since F.D.R. Like politics, science, and business, people have undergone profound

Frances R. Link, Director of Curriculum and Research, School District of Cheltenham Township, Elkins Park, Pennsylvania. In 1968, Coordinator of Secondary Education, School District of Cheltenham Township

change. "The marines we have in Vietnam are a lot smarter than the ones we had at Guadalcanal," says a veteran marine, quoted in a recent news account, "but they are a lot harder to discipline."

The "now" generation, we are told, is alienated and mobile, has empathy and stimulated imaginations. What has happened? Toronto scholar, Marshall McLuhan, gives one kind of explanation, with his complicated theories of the effect of television and modern communications.

I seem to blow a fuse every time I *read* a McLuhan book. Perhaps this is what he means when says that television, with its instantaneous communications of myriad events, has educated children in a different way than did the book, which presents information in a one, two, three sequential way. He believes that printing, with its absolutely clearly defined character, causes the reader to receive information passively.

Television, by contrast, is a vaguely defined picture and the need for one's eye to connect the thousands of dots makes it an involving experience, one that not only draws the child into action, but tends to make him desire immediate action. What is important here is the powerful influence that media participation presents in planning for change. Our schools, the staff, and the curriculum must unfold and become tomorrow-oriented.

Media participation, city and suburban living, technology and scientific research are creating global, new life styles at a whirlwind pace. Architecture and the Peace Corps are making societies, "look alikes" all over the world. The vast recent increase in the sheer number of human beings has further complicated our understanding of the consequences of change. And the fact that this generation in America and abroad has been subjected to faster and more bewildering change than previous ones has made us oblivious to some of the more subtle but important changes that affect the quality of human living and learning.

For Social Reality

This generation seems more interested in the role of education, beyond a mastery of the three R's. John Dewey's philosophy, which stressed group experience and the utilizing of the school to prepare for life, is being discovered by the "now" generation. They are discovering much more of Dewey—they are using the school as a testing ground against social rigidity and, in some cases, for social reality. Witness the recent race riots in the schools and during extracurricular games. Many administrators are so bewildered by expressions of youth to demonstrate on the one hand, and by their desires for flexibility and opportunities for creativity on the other hand, that they are in a constant state of "floating anxiety." This generation is forcing the notion that the school is "everywhere"—everywhere they find *meaning*. It is up to us to remake the schools in styles less dull and more worldly.

I believe that our schools have become so highly structured that the policies and goals being set by school boards and administrators, and the work actually being done, seem unconnected. When this happens, we have one of the outstanding manifestations of alienation. As schools become increasingly large and complex, the traditional organizational hierarchy or power structure loses its usefulness.

The most effective decision making and policy determinations seem to evolve when key people *directly* related to an issue are brought together: sometimes parents, sometimes teachers, sometimes the police, sometimes students, etc.; this brings "instant" psychological recognition and personal satisfaction—especially when things begin to happen. Some university campuses are organized in this fashion, where the professors are under the loosest bureaucratic control. Within many corporations, research departments already operate this way—as virtually independent organizations made up of independent projects.

Leonard Duhl, a Washington psychiatrist and government advisor, sees corporate organization emerging as a "floating crap game." Rather than becoming a solid organization in the old sense, Duhl says, corporations will draw people together for a problem. As a solution evolves, they will break apart and reassemble in other groups. For example, a new nonprofit company in Cambridge, Massachusetts, the Organization for Social and Technical Innovation (OSTI) retains a permanent staff of ten generalists. For any particular project it picks up key men from all over the country. The trick is to find the specialist and the generalist and bring them together to bear on a problem. For the problems we face in education, we will have to learn how to move people "horizontally as well as vertically." Done skillfully, this assignment-by-task can solve not only a specific curriculum problem, but also the problem of teacher motivation.

Many companies are adding to this concept a change in salary structure. For example, a *valuable* technical man might earn more than his boss (although the technical people never believe it). This might solve the age-old problem: How to promote the master teacher without making him a second-rate supervisor or administrator? In industry, "There is a change taking place in the old concept of line and staff," says Frank Metzger, ITT's director of personnel planning and development. "A blurring is taking place. You no longer have a strict allegiance to hierarchy. You try to forget about seniority and organize to get the job done."

Persons in the Process

Why weren't we in education smart enough to figure this out? As supervisors, we have been struggling with line and staff organization for years—mostly because we were unable to work in such a "tight" structure. We just did not fit the old pattern. The very nature of supervision and curriculum development requires that we have authority and responsibility to organize and constantly reorganize, with different people involved, to get the jobs done. We must work at establishing ourselves as "persons in the process," not at establishing our power or authority in the organization.

The very nature of the struggle suggests that the pyramidal structure of our schools was established to handle routine tasks and there is nothing routine about working with people in the processes of supervision and curriculum development. ASCD has been the spokesman for this structural style—a style of communications, up, down, and sideways. The style will need to be high-fashioned. We will need to bring more specialists and generalists into schools to work on specific curriculum problems.

The interdisciplinary process of bringing together people who have never met before to solve problems, and to develop curriculum will acquire spontaneity and require new skills. Regrouping of educators for decision making will make "sensitivity training" a relevant prerequisite. Each school person will have to understand himself in relationship to others. He will have to learn to build a culture out of each group in which he finds himself. Many educators who have been through leadership training experience soon accept it as just another happening, mostly because school systems are operated more like Prussian armies than like human interaction systems.

New Social Skills

The changeover from hierarchical structures to participative management techniques will evoke new social skills and feelings. It will create some new anxieties, too. Some administrators will constantly worry about "who's in charge?" To a degree, the inflexible "older" supervisors and administrators (and there are just a few) will discover that an "open-system" has the built-in power and capacity to bring everyone involved the illusive psychic and psychological rewards and far less work-boredom and worry about loss of power.

Participative management approaches in education need to be discovered and no doubt they will bring new social problems; for in most traditional systems, seniority has been equated with wisdom. The "new" system will draw on the expressive talents of both young and older personnel. The person with the *ideas* and the *ability* to make them live will emerge to do the task. Young and older educators will find that they need to keep on learning, consequently the very nature and need for in-service education will change radically. The chief source of need for continuing learning will be the commitment of the people involved to study and understand social change and its effect on children in the home and on youth and teachers in the school.

Many of us have been working and planning this way in part. I am convinced that too many have not because of the demands of teachers and the negotiations and contracts which have emerged in the past few years and which have been dumped in our laps.

If curriculum negotiations spread, they will not bring about participative management, but will lead only to role reversal and the same hierarchical organization, but with a different power-questing group pulling the strings.

It is not only the young generation of teachers who are pushing the negotiations movement. It is also a segment of a "middle-aged generation" of teachers who are now discouraged, bored, bitter, and rebellious. These teachers are discouraged because they have had to *insist* on getting simple monetary recognition for recognition as professionals.

It seems that in the process they have become "packaged personalities," attracted to higher salaries on the teacher market. As teacher negotiations become institutionalized, the individual teacher is quite likely to suffer a greater loss of dignity and sense of self.

School as a tightly scheduled island has also contributed to teacher alienation. The boredom of routine (just fitting into one of the schedules) gives one a sense of nothingness, and a loss of feeling unique. To make matters worse, a growing number of middle-aged teachers just cannot understand the "now" generation of students in their classes, or even the younger generation of teachers in the school.

The middle-ager has lost "teacher" power in the classroom where once his word was law. The "now" generation of students question teacher authority. The "now" generation act as though no one had ever lived before them.

It seems to me that both these generations are exhibiting many of the same tendencies: intolerance of existing conditions; lack of respect for authority; a desire to participate physically in significant activities and relationships.

What I can't figure out as I am writing this is: To which generation do I belong? To which do *you* belong?

What I *can* figure out is: That the next generation of effective supervisors, teachers, and administrators will emerge as individuals who are willing to take risks; that educational technology will force us to take a new look at instructional theory as well as force us to deal with costly obsolescence. However, the immediate challenge before us is to use the evaluation data we accumulate to change the curriculum: a curriculum which must emerge to help develop individuals of global stature in their thinking and in their performance. ☐

Index

Page numbers in italic indicate quoted material. Page numbers in bold type refer to articles in this book.

Abbott, Max G., 242-43
Accreditation, influence on instructional change, 231; of teacher education institutions, 44
Action research, 102-106, 140, 179, 205-206; *see also* Change, instructional
Administrators, interaction with staff, 126-28, 183-85; interaction with supervisor, 133; interaction with teacher, 201, 239, 242; problems of, 126-27
Alberty, Harold B. and Elsie J., 95
Alexander, Ray, 71
Allen, Dwight W., 119-20
Allen, Rowannetta S., **62-65**, 80
American Association of Colleges for Teacher Education (AACTE), 221
American Association of School Administrators (AASA), 43, 56, 58
Analysis, *see* Bloom, Benjamin S.
Arts, 190
Argyris, Chris, 15-16, 225, 243-44
Association for Childhood Education International, 141
Association for Supervision and Curriculum Development (ASCD), 43-44, 57-58, 59, 63, 64, 65, 72, 77-78, 80, 156, 161, 173, 174, 233-34

Audio-visual aids, in supervisor reporting, 130-31; poor utilization of, 147

Bagley, William, *70*
Bandura, Albert, 119
Bartlett, Sir Frederick, *113*
Behavior, changed by modeling, 118-22; dimensions of, 28
Behavioral science, contributions to supervision, 227, 245
Bellack, Arno, 176
Berman, Louise M., **113-18, 193-95,** 227
Better Than Rating, 173-74
Black box, *see* Systems analysis
Blair, Medill, 167
Bloom, Benjamin S., 116, 119
Board of education, curriculum as area for collective bargaining, 225; proponent of merit rating, 173; role in leadership plan, 144
Boguslaw, Robert, 228
Boulding, Kenneth, 229-30
Bowers, Norman D., 111, 220
Bradfield, Luther E., *25*
Brannen, Jeanne Floy, 89-90
Brickell, Henry M., *141,* 184
BRIDGE: A Teacher Education Project, 206-209
Broudy, Harry S., 220
Browning, Elizabeth Barrett, *125*
Bruner, Jerome Seymour, 116, 130, 138, 139
Buber, Martin, *3*
Bulletin, device for supervisor

communication, 127, 128, 135-36, 206
Bulletin boards, 131
Burch, Gilbert, 231
Bureaucratic model, 242-43
Burnham, Reba M., **45-49,** *103,* 138
Burke, Edmund, *6*

California, deficiencies in secondary English teachers, 157; evaluation of educational goals, 197-98; experiment in instructional change, 202-203
Castetter, William B., 171
Central office consultant, *see* Supervisor
CERLI Matrix, 152
Certification of supervisors, 53-56; and curriculum workers, 66-67, 72-74, 79
Change, 11-13, 17; behavioral, 22-23, 254-56; instructional, 19-21, 92, 149-53, 191-93, 200-203, 205-206, in subject fields, 41-42, 43, 190, problem solving approach, 133, influence of accreditation on, 231; in teacher behavior, 17, 111-12, by modeling, 119-22; teacher resistance to, 94-98, 201, 212-13; *see also* Innovation
Cheltenham (Pa.) plan of merit rating, 172
Citizens committee, in Cleveland, Ohio, 143, 144; in

Index

Dearborn, Michigan, 129-30
Clark, Harold, 17
Classroom observation, *see* Visitation
Claus, Karen, 120
Collective bargaining, *see* Negotiation
Combs, Arthur W., *22-23, 95-96,* 234
Commission on Preparation of Instructional Leaders (ASCD), 43-44, 57-58, 59
Commission on Supervision Theory (ASCD), 233-34
Commission on Teacher Education and Professional Standards (NEA), 56
Commission on Teacher Evaluation (ASCD), 173, 174
Committee on Professionalization of Supervisors and Curriculum Workers (ASCD), 57-58, 59, 63, 64, 65, 72, 78, 80
Communication, 4-5, 6, 192-93; as function of supervisor, 128-32; between school and community, 196; between staff and administration, 126-28
Computerized instruction, 232-35
Conant, James B., 175
Conference, as technique of supervisor, 18-19, 133, 134-35, 205
Conlin, Marcia R., **209-14**
Consultation, *see* Conference
Coon, Herbert, 95
Coordinator, *see* Supervisor
Corey, Stephen, **13-15,** *104, 106,* 205
Cox, Johnnye V., **75-77, 87-90**
Creason, Frank, **250-53**
Cremin, Lawrence, *249*
Crosby, Muriel, *104,* **125-28**
Cuban, Larry, **214-17**
Cunningham, Luvern L., **30-35**
Curriculum, concept of, 138-39; negotiation, 225, 238-41, 256; packaged, 223-27; *see also* Instructional materials

Curriculum change, *see* Change, instructional
Curriculum design, problems of, 226, 228-29; systems analysis approach to, 228-32
Curriculum workers, certification of, 66-67, 72-74, 79; characteristics of, 70, 216; functions of, 62-65, 215; internship of, 73; preparation of, 70-71, 78-79; professionalization of, 59, 61, 65, 77-80; recruitment of, 71-72; selection of, 70-71; *see also* Supervisor

Dalkey, Norman, 231
Davies, Daniel R., *92*
Davison, Hugh M., *205-206*
Decentralization of schools, 18
Delaware, survey of beginning mathematics teachers, 163-64
Delphi method, 231
Demography, and education, 69
Demonstration, as technique of supervisor, 134, 170
Department of Elementary School Principals (DESP), 43, 56, 58
Dewey, John, *4-5, 7, 145,* 254
Diagnosis, concept of, 32-34; of teaching problems, 108-109
Disadvantaged, needs of teachers of, 215-16; schools for, 206-209; supervising teachers of, 209-14; teacher perceptions of, 210-11
Discipline, 149
Discovery learning, 139
Doll, Ronald C., 105
Downing, Gertrude L., **206-209**
Drummond, Harold D., **21-23**
Duhl, Leonard, 255
Dull, Lloyd, 247-48

Eash, Maurice J., **65-69,** *79,* **223-27, 227-32**
Edelfelt, Roy A., **153-56**
Edmonds, Fred, **49-52**

Education, and technology, 237; definition of, 12; federal aid to, 43, 161-62, 190, 191, 220, 236; foundation aid to, 42, 43, 190, 191; goals of, 22, 189, 197-98, 251-52; politics of, 145; trends in, 193-94; *see also* In-service education
Educational Development Cooperative, 149-53
Educationist, 8-11; definition of, 8; in ASCD, 10; traits of, 10
Elementary schools, English instruction in, 157; foreign languages in, 190
English, deficiencies of teachers of, 157-58; instruction of, 157-62; poor usage by teachers, 148-49
Ennis, Robert H., 116
Etzioni, Amitai, 183
Evaluation, of instruction, 151; of peers in teaching team, 168; of schools, 231; of teachers, 172-76, 181; self-evaluation by supervisor, 89-90, 105
Evans, N. Dean, *24, 204,* 218
Eye, Glen G., 204

Fattu, N. A., 176
Feedback, 119-21, 151
Ferguson, Charles, 162
Flanders, Ned A., 111, 117, 176, 220, 246
Flintom, Margaret, **53-56**
Flexner Report, 59-61
Foreign languages, 190
Foster, Howard G., *225*
Foster, Richard L., **15-21**
Franseth, Jane, *106, 182, 197,* 205
Frazier, Alexander, **136-41**
Frost, Robert, *11*
Frymier, Jack R., **94-98**

Gage, N. L., 219, 249
Gagné, Robert M., 119
Georgia, preparation of supervisors, 75; program of in-service education of supervisors, 45-49; program of supervisor recruitment, 75-

77; study of perceptions of supervisor, 87-90
Georgia Teacher Education Council, 75-77
Gerhardt, Frank, **142-45**
Getzels, Jacob W., 28, 31, 34, 116
Getzels-Guba Model, 28, 34, see also Leadership, styles of
Gibran, Kahlil, *6-7, 23, 25*
Granite, Harvey, **180-85**
Greer, Edith S., 170, 171
Gross National Product, as example of modeling, 230
Grouping, problems of, 147
Guba, Egon G., see Getzels-Guba Model
Guss, Carolyn, **83-86,** *247*

Haberman, Martin, *182,* **209-14**
Hagen, Everett E., 96
Hallberg, H. Irene, **72-74,** *79*
Hansen, Carl F., 138
Harris, Ben M., 24, **35-37, 98-102, 107-10,** *204-205,* 218
Hartsig, Barbara A., **77-80**
Havighurst, Robert J., 189-90
Hawthorne effect, 234
Helmer, Olaf, 231
Hemingway, Ernest, *21*
Hill, Clyde, 128-29
Hill, O. E., 143
Hill, Richard J., 99
Hogan, Robert F., **157-63**
Hudspeth, DeLayne, **235-38**
Hughes, Marie, 99
Human association, 4, 5, 6
Human relations approach to supervision, 245-46, 247
Human relations model, 234

Iannaccone, Laurence, *92*
Idiographic, see Leadership, styles of
Illinois, Program for Instructional Improvement, 149-53; survey of supervisor functions, 133
Imitation learning, 119
Indiana, study of perceptions of supervision, 83-86, 247

Ingils, Chester, *183-84*
Innovation, definition of, 11; in the school, 237-38; see also Change
In-service education, centers in schools, 217; of English teachers, 158-62; of supervisors, 45-49, 222; of teachers, 140, 158-62, 170-71, 177, 206-209, 220, 230; see also Internship; Supervisor, Teacher, preparation of
Institutes, for English teachers, 159; for science teachers, 220; for supervisors, 48, 209-14
Institutions for teacher education, 73-74, 78, 206
Instruction, computerized, 232-35
Instructional change, see Change, instructional; Supervision, goals of
Instructional leader, see Supervisor
Instructional Leadership Program, Cleveland, Ohio, 143-45
Instructional materials, 199
International Reading Association, 160
Internship, of curriculum workers, 73; of supervisors, 45-46, 51, 73, 179, 195; see also In-service education, Supervisor, Teacher, preparation of
Intervention, by supervisor, 33, 34
Interview Guide, see Thinking, processes of
Inventory of Thinking Behaviors, see Thinking, processes of
Iteration, 230
Ivins, Wilson, 166

Jackson, Philip W., 116
Jacobson, Paul B., 166
Jersild, Arthur T., 103
Johnson, Earl S., **3-8**
Johnson, Harold, 243
Joint Committee on the Professionalization of Administrators and Supervisors, 57-58
Jordan, William C., **200-203**

Kahn, Herman, *233*
Kaplan, Abraham, 229
Kelley, Earl C., *25,* *199, 234*
Kentucky, program for preparation of supervisors (PEPES), 49-52; study of supervisors, 71; ungraded school in Jefferson County, 130
King, Martha L., *103,* 138
Koerner, James D., 175
Koran, John J., Jr., **118-22**
Koran, Mary Lou, 119
Koontz, Elizabeth, *242*
Kyte, George C., **146-49**

Language arts, see English
Language laboratories, 190
Lawler, Marcella R., **189-93**
Lay committee, see Citizens committee
Leader, description of, 128-29
Leadership, definition of, 36; factors of, 145; instructional, 142; styles of, 17-18, 28, 32-33, 34
Leadership for Improving Instruction, 93
Lear, John, 60
Learning, 119, 139, 204, see also Modeling
Learning process, supervisor knowledge of, 129-30
Leeper, Robert R., **vii-viii, 11-13,** 59
Lesson plan, example of, 150-52, see also Planning
Lewin, Kurt, 31
Likert, Rensis, 225
Lindsey, Margaret, see New Horizons Project
Linguistics, 162
Link, Frances R., **172-76,** **253-56**
Lippitt, Ronald, 32
Logsdon, J. D., 166
Lonsdale, Bernard J., **196-200**
Lott, Jurelle G., 87
Lovell, John T., **241-44**
Lucio, William H., **90-94,** 170, *218,* 227, 233, *234*

260 • Index

McDonald, F. J., 119-20
Macdonald, James B., **110-12,** 215
McKean, Robert C., *180-81, 182, 184-85*
Mackenzie, Gordon N., **41-45,** *63,* 140
McLuhan, Marshall, 254
McMaster, Alice L., **23-27**
McNamara, Robert S., 227
McNeil, John D., *92,* 170, *218*
Maccia, Elizabeth S., 176
Mallan, John T., **250-53**
Manley, Jo Ann Seagraves, 88
Maryland, supervisory legislation, 62-63; survey of beginning teachers of mathematics, 163-64
Maslow, Abraham, 234
Master teacher, 137, 167, 246
Mathematics, supervision of beginning teachers, 163-65
Mayo, Elton, 234
Media, instructional, 43, 190-91, 192, 235-38; definition of, 235-36; research, 236; role of supervisor, 236-38; role of teacher, 237
Merit rating, 172-76
Methodology of teaching, 198-99, 220, 221-22
Meux, Milton, 246
Michigan, Citizens Advisory Committee, 129; use of audio-visual devices, 131
Microteaching, 120-21
Middle States Association, 163
Miles, Matthew B., 242-43
Miller, Elwood E., **235-38**
Mills, H. H., *180-81, 182*
Modeling, 119-22, 229-31; and supervision of computerized instruction, 233-35
Modern Language Association, 161
Moeller, Gerald H., 242-43
Mooney, Ross L., *105*
Morris, Charles, *25*
Moser, Robert P., *32*
Motivation of teachers, 171, 174, 203-206
Myers, R. E., 96

Nance, Afton D., 197-98
National Association of Secondary School Principals (NASSP), 43, 57, 58, 161
National Council for Accreditation of Teacher Education (NCATE), 44, 57, 58
National Council of Teachers of English, deficiencies in secondary English teachers, 157; survey of in-service education, 158-162
National Education Association (NEA), 56, 226; New Horizons Project, 43; Project on Instruction, 95
National School Boards Association, 225
National Science Foundation institutes, 220
National Study of High School English Programs, 161
NDEA Institute for supervisors of teachers of disadvantaged, 209-14
Neagley, Ross L., *24, 204,* 218
Negotiation, curriculum, 225, 238-41, 256; interference with supervisory functions, 223-27; professional, 238-41, 241-44
Netzer, Lanore A., 204
Neville, Richard F., *215,* **244-50**
New Horizons Project, 43
New Jersey, survey of beginning teachers of mathematics, 163-64
New York, schools for disadvantaged, 206-209; supervising teachers of disadvantaged, 209-14; survey of beginning teachers of mathematics, 163-64
Noda, Daniel S., 95
Nomothetic, *see* Leadership, styles of
North Carolina, certification of supervisors, 53-56

Observation, *see* Visitation
Ogletree, James R., **49-52, 56-58**
Ohio, Instructional Leadership Program, 143-45; study of characteristics of principals, 19; study of leadership style, 28; study of teacher resistance to change, 96-97
Olds, Henry F., 165
Openshaw, Karl, 54
Operational gaming, 231
Organization for Social and Technical Innovation, 255
Organization, school, effect on supervision, 194, 225
Ort, Lorrene Love, 103

Pedaguese, 196-200
Pennsylvania, Cheltenham plan of merit rating, 172; deficiencies of secondary English teachers, 157; survey of beginning teachers of mathematics, 163-64
Perceiving, Behaving, Becoming, 22-23, 25, 104
Personality and social change, 96
Personnel administration, supervisor's role in, 168-72
Petrie, Thomas A., **149-53**
Phillips, Ray, 243
Phipps, Doris G., **203-206**
Planning, curriculum, 181; instructional, 146-47, 150-52, 167
Prater, John, **132-36**
Prejudice, 211-12
Preparation, *see* Supervisor, Curriculum workers, Teacher, preparation of
Principal, characteristics of, 19; goal of, 132; interaction with supervisors, 27-30; role in team teaching, 167, 168
Problem solving, 254-55; approach to instructional change, 133
Profession, characteristics of, 59, 68, 73, 78-80
Professionalization, ASCD state unit contributions to, 58, 83-86; elements of, 65; of supervisors, 44-45; of supervisors and curriculum workers, 59, 61, 65, 77-80, 191-92; of teachers, 137-41, 191-92, 221; *see also*

Committee on Professionalization of Supervisors and Curriculum Workers
Programmed learning, 92-93, 191
Progressive education, 107
Psychology, 191
The Pursuit of Excellence, see Rockefeller Report

Quade, E. S., *227*, 230
Questioning, developing skill in, 119, 120-21

Rasey, M. I., *199*
Radtke, Muriel, **113-18**
Rating, *see* Evaluation; Merit rating
Reading, individualized, 104; instruction of, 162, 208-209
Reavis, W. C., 166
Recruitment, of supervisors, 75-77; of supervisors and curriculum workers, 71-72
Reinforcement, 119-21
Research, 192-93, 205-206, media, 236, on methodology, 198-99, 220; on supervisory programs, 100; on teaching, 246; *see also* Action research
Research Division (NEA), 226
Research Institute (ASCD), 110, 112
Revisionist model, 234
Rockefeller Report, 16, 17
Rodgers, Mary Columbro, **102-107**
Roethlisberger, Fritz J., 234
Rogers, Carl, 99, 234
Ross, D. and S., 119
Russell, David H., *113*, 116, *199*
Rutrough, James E., **168-72**
Ryans, David G., 17-18, 99, 100, 246
Ryder, N. B., 69

Saunders, Robert L., **241-44**
Scenario writing, 231
School, as change agent, 22; as social system, 31; decentralization of, 18; for disadvantaged, 206-209; ungraded in Jefferson County, Kentucky, 130
School board, *see* Board of education
School organization, effect on supervision, 194, 225
Science—A Process Approach, 119
Scientific management model, 233
Scientific supervision, 91
Seeman, Melvin, 28
Selmeier, H. Leroy, **128-32**
Seminars, as technique of supervisor, 135; for supervisors, 46-47
Shafer, Harold T., **59-61**, 78
Shaftel, Fannie R., 91
Shaplin, Judson T., 165
Shumsky, Abraham, 104-105, 205
Simon, Herbert A., *92*
Skinner, B. F., *91, 93,* 233
Smith, B. Othanel, 176, 246
Smith, Sandra Noel, **163-65**
Snygg, Donald, 95-96
Soar, Robert S., 111, 220
Social system, concept of, 31-32; school as, 31
Soper, Daniel W., 96
Spock, Benjamin, 128
Squire, James R., **157-63**
Stanford Teacher Competence Appraisal Guide, 117
Stanford University, microteaching clinic, 120
Strickland, Ruth, 159
Students, participation in leadership plan, 144
Subject fields, instructional change in, 41-42, 43, 190; *see also* English; Mathematics
Supervision, concerns of, 64; contributions of behavioral sciences to, 227, 245; definition of, 24, 85, 166; factors in, 24-25, 132; functions of, 92, 125, 194-95, 197, 218, 221; goals of, 24, 85, 91-92, 99, 118, 219, 252-53; history of, 107, 166, 180; human relations approach to, 91, 245-46; perceptions of, 83-86, 247, 248-49; program development, 108-10; scientific, 91; techniques of, 133-36, 166, 204-206; terminology of, 24
Supervisor, and computerized instruction, 233-35; and instructional media, 237; and personnel administration, 168-72; attitude toward others, 25; beginning, time study of, 89-90; certification of, 53-56, 66-67, 72-74, 79; characteristics of, 70, 76, 87-88, 100-101, 132-33, 182, 216, 221, 246, 249; definition of, 41; elementary, function perceived by principal, 28-29; historical functions of, 41-43, 63, 91, 168; in-service education, 45-49, 222; internship of, 45-46, 51, 73, 179, 195; preparation of, 44, 49-52, 53-56, 65-69, 70-71, 75, 78-79, 182-83, 195, 219, 222, 225, *see also* Internship, In-service education; problems of, 141, racial, 211-12; professionalization of, 44-45, 59, 77-80, 191-92; recruitment of, 61, 71-72, 75-77; rewards of, 26; selection of, 44, 70-71, 75-77; self-evaluation of, 89-90, 105; use of action research, 103-106
Supervisor, functions of, 23-26, 30-31, 62-65, 84-85, 87-89, 93, 99, 103, 113, 132, 133-36, 169-71, 176-79, 180, 192-93, 204, 206, 215, 221, 225, 244-49; as central office consultant, 180-81; as change agent, 31, 33, 215, 245; as generalist, 161; as teacher-leader, 3-8; communication, 128-32, 135-36, 206; evaluation, 14; facilitation, 194-95
Supervisor, interaction of, social, 251; with administrators, 133; with principals, 27-30; with supervisees, 14;

with teachers, 18-19, 103-105, 106, 126, 132, 133, 141, 146-49, 151, 153-56, 166-67, 169-70, 181-82, 201, 205, 212, 223, 237
Supervisor, techniques of, conferences, 18-19, 133, 134-35, 205; demonstrations, 134, 170; group meetings, 135; seminars, 135; visitation, 133-34, 146-49, 181, 204-205, 216; workshops, 135
Supervisory personnel, 194
Supervisory program, 44, 125-28, 136, 204; criteria for evaluation of, 247-49
Swearingen, Mildred E., *205, 218*
Sybouts, Ward, **165-68**
Systems analysis, 227-32; in preparation of supervisors, 66-69; definition of, 227

Taba, Hilda, *106,* 176, 205
Taylor, Frederick W., 233
Teacher, and action research, 104-105; and computerized instruction, 233, 234; and instructional media, 237; as perceived by administrators, 242; beginning, as team teacher, 167-68, demonstrations for, 134, 170, in-service education of, 217, workshops for, 170; behavioral change in, 111-12; career, 155-56; criteria for selection of, 17-18; incentives for, 155-56; in-service education of, 140, 158-62, 170-71, 177, 206-209, 220, 230; motivation of, 203-206; perceptions of disadvantaged, 210-11; perceptions of supervision, 247, 248-49; preparation of, 155, 175, 182, 220, *see also* In-service education; professionalization of, 137-41, 191-92, 221; resistance to change, 94-98, 201, 212-13
Teacher interaction, with administrators, 201, 239, 242; with supervisors, 18-19, 103-105, 106, 126, 132, 133, 141, 146-49, 151, 153-56, 166-67, 169-70, 181-82, 201, 205, 212, 223, 237
Teacher-leader, *see* Supervisor
Teachers of disadvantaged, beginning, 206-209; needs of, 215-16
Teaching, areas for improvement, 146-49; audio-visual aids, 147; class control, 149; English usage, 148-49; grouping, 147; learning activities, 147-48; planning, 146-47
Teaching machines, 93, 190, 192
Team teaching, 165-68, 193-94, 208-209; role of principal in, 167, 168
Technology, and education, 237; *see also* Media, instructional
Television, *see* Media, instructional
Tennyson, Alfred, 253
Thelen, Herbert A., *17,* 31
Thinking, definition of, 113; processes of, 113-18
Thompson, Victor A., 228
Thurman, Howard, *26*
Thurman, Robert S., **69-72**, 78
Tolstoi, Count Leo, *6*
Torrance, E. Paul, 96, 116
Toynbee, Arnold, *199-200*
Transactional, *see* Leadership, styles of
Trow, Martin, 228
Turner, R. L., 246

Turney, David T., **218-22**
Turpin, Henry Russell, *89*

Ungraded school, in Jefferson County, Kentucky, 130
University Council on School Administration, 44
U.S. Office of Education, 161, 236
Urick, Ronald, **94-98**
Usery (White), Mary Lou, **113-18,** 227

Van Til, William, **232-35**
Van Zwoll, James A., 169, 170, 171
Varner, Glenn F., *167*
Vigilante, Nicholas J., **27-30**
Visitation, classroom, as technique of supervisor, 133-34, 146-49, 181, 204-205, 216

Wahle, Roy, 64
Walters, R., 119
Watson, Jeanne, 32
Wear, Pat W., **49-52, 176-79**
Westley, Bruce, 32
White, Mary Lou Usery, **113-18,** 227
Whitehead, Alfred North, *16,* 229
Wiener, Anthony J., *233*
Wilcox, John, *166*
Wildman, W. A., 166
Wiles, Kimball, 218, 226
Wilhelms, Fred T., **ix-xi, 8-11,** 176
Williams, Stanley W., 166
Woodward, Richard G., 167
Workshop, as technique of supervisor, 135; for beginning teacher, 170

Young, William F., **238-41**